Girl Wide Web 2.0

mediated youth

Sharon R. Mazzarella
General Editor

Vol. 9

This book is part of the Peter Lang Media and Communication list.
Every volume is peer reviewed and meets
the highest quality standards for content and production.

PETER LANG
New York • Washington, D.C./Baltimore • Bern
Frankfurt • Berlin • Brussels • Vienna • Oxford

Girl Wide Web 2.0

Revisiting Girls, the Internet, and the Negotiation of Identity

EDITED BY Sharon R. Mazzarella

PETER LANG
New York • Washington, D.C./Baltimore • Bern
Frankfurt • Berlin • Brussels • Vienna • Oxford

Library of Congress Cataloging-in-Publication Data

Girl wide Web 2.0: revisiting girls, the Internet,
and the negotiation of identity / edited by Sharon R. Mazzarella.
p. cm. — (Mediated youth; vol. 9)
Includes bibliographical references.
1. Teenage girls—Psychology. 2. Identity (Psychology)
3. Internet. 4. Adolescent psychology. I. Mazzarella, Sharon R.
HQ798.G5253   305.235'20285—dc22   2010029954
ISBN 978-1-4331-0550-0 (hardcover)
ISBN 978-1-4331-0549-4 (paperback)
ISSN 1555-1814

Bibliographic information published by **Die Deutsche Nationalbibliothek**.
Die Deutsche Nationalbibliothek lists this publication in the "Deutsche
Nationalbibliografie"; detailed bibliographic data is available
on the Internet at http://dnb.d-nb.de/.

FSC
Mixed Sources
Product group from well-managed
forests, controlled sources and
recycled wood or fiber
Cert no. SCS-COC-002464
www.fsc.org
©1996 Forest Stewardship Council

The paper in this book meets the guidelines for permanence and durability
of the Committee on Production Guidelines for Book Longevity
of the Council of Library Resources.

© 2010 Peter Lang Publishing, Inc., New York
29 Broadway, 18th floor, New York, NY 10006
www.peterlang.com

Printed in the United States of America

To my niece and nephew Amanda and Matthew Mazzarella
for being such amazing, cool kids.

Contents

Section Two: Girls as Cultural Producers

Section Three: Online "Spaces" for Girls

Foreword

DAFNA LEMISH

There is an exciting, vibrant boom in the study of girlhood, as demonstrated by publication of numerous new articles in our major journals and books, an encyclopedia, a journal—*Girlhood Studies: An Interdisciplinary Journal,* and several recent academic conferences and panels devoted entirely to girls. Naturally, in these early stages of the development of this new interdisciplinary, multi-method field, there is an exploration of the core identity and defining of boundaries. To date, this search has been focusing on many important domains, such as: agency and voice, identity construction, "Girl Power," notions of femininity and feminism, everyday cultural practices, leisure, sexuality, and hetero-normativity.

The common thread interwoven throughout these efforts is that girls and girlhood are at the center of inquiry and concern. However, "girls" is not a homogenous category, as a number of scholars have pointed out (Driscoll, 2008; Mazzarella & Pecora, 2007). Yet, all too often in studies of girlhood conducted to date, we find that girls of color and/or non-Western backgrounds remain mostly invisible and voiceless. That is, claims of what it means to be a girl are often generalized from the experiences of White, Western, middle-class girls. But, surely we all agree that the lived-experience of Judy in the U.S. is not the same as that of Manisha in Nepal, Laticia in Brazil, or Naamah in Jordan. As a matter of fact, it is not the same for the different "Judys" throughout the broad expanse of the U.S., be it in urban, suburban, and rural settings. Thus, while researchers search for universalized commonalities of girlhood and explore global processes that affect them (such as pressures of the profit-driven market, global flow of programming and merchandizing, global digital divides, and the like), there is also a dire need to examine nuanced culturally contextualized differences. If so, then research efforts must expand beyond middle-class White Western girls' cultural experiences and practices to study the diverse worlds in which girls colored by race, class, religion, culture, geography (among others) come to age around the globe. Indeed, "we need to make an effort to attend to the voices and lives of *all* girls," advocated Sharon Mazzarella and Norma Pecora (2007, p. 117) in their assessment of the growing domain of girls' studies.

Girl Wide Web 2: Revisiting Girls, the Internet, and the Negotiation of Identity is exactly such an effort: It opens up our intellectual door to the "wide web" not only of the Internet, but literally the nature of girls' engagement with it, around the world. The scope of the book's inquiry into girls' Internet and identity construction activities and practices brings us authentic voices from diverse cultures and geographical regions: from Arab girls in Qatar to Latina girls in the Dominican Republic; from Korean girls in the U.S. to rural South African girls. Located in and outside of the U.S., and studied by diverse scholars ground in those cultures, the lives of the girls who are the subjects of this book are at the center of the reader's attention and their experiences are visible, present, and valued.

The notion of empowering under-represented and mis-represented groups by giving them a voice in the media has been discussed extensively by scholars with diverse interests from a variety of theoretical approaches (Couldry, 2008). It is this inclusive aspect of the Internet technology that has stimulated most deliberations and the high hopes underlying feminist inquiry of new technologies: Does the Internet platform enable marginalized groups to be present? Does it serve as a tool for participatory democracy and empowerment? Is it utilized to realize the potential for women's empowerment and transformation of gender relations (Van Zoonen, 2002; Wajcman, 2004, 2007)?

The unique characteristics of the Internet—its expansiveness, accessibility, and decentralized nature—feed the aspiration and hope that it will serve to facilitate breaking down traditional power structures. Readings of the collective and most recent research literature offers a very mixed evaluation of the materialization of this promise. Indeed, a social analysis of technology from a feminist perspective (Cockburn, 1992; Riccini, 2003) suggests that technology has many more implications than being just hardware. It is also a process of production and consumption, a form of knowledge, a site of gender domination as well as power struggle. Further, gender relations in both the private and public spheres, with their varying characteristics, shape the way technologies—including the Internet as a communication and leisure activity—are adopted and used in everyday life. In addition, exploring its roles in girls' lives, involves dissecting the interwoven inequalities brought about not only by gender and a host of other social markers, but also age hierarchies so prevalent in our respective societies.

The limited range of representations of childhood, to date, in all cultural and media forms, means that not only are children absent but so, too, are expressions in their own voices of their concerns, interests, views, pleasures, etc., as well as exemplars of children's agency in these media. The limited presentation and analysis of children's voices in research has led some scholars to question our ability to make sense of "girls' voices" (and for that matter, boys' voices as well, although they have received less attention until more recently) and of what can be concluded about their inner worlds. Currie (2008) issued a call to develop "a method for listening 'beyond and around' girls' words, interrogating especially troublesome talk rather than simply recording 'obvious' meanings." Studying girls' Internet use as a form of "participatory culture," (Jenkins, 2006) offers one such direction for listening to girls.

As they navigate their ways through the hybrid world of the Internet, girls join in the world of possibilities for blurring the boundaries between being consumers of Internet content to being producers and distributors of new content (Bennett, 2003). In doing so, they adopt existing genres, create new ones, and imitate others. While some of the efforts seem to be subversive and work against the grain, others embrace conventional expectations about appearance, sexuality, and femininity. But, as the chapters in this book demonstrate, through the variety of possibilities of engaging others online, girls do explore new opportunities to express their voices, and so the Internet is involved in self-growth. Some practices involve the construction of very private and individual identities and a creative process of expression. Others experiment with social relationships and create communities of "sisterhood." A minority of them is also involved in advancing civic initiatives, and hence the Internet provides them with the opportunities to engage in activism and collaborative teamwork. Hence, girls' cultures online incorporate all of these practices and goals, as several scholars studying girlhood have demonstrated in previous work on a variety of media (Kearney, 2006; Mazzarella, 2005; Stern, 2007).

While this book is grounded in the two areas specified earlier of girlhood studies and feminist inquiry into the gendered nature of technology, it also draws from the increasing expansive work being undertaken in the area of children, youth, and Internet studies. As Stern (2008) argued, one way to forefront girlhood studies is to contextualize it within the larger body of work on youth Internet studies, suggesting its unique contribution to other research approaches and theorizing of the field. Trying to avoid both the traps of celebratory discourse of the application of Internet in everyday lives of children and youth, as well as, moral panics over possible harm (particularly for girls), Livingstone (2009) locates the "great expectations" and "challenging realities" of children and the Internet in the more general historical analysis of the nature of changing childhoods and the media's role within them. Such an approach argues for the ease with which contemporary children's off-line and on-line lives are intertwined and reinforce each other (Mesch & Talmud, 2010). Clearly, the cultural and social structures in which girls live today and the role new information technologies play in their lives mutually affect each other in inseparable ways, making it impossible (and perhaps, even unnecessary) to distinguish the boundaries between their whereabouts in reality and in virtual reality, as for girls coming-of-age in the Internet era, both are integrated in their experienced life. Furthermore, the Internet itself has somewhat made girls private off-line lives more public and accessible to others, offering simultaneously a complementary perspective on popular discourse of potential vulnerability of girls on-line, yet also reinvigorating the debate over "troubled girls'" sexuality (Lemish, 2010).

Thus, understanding the role of the Web in girls' diverse lives exemplifies the interdisciplinary nature of the more general field of girlhood studies, as it requires pulling together work undertaken in multi-cultural contexts through a variety of scholarly research traditions. Doing so, engages questions about the gendered nature of technology, the democratic potential of the Internet, implications of the digital divide, empowerment and agency, identity construction, roles of leisure and popular culture, networking, and sociality. It moves forward the agenda of considering girls as active producers of texts and meanings, rather than solely passive victims of hegemonic culture. At the same time, we are advised to recognize the limitations of both of these discourses, as suggested by Driscoll (2008, p. 78): "Girl culture capital is neither 'cultural capital' nor 'sub-cultural capital,' and it is neither 'conformist' nor 'resistant,' but exceeds and questions those oppositions by encompassing multiple variations to them."

Such is the spirit and the method driving the collection before us, as a contribution to efforts to move forward the girlhood studies agenda by assisting us attain a richer understanding of what it means to be a girl today, globally, in their off-line and on-line lives. In doing so, this book continues the trend of taking the study of girlhood out of girls' bedroom culture, where it originated (with the formative McRobbie & Garber, 1976 study and the many since inspired by it). In doing so, it introduces us to a whole new vocabulary of virtual places and on-line activities that are *terra incognita* to many of us who are not girls anymore, or researchers who never experienced this culture; such as, Cyworld, blogrings, fangirls, MySpace, and Whyville. Along the way, we learn about their play, activism, sisterhood, and pleasures. Hence, accumulatively, this collection of research studies makes a major contribution to understanding and theorizing the field of girlhood studies as well as to honing our capacity to listen to, make sense of, acknowledge, and respect *ALL GIRLS*.

REFERENCES

Bennett, W. L. (2003). New media power: The Internet and global activism. In N. Couldry & J. Curran (Eds.), *Contesting media power: Alternative media in a networked world* (pp. 17–28). Lanham, MD: Rowman & Littlefield.

Cockburn, C. (1992). The circuit of technology: Gender, identity, and power. In R. Silverstone & E. Hirsch (Eds.), *Consuming technologies: Media and information in domestic spaces* (pp. 32–37). London: Routledge.

Couldry, N. (2008). Media and the problem of voice. In N. Carpentier & B. De Cleen (Eds.), *Participation and media production: Critical reflections on content creation* (pp. 15–26). New Castle, UK: Cambridge Scholars.

Currie, D. H. (2008). Talking with girls: Methodological challenges and the need to sharpen our methods of inquiry. *Journal of Children and Media, 2*(1), 76–77.

Driscoll, C. (2008). Girls culture capital. *Journal of Children and Media, 2*(1), 78–79.

Jenkins, H. (2006). *Convergence culture: Where old and new media collide.* New York: New York University Press.

Kearney, M. C. (2006). *Girls make media.* New York: Routledge;

Lemish, D. (2010). *Screening gender on children's television: The views of producers around the world.* New York: Routledge.

Livingstone, S. (2009). *Children and the internet: Great expectations, challenging realities.* Cambridge, UK: Polity Press.

Mazzarella, S. R. (Ed.). (2005). *Girl wide web: Girls, the Internet, and the negotiation of identity.* New York: Peter Lang.

Mazzarella, S. R., & Pecora, N. (2007). Revisiting girls' studies: Girls creating sites for connection and action. *Journal of Children and Media, 1*(2), 105–125.

McRobbie, A., & Garber, J. (1976). Girls and subcultures. In S. Hall & T. Jefferson (Eds.), *Resistance through rituals: Youth subcultures in post-war Britain* (pp. 209–222). London: Harper Collins Academic.

Mesch, G. S., & Talmud, I. (2010). *Wired youth: The social world of adolescence in the information age.* New York: Routledge.

Riccini, R. (2003). Women's identities and everyday technologies. In L. Fotunati, J. E. Katz, & R. Riccini (Eds.), *Mediating the human body: Technology, communication, and fashion* (pp. 113–122). Mahwah, NJ: Lawrence Erlbaum.

Stern, S. (2008). Girls as internet producers and consumers: The need to place girls' studies in the public eye. *Journal of Children and Media, 2*(1), 85–86.

Stern, S. T. (2007). *Instant Identity: Adolescent Girls and the World of Instant Messaging.* New York: Peter Lang.

Van Zoonen, L. (2002). Gendering the Internet: Claims, controversies and cultures, *European Journal of Communication, 17,* 5–23.

Wajcman, J. (2004). *TechnoFeminism.* Cambridge, UK: Polity Press.

Wajcman, J. (2007). From women and technology to gendered technoscience. *Information, Communication and Society, 10,* 287–298.

Acknowledgments

As I type this on April 2, 2010, I am thinking back to November 2008 when an amazing group of scholars first responded to my call for chapter proposals for this book. I was thrilled with the responses I got then, and am even more excited with the finished product! Thanks to all of the chapter authors for undertaking such rigorous and thought-provoking research, meeting deadlines, being responsive and open to my suggestions for revisions, and for just being a pleasure to work with!!! I have enjoyed this experience tremendously.

Thanks also to Mary Savigar, Senior Acquisitions Editor for Media and Communication Studies at Peter Lang Publishing, for being supportive and enthusiastic not only about this book, but about all of my projects with Peter Lang. It is always great to work with her.

Thanks also to the international community of Girls' Studies Scholars for both the excellent work they do and for inspiring my own scholarship. I must acknowledge one such scholar in particular, Dafna Lemish, whose compelling foreword to this book blew me away. When I asked her to write it, I knew she'd do a great job, but she exceeded my wildest expectations. Thanks, Dafna, for being an incredible feminist colleague and friend.

I would be remiss if I did not acknowledge the support I received from two educational institutions—James Madison University, my current institution, and Clemson University, where I began this project. My colleagues and superiors at both schools have been tremendously encouraging and supportive, and I value them greatly.

Finally, thanks to the girls who shared their stories, experiences, and creative projects with us. Without them, this book would not exist.

Introduction

SHARON R. MAZZARELLA

Since the foreword by Dafna Lemish has so brilliantly captured the current state of Girls' Studies scholarship and the place of this book within it, I've opted instead to structure this introduction as an explanation for why I felt it was important to revisit the subject of my 2005 anthology *Girl Wide Web: Girls, the Internet, and the Negotiation of Identity* (Peter Lang). As I sit here typing this, I find it hard to believe that over five years have passed since the initial publication of that book. While the original book has been well received, I felt it was necessary to take a fresh look at the subject matter in order to more accurately reflect the current state of "girls, the Internet, and the negotiation of identity." My original thought was to do a revised version, but how does one "revise" an anthology? Does she keep some chapters/authors and discard others? On what basis does she make that decision? What if the original chapter authors do not want to revise their work? Given the logistical questions involved in producing a revised anthology, I opted instead to do a "sequel." No, sequels are not common in academic publishing, and I certainly do not intend for this to be the start of a *GWW* franchise. But I felt the best way to take another look at the topic was to do so within the realities of our current world—the realities in which today's girls and young women live. Since the mid-2000s, a great deal has changed in terms of computer technology itself (hence the title's reference to Web 2.0), the ways girls use that technology, and the way we as scholars study girls and the Internet. Each of those changes is reflected in the content of this volume.

Two reviews of the original book, while applauding the content and approach overall, pointed out three gaps in the topics covered and methodologies employed. This book sets out specifically to fill these gaps. First, in a 2006 review published in *Communication Research Trends* Chad Raphael points out that the book's "perspective is limited mainly to American girls and U.S.-based Web sites" (p. 38). With the exception of Divya McMillin's chapter on girls in Bangalore, India, the original book was, indeed, U.S.-centric. The current book, however, includes chapters on girls in the Dominican Republic, Qatar, Thailand, and South Africa, as well as Korean diasporic girls in the United States.

Second, Denise Bortree (2006, p. 852), in *New Media & Society*, suggests that the studies in the original book "would have benefited from validation through interviews with primary sources: the teen girls themselves. A triangulation of methods would have strengthened the analysis and given more credence to the claims of how identity is, in fact, negotiated online." While many of the chapters in the original book employed content analysis methodology (as was typical of girls' studies scholarship at the time), all but a couple of chapters in this book privilege studies of girls themselves, in particular through the use of interviews.

Third, Bortree writes that "one regrets a lack of discussion in the book about other common uses of the internet among girls, such as blogs, games and downloading music. Teen girls are the largest group of creators and readers of blogs, so a chapter on that format would have fit into the book nicely" (p. 852). From social networking sites to game design, from blogs to game play, and from fan fiction to commercial web sites, *Girl Wide Web 2.0: Revisiting Girls, the Internet, and the Negotiation of Identity* offers a complex portrait of millennial girls online. Grounded in an understanding of the ongoing evolution in computer and internet technology and in the ways in which girls themselves use that technology, the book privileges studies of girls as active producers of computer/Internet content and incorporates an international/intercultural perspective so as to extend our understanding of girls, the Internet, and the negotiation of identity.

The book is divided into three sections—"Representing Self, Identity, and Lived Experience," "Girls as Cultural Producers," and "Online 'Spaces' for Girls." Many of the chapters could easily have been included in two or more sections, and I could have used a completely different organizational scheme altogether. The final organization of the book is what made sense to me at the time.

The book begins with Paola Prado's chapter on girls and young women in the rural town of El Seybo, Dominican Republic. Based on her interviews, Prado shows how affordable public Internet access at a local telecenter has enabled her respondents to pursue advanced schooling, communicate with friends and relatives abroad, and envision a range of future possibilities. One use of the Internet discussed by Prado was social networking, a topic taken up more specifically by Rodda Leage and Ivana Chalmers in Chapter Two. Specifically, they document the creative ways girls in the conservative Arab country Qatar express themselves on Facebook. Based on their interviews with girls aged 18–22, Leage and Chalmers document a range of "approaches" used to negotiate the cultural restrictions against public displays of identity for females in this country. While some informants have chosen not to use Facebook, others have found creative ways to express themselves while staying within the conventions of the culture. Others still have chosen to disregard some cultural conventions in order to obtain more freedom of self expression.

Continuing the discussion of social networking sites and girls' online identity construction, Chapter Three focuses specifically on issues related to sexuality. From her longitudinal analysis of Black American girls' postings on the social networking site she identifies by the pseudonym "NevaEvaLand," Carla Stokes documents the double-edged nature of Black American girls' online construction of their sexual identities. On the one hand, they are creating a space to talk about and navigate the complexities of their sexual development and relationships, while simultaneously often reproducing repressive and hegemonic sexual scripts and beauty ideals found in hip-hop culture, music lyrics, and music videos.

In their comparative analysis of the home pages of Thai and American girls Narissra Maria Punyanunt-Carter and Jason M. Smith (Chapter Four) seek to understand whether there are differences in how girls negotiate their identities and in how they choose to present themselves online. While they find some differences between girls growing up in a collectivistic culture (Thailand) and in an individualistic culture (the United States), they find more similarities. The final chapter in Section One continues the discussion of girls' use of personal homepages in their negotiation of identity. Specifically, in Chapter Five, Michelle Bae looks at how diasporic Korean girls in the United States use their cy *hompis* (personal homepages) on the Korean social networking site Cyworld to construct a culturally hybrid form of ethnic femininity. Through her focus primarily but not exclusively on girls' pictures, Bae documents the playful and nostalgic way in which these girls are recreating an imagined Korean girlhood.

Moving into Section Two on "Girls as Cultural Producers," Jaime Warburton (Chapter Six) examines online fan fiction written by young female fans of the wildly popular *Harry Potter* and *Twilight* franchises. Surveying authors on a variety of fan fiction sites, she shows how active involvement in online fan communities facilitates the fluidity of "fangirls'" identity construction. While there are online spaces for girls to post and share their writings, the Internet also offers girls opportunities to create content specific to computer technology. The next three chapters in Section Two focus on girls actively learning about and using computer technology—notably game designs and blogs. In Chapter Seven, Kristine Blair, Erin Dietel-McLaughlin, and Meredith Graupner Hurley take us on a journey through the Digital Mirror, a 4-day computer game camp for middle-school girls. Focusing primarily but not exclusively on Web portfolios designed by three campers, the authors document the girls' growing digital, critical, and rhetorical literacies as a result of their experiences at the camp—literacies that they then employed in their identity work.

Highlighting the work of another adult-run program designed to expose girls to computer technology, Claudia Mitchell, John Pascarella, Naydene de Lange, and Jean Stuart reflect on a series of workshops designed to educate girls about computer use in a rural secondary school in the KwaZulu-Natal province of South Africa, a region hard hit by HIV and AIDS. The chapter, which focuses on the blogs of five Zulu girls who participated in the workshops, reveals how such a "youth-centered approach to knowledge production and behavior change in the context of HIV and AIDS" could potentially be used as an educational tool. Situating blogrings as online communities, Jacqueline Vickery in Chapter Nine conducted an in-depth analysis of blogs authored by girls aged 14–19. The chapter, which highlights the blogs of three specific girls, demonstrates how creating blogs enables girls to both find their own voices and to create communities, in particular when opportunities to do so are missing from their online lives.

While many of the previous chapters address online spaces for girls, as well as the opportunities provided by such spaces, the chapters in Section Three foreground the concept. In Chapter Ten, Jill Denner and Jacob Martinez study 16 middle school girls who participated in the Girl Game Company (GCC). Designed to introduce computer literacy skills and game design to girls who otherwise would not have such opportunities, GCC provides a fertile ground from which to examine Internet spaces for girls. Specifically, Denner and Martinez compare two groups of girls distinguished by their affinity for either the social networking site MySpace or the virtual world Whyville, and find fascinating differences in girls' use of the sites for negotiating their identities.

Taking us in a slightly different direction in Chapter Eleven, Lillian Spina-Caza offers suggestions for researchers seeking to study girls' online play, specifically play on popular commercial pet adoption sites such as Webkinz.com and virtual communities such as Millsberry.com. Using unique methods for capturing and coding the real-time online play of her daughters, Spina-Caza's exploratory study provides researchers with the beginnings of a "methodological framework," for understanding girls' online play.

The last two chapters in the book offer content analyses of commercial websites targeted to girls—teen girl magazines and "magalogs." Denise Sevick Bortree specifically examines how environmentally focused articles in online teen girl magazines such as *CosmoGirl* and *Seventeen* enable girls to engage in a conversation about environmental issues. Through her examination of nearly 600 responses by girls posted to a variety of articles, Bortree documents the manner in which consumerism rather than activism is often presented as the primary way for girls to respond to the environmental crisis. Consumerism is again raised in the last chapter by Sharon R. Mazzarella and Allison Atkins who conduct an analysis of the online "magalog" alloy.com. The authors argue that, while serving ostensibly as an online catalog for girls seeking access to the latest fashions, alloy.com has become an interactive, magazine-like virtual community for tween/teen girls, one that celebrates commodity femininity, a celebrity-based cult of personality, and enforced heterosexuality. They find that alloy.com constructs an idealized, normative tween/teen girl identity while simultaneously providing spaces for girls to interact with each other.

Lynne Edwards chapter in the original *Girl Wide Web: Girls, the Internet, and the Negotiation of Identity* documented the mainstream news media's proclivity to frame the Internet as a dangerous place for girls, and to frame girls themselves as passive victims of untold evils lurking online (Edwards, 2005). While the general public and journalists alike often focus on the negative potential of the Internet in girls' lives, taken together, the chapters in this book paint a compelling picture of girls as active and engaged users of the technology—using it to negotiate their identities, flex their creative muscles, educate others, and just have fun.

References

Bortree, D. (2006). [Review of the book *Girl Wide Web: Girls, the Internet, and the Negotiation of Identity*]. *New Media & Society*, 8, 851–853.

Edwards, L. Y. (2005). Victims, villains, and vixens: Teen girls and Internet crime. In. S. R. Mazzarella (Ed.) *Girl wide web: Girls, the Internet, and the negotiation of identity* (pp. 13–30). New York: Peter Lang.

Mazzarella, S. R. (Ed.). (2005). *Girl wide web: Girls, the Internet, and the negotiation of identity.* New York: Peter Lang.

Raphael, C. (2006). [Review of the book *Girl Wide Web: Girls, the Internet, and the Negotiation of Identity*]. *Communication Research Trends*, 25 (2), 38–39.

SECTION ONE

Representing Self, Identity, and Lived Experiences

CHAPTER ONE

The Girls of El Seybo

Logging in to a Different *Mañana*

PAOLA PRADO

Every first week of May, the rural town of El Seybo in the Dominican Republic holds *fiestas patronales*, a weeklong celebration to honor the Holy Cross. The festivities are crowned by bull runs where horse riders and bull "fighters" who taunt and daze, but do not kill, the bulls, are cheered on by onlookers perched on wooden bleachers. The ritual dates back to the years of Spanish colonial rule. This Spanish-speaking Caribbean rural province holds the distinction of being the longest continuing European settlement in the Americas, established in 1506, following the arrival of Christopher Columbus.

These performances are unlike traditional Spanish bullfights. For one, the bulls survive uninjured. Secondly, bucking macho tradition, the El Seybo bull runs feature a female teenager in the role of official bugle player. Atop the VIP balcony that overlooks the bull ring, her horn signals the start of the bull run, whereupon a female horse rider escorts the bull into the ring, alongside her male counterparts. Sitting close to the bugle player, a more traditional vision of womanhood is on prominent display: the crowned teenage beauty queen sports a tiara and a satin sash, smiles, and waves to the crowd.

Across the developing world, women are living through a transition, stepping beyond traditional roles and engaging in new activities that were once forbidden or frowned upon. These changes, often brought about by economic necessity, also result from increased access to information from global trends happening in the outside world. In Latin America, where a culture of machismo remains widely prevalent, socioeconomic and gender inequality is particularly pronounced. Many women of childbearing age, including those with a formal education, often remain bound by tradition, relegated to activities in the home sphere.

In recent years, the United Nations moved to address such patterns of gender exclusion by establishing the Millennium Task Force on Gender Equality. As a result, governments and development agencies worldwide are now reassessing the role of women in promoting community prosperity, and acknowledging that women who are digitally literate can improve their own prosperity and become active agents of community development (Huyer, 2006b; Melkote & Steeves, 2001). Digital literacy is now considered an integral tool in the arsenal against gender exclusion and poverty.

WOMEN AND DIGITAL INCLUSION

In 2003, the World Summit on the Information Society (WSIS) identified digital literacy as one of the top components of human development (International Telecommunications Union, 2003). It consequently recommended that United Nations member countries adopt initiatives to foster information and communication technologies for development that would promote an equitable information society. These recommendations are in keeping with the Millennium Development Goals (MDGs), which set human development benchmarks aimed at improving conditions among the poorest segments of society by the year 2015.

The concept of digital inclusion is rooted within the human development paradigm espoused by the United Nations Development Program (UNDP, 2008), which calls for expanding opportunities for all people, so that they may lead healthy, creative, and prosperous lives. Equitable access to the information society and an end to digital poverty are identified as key components of this equation. So are women. The MDGs clearly identify digital literacy among women as a central piece of the human development puzzle. World Bank (2009a) studies indicate that nations that educate their girls see a rise in health indicators and a decline in mortality and fertility rates. One of the reasons is that a mother's educational achievement is a significant marker for better childhood nutrition (World Bank, 2001). Another is that education is essential to combating poverty. All of these reasons prompted the MDGs to call for an end to gender disparity in education, a goal that is now close to being met in many regions of the world.

In Latin America, the Dominican Republic is one such country where new initiatives in education and digital literacy have kept pace with the MDGs and the digital inclusion guidelines set by the WSIS. The recent adoption of neo-liberal free-market policies and structural reforms during the three-term government of President Leonel Fernández has substantially modernized the economy. A modernizing economy requires skilled workers. Therefore, the government launched educational initiatives aimed at reducing digital poverty. One such program established public access community technology centers, or telecenters, in the poorest areas of the nation. Known locally as *Centros Tecnológicos Comunitarios* (CTCs), the telecenters are managed by the Office of First Lady Margarita Cedeño de Fernández, whose commitment to digital literacy earned her the 2007 World Information Society Award, bestowed by the International Telecommunications Union.

While those of us in the Global North increasingly enjoy reliable and affordable connectivity almost everywhere, most people in the developing world cannot count on reliable or affordable Internet access. In many countries, poverty and long-standing structural deficiencies place computer access beyond the reach of most individuals. In such settings, and wherever home computers represent a prohibitively costly luxury, public Internet access points at telecenters, libraries, government agencies, Internet cafés, and kiosks provide the only means for affordable online access.

In Latin America, public access telecenters have sprouted in almost every nation over the past decade. Whether public or privately run, these facilities provide an affordable and accessible way for the poor to connect to the Web. As a result, telecenters that serve rural populations, far removed from urban centers, have assumed an important social dimension in the lives of those communities. More than a place to make a phone call or send a fax, they often also become a meeting ground where communities share information received from the Web and join together to find solutions to common problems (Heeks & Kanashiro, 2009; Schilderman, 2002; Sorj, 2003; Warschauer, 2003). In remote locations, telecenters can make it possible for entire communities to overcome capital and technical barriers, open new markets for their goods, and benefit from global information flows (Baggio, 2008; Blattman, Jensen, & Roman, 2003; Jensen, 2007; Roman & Colle, 2002).

Indeed, in rural areas where connection to the outside world requires hitching a ride over treacherous unpaved roads, riding a mule, or walking miles to the nearest town, the inauguration of a telecenter with satellite connection to the Internet can vault an entire community from the nineteenth to the twenty-first century at the click of a mouse.

Challenges of social inclusion in the developing world

The knowledge and the ability to use the Internet and other information and communication technologies can be particularly empowering to women and beneficial to entire communities (Garrido & Roman, 2006; Parmentier & Huyer, 2008). A woman's ability to learn and leverage new information can drastically improve her self-esteem and allows her to engage with technology in a way that widens the opportunities for her professional and civic engagement in society (Parmentier & Huyer, 2008; Sorj, 2003; Tolbert, Mossberger, King, & Miller, 2007). Digital literacy can also give women an edge in competing for highly valued technical jobs such as those found in call centers, where social skills are at a premium (Kelan, 2008). Among those in remote rural communities, the ability to connect to global markets through access to the Internet can promote business and trade, and help reduce economic disparities (Hosman & Fife, 2008).

Unfortunately, many women in the developing world are constrained by poor education, limited financial resources, and cultural taboos that limit their ability to learn and practice digital literacy, leaving them marginalized (Huyer, 2006a; Roman & Colle, 2002; Warschauer, 2003). Age, gender, and educational level have been well established as factors that can limit access to information and communication technologies (Proenza, Bastidas-Buch, & Montero, 2001; Tolbert et al., 2007; van Dijk, 1999; van Dijk & Hacker, 2000). Such challenges can prevent women from participating in the information society and effectively exclude them from producing or consuming technological goods and services. In doing so, they contribute to aggravate patterns of gender inequality and discrimination (Munévar & Arrieta, 2005).

One way to overcome these barriers is to engage students in digital literacy education early and often, with the help of supportive social networks. Learning and practice occurs best in settings that provide user-friendly information and communication technologies, speedy online connections, and Web content that is relevant to the personal lives of students (Massey & Levy, 1999; Morris & Ogan, 1996; Rafaeli, 1988; van Dijk, 1999; van Dijk & Hacker, 2003). The regular practice of digital literacy among women, established from an early age, is essential to societies that hope to end gender inequality and digital poverty. In order to push this agenda, developing world countries first need to address the challenge of Internet access. Whereas the near ubiquity of Internet connectivity in the U.S. makes it possible for almost everyone to go online with great ease and frequency; in the developing world, most people remain unconnected to the Internet.

Logging on in the Dominican Republic

Those of us who spend most of our time in the Global North may easily forget the difficult living conditions that pervade much of the developing world. In the Dominican Republic, one out of every three people live in homes without indoor plumbing and one-half of those dispose of their trash by dumping or burning it—

waste removal services are only available in major urban areas. People everywhere lack access to proper sanitation, nutritious food, and adequate shelter. Many among the poorest make their home in rural areas, where 55.7% live below the poverty line (Oficina Nacional de Estadística [ONE], 2004; World Bank, 2008).

Given such conditions, it is not surprising to find that severe structural and economic barriers limit Internet access to two out of every 10 people (International Telecommunications Union [ITU], 2008). That places the Dominican Republic on par with the rest of Latin America, where on average only 20% of the population enjoys Internet access. The few Dominicans who are online connect mainly through slow dial up connections; only 2% of the population has broadband access. Nine out of 10 people lack access to a fixed telephone line nationwide (ONE, 2009). Outside major metropolitan areas, fixed line access is considerably more restricted (Rey, 2006). By comparison, in the U.S., 87% of all girls and boys aged 12–17 were online by 2004, logging in mostly from home or school (Lenhart & Madden, 2006).

This chapter examines how girls in the rural community of El Seybo, in the Dominican Republic, having overcome many of these challenges, are going online and surfing the Web. While a number of studies have examined the online behavior of girls in the developed world, little attention has been paid to the impact of the Internet on girls who live in traditional rural societies. The near ubiquity of Web access in the Global North, where most of the studies that have been done take place, presents scholars with conditions that differ markedly from those that prevail in developing nations. Furthermore, very little has been written about gender and the media in Latin America (Lozano & Frankenberg, 2008; Peimbert Reyes, 2007), and the author could not find any studies on the topic of the online behavior of girls in Latin America. This chapter presents an exploratory case study[1] that describes how Dominican girls perceive and use the Web. What has been the impact of the Internet in their lives? What do they do online? Does use of the Web impact their self-identity, their attitude toward education, and their plans for the future?

The information for this chapter was collected in 20 individual face-to-face interviews[2] conducted in Spanish on three consecutive weekdays in May 2009 in or near the community technology center located in El Seybo. The community technology center is a public educational facility that provides public Internet access at a nominal cost. Each hour of Internet access at a public Windows-based computer station costs the equivalent of U.S. 42 cents.

The convenience sample was filtered so that all respondents met common criteria for gender, age, and Internet use. All of the respondents were girls or young women between the ages of 13 and 25,[3] and all used the Internet regularly (at least twice weekly). Ten of the 20 girls interviewed were young adults between the ages of 20 and 25, and 10 were teenagers between the ages of 13 and 19. Their responses,[4] along with my observations, allowed me to analyze and compare the themes that emerged as the girls shared their perceptions about the value of the Web in their lives.

THE GIRLS OF EL SEYBO

Restricted for the most part to Web use at public facilities, the girls of El Seybo go online less frequently and stay connected for shorter periods of time than those who log in from a home in the U.S., where the average teen spends 11 hours and 32 minutes online each month (Nielsen, 2009). Most of the girls interviewed for this study went online a few days each week, logging in for 15 or 20 minutes at a time each day to check e-mail. The heaviest Internet users among these Dominican teens stayed online at most up to 2 hours at a time. This is due in part to the fact that home computers are uncommon in this rural area. Only five of the girls I interviewed had a computer in their houses. All others connected to the Internet through a telecenter or other public access facility. This reality is markedly different from that of teens in the U.S., where three out of every four, who are online, access the Internet mostly from home (Lenhart & Madden, 2006).

Dominican girls also did not log in from mobile phones. In a country where fixed telephone lines are a rarity, three out of every four people subscribe to cellular service, mostly of the pre-paid variety (ONE, 2009). Yet very few of the young women interviewed for this study carried a cellular phone of their own. Personal electronic devices remain a consumer luxury in rural areas, where 50.3% of the population is classified as moderately poor, living on less than the equivalent of US$2.00 per day (World Bank, 2009b). New generation phones that connect to the Web have yet to enter the market at rates that would make their use widespread among the average Dominican subscriber.

Once school lets out and they have been home to eat lunch, children stream into the telecenter to attend computer classes. Girls and boys between the ages of 7 and 12 learn how to run Microsoft Office Suite and play with age-appropriate educational software. On days when they do not have computer class, they pay the equivalent of U.S. 42 cents for an hour of online access in which they surf the Web or check their e-mail.

"It's changed my life a lot and has made many things easier."

The importance of local Internet access for those who live in remote areas cannot be overstated. Rural telecenters place a wealth of resources within reach of populations that may be too poor or overworked to travel to the nearest urban center. El Seybo can be reached in a two-hour drive from the capital of Santo Domingo. The last half of the trip requires careful driving on a paved two-lane road where people and animals roam freely, making night travel extremely perilous. What may seem to be a short distance from the capital to an outsider represents substantial travel to locals, who pay to travel in buses or on the backseat of motorcycles, the ubiquitous "*motoconchos*," to get to the capital. Sonia,[5] a 22-year-old university student, was grateful for local access to the Internet, which significantly saves her time and money,

> It's much easier. Can you believe that we used to have to spend a ton of money on bus fare to travel from here to Santo Domingo or Higuey? Now we log on right here, and pay by the hour or by the download. That saves us a lot of money.

College or university students, who must travel out of town to attend classes or meet with professors, were especially pleased with the option of obtaining school information through the Web. Many can now follow up on school assignments, or register and attend classes online, without the need to travel. The ability to register online or contact professors on e-mail represents a significant cost savings for these students, and helps them to avoid frequent travel on dangerous roads. Flor, a 22-year-old who also attends classes at the university two towns over, remembered how she struggled to find information before the Internet,

> I had no Internet access when I first started college. I had to go to different places to gather information. I had to physically go somewhere else because I could not do anything from home. Now I log in from home to find what I need, or do my homework or whatever. I save time and have access to a lot of information.

Access to information that is readily available at a minimal cost has changed the way these girls live their lives. Most Internet users care about technology if it helps them save time or effort (Hammond, Turner, & Bain, 2000). Dominican girls are no different, relying on the Web to retrieve information that would otherwise be found only in schools or libraries. Alma, a 19-year-old nursing student compared her life before and after she learned to search the Web for information,

> The Internet has improved my life 100%. I used to have to sometimes go someplace far away to find information in books and such. Those days are gone. I can now easily access the Net at the telecenter nearby, and find plenty of information quickly and efficiently.

"It's one of the best tools available to students."

In the Dominican Republic, levels of functional literacy hover around 89% for women and men alike, but women are more likely to finish elementary school, and outpace men in high school and college enrollment (World Bank, 2008). Still, the overall number of those who pursue secondary education is low; teenage student retention drops to 48% by middle and high school (World Bank, 2008). This poses a significant challenge; the majority of the population is unskilled, and their literacy skills fall short of the level required for employment in a modernizing workforce. The average Dominican woman may stay in school longer than her male counterpart, yet fewer women than men join the labor force despite the absence of systematic wage discrimination in the workplace (World Bank, 2001).

In this context, the girls of El Seybo may be bucking a national trend. Every girl gushed about their schoolwork and spoke about their college plans. When prompted, they proudly discussed their school accomplishments and spoke of using the Web to search for information that helped them complete homework and school assignments. Diana, a 19-year-old journalism student, explained the significance of Web access thus,

> The Internet has had a big impact on our lives. One usually refers to the before and after of online access. Those who are not online and don't know how to use the Internet are "out." Those people are out of touch because the Internet is the greatest technology source. It's also one of the best tools for students.

Access to online resources represents a significant benefit given the dearth of public or school libraries, and the prohibitive cost of printed materials. Fifteen-year-old Andrea agrees that the Internet has made studying easier than before when, "One had to rely on whatever materials one found in class or in dictionaries. Now you go online, do a Google search, a page pops up and everything is there." Rosa, a 24-year-old nursing student, also relies on Google for her school work,

> This has been a positive change for me. In my case, I used to do a lot of research at the library, looking for books and checking one topic at a time. Now, with the Internet, I type in my search term into Google and there it is.

Students in El Seybo also benefit from the educational materials and lesson-planning resources local educators now find online. Information found on the Web supplements worn instruction guides and sparse library supplies. Patricia, a 25-year-old nursery school aide employed at the local telecenter, explained that she relies on the Internet to plan activities for her class, "Oftentimes, when I am preparing a lesson plan for my class, I find the information I need online. It's been very helpful to me. It makes it easier for me to find new information."

"I want to move up, to be someone in life."

The sight of poverty and joblessness provides these girls with a powerful incentive to pursue an education as a path to a better life. The ravages of poverty are every-where around them. At least once a month, a crowd of adults line up for subsidized food packages of rice, sardines, and cooking oil distributed by armed military troops outside the sports court behind the public telecenter.

A college education is widely considered to be a ticket out of rural poverty. Each girl spoke of pursuing a college education, dreaming of professional careers in architecture, broadcast journalism, communication, dentistry, education, engineer-ing, filmmaking, law, medicine, nursing, psychology, and tourism. Twelve-year-old Sandra already has plans for college, "Once I'm done with school, I plan to study psychology at the university so I can work with children. I would like to work with small kids in a school setting. That's my passion." Also fond of small children, Andrea said she was undecided between a career as a pediatrician, engineering, or the law. Some believe that they need more than one college degree in order to suc-ceed professionally. That is the case with Marina, 24, who's almost done with a bach-elor's degree in communication, and is thinking of going on to law school and beyond,

> Here in the Dominican Republic, there are not many media outlets where those of us who studied mass communications can make our voices heard. A law degree gives one a better chance to make money and have a second career....I would also like to get a master's so I can one day teach kids.

Whatever their plans for college, some are already aware that it is unlikely they will be able to find work in the field of their choice in the countryside. Whereas two of the girls boldly spoke of working abroad in the U.S. or in Spain. Flor betrayed some of the anxiety associated with moving away from home when she spoke about her future career,

> I want to work in [tourism]. I believe that when I finish my degree I will have to move elsewhere because the tourism trade is not very developed in El Seybo. So, I would like to work in Higuey or Bavaro, where tourism has taken off. I've never been anywhere else and I've always lived at home with my family.

Tourism is a principal source of employment and a top career choice for young adults who live in the area surrounding El Seybo, where beach resorts abound. Across the country, most of the labor force (67.3%) works in the service sector, many in the thriving tourism industry that hosts more than four million tourists each year in a country nine million people call home (Banco Central de la República Dominicana [Banco Central], 2009). Yet almost half of all Dominicans (47.6%) work in the infor-mal economy (Organisation for Economic Co-operation and Development [OECD], 2009) and endemic poverty contributes to a strong migratory outflow, mostly directed at the U.S. Women face much higher unemployment rates than men: 28.8% of working age women is out of work, compared to 11.3% of men (World Bank, 2008). Yet women still run one-third of the households in the country (ONE, 2004) and these households are more likely to be poor (World Bank, 2001).

"I hope to study to be a doctor. I like the health professions."

One new area of job growth for skilled workers is the health industry: the Fernández administration has stepped up health training in the countryside. The results are visible in improved health indicators, a life expectancy rate of 72 years of age and declining fertility rates, the latter linked to increased use of contraception (ONE, 2004). Three-quarters (77.1%) of all Dominican women of childbearing age rely on birth control pills or the rhythm methods to prevent unwanted pregnancies, contributing to a relatively low birth rate of 2.4 births per woman (World Bank, 2008). This is particularly important in a society where early marriage remains the norm; the average Dominican girl is married for the first time at the age of 21 (World Bank, 2008).

During my visit to El Seybo, I saw several young female social workers on the streets, toting white Styrofoam coolers filled with doses of vaccines to be used in childhood inoculation.

Meanwhile, on the yard outside the telecenter, a group of older girls enrolled in vocational training in nursing studied common parasitic diseases, sitting in plastic chairs under a tin-roofed open air gazebo. The young nurses-in-training discussed common disease vectors and their cures. Their teacher encouraged them to research their assignments on the Web. When asked why she was learning to use the computer, 23-year-old Vera replied, "…it's important because almost everything you do is now computerized. For that reason, we ought to learn it well and use it to our benefit." Several of these students spoke with a sense of wonder about how they were now able to track down health-related information online, and how this would help them better serve their communities. Sonia, who interrupted her college career when money was tight and is now studying to be a nurse, hopes her training will help patients locally, "I plan to work helping patients and all those in need. I want to provide the best possible service based on what I'm being taught here, and to share that knowledge with others." Whether thinking of a career in nursing or hoping to go on to medical school, these trainees all expressed a deep sense of commitment to their local community.

"I admire my mom because she is a fighter."

Early marriage signals the critical importance of family life among Dominican girls.

Whereas external friendships may be important to them, those come second to the nuclear family. The girls are fiercely proud of their families, show strong attachments to their parents, and freely admit to looking up to them as role models. In this regard, their discourse is notably different from that of their U.S. counterparts, who derive strength from friendships as a way to assert their independence from the family unit (Spear, 2000). Diana's appreciation for her family life echoed the comments of many other girls. Speaking about role models, Diana replied,

> My family [is my role model] because I've realized that although our resources are scarce compared to that of other people, we are rich because we have all we need, that is we are together. Everything else is meaningless wealth; it only amounts to physical comfort, which is not as...essential as people like to think.

In addition to praising family life, almost every single girl spoke affectionately and admiringly of her mother, many citing the sacrifices they made to provide the children with food, shelter, and education. Among the younger girls, Sandra and Andrea spoke with admiration about the contributions their working mothers made to the overall welfare of the family. Among the older ones, Marina, herself a single mother of a baby boy, praised her own mother for working hard to support her and her child, as well as other siblings, all of whom continue to live in the family home. It is somewhat common for extended families in the Dominican Republic to share a single roof, an arrangement which allows for grandmothers to remain actively engaged in childrearing across generations. Many of the girls spoke adoringly of grandmothers and fathers who were active in their upbringing.

When asked about their role models, very few thought to name anyone other than their parents. Those who did cite local celebrities, such as former President Juan Bosch, First Lady Margarita Cedeño de Fernández, and the Dominican broadcast reporter Yolanda Martinez. Hoping to become a journalist, Diana explained her admiration for Martinez thus,

> The Dominican journalist Yolanda Martinez is one of the women who have achieved the most distinction in the mostly male news media. She's a prominent columnist who's succeeded as a journalist in a field dominated by men, without sacrificing her personality and standing her ground despite working in a male profession. She's made sure her voice is heard.

The only mention of foreign celebrities came from an aspiring scriptwriter, who cited Colombian Nobel Prize-winning author Gabriel García Márquez, and from a young woman who cited her admiration for Oprah Winfrey, "because she is a woman who managed to achieve much, despite her humble origins."

While most stayed close to home in their search for role models, the girls of El Seybo nevertheless surf the Web for news about their favorite soap opera and musical stars, looking for photos of celebrities and the latest fashion trends. Marina explained that she relies on YouTube to catch up on the any soap opera episode she may have missed on television. The much younger Sandra checked for news of the stars from her favorite sitcom, while her 13-year-old classmate Blanca surfs the Walt Disney Web site and downloads music.

"The Internet had an impact in my life. I no longer stay home bored."

Internet access provides an important source of entertainment in this small community. In the eyes of Norma, 13, the Web offers an alternative to boredom by offering "many beautiful things, there's so much to see on the Internet." Almost none of the girls I spoke to showed any interest in the computer games which captivate the attention of the boys. Instead, the girls logged on to the Hi5 social networking site to check out the latest photos posted by their friends, listened to music, or checked their Hotmail accounts.

More than half of the content that is available on the Web is presented in English (Ebbertz, 2002), yet the majority of the girls are unfamiliar with any language other than Spanish. This restricts their choice of Web sites, compared to the many alternatives available to English-speaking youth. When they logged on to Google or Wikipedia, the settings on the PCs defaulted to the Spanish-language versions of the sites. Navigating beyond the search engine, the girls checked the Web for fashion tips, celebrity news, cooking recipes, and information related to their own health. Those who watched videos and music clips on YouTube bore frequent delays as they waited patiently for streams to buffer at slow connection speeds.

Another way in which the girls' experience of the Web varies markedly from that of U.S. teenagers is that almost none of them had ever shopped online. Online shopping is not only prohibitively expensive for girls in rural areas; it is also difficult to do. Most Dominicans do not hold credit cards, and those who do and know how to order goods online may not find Web merchants that fulfill deliveries in the Caribbean.

"I'm proud of having so many friends everywhere."

Online surveys and virtual ethnographies that examine teenage behavior online have established that girls and boys use the Web differently, albeit at the same rate (boyd, 2008; Livingstone, Bober, & Helsper, 2005). Whether on social networking Web sites, surfing for information, or blogging, girls are more likely than boys to use the Web to build social relationships and maintain friendships (Boneva et al. as cited in Subrahmanyam & Lin, 2007; Bortree, 2005). The girls of El Seybo are no different in this regard; they use the Web to e-mail and chat, as a way to socialize with friends, acquaintances, schoolmates, and co-workers near and far. The sizable Dominican expatriate community residing abroad fuels e-mail communication and chat sessions with relatives and friends who live abroad. More than one million Dominicans resided in the U.S. alone in 2007, according to the U.S. Census Bureau (2007).

Girls as young as 13-year-old Norma already relied on e-mail and chat to stay close to relatives and friends who moved away from the community. Twenty-year-old Rosa was alone in claiming that she only checked e-mail because the university required her to do so. All others spoke of relying on chat and e-mail on a regular basis. Among them, 18-year-old Eliane, for whom, "My favorite Web site is my e-mail inbox because I see all that is happening and everything people send me and all that I can send others." Most are nonetheless mindful of the possibility of having one's privacy disrupted online, and of the potential pitfalls of chatting with strangers. In Vera's words,

> The Internet also has disadvantages. We've been told of many cases where people are even kidnapped, or people get undressed in front of them—they set a bad example for the kids. But not everybody does that. It all depends on how you use it, you know.

Unfortunately, concern over online predators might be misplaced. The risks associated with sexual predators may extend beyond the online world. While struggling to learn basic computer skills at the telecenter, a 15-year-old teen boasted publicly about being courted by a married man. Soon after this exchange, a more cautious peer explained to me that she herself was judicious about her online contacts, which nonetheless spanned the globe, "I only use the Web to connect with friends, but only with special friends. I don't socialize with people I don't know, only with schoolmates, and with friends abroad in the United States and in Spain."

CONCLUSION

As the world economy turns increasingly more connected, the challenge of digital inclusion in the developing world becomes more pressing. The factors that contribute to restrict individual access to information and communication technologies can be structural, physical, financial, or cultural in nature (Norris, 2001; Servon, 2002). This digital divide continually shifts participation in the global economy beyond the reach of those who lack the skills or the ability to navigate the Web.

Women in developing countries stand to benefit from learning and practicing the use of information and communication technologies, and from gaining access to information found on the Web. This knowledge is critical to enacting positive social change, combating poverty, and promoting gender inclusion in the developing world (Parmentier & Huyer, 2008; Hafkin & Huyer, 2006). Thanks to their continued practice of digital literacy, the girls of El Seybo are better equipped to positively change and improve their lives, and that of their communities.

Taken together, the findings in this chapter point to an alternative path for rural communities intent on ending digital poverty and gender inequality. The girls of El Seybo have bridged the divide thanks to the affordable public Internet access. The girls looked to the Web at the local telecenter to help them with their studies and to socialize with friends. Web access provided them with an alternate means of information gathering, placing within reach knowledge that would be otherwise costly to obtain, or beyond reach. As Hammond et al. (2000) suggested, the opportunity to save time and effort comprises a powerful driver for digital literacy.

Once online, the girls embraced the Web as a tool for academic achievement. Their ability to complement their school work with information found online supported their aspirations, boosting their hopes for college in a setting where poverty conspires to limit those dreams. Unperturbed by the daunting challenges facing her, Diana spoke about one of the many projects she was involved in,

> Right now I'm writing a book that I hope to finish…it's titled *Cotton Dreams*, and tells the story of a child who decides to be mute because he's used to the fact that no one ever listens to him. So he decides to no longer speak to his family, or to anyone else. Then he happens to read a book, which helps him to realize there are things worth talking about. So, at the end of the story, he decides to speak. His first words are spoken to thank God for a new day. That's how the story goes. The ending is like a beginning.

In El Seybo, girls young and old, the daughters and granddaughters of women who lived lives muted by inequality and oppressive poverty, are also finding their voices and a reason to speak up, as they open the pages of the Web. This is a new beginning.

NOTES

1. According to Creswell (2007), case studies provide an appropriate method of investigation when cases meet clear boundaries, as in this study of the online habits of Dominican girls, which is bound by time and place.
2. The structured interview questionnaire was written in Spanish by the author, who also conducted, recorded, and transcribed the data. The questionnaire was built following Creswell's (2007) recommendations for qualitative research, which suggest the use of open-ended questions. The researcher rephrased and repeated the answers to the respondents, in order to verify and ensure that the meaning of each reply was correctly understood.
3. The inclusion of young women as old as 25 years of age is informed by the work of Baumrind (1987), who defines it as the age margin of late adolescence.
4. The interviews were recorded and transcribed by the author, and the transcripts were analyzed using NVivo software.
5. All names have been changed to ensure confidentiality.

REFERENCES

Baggio, R. (2008). *Committee for Democratization of Information Technology (CDI).* Retrieved March 18, 2008, from http://www.cdi.org.br

Banco Central de la República Dominicana [Banco Central]. (2009). Sector turismo [Tourism sector]. Banco Central de la Republica Dominicana. Retrieved March 28, 2009, from http://www.ban-central.gov.do

Baumrind, D. (1987). A developmental perspective on adolescent risk taking in contemporary America. In C. E. Irwin, Jr., (Ed.), *Adolescent social behavior and health* (pp. 93–125). San Francisco: Jossey-Bass.

Blattman, C., Jensen, R., & Roman, R. (2003). Assessing the need and potential of community networking for development in rural India. *Information Society, 19*(5), 349–364.

Bortree, D. S. (2005). Presentation of self on the Web: An ethnographic study of teenage girls' weblogs. *Education, Communication & Information, 5*(1), 25–39.

boyd, d. m. (2008). Taken out of context: American teen sociality in networked publics. Doctoral dissertation, University of California, Berkeley. Retrieved June 12, 2009, from http://www.danah.org

Creswell, J. W. (2007). *Qualitative inquiry and research design: Choosing among five traditions.* Thousand Oaks, CA: Sage.

Ebbertz, M. (2002). *Das Internet spricht Englisch...und neuerdings auch Deutsch.* [*The Internet speaks English...and now German too.*] Retrieved October 11, 2009, from http://www.netz-tipp.de/sprachen.html

Garrido, M., & Roman, R. (2006). Women in Latin America: Appropriating ICTs for social change. In N. J. Hafkin & S. Huyer (Eds.), *Cinderella or cyberella? Empowering women in the knowledge society* (pp. 165–190). Bloomfield, CT: Kumarian Press.

Hafkin, N. J., & Huyer, S. (2006). *Cinderella or cyberella? Empowering women in the knowledge society.* Bloomfield, CT: Kumarian Press.

Hammond, K., Turner, P., & Bain, M. (2000). Internet users versus non-users: Drivers in Internet uptake. *International Journal of Advertising, 19*(5), 665–681.

Heeks, R., & Kanashiro, L. L. (2009). Remoteness, exclusion and telecentres in mountain regions: Analysing ICT-based "information chains" in Pazos, Peru. Working Paper Series, Paper No. 38. Development Informatics Group. Institute for Development Policy and Management. University of Manchester. Retrieved March 23, 2009, from http://www.sed.manchester.ac.uk

Hosman, L., & Fife, E. (2008). Improving the prospects for sustainable ICT projects in the developing world. *International Journal of Media & Cultural Politics, 4*(1), 51–69.

Huyer, S. (2006a). Cyberella in the classroom? Gender, education, and technology. In N. J. Hafkin & S. Huyer (Eds.), *Cinderella or cyberella? Empowering women in the knowledge society* (pp. 95–118). Bloomfield, CT: Kumarian Press.

Huyer, S. (2006b). Understanding gender equality and women's empowerment in the knowledge society. In N. J. Hafkin & S. Huyer (Eds.), *Cinderella or cyberella? Empowering women in the knowledge society* (pp. 15–47). Bloomfield, CT: Kumarian Press.

International Telecommunications Union [ITU]. (2003). *World Summit on the Information Society.* Retrieved June 1, 2009, from http://www.itu.int/wsis/docs/geneva/official/poa.html

International Telecommunications Union [ITU]. (2008). *ITU ICT-Eye.* Retrieved May 22, 2008, from http://www.itu.int

Jensen, R. (2007). The digital provide: Information (technology), market performance and welfare in the South Indian fisheries sector. *Quarterly Journal of Economics, 122*(3), 879–924.

Kelan, E. (2008). Emotions in a rational profession: the gendering of skills in ICT work. *Gender, Work & Organization, 15*(1), 49–71.

Lenhart, A., & Madden, M. (July 11, 2006). *Teens and the Internet.* Findings submitted to the House Subcommittee on Telecommunications and the Internet. Washington, DC: Pew Internet & American Life Project.

Livingstone, S., Bober, M., & Helsper, E. J. (2005). Active participation or just more information? *Information, Communication & Society, 8*(3), 287–314.

Lozano, J. C., & Frankenberg, L. (2008). Enfoques teóricos y estrategias metodológicas en la investigación empírica de audiencias televisivas en América Latina: 1992–2007. [Theoretical focus and methodological strategies in the empirical investigation of Latin American television audiences: 1997–2007.] *Comunicacion y Sociedad (0188–252X), 10,* 81–110.

Massey, B. L., & Levy, M. L. (1999). Interactivity, online journalism, and English-language Web newspapers in Asia. *Journalism & Mass Communication Quarterly, 76*(1), 138–151.

Melkote, S. R., & Steeves, H. L. (2001). *Communication for development in the Third World: Theory and practice for empowerment.* Thousand Oaks, CA: Sage.

Morris, M., & Ogan, C. (1996). The Internet as mass medium. *Journal of Computer-Mediated Communication 1*(4), 39–50.

Munévar, D. I., & Arrieta, J. A. (2005). Gender-net: A political goal of communication technologies. In C. Ng & S. Mitter (Eds.), *Gender and the digital economy: Perspectives from the developing world* (pp. 211–230). London: Sage.

Nielsen. (2009). *How Teens Use Media.* Retrieved October 16, 2009, from www.nielsen.com

Norris, P. (2001). *Digital divide: Civic engagement, information poverty, and the Internet worldwide.* Cambridge; New York: Cambridge University Press.

Oficina Nacional de Estadística [ONE]. (2004). *Resultados definitivos VIII censo nacional de población y vivienda 2002: Características económicas. [Definitive results of the eighth national census of population and households 2002: Economic characteristics.]* Vol. V. Santo Domingo, Dominican Republic.

Oficina Nacional de Estadística [ONE]. (2009). *Teledensidad por tipo de servicio, según año, 1996–2008. [Teledensity by type of service and by year, 1996–2008.]* Retrieved October 17, 2009, from http://www.one.gob.do

Organisation for Economic Co-operation and Development [OECD]. (2009). *Is informal normal? Towards more and better jobs in developing countries.* Development Centre Studies. Retrieved April 3, 2009, from www.oecd.org

Parmentier, M. J. C., & Huyer, S. (2008). Female empowerment and development in Latin America: Use versus production of information and communications technology. *Information Technologies and International Development, 4*(3), 13–20.

Peimbert Reyes, A. (2007). ¿Qué investigan los estudios de género en la prensa? Revisión de temáticas, 1989–2004. [What is examined in research studies about gender in the media? A review of topics, 1989–2004.] In *Comunicación para el Desarrollo en México* (pp. 151–167). Mexico, DF: Asociación Mexicana de Investigadores de la Comunicación.

Proenza, F. J., Bastidas-Buch, R., & Montero, G. (2001, May). *Telecenters for socioeconomic and rural development in Latin America and the Caribbean: Investment opportunities and design recommendations, with special reference to Central America.* Washington, DC: Inter-American Development Bank. Retrieved April 3, 2009, from http://www.iadb.org/regions/itdev/telecentros/index.htm

Rafaeli, S. (1988). Interactivity: From new media to communication, In R. P. Hawkins, J. M. Wiemann, & S. Pingree (Eds.), *Sage annual review of communication research: Advancing communication science, 16*, (pp. 110–134). Beverly Hills, CA: Sage.

Rey, N. (2006). *Acceso universal en Latinoamérica: Situación y desafíos, 2006.* Geneva, Switzerland: International Telecommunication Union [ITU].

Roman, R., & Colle, R. D. (2002, July 21–26). *Creating a participatory telecenter enterprise.* Paper presented at the Participatory Communication Research Section in the annual meeting of International Association for Media and Communication Research, Barcelona, Spain.

Schilderman, T. (2002). *Strengthening the knowledge and information systems of the urban poor.* Practical Action, ITDG. Retrieved December 10, 2008, from http://www.eldis.org/cf/search/disp/docdisplay.cfm?doc=DOC10072&resource=f1

Servon, L. J. (2002). *Bridging the digital divide: Technology, community, and public policy.* Malden, MA: Blackwell.

Sorj, B. (2003). *Brasil@povocom: A luta contra a desigualdade na sociedade da informação.* [*Brasil@povocom: The fight against inequality in the information society.*] Rio de Janeiro: J. Zahar.

Spear, L. P. (2000). The adolescent brain and age-related behavioral manifestations. *Neuroscience Bio-behavioral Review. 24*(4), 417–463.

Subrahmanyam, K., & Lin, G. (2007). Adolescents on the Net: Internet use and well-being. *Adolescence, 42*(168), 659–677.

Tolbert, C., Mossberger, K., King, B., & Miller, G. L. (2007). Are all American women making progress online? African-Americans and Latinas. *Information Technologies and International Development, 4*(2), 61–88.

United Nations Development Programme [UNDP]. (2008). *Human development report 2007–2008.* New York: United Nations.

United States Census Bureau. (2007). *American Fact Finder: American Community Survey.* Washington, DC: United States Government Printing Office.

van Dijk, J. A.G. M. (1999). *The network society: Social aspects of new media.* London: Sage.

van Dijk, J. A.G. M., & Hacker, K. (2000). *Digital democracy: Issues of theory and practice.* London; Thousand Oaks, CA: Sage.

van Dijk, J. A. G. M., & Hacker, K. (2003). The digital divide as a complex and dynamic phenomenon. *Information Society, 19*(4), 315–326.

Warschauer, M. (2003). *Technology and social inclusion: Rethinking the digital divide.* Cambridge, MA: MIT Press.

World Bank. (2001). *Dominican Republic poverty assessment: Poverty in a high-growth economy (1986–2000).* Report No. 21306-DR. Washington, DC: World Bank.

World Bank. (2008, September). *Dominican Republic at a glance.* Retrieved March 29, 2009, from http://devdata.worldbank.org

World Bank. (2009a). *Gender Stats.* Retrieved March 29, 2009, from http://web.worldbank.org/
World Bank. (2009b). Country partnership strategy for the Dominican Republic for the period
     FY10-FY13. Report No. 49620-DO. Washington, DC: World Bank.

CHAPTER TWO

Degrees of Caution

Arab Girls Unveil on Facebook

RODDA LEAGE & IVANA CHALMERS[1]

When we asked Arab girls taking part in our study how they expressed their identity they had little trouble discussing their appearances, their interests, their religions or their families. However, when asked how they expressed themselves on social network sites like Facebook they often seemed confused and uncertain. Most of our participants explained that Facebook was a place to communicate, and not a place to express their identity. As residents of a conservative Arab country and social network site (SNS) users ourselves, we were curious to learn more about how Arab girls express themselves on a site like Facebook. What methods would they use? Would they feel comfortable expressing themselves publicly in a culture that values discretion and privacy? Would they take more liberties online than offline? How would Arab girls negotiate other aspects of the site that might conflict with their cultural values? In order to address these questions, our study explores how Arab girls use social network sites as a means of achieving identity expression.

THE LITERATURE

Expressing Yourself on Facebook

Researchers have consistently shown that people use SNSs as a vehicle for expressing their identities (Tufekci, 2008a). As Livingstone (2008, p. 394) suggests, posting content online and networking with others is an "integral means of managing one's identity, lifestyle and social relations." Goffman's (1959) view of identity as a kind of performance for an intended audience or imagined community speaks to Facebook users' practice of making implicit identity claims and appeals to group identities (Merchant, 2006; Pearson, 2009; Zhao, Grasmuck, & Martin, 2008). Such behavior signals that the user intends to be perceived in a certain way (Donath, 2007).

Because the relationships that people pursue on Facebook are usually with people whom users know in their offline environments (boyd & Ellison, 2008), there are limitations to the level of creative performance and identity construction that can occur (Albrechtslund, 2008; DiMicco & Millen, 2007). As a result, those who reveal their identity online (Sundén, 2003), often present themselves in a way that will be perceived as realistic but also positive (Pearson, 2009; Strano, 2008; Vazire & Gosling, 2004). Additionally, the honesty of this presentation affects the extent to which newly formed relationships online can be brought into the offline world (Bargh, McKenna, & Fitzsimons, 2002; McKenna, Green, & Gleason, 2002).

Facebook users make choices in how they will use the technology's features to express their identity. The profile picture is one primary feature that is often used to convey one's sense of self to others. Researchers estimate that users change their profile pictures, on average, seven times a year (Strano, 2008). In the digital age, photographs are seen as building blocks for personal identity and users' choice of posted photographs is indicative of identity expression (Van Dijck, 2008). In addition to actively controlling information displayed on their Facebook profiles, users can also limit their visibility (Tufekci, 2008b). By restricting who can be their Facebook friend and who can view their posts and activities, users delicately negotiate simultaneous connections to a range of people who belong to distinct, separate social networks in their offline life (DiMicco & Millen, 2007; Hewitt & Forte, 2006).

The Middle East Joins Facebook

Much of the research on identity expression on SNS is focused on American and European youth. The lack of research on SNS in the Middle East could be a consequence of many factors; however, the lack of Internet access, low Internet literacy levels, and low numbers of users are all contributing factors (Arrington, 2007; Julfar, 2006; Wheeler, 2005).

Having been looked at most extensively, Facebook proves to be a good starting point for researchers wishing to supplement existing knowledge on SNS from other parts of the world. Research on women's use of technology in the Middle East has focused on its ability to empower, democratize, and allow women entry to the public sphere (Al-Jassem, 2006; Al-Zubaidi, 2004) thereby allowing the emergence of new identities (Anderson, 1999). Women in this region are enabled by modern technologies to produce alternative discourses about their womanhood, citizenship, and political participation in society (Skalli, 2006) and are able to experience enhanced freedoms of expression and expanded choices for social interaction (Wheeler, 2005). The impact of Twitter in the recent Iran elections is a good example of ways in which enhanced technology is making it possible for citizens to voice their opinions and concerns to a global audience (Cardwell, 2009).

Facebook has caused a stir in the Middle East, evident by recent news coverage of it being used as a platform for protest by "giving voices to the voiceless" (An unseen burqa revolution, 2009; Eltahawy, 2009). A Saudi Arabian woman was recently beaten and killed by her father after he discovered she had been conversing with a man on Facebook (McElroy, 2008). While extreme, this example illustrates the tension that Facebook has created in the Arab world and the threat to cultural norms is the likely reason for Facebook censorship by governments (Al-Zubaidi, 2004). Despite these problems, Facebook remains pervasive and is now available in Arabic through Facebook Beta. The demand for more Arabic-centered or Arabic language sites (Jafaafar, 2009) is evident in the large number of sites such as www.kalamarab.com, www.ArabFriendz.com, and iMatter, a network site with relevant issues by and for Arab women.

Our Study

Because so few studies have focused on how SNSs are used in the Arab world, in general, or by Arab girls, in particular, we decided to use an inductive approach to our data collection and analysis. We interviewed 42 girls between the ages of 18 and 22, all of whom were university students. All participants were unmarried, lived with their parents, and most practiced Islam. Our study received IRB approval through Northwestern University and each participant was informed of their rights before signing a consent form. All but eight spoke Arabic as their first language, and all were fluent in English as a second language. Although they traced their origins to a number of countries in the Middle East, including Syria, Egypt, Lebanon, and Saudi Arabia most participants grew up in Qatar. Despite differences in national origin, participants shared many of the overarching commonalities in cultural codes identified by Al-Jassem (2006) such as shared understandings of religion, politics, and family responsibility and most referred to themselves as "Arab." It is highly problematic in Middle-Eastern Arab countries to refer to unmarried females as "women," since the title signifies that the female has engaged in sexual intercourse; therefore, our participants referred to themselves as "girls." Hence, throughout our chapter, we use the nomenclature provided by our participants and refer to them as "Arab girls."

Our data collection took place in Doha, Qatar. Qatar, located on the Arabian Peninsula, is one of the world's wealthiest countries thanks to prodigious oil and national gas reserves (Stasz, Eide, & Martorell, 2007). It is regarded as one of the most conservative Arab countries and places a high value on its cultural and religious traditions (Bahry, 1999). Qatar is an ideal place to study online identity expression among Arab girls for several reasons. First, due to its wealth, Qatar has seen an influx of immigrants from neighboring Arab countries in recent years. Thus we were able to interview a wide range of Arab girls. Nineteen of the 42 girls that we interviewed were Qatari nationals and 15 claimed patrimony from other Arab countries. Second, despite their diverse national backgrounds, participants growing up in Qatar all experienced the country's strong cultural norms regarding the role of women in society. Women's primary role is defined as heads of households, mothers, and wives (Rashad, Osman, & Roudi-Fahimi, 2005), yet women in Qatar have the ability to vote and have already attained a number of high-level government positions (Bahry, 1999; Hoveyda, 2005). Third, due to Qatar's high socioeconomic status, the average college-age girl has numerous computer-enabled devices at her disposal, including laptop computers, smart phones, and PDAs that they can use to connect to SNS such as Facebook. Finally, because English is the *lingua franca* in Qatari higher education, and because most girls have taken English classes every year since their primary education, most are fluent in English. This means that they have access to a wide array of English language web sites and that we, as researchers from English speaking countries, could communicate with our participants easily.

We constructed and pilot tested a standard interview protocol that asked participants three series of questions. First, we inquired about how participants expressed themselves to others. Specifically, we were interested to learn what types of strategies they used to perform their identities to themselves and others, and how cultural norms regarding the behavior of Arab girls affected these processes. Second, we asked participants about the kinds of SNS technologies they regularly used. We queried them about how and when they used the features. We also asked how their online identities either coincided or clashed with their offline presentations. Finally, we asked questions about whether or not participants felt that they were more free or less free to enact their identities online than offline. Each author conducted approximately half of the interviews, which normally lasted between 30 and 40 minutes. All interviews were audio-recorded and were later transcribed verbatim.

As we coded our interview data, we were struck by the pervasiveness of participants' discussion of reputation and the important role that it played in moderating identity construction. The girls in our study consistently mentioned that they actively monitored their reputation because so much of their standing within Arab culture, in general, and Qatari society, in particular, depended upon how one conducted herself in public. For example, girls mentioned that they must wear the appropriate, modest dress (for Qatari girls this is the *abaya*[2] and *shayla*[3]), have limited or no contact with non-related males, and in general be modest and demonstrate that their families have instilled these qualities in them well. Consider, for example the explanation of the importance of reputation in Qatari society by Hadal, 19[4]:

> What Qatari people worry about the most is reputation. And reputation is a very, very, very important thing for men and women, but specifically women because reputation is all about who you are. We have specific regulations for women that for instance, if she puts her picture on Facebook, she's very open-minded, she doesn't stick to her cultural beliefs or traditional beliefs, so she is not really—she doesn't really come from a good family. That's how typical minds think.

Quotations like the one above abounded in our data. Girls suggested again and again that a female's reputation defines her character and that if she were to do something that was *haram*,[5] she would permanently damage her reputation and shame her family. Our data suggested that actively working to establish and maintain her reputation is a major factor in Arab girl's identity construction. Thus, we decided to focus our analysis efforts to understand how this strong desire to establish a good reputation affected the ways that girls' used Facebook to perform their identities.

Findings

We have divided this section into four areas or "approaches" used by girls to express their identity. In the first approach, girls, for a variety of reasons, chose not to participate in social network sites. In the second approach, girls used Facebook but were careful to follow the conventions of the culture and, as a result, used it as a means of limited self-expression. In the third approach, creative methods were implemented to allow for more self-expression, while staying within the conventions of culture. In the fourth and final approach, users disregarded certain cultural mores in order to have greater freedom of expression. In our interviews we found that girls' approaches were not mutually exclusive. Participants expressed themselves using a variety of methods, and while each girl did not necessarily fit into only one category, the range of responses showed some distinct ways that girls negotiated identity expression within their culture.

Danger Zone: Reasons to Not Join Facebook

> It's just inevitable. I think you're going to misconvey to people who you really are [on Facebook] even without thinking or meaning to. (Amina, 18)

Facebook is popular in Qatar. Girls are excited by new technology in general and are interested in how it can be used to enhance their lives. Students write papers extolling the virtues of technology, and are eager to take classes that teach them more about technological innovations.

However, despite its growing popularity, a few girls that we talked with chose not to participate in SNSs like Facebook. Leila tried Facebook for about 10 days but quit because it was boring and she didn't enjoy it. She signed up, in part because all of her friends had joined but decided that she was too busy to participate. She explained that she preferred using her phone as a way to stay in touch. However, when pressed as to why she decided to stop using Facebook Leila, 21, said that it also bothered her that some people misrepresented themselves,

> That's just sad to me. That's why I just didn't want to get involved in all that. I just think I'm—I don't want to say I'm higher than this because obviously it's not like that. It's not classified like that, because my friends have Facebook and I know them very well.

Here Leila touches on two important issues in Qatari culture. The first is misrepresentation: photographs, comments, or even friends (namely, the opposite sex) seen as inappropriate can seriously damage a girl's reputation and future. Leila's apprehension at "get[ting] involved" with a site that has the potential to harm her reputation, touches on one of the underlying concerns in Arab girls' participation on Facebook. A second issue, stressed by Leila throughout our conversation, is the importance of family for a young woman. She explained that, all Qatari girls have a commitment to their religion and their family. While she never used the word "reputation," she did say, "I really do care about my image, and how people would look at me, because I just don't want to send the wrong message." The anxiety over sending the wrong message seems to be concern among many of the Arab girls with whom we spoke.

Like Leila, many girls expressed that family is one of the most important influences on a girl's life, and it is important that she maintains her reputation as a way of honoring them. While it is probable that Leila does prefer the phone to Facebook for its convenience, her denial that, "I don't want to say I'm higher than this because obviously it's not like that," suggests that it may be exactly like that. The reason isn't that Leila actually thinks she's better than her friends who use Facebook, but that because she has been raised to place a high value on her reputation as an extension of her family's reputation, she will take precautious measures in order to protect it. After trying out Facebook, Leila opted out of using it, citing that she didn't have the time and that it bored her, but she also mentioned that, "I was shocked when I saw [friends'] pictures and you know, like if their parents knew that . . ." Leila had multiple reasons for opting out of Facebook, one of them being her concern that Facebook could potentially hurt her family's reputation.

Leila isn't the only one who is concerned with reputation. Amina also had similar concerns. Like Leila, she prefers to engage in types of communication that are less likely to be misunderstood, and she is anxious over how she appears online, stressing the importance of context:

> Even a full stop or an exclamation mark used incorrectly can give off the wrong signals. A photo taken out of context can give off a lot of wrong signals and wrong messages. Facebook, I think, is the most powerful tool to facilitate [rumors] and [other girls] use it as a weapon to arm their gossip.

Further, Amina described posting images as, "putting myself up for sale," and she displays anxiety over the power of Facebook when she described it as a "weapon." The strong language that she uses to describe her reasons against joining Facebook shows that some girls feel pressure to live up to the social expectations in Qatar. Underlying both girls' comments appeared to be concern about being misunderstood or misjudged within their community and potentially damaging their reputations.

Better safe than sorry: Minimal self-expression on Facebook

> There's no freedom on Facebook. (Alma, 19)

In the first approach girls chose to not participate on Facebook, but these examples are the exception rather than the rule; only three out of 42 participants were not currently on Facebook. Our second approach was much more common. In this approach girls used Facebook, however, they were very careful not to express themselves in ways that could be viewed as inappropriate by the culture. The approach used in this section allowed girls to participate on Facebook, while avoiding cultural conflicts. In this approach many girls, according to Kaliyah, 18, use it "just to keep in touch," and Facebook wasn't generally seen as a safe place for self-expression. In reality, some of the girls did use it to express themselves, but they gave many reasons for limiting what type of information they included on their site. We found a wide range of styles in this approach, with some participants showing almost no identity expression and others displaying a high degree. The following section will look at identity expression on a variety of Facebook features.

Status Updates

Many girls commented on their discomfort with emotional statements on status updates. There were two main reasons for this. The first is that they often felt that they could easily be misunderstood; the second is that they didn't think it was appropriate to express strong emotions in public. Kaliyah captures both of these sentiments when she says,

> I really hate that anyone can misunderstand [status updates] and I would rather not have a Facebook status. I don't want everyone knowing what I'm doing all of the time. The idea disturbs me.

The discomfort with public displays of emotion was a common sentiment among our participants. Many expressed that they felt that it was inappropriate to be overly expressive in a public setting. Concern was shown for girls who chose to display too much emotion, be it positive or negative, in both offline and online shared spaces. Furthermore, many felt that they were under scrutiny from friends and families regarding their public behavior. Whereas individuals in the West often underestimate the public aspect of Facebook, girls in the Middle East are extremely aware of this reality.

Images

Most of the girls with whom we spoke had no images of themselves on their site, while some girls had a few images, and a few posted many images. Instead, many found creative ways to post images that still allowed them to express themselves. Rasha, 18, explains why she doesn't post her picture,

> Yeah, I do [post images] but not my picture, because I can't. I'm a Muslim, so I can't put my pictures up because I'm a woman. And the culture, people will say, "Oh, she has her picture on Facebook. She is very open-minded. She is not a respected good girl." They'll think that I'm bad.

Rasha, like many girls that we interviewed, frequently used black and white language like "good/bad," "wrong/right," and "*haram*/permitted" to describe her actions. These participants perceived that they had little latitude in how they presented themselves on Facebook. While this cautious approach allows for some negotiation within the culture, in this category participants generally follow the rules set out by their parents, even when they don't personally understand them or agree with them. As Dima, 20, explains,

> I decided [to remove photos on Facebook] to avoid trouble from my parents. So I don't necessarily like totally think it's right, but still to avoid any trouble. It's like a double identity where within yourself you might be thinking things are right, but unfortunately your culture does not think it's right.

It was common to hear girls adapting their site to please their parents, brothers, or friends. They would remove pictures, change the types of information they post, and "unfriend" people if their siblings didn't approve of them. Some even had friends who had stopped using Facebook entirely at the request of a family member.

Additionally, as we have seen in earlier examples, there is a strong mistrust of the Internet and social network sites. Samar, 19, shares her reasons for not posting images of herself:

> The Internet isn't a very safe place. I'd hate it if I saw someone else take my picture and uses it as their own. It's a lot of risk. You don't know how they'd use your picture. You don't know how they're going to interpret it. And I'm just not willing to take that risk.

This response was common among our participants. This concern over the tampering of images was always hazily explained; however, their concern was very real. While many changed their behavior on Facebook in order to avoid problems, some did find ways to express themselves while still remaining inside the cultural boundaries. Interestingly, the girls we interviewed rarely felt that not being able to post their image was a problem, as Kaliyah said, "There are so many things that define me other than my face."

Tools of Expression

Despite the culture boundaries that some girls experienced in Qatar, some managed to both abide by the customs and find culturally acceptable ways of expressing themselves. One example was a friend of an interviewee who used the "Notes" feature as a journal, which she shared with selected friends. The interviewee perceived it as a way that her friend could express her emotions and concerns on Facebook and shares them with selected friends, choosing who had access to her Notes and who did not. Restricting access was a method used by many girls and became more frequent as a girl attempted broader self-expression.

A second example of self-expression can be seen here from Anisah, 18:

> We can spend hours just looking at the bumper stickers and laughing at them. I like sending them out. And then when it shows who sent it, it shows kind of who you are, like if you send a really good one, it kind of shows who you are.

Anisah feels that sending *Bumper Stickers*—virtual "stickers" with images and humorous messages that can be sent to friends and displayed on profiles and in streams—enables her to show her personality and have fun with her friends. This type of expression, as long as it isn't sexually explicit or in poor taste, is perfectly acceptable in the culture and it allows her to freely interact with her friends online.

Freedom on Facebook

Despite opportunities for self-expression, when participants were asked if they felt that overall Facebook gave them the freedom to express themselves, most participants responded that it did not. They often spoke about the possibility for self-expression, but few said that they were currently experiencing it. The following excerpt from Maram, 22, who was asked how she decided what information to post on Facebook and what information to leave out, might help explain why:

> According to what people would think. My family. I have to keep into consideration, every time I upload something, I upload a picture, what would people think? And sometimes I would ask my friends to untag me. If they have a picture of me, they must untag me, so that people I know won't see the picture.

Maram believes that she must manage the content on both her site and to some extent her friends' sites in order to guarantee that she is presented properly. While many people would claim to have similar concerns on SNS, the vigilance that girls like Maram keep is much more demanding. While Facebook allows her a certain amount of self-expression she must constantly manage that "freedom," begging the question of whether or not the payoff is actually worth it.

While we have shown examples of self-expression on Facebook, girls in this approach primarily choose to play it safe, avoiding language or images that might offend someone. In the next approach we'll observe girls expressing themselves more fully by using creative methods in their Facebook approach, while remaining within cultural boundaries.

Proceeding with Caution: Using Creative Approaches on Facebook

> I have one identity, but my friends can't see all of it. (Anisah)

Rather than not participating like those in our first approach, or minimally expressing themselves by limiting their participation on Facebook like those in our second approach, the behavior in the third approach stayed within the cultural bounds but employed more creative techniques.

Status Updates

As we saw with the previous approach, many girls were concerned about putting too much information on their status updates, but Anisah found a creative solution to this dilemma. In order to negotiate the privacy challenges on Facebook while still expressing herself, she created a system for pleasing both of her competing desires—identity expression and privacy. She would often write a string of nonsequiturs that didn't appear to relate, but to her close friends revealed or at least suggested specific information about her current status. For example, she once wrote, "red lipstick" on her Status Update to communicate that she was going to a party. Her close friends could "decode" her status update and knew that she would be at the party, but most people wouldn't know that she was referring to her evening plans.

Images

Many participants responded creatively to the cultural expectation that images of females should not be posted online. They found imaginative ways to express their identity through their profile pictures. Janan, 20, described posting an advertisement of a perfume bottle. On the surface this seemed to signify little, but she went on to describe that the ad was created by an artist that she and her friends had learned about in an art class. Janan's friends commented on the profile picture and it helped to connect them and remind them of this shared experience from high school. Kalila, 20, posted a picture that revealed her lower body feeding ducks at Hyde Park, which she felt was permissible since it didn't show her face. Digitally altering your face so that only half of it shows (scored vertically) is another approach; in this way, a girl might be allowed by her family to show her picture, the rationale being that the face, since it isn't entirely there, can't be tampered with online. Taking this idea to a greater extreme, Facebook groups with names like "hottest hair" and "hottest stomach" are well-known to some of our participants. These sites invite members to post images of a specific body part for general viewing, but no one's identity is ever revealed. While these sites don't seem to support authentic identity expression, they do suggest that many girls, despite the cultural expectations, are eager to renegotiate these boundaries, and the variety of examples of profile pictures stand as a testament to the girls' creative impulses.

Another interesting profile picture example can be seen in the strategy of Fadia, 18. For her profile picture she asked someone to take a photograph of the back of her head as she looks through her camera lens at a female model in stylish clothing that she was shooting for a class project. The picture showcases her interest in photography and cleverly avoids showing her face while still showing her body in action. The photograph's inventive angle further serves as an example of her talent in the art of photography. Fadia originally said that she didn't think that Facebook was an appropriate place for identity-expression, but after describing her profile picture she commented with surprise that she had been engaged in identity expression without even realizing it.

Creative Approaches

As seen above, many girls in our third approach often limit access in some way, only allowing certain people to see or understand certain information, thereby giving them the opportunity for more expansive identity expression. Participants employing this approach used the privacy settings in a variety of ways, including putting friends on limited profile, customizing specific photo albums that include photos that might not be deemed acceptable by some friends, or by "unfriending" individuals that may share what's on the individuals Facebook page with others who can damage their reputation.

Taking this approach to another level, some of our participants created fantastic, fabricated identities on Facebook, inventing characters with Facebook profiles that had the opportunity to participate in activities that the girls would not actually be allowed to take part in. Writing about these characters' adventures on Facebook allowed them to express their unspoken desires. Samar, 19, spoke about girls who,

> Make up amazing, amazing characters and they talk about their adventures and what I did last week in the city and what I am going to do with my boyfriend and stuff like that, so it creates like a split personality. But to them, it's not real, they're just doing it to vent. Like to get what they want out of their system, like if they can't say this in front of their parents, hey, what the heck, I'll say it on the Internet. Nobody knows who I am.

In this example we see the anonymity of Facebook again being used to allow for greater self-expression. According to Samar, girls could be creative and express their desires for a life that was currently out of reach. By creating an alternative identity on Facebook these girls expressed, not their realities, but their hopes for the future. In this way the girls used an online tool to "vent" about their frustrations to friends and take pleasure in their imaginary life.

A very different approach was used by Hana, 20, a member of three social network sites: Facebook, MySpace, and an ethnic-specific site. She used the sites to display different aspects of her identity and her friends on each site differed based on the site's identity. For example, on MySpace she posted pictures of concerts and more intimate photographs of her and her friends because she felt that she had more privacy there than the other two sites. On the ethnic-specific site she has photographs of her in traditional dress and posts information that relates more to the shared culture of the friends she has on this site. Overall she believed that the privacy of the different sites granted her more freedom to express herself. Like all of the girls in this section, Hana found an innovative way to have a high degree of identity expression while still remaining within the cultural expectations.

Calculated Risk: Disregarding Cultural Mores on Facebook

> People think it's really bad for girls to have—especially Arab girls who are restricted in their own real environment—to have other personalities online, but I think it's really helpful. (Samar)

Girls desiring more communication on Facebook than the Qatari culture deemed acceptable found themselves taking greater risks online. For Nashwa, 19, this meant joining an Arab dating site, despite the fact that, for Qatari females, dating is strictly forbidden. She enjoyed being a member of the site because it allowed her to befriend and chat with males online whom she wouldn't be allowed to converse with offline. While the custom in Qatar is currently such that parents play a large role in determining their children's marriages, Nashwa hoped that she would meet her future husband through an online dating site, thus giving her more control over who she married. Interestingly, Nashwa's three brothers were also on dating sites and although this is becoming more acceptable for boys, it is currently never acceptable for girls. When asked if this gender difference bothered her she said,

> It frustrates me, and it's not part of Islam. It's just part of our culture, because Islam sees women and men at the same level. Men are not superior. But the culture gives extra opportunity for men to do whatever they want. In education, we are equal. But in real life, we are not.

Throughout our interviews many Arab girls expressed that the reality for them in Qatar is that they currently must live with inequality—both offline and online. While one may assume that SNSs like Facebook actually allow girls more freedom of expression, the truth is that living in a close-knit community—"Being judged 24/7" as Rasha, 19, expressed it—means that online information quickly reaches the offline world where it can potentially be used to damage a girl's reputation. When pressed about what consequences she would face if her family found out that she was participating on a dating site, she admitted that, "My brothers will have the right to maybe beat me." Currently, Nashwa is willing to take this risk in order to "meet her soul mate" and have more freedom online.

While Nashwa's story may seem extreme, Samar echoed a similar story. Friends of hers have used alternative identities on Facebook in order to "friend" boys and communicate with them on the site. She talked about friends getting beaten up for this type of behavior, and had a friend who was taken out of school because she had started a relationship with a boy who attended. While some girls are clearly willing to violate certain cultural rules in order to communicate more freely online, the consequences may be quite severe.

Both of these stories raise the question of whether this type of communication can really be classified as reaching greater "identity expression." Perhaps this is nothing more than an example of teens attempting to date? The distinction seems to be that while their desires may be romantically inclined, the act of using an online tool like Facebook to communicate your personality, interests, and attitudes speaks directly to identity expression. They seem to have two related goals in mind through their use of SNSs: challenging cultural norms and achieving identity expression, and are willing to take risks in order to have both.

However, some girls have turned meeting people on Facebook into a game. As Kalila explained,

> Me and my friends, if we like a guy or something, we have a fake profile and all of us know the password and all of us go on it like a million times a day. Like we don't even

go on our own profiles, but we go on that profile, just to like spy on people, and it's kind of fun. We like—we'll learn more about them that way. They do use privacy settings, but we add them as a friend and they accept. We're afraid if we contact them, they'll realize we—we don't—they don't know each other and they'll delete us, so we're just like completely quiet about the whole thing.

Although the girls clearly enjoyed the game of "spying" on the boys, the fact that they chose to create an alternative identity in order to learn more about the boys demonstrates their desire to express their interest through Facebook. It isn't surprising that they turn to SNSs since they generally aren't able to openly befriend boys offline. Since they aren't supposed to befriend boys online either, they have devised a way to learn about them secretly, albeit in this example the communication flows only one way.

Alternative identities, as we have mentioned numerous times, are used often by Arab girls seeking more freedom online. Anisah shared an example of a friend who used an unusual spelling of her name for her Facebook account so that only people that she wanted to be able to find her on the site could do so. In this way, she posted pictures of her "partying" that her parents wouldn't approve of and other information that she wouldn't want to be made public if she felt pressured to add friends that would look her up on Facebook's "Find a Friend" feature. While her photos could be made public by those who visited her site she felt that she had control over who was invited to view her site and the unusual spelling would detract friends that might search for her under the "Find a Friend" feature. By changing the spelling of her name she gave herself the opportunity to communicate more freely online.

DISCUSSION

The purpose of this chapter was to explore whether or not Arab girls, living in a conservative and close-knit community such as Qatar, would use Facebook as a place for identity expression. We would argue that the pressure that many girls feel to comply with their culture and protect their reputation often limits their ability to express themselves as fully as they would like. For a few girls this meant choosing not to join Facebook because it was perceived as too dangerous. Others enjoyed being on Facebook, using it primarily as a way to "stay in touch" rather than express their identity. Some were able to simultaneously express themselves and respect their culture by being creative in their approach. For others, rebelling against the cultural norms requires subversion, most often through communication with males, which is not looked upon favorably.

Negotiating the cultural expectations of Arab girls in a rapidly changing social landscape is no easy feat. While all Qatari females are expected to wear the full-length *abaya* and *shayla* in public, underneath that you will often find typical, fitted, Western clothing, and tall heels. On Facebook they are once again caught between two worlds: using a Western-based technology but adapting it to their own culture.

One encouraging finding from our study was that girls who used creative methods to express themselves on Facebook generally had positive experiences both publicly and privately. Their ability to balance cultural expectations and their desire for identity expression may be a good model for approaching this research topic in the future.

Perceptions of Facebook in Qatar do show signs of changing. Through talking with girls, we learned stories of Arab couples meeting on Facebook and later marrying, and of parents who enjoy using Facebook and don't mind their daughters posting personal photographs. Perhaps Nashwa will even meet her soul mate online. The girls we spoke with were optimistic about the opportunities that social network sites like Facebook could provide, even if our study suggests that many girls feel that cultural conventions currently limit some aspects of their identity expression.

As Facebook and similar social network sites increase in popularity around the globe, they undoubtedly cause a shift in the perception of identity and in identity management. While many of our participants were initially hesitant to agree that they used Facebook as a tool for self-expression, many ended the interview excited by the realization that they did in fact express themselves online. Limitations on their self-expression were often approached as a challenge to be overcome or a reality to accept. How girls in conservative Islamic countries like Qatar will continue to negotiate these new technologies is left to be seen; however, it seems that they are prepared to continue finding new ways to express themselves. As Samar said, "If a girl wants to do something, nothing in the world will stop her, nothing in the world."

NOTES

1. The order of our names on this chapter should not be taken as an indication of lead and second authorship. We are co-authors in every sense of the word.
2. An *abaya* is a scarf worn around the head which covers the hair.
3. A *shayla* is a loose, modest gown worn over clothing.
4. All girls' names are pseudonyms.
5. *Haram* is a commonly used word in Arabic, which translates loosely to "forbidden."

REFERENCES

Albrechtslund, A. (2008, March). Online social network as participatory surveillance. *First Monday*, *13*(3). Retrieved April 22, 2009, from http://www.uic.edu/htbin/cgiwrap/bin/ojs/index.php/fm/article/viewArticle/2142/1949

Al-Jassem, M. (2006). The impact of the electronic media on Arab socio-political development. In *Arab media in the information age* (pp. 169–182). Abu Dhabi, UAE: Emirates Center for Strategic Studies and Research.

Al-Zubaidi, L. (Ed.). (2004). *Walking a tightrope: News media & freedom of expression in the Arab Middle East*. Beirut: Heinrich Böll Foundation.

An unseen burqa revolution. (2009, May 11). *Christian Science Monitor*, p. 8.

Anderson, J. W. (1999, September). *Technology, media, and the next generation in the Middle East*. Paper presented at the Middle East Institute, Columbia University, New York, USA. Retrieved April 28, 2009, from http://www.mafhoum.com/press3/104T45.htm

Arrington, M. (2007, November 21). Facebook is almost 2/3 women and other stats. *TechCrunch*. Retrieved April 26, 2009, from http://www.techcrunch.com/2007/11/21

Bahry, L. (1999, June). Elections in Qatar: A window of democracy opens in the Gulf. *Middle East policy*, *4*(4). Retrieved May 15, 2009, from http://www.mepc.org/journal_vol6/bahry.html

Bargh, J. A., McKenna, K. Y. A., & Fitzsimons, G. M. (2002). Can you see the real me? Activation and expression of the "true self" on the Internet. *Journal of Social Issues*, *58*(1), 33–48.

boyd, d. m., & Ellison, N. B. (2008). Social network sites: Definition, history, and scholarship. *Journal of Computer-Mediated Communication*, *13*, 210–230.

Cardwell, S. (2009, June). A Twitter timeline of the Iran election. *Newsweek*. Retrieved July, 2009, from http://www.newsweek.com/id/203953

DiMicco, J. M., & Millen, D. R. (2007, November). *Identity management: Multiple presentations of self in Facebook*. Paper presented at the ACM GROUP'07, Sanibel Island, FL, USA.

Donath, J. (2007). Signals in social supernets. *Journal of Computer-Mediated Communication*, *13*(1), article 12. Retrieved April 28, 2009, from http://jcmc.indiana.edu/vol13/issue1/donath.html

Eltahawy, M. (2009, January 5). Blogging for freedom. *The Jerusalem Post*, p. 25.

Goffman, E. (1959). *The Presentation of self in everyday life*. New York: Anchor Books.

Hewitt, A., & Forte, A. (2006, November). *Crossing boundaries: Identity management and student/faculty relationships on the Facebook*. Paper presented at the ACM Conference on Computer Supported Cooperative Work CSCW'06, Banff, Alberta, Canada.

Hoveyda, F. (2005). Arab women and the future of the Middle East. *American Foreign Policy Interests*, *27*, 419–488.

Jafaafar, A. (2009, March 23). Finding the right niche. *The Guardian (London)*, Newsprint Supplement, sp. 2.

Julfar, A. A. (2006). Empowering the Arab media through the internet. In *Arab media in the information age* (pp. 183–198). Abu Dhabi, UAE: The Emirates Center for Strategic Studies and Research.

Livingstone, S. (2008). Taking risky opportunities in youthful content creation: Teenagers' use of social network sites for intimacy, privacy and self-expression. *New Media & Society*, *10*(3), 393–411.

McElroy, D. (2008, April 1). Saudi woman killed for chatting on Facebook. *The Daily Telegraph* (London). p. 16.

McKenna, K. Y. A., Green, A. S., & Gleason, M. E. J. (2002). Relationship formation on the internet: What's the big attraction? *Journal of Social Issues*, *58*(1), 9–31.

Merchant, G. (2006). Identity, social networks and online communication. *E–Learning, 3*(2), 235–244.

Pearson, E. (2009, March). All the World Wide Web's a stage: The performance of identity in online social networks. *First Monday, 14*(3). Retrieved April 28, 2009, from http://www.uic.edu/htbin/cgiwrap/bin/ojs/index.php/fm/article/viewArticle/2162/2127

Rashad, H., Osman, M., & Roudi-Fahimi, F. (2005). *Marriage in the Arab world.* USA: USAID www.prb.org

Skalli, L. H. (2006). Communicating gender in the public sphere: Women and information technologies in the Mena. *Journal of Middle East Women's Studies, 2*(2), 35–59.

Stasz, C., Eide, E. R., & Martorell, F. (Eds.). (2007). *Post secondary education in Qatar: Employer demand, student choice and options for policy.* Doha, Qatar: RAND Corporation.

Strano, M. M. (2008). User descriptions and interpretations of self-presentation through facebook profile images. *Cyberpsychology: Journal of Psychosocial Research on Cyberspace, 2*(2). Retrieved April 28, 2009, from http://cyberpsychology.eu/view.php?cisloclanku=2008110402&article=(search%20in%20Issues)

Sundén, J. (2003). *Material virtualities: Approaching online textual embodiment.* New York: Peter Lang.

Tufekci, Z. (2008a). Can you see me now? Audience and disclosure regulation in online social network sites. *Bulletin of Science, Technology and Society, 28*(1), 20–36.

Tufekci, Z. (2008b). Grooming, gossip, Facebook and MySpace. *Information, Communication & Society, 11*(4), 544–564.

Van Dijck, J. (2008). Digital photography: communication, identity, memory. *Visual Communication, 7*(1), 57–76.

Vazire, S., & Gosling, S. D. (2004). e-Perceptions: Personality impressions based on personal websites. *Journal of Personality and Social Psychology, 87*(1), 123–132.

Wheeler, D. L. (2005). Gender matters in the internet age: Voices from the Middle East. In M. Thorseth & C. Ess (Eds.), *Technology in a multicultural and global society* (pp. 27–42). Trondheim, Norway: NTNU University Press.

Zhao, S., Grasmuck, S., & Martin, J. (2008). Identity construction on Facebook: Digital empowerment in anchored relationships. *Computers in Human Behavior, 24*, 1816–1836.

CHAPTER THREE

"Get on My Level"

How Black American Adolescent Girls Construct Identify and Negotiate Sexuality on the Internet

CARLA E. STOKES

Black American adolescent girls are surrounded by unhealthy messages and images of Black women and girls as hypersexual and deviant in the mass media and popular culture including the Internet and hip hop music videos (Stokes, 2007; Stokes & Gant, 2002). In fact, Google search results for "Black girls" and "Black teen girls" are dominated by sites that exploit their sexuality by advertising "Black teen pussy," "Black porn," "Ebony dirty girls," "nude Black girls," and opportunities to "pimp my Black teen." This is of particular concern given the popularity of the Internet among Black adolescent girls (MEE Productions, 2004). Despite controversy surrounding sexually explicit and misogynistic rap lyrics, images, and portrayals of women and girls in hip hop-influenced popular culture and on the Internet, few researchers have investigated how sexual media affect Black adolescent girls' sexuality (Stokes, 2007). Although widespread concern regarding the harmful effects of the sexualization of girls on their physical and emotional health and well-being has been the focus of academic study and media attention, the majority of research to date has focused on White girls (American Psychological Association, 2007). Consequently, there is a limited understanding about the potential influence of sexual media on the sexual and psychological development of Black adolescent girls, including their beliefs and attitudes about sexuality, dating, relationships, and body image (Stokes, 2004). Given the disproportionate impact of negative sexual health outcomes in this population, it is critical for scholars to empirically investigate the sexual development of Black adolescent girls and how they relate to their bodies in the context of an increasingly media and technology-saturated society (Stokes, 2004, 2007).

Although qualitative research has demonstrated that some girls resist media messages by creating their own media such as zines and films (Kearney, 2006), few studies of girls' media productions have focused on Black girls (Emerson, 2002; Stokes, 2007). A growing body of literature explores sexuality, identity construction, and community building in adolescent girls' personal home pages, Web sites, social networking profiles, and instant messaging conversations; and a few girls' studies scholars have reported that girls discuss sexuality, body image issues, and their desire to attract boys in these online spaces (Grisso & Weiss, 2005; S. Stern, 1999, 2000a, 2002a, 2002b; S. T. Stern, 2007; Stokes, 2007; Takayoshi, Huot, & Huot, 1999). However, while a handful of scholars have begun to include a small number of Black adolescent girls in their studies of girls' instant messaging practices and MySpace profiles (McCormick, 2008; S. T. Stern, 2007; Willett, 2008), among the existing studies of adolescent girls' Internet activities, Black adolescent girls are generally lumped into broader samples of adolescents. Thus, Black adolescent girls who produce online content have been largely overlooked in the published academic literature, and deserve serious attention. Given this oversight, it is not surprising that the sophisticated ways in which Black adolescent girls use the Internet to express their everyday lives and negotiate key developmental tasks such as sexual self-definition and identity formation have heretofore not been adequately investigated (Stokes, 2004, 2007).

This chapter begins to fill the research gaps by relocating Black girls to the center of the girls' studies literature on girls' media productions—illuminating the innovative and meaningful ways in which this socially marginalized group has claimed their space on the Web. The main research questions were: How do Black adolescent girls use the Web to create cultural productions and negotiate identity? What do Black adolescent girls reveal about their attitudes and beliefs around issues of sexuality, dating, relationships, body image, and physical attractiveness in their online profiles? How are Black adolescent girls' online self-representations and body image portrayals related to dominant discourses in the media and hip hop culture? I explore these questions through a longitudinal examination of how Black American adolescent girls use new media to construct identity and negotiate sexuality (Stokes, 2004).

SETTING

I was initially inspired to conduct this study as a result of my insider knowledge of the norms of Black youth cyberculture and hip hop culture. My interest in Black adolescent girls' personal home pages emerged during my early twenties, when I created my first home page in a social networking Web site, "NevaEvaLand" (pseudonym), with thousands of Black American youth members, which I joined in 1999 (Stokes, 2004). Although the Web site pre-dated MySpace, NevaEvaLand contains similar features including an online space for youth to hang out, express themselves, construct identity, connect with offline friends, and meet new people. (Many of the users have since joined MySpace and other social networking sites.) The site provides template-based home page publishing tools, which allow girls to create personalized, publicly searchable profiles[1] without requiring knowledge of HTML or Web design. NevaEvaLand users create and modify their profiles, which are connected to others via hyperlinks to friends' profiles in the site. They receive feedback and validation from other users who can send private messages and post public comments on profiles.

Shortly after creating my first home page, I became deeply immersed in the activities of NevaEvaLand by exploring home pages, participating in bulletin board and chat room discussions, and making online friends. I also became fascinated by the creative ways Black youth used the Web—and their home pages in particular— for the presentation of self and to explore their sexuality and identity. Further, I noticed the creative ways that hip hop culture appeared to shape these expressions and self-narratives.

After returning to graduate school to pursue my doctorate in health behavior and health education in 2000, I became intrigued by the potential of my experiences to inform Internet-based health education and HIV/AIDS prevention initiatives for youth and people of color. As I investigated existing online health education initiatives and Web sites, I created an informational HIV/AIDS home page in NevaEvaLand. The overwhelming positive response I received motivated me to create a hip hop-infused educational home page for Black adolescent girls about HIV/AIDS. The following year, I launched an online HIV/AIDS awareness campaign, which inspired me to establish Helping Our Teen Girls In Real Life Situations, Inc. (HOTGIRLS), a 501(c)3 nonprofit organization dedicated to advancing the health and lives of Black young women and girls through media education and youth development. Over the years, I have collaborated with Black adolescent girls to develop educational Web sites that raise awareness about health and social justice issues.

METHODOLOGIES

The data presented in this chapter are part of an ongoing investigation that formally began in 2001 with a pilot study of Black adolescent girls' personal home pages ("profiles") constructed in NevaEvaLand. This longitudinal study introduced pioneering data collection and analysis methods for observing girls' online interactions through the use of multiple methodologies and software programs in unconventional ways. The profiles described in this chapter were primarily collected from December 2003 to February 2004; however, I revisited the profiles periodically to collect follow-up data. I used the NevaEvaLand search engine to locate profiles authored by girls who were online during times of the day when adolescents were most active in the Web site (e.g., after school, evenings, and weekends).[2] Using domain-driven and opportunistic sampling, I selected profiles that contained substantive, information-rich textual narratives and references to constructs of interest (e.g., sexuality, gender roles, dating, partner seeking, self-definition, hip hop, etc.). Given the disproportionate impact of HIV/AIDS on Black women and girls in the South, other eligibility criteria were: female author between the ages of 14–17 years, who self-identified as "Black," "African American," or otherwise of African descent, and resided in the District of Columbia or one of seven southern states with Black Americans constituting 60% or more of the cumulative AIDS cases through June 2002 *and* incident AIDS cases reported from July 2001 through June 2002 (Alabama, Delaware, Georgia, Maryland, Mississippi, North Carolina, and South Carolina). Age, gender, and race/ethnicity were determined from explicit references (i.e., self-reported demographic information in the authors' profile). Because NevaEvaLand profiles are in the public domain, the University of Michigan institutional review board (IRB) granted an exemption for examining these documents, without contacting the authors.

I used ethnographic and quantitative content analysis methods to code eligible profiles and to analyze their narratives, sounds, and images. Consistent with ethnographic content analysis (ECA) methods (Altheide, 1996) and existing studies of girls' home pages (S. Stern, 2002a), a protocol was used to guide data collection. Descriptive summaries of each page were written, including a general description of the tone, stylistic features, images, multimedia content (songs and music videos), appropriation of hip hop and youth culture, and the page authors' description of her appearance. Profiles were collected until the content became redundant. The final sample included 216 profiles ("core sample"), which were approximately evenly distributed across states, and by ages within states, with the exception of the selection of 101 profiles from Georgia, which were over sampled. Because profiles are evolving documents that are updated and deleted unpredictably, electronic copies of each profile were downloaded using a range of software programs to facilitate ongoing coding (Stokes, 2004). The profiles were visited repeatedly and compared to each other until the main themes became clear.

A smaller sample of 27 Georgia profiles that reflected the preliminary themes uncovered in the larger sample was selected to facilitate in-depth analyses ("in-depth sample"). I used ECA methods (using ATLAS.ti) to analyze the in-depth sample.

Emergent coding was used as new patterns and themes emerged (Altheide, 1996), and whenever possible, in vivo codes (Strauss & Corbin, 1990) were used to retain the original language and meanings. This technique generated a rich and useful context for understanding the content. Data were reduced into major categorical themes, and profiles were coded until new categories and relations among categories were no longer being discovered. The in-depth analysis revealed themes related to sexuality, relationships, and body image that were present in the core and in-depth samples. Conceptually clustered matrices were created to display the data related to sexuality, self-definition, and ideal partner preferences for each page in the in-depth sample. Matrices assisted with detecting themes across and within the profiles and verifying descriptive conclusions (Miles & Huberman, 1994).

Preliminary conclusions were verified by consulting with an expert panel of 10 Black adolescent girls (ages 14–18 years) who resided in the Atlanta, Georgia area, were familiar with the Internet and/or were NevaEvaLand members, and were knowledgeable about hip hop and southern Black youth culture. To address regional differences in Black adolescent girls' vernacular and music preferences, the panelists were recruited from Atlanta-based mentoring programs for Black adolescent girls (two were recruited through snowball sampling). The demographic characteristics of the panelists were similar to the NevaEvaLand page authors. Informed consent was obtained from parents and legal guardians of the panelists and note takers, and written assent was obtained from each girl. Each participant was given a $15 cash incentive at the end of the meeting. IRB approval was obtained for consulting with the panelists. During the meeting, feedback was solicited on page content that illustrated the most salient themes. The panelists confirmed the emerging themes and clarified questions about Black online youth culture, girls' profiles, songs, celebrities, geographic nuances, images, and vernacular. I assigned a pseudonym for the panelists' names and page authors' screen names to respect their privacy. The following analysis highlights findings from the core sample and includes relevant data from the pilot and follow-up studies.

WHO ARE THE GIRLS?

The ages of the 216 girls selected for this study were evenly distributed, with a mean of 15.5 years. Most of the girls (83.3%) reported that they were enrolled in high school; 13.9% reported that they were in junior high (2.8% did not respond). During the registration process, prospective NevaEvaLand members were asked to check one or more boxes corresponding with their "race." The majority (73.1%) self-identified solely as "Black." The remainder selected "Black" and "Native American" (10.6%); "Black" and "Latino" or "Black" and "Puerto Rican" (5.1%); "Black" and

"White" (2.8%); "Black" and "Asian" (1.9%); or selected three or more racial/ethnic categories including "Black" (6.5%). Of the 47.7% who reported their religious denomination, the majority (30.6%) selected Baptist. Although the girls reported listening to a range of musical genres, the most popular were R&B (93.5%), rap (90.7%), Caribbean/reggae (35.6%), and pop (26.4%). The girls were also asked to report their relationship status from a list of options. The majority of the girls (69.4%) reported that they were single. A smaller percentage reported that they were "dating" (11.6%). The reminder reported that they were in a relationship.

A LOOK INSIDE BLACK GIRLS' VIRTUAL LIVES

In my work as a researcher, educator, and activist during the past decade, I have identified several persistent themes and patterns of interest regarding how Black girls' use Web 2.0 technologies to construct identity and negotiate sexuality in a variety of online settings. In general, many girls construct sexual self-definitions that resemble hegemonic sexual scripts and gender roles portrayed in the media and hip hop culture (Stokes, 2004, 2007), which I have also observed in my interactions with Black girls through HOTGIRLS. It is interesting to note that even though girls have adopted new Web sites and technologies since the emergence of Web 2.0, I have found that the themes described in this chapter continue to dominate Black adolescent girls' online performances in sites such as MySpace, bebo, Facebook, Hi5, and YouTube.

Common Features

NevaEvaLand is more than an online hangout. The girls use the site to negotiate their sexuality, gender, race, and relationships through their profiles within a highly competitive virtual environment (Stokes, 2004). As Stern pointed out, the girls' home pages typically included well-established conventions such as autobiographical information, blogs, photo galleries, original writings, comments, links to friends, music archives, and listings of favorite links (see Table 3.1) (S. Stern, 2002a, 2008). The two most common content features were desirable attributes/qualities in ideal romantic and/or sexual partners (i.e., "What I Like in a Guy") and self-description of appearance—with the overwhelming majority of girls including at least one of these themes in their profiles, which may reflect in part, some of the expert panel members' descriptions of NevaEvaLand as a "hook-up" site. As such, the primary motivation for creating and maintaining a home page for many of the girls in the core sample appears to be to attract a romantic and/or sexual partner.

Table 3.1

	Core Sample	
What percentage of profiles contain the feature listed?	Frequency	%
Desired attributes/qualities in a romantic partner (likes)	199	92.1
Self-description of appearance	185	85.6
Shout-outs	149	69.0
Autobiography	136	63.0
Undesirable attributes/qualities in a romantic partner (dislikes)	124	57.4
Photograph(s) of the author	79	36.6
Alternate contact information provided	73	33.8
Quizzes	69	31.9
First name disclosed	63	29.2
First and last name disclosed	38	17.6
Quotes	21	9.7
Original writings	16	7.4

Stern's work has demonstrated that the appropriation of mass media representations such as images, song lyrics, and audio clips is a common phenomenon in girls' home pages (S. Stern, 2000b, 2002a). Similarly, a key finding in the present study is that Black girls commonly included hip hop and R&B music lyrics, listings of favorite rap and R&B artists and celebrities, audio clips, and music videos in their profiles. Similarly, half of the girls in the core sample (49.5%) played music in their profiles. The inclusion of music videos in girls' profiles emerged over the course of the study with the introduction of YouTube and technological advancements. In addition, male celebrities were the most popular wallpaper background selected by the girls in the core sample, with 72 girls (33%) selecting Black male rap artists, R&B

artists or groups (14 girls/6.5%), actors (2 girls/.9%), and the professional basket-ball star, Allen Iverson (5 girls/2.3%).

Original Writings, Quotes, and Quizzes

A small number of girls in the present study included original writings (7.4%) or favorite quotes (9.7%) in their profiles. A few of the girls linked to blogs and inde-pendent web sites they created outside of NevaEvaLand, which also included con-tent that mirrored their profiles (Stokes, 2004). Girls also appropriated graphics and poetry related to sexuality, relationships, and heartbreak, which are consistent with the topics addressed by girls in Stern's research (S. Stern, 2000a, 2002a). Many of the graphics selected by girls expressed their desire to have loving relationships that reflected the idealistic heterosexual romantic scripts portrayed in popular songs, nov-els, women's and teen girls' magazines, soap operas, movies, and television shows (see Figure 3.1) (Stokes, 2004).

Figure 3.1 *Example of popular poems*

In addition, one third (31.9%) of the girls includ-ed images featuring the results from online quizzes, which are also popular in girls' Web sites and profiles in MySpace, Facebook, and other social networking sites. The girls used quiz results for self-definition, sexual self-expression, and to elevate their social status by aligning themselves with popular brands, corporations, and status symbols (i.e., "What sexual position are you?," "What type of nipple are you?," "In Those Jeans: What Jeans Are You?...You are...Baby PHAT. You have a bold, fun, and sexy attitude," etc.) (Stokes, 2004).

Feedback Mechanisms

Internet researchers have interpreted the use of feedback mechanisms in home pages as indicative of the authors' desire for social approval, validation, and interperson-al communication (Papacharissi, 2002; S. Stern, 2008), which also supports adoles-cent developmental literature. The overwhelming majority of girls solicited feedback from visitors by inviting them to contact them and/or asking them to leave com-ments. Some of the girls hoped to gain status and prestige for their Web design skills, while others strived to gain online recognition and popularity by obtaining the highest numbers of "hits" (page visits) and/or comments. Approximately 33.8% of the girls in the core sample encouraged feedback by providing alternate ways for persons to contact them outside of NevaEvaLand (i.e., e-mail addresses, instant messaging aliases, and even cell phone numbers). Moreover, many of the girls provided guidelines for posting public comments in the guest books linked to their pro-files, and some cautioned their visitors that negative feedback would be reciprocated.

One of the most fascinating aspects of girls' feedback mechanisms is the wide-spread use of sexual language to entice visitors to leave feedback. For instance, girls commonly eroticized the feedback process by encouraging visitors to "lick" their "G-Spots" (guest books) and to make them "wet." Similarly, "CandieCane" (16/AL) wrote, "sign ya name 2 my g-spot and tell me what flava yo milkshake iz."[3] Moreover, the comments in girls' guest books often included sexual content includ-ing pornography, sexual language, and sexual solicitations posted by their profile vis-itors. It is also customary for the first person who leaves a comment to make sexually suggestive comments about being the author's "first," "taking" his/her "vir-ginity," or "popping" her "cherry." For instance, "LegzWideOpen" (16/MD) wrote:

SoMe NoTeS tHaT i HaTe WhEn PpL sEnD tHeM aRe: "*WUZ UP MA, U SOUND LIKE U ALWAYZ DOWN WIT, I, MEAN IF YOU KNOW HOW TO S^CK D^CK. I CAN HANDLE THA REST. I HOPE UR PUZZY IS READY FOR 9 INCHES, CUZ U SOUND LIKE YOU NEED SUM.....*

This example reflects the sexual innuendos that pervade the normative code of behavior in NevaEvaLand (Stokes, 2004), as well as the sexualization that Black girls experience in their daily lives through harassment in public spaces (Miller, 2008).

Technological Innovation

All of the girls used a variety of stylistic features including textual narratives, images, sparkly "glitter text" graphics, favorite songs, streaming music videos, and web design effects. Although it is possible that some girls may have had assistance from others, the vast majority of the girls (70.8%) demonstrated moderate Web design skills. These girls selected profile layout templates provided by NevaEvaLand or used simple HTML codes to change the background image. In addition, the girls with moderate Web design skills used HTML programming (including "copy and paste" codes) to create effects such as basic and multi-directional scrolling marquees, drop down menus, page borders, and creative font manipulations (Stokes, 2004).

An additional 23.1% of girls demonstrated advanced Web design skills. Although some of the more technologically savvy girls complained that the home page builder restricted their Web design freedom, creativity, and innovation (Stokes, 2004), some girls used creative HTML programming to manipulate the standard layout to gain control of the page design and some created customized profile lay-outs for other members. For instance, many of the girls included marquees that scrolled horizontally across their profiles and pop-up windows that displayed friendly greetings (i.e., "Welcome to Mah Page"), shout-outs, and self-promotional messages that reflected technological innovation influenced by hip hop elements and styles. These messages included the girls' real names, nicknames, and user names written in attention-grabbing font type that was often enhanced with creative coloring, shadowing, filtering, glowing, and "flaming text" techniques—virtual "tags" so to speak, that bring to mind the individualized styles and artistic techniques used by graffiti writers and DJs (Rose, 1994)—generating energy reminiscent of rap music's repetitive beats and rhymes. These textual messages (Guevara, 1996), and images were disseminated in profiles and posted in comments sections through marquees that scrolled repeatedly forward and backward horizontally—and up and down vertically—across the profiles. For example, "ghettochic" (15/GA) greeted visitors with the words "HATERS GET ON MY LEVEL," which scrolled horizontally across her home page—referencing lyrics from "Neva Eva," a rap song by Trillville featuring Lil Jon and Lil Scrappy (2003), which was extremely popular in NevaEvaLand during the primary data collection period.

It is interesting to note that several years after the primary data collection period, NevaEvaLand adopted an optional "2.0" page layout for users that closely resembled MySpace, which had become popular among NevaEvaLand members. The profiles constructed by girls who utilized the NevaEvaLand 2.0 page layout were noticeably less creative and technologically sophisticated than those constructed prior to the new page layout. One girl commented that her profile design services would not be needed after the page 2.0 layout templates became available. Moreover, some users complained that the layout was too similar to MySpace. Among the girls who linked their profiles to their pages in other sites, I noticed that although there were many similarities with respect to content and stylistic effects, the MySpace and Facebook pages were less technologically impressive and more "cookie-cutter"—perhaps because girls commonly upload popular pre-designed layouts to their profiles.

The Importance of User Names

Several studies have found that user names are a vital part of girls' online identities (S. T. Stern, 2007; Stokes, 2004, 2007), and are used by girls to stand out from the millions of other online profiles and to facilitate the negotiation of sexuality, gender-role identity, and relationships (Stokes, 2004, 2007). Similarly, members of NevaEvaLand make decisions about whether to visit particular profiles in part, on the basis of user names, and the messages they convey about the page author. User names are connected to girls' reputations; therefore, their importance cannot be overstated. In response to sexual advances and unwanted feedback, "LegzWideOpen" defended her user name and right to express her sexual desires without being labeled as a "hoe":

Well most ppl just see me as being a hoe just cuz of my screen name but that ain't sh^t . . . A SCREEN NAME IS JUST WHAT IT IS A SCREEN NAME. DONT COME UP IN HERE ASKING ME WHAT MY NAME MEANS CUZ IT SAYS IT FOR ITSELF. I LIKE TO GET LYCKED AND *bleep*ED!. IF THERE IS A PROBLEM THEN *bleep* U!!!!!!

In addition to user names that align girls with celebrities, popular songs, and neighborhoods, girls commonly created user names that express gender-role identities and sexual scripts portrayed in the media and hip hop culture (i.e., variations of the word "pimp") (Stokes, 2004, 2007). This finding supports Steele's (1999) research, which reveals that adolescents incorporate media content into their identities. Moreover, user names often describe girls' appearance (i.e., skin color, body parts, etc.), racial/ethnic heritage (i.e., "dominicanmami"), feminine markers (i.e., user names that ended in "ette" and variations in the spelling of the words "girl/gurl," "chic," "Ms/Miss/Mrs/Mz," "baby," etc.), personality traits (i.e., "24_7crunkgirl"), personal characteristics (i.e., graduation dates and birth dates and/or years), and sexual orientation (i.e., "bi," "les/lez," "stud," "fem/femme," "dom," etc.). Given Black girls' multiple social locations, user names frequently include a combination of descriptors (i.e., "ATLdominicangurl2007"). Additionally, user names also assist in attracting potential romantic interests (Stokes, 2004, 2007).

Moreover, user names are updated to reflect the fluid nature of hip hop and youth culture. Thus, when new songs and movies are released, members of NevaEvaLand quickly respond by integrating these new developments into their online identities (Stokes, 2004). Similarly, studies of adolescent girls' instant messaging practices report that girls adopt sexually explicit lines from rap songs as their log-in names (S. T. Stern, 2007; Thiel, 2005). Consequently, it is not uncommon for girls to create new profiles that reflect the identities they wish to portray online, reflecting the common practice of "reinvention and self-definition" within the hip hop community (Rose, 1994). For instance, one girl in the core sample wrote the following on her new page: "some of ya'll may know me as "ghettomistress," but I wasn't really feelin the name anymore ya know, so had to move on." In a similar fashion, "Rappers, DJs, graffiti artists, and breakdancers all take on hip hop names and identities which speak to their role, personal characteristics, expertise or 'claim to fame'" (Rose, 1994, pp. 79–80). Because certain themes are popular in NevaEvaLand, girls often create innovative and alternative spellings (i.e., 2009pimpette, 2009_pimpette, 09p!mpette, 2009pimpett, 2009pimp3tte, etc.) since each user name must be unique (Stokes, 2004).

"Strictly Dickly": Sexual Orientation and Homophobia

NevaEvaLand members were also asked to select their sexual orientation from a standard list of options during registration. While the majority selected "heterosexual" (48.6%), the remainder selected "lesbian" (2.8%), "none of your business" (2.8%), "bisexual" (2.3%), or deliberately concealed their sexual orientation (43.5%). Several of the heterosexual girls provided their own descriptions of their sexual orientations, such as "I love dick," "Dick," "I love boys," "Strictly Dickly" (collectively, these girls were included in the "heterosexual" category) and "Strictly Clitly" (I included these girls in the "lesbian" category). In general, the girls who identified as "strictly dickly" exhibited homophobic attitudes and adopted this terminology to warn their virtual audience that they are only interested in dating males. For instance, a 15-year-old girl in the pilot study from Austin, Texas, wrote, "...just to put this out there im STRICTLY DICKLY so if u a female dont try to holla at me." Moreover, some of the girls described themselves as "studs" or "femmes/fems," and often mentioned whether they were attracted to "studs," "femmes/fems," or both in their online narratives. These alternate descriptions reflect girls' own conceptualizations of their sexual orientation, as opposed to labels imposed by the dominant culture and academicians (Stokes, 2004).

Interestingly, 43.5% of the core sample deliberately concealed their sexual orientation from public display and 2.9% selected "None of Your Business." The large number of girls who concealed their sexual orientation may be explained by several factors. Some girls who identify as lesbian, bisexual, bi-curious, or transgender (or who are questioning their sexualities) may feel uncomfortable disclosing their sexual orientation in NevaEvaLand because of the risk of stigma from their audience (and possibly individuals who are part of their lives offline) (Stokes, 2004). Other girls may consider their sexual orientation to be a private matter or may not identify with the options provided during the registration process. To this end, one 17-year-old girl wrote:

> As far as my preference goes...right now I can't really say. boys are a turn off cuz almost all of them come off to me as wantin one thing . . . they don't know how to treat a good girl when they have one. I don't understand it. And girls have the tendencies to play games too. So right now I have no preference...if you are a real down-to-earth person and I'm happy with you, it doesn't matter to me what you are.

Although some girls openly expressed their tolerance for gay, lesbian, and bisexual youth, homophobic comments, threats, and graphics were common among girls in NevaEvaLand, with 19% of the girls including derogatory comments or images about gays, lesbians, and/or bisexual in their profiles (i.e., some girls warned "dykes" to stop viewing their profiles) (Stokes, 2004), which is consistent with previous research that documents homophobic attitudes among Black pre-adolescent girls (Stephens & Few, 2007a). For instance, "BrownEyez," a 15-year-old girl from Delaware wrote, "IF YOU IS GAY, YOU BETTA FALLBACK CUZ I'M FOR DA SEXY GUYS ONLY!!!!" Conversely, many of the girls who openly identified as lesbian or bisexual included graphics and narrative content associated with gay pride in their profiles (i.e., rainbow-colored graphics) (Stokes, 2004).

Sexual Self-Expression and Self-Definition through Cartoon Dolls

In NevaEvaLand (and other popular teen-oriented Web sites), cartoon dolls, which are created by independent doll artists and other Web sites featuring dress-up games such as CartoonDollEmporium.com and Stardoll.com, are an important part of girls' online peer culture and their daily lives in cyberspace (Stokes, 2004)[4]. Although I did not code all of the girls' profiles for the inclusion of cartoon dolls, almost half of the girls in the in-depth sample included dolls in their profiles (13 girls/48%). Girls appropriated cartoon dolls to convey various messages related to sexuality, gender-role identity, and relationships (Stokes, 2004).

What is most interesting about the appropriation of dolls in NevaEvaLand is that some of the dolls that were circulated widely in girls' (and boys) profiles included "thug" dolls and other graphics that depict "ghetto" themes, criminality, gun imagery, sexual activity, misogyny, strip club culture, gang culture, violence, and illegal drugs. The majority of the dolls selected by girls were adorned in popular street fashions associated with Black urban youth and hip hop culture (i.e., baggy jeans that hang below the waist, diamond-adorned jewelry and teeth, designer fashion labels, etc.). Many of the dolls were sexualized, racialized, and gendered in nature, and often mirrored the hegemonic sexual scripts and gender-role ideologies stereotypically associated with blackness in the media and hip hop culture. It is also interesting to note that many of the female dolls mirrored the role of music video "models/actresses" in that they are featured as "eye candy" and objects of male fantasies. As such, many were dressed in trendy, revealing, and tight clothing that accentuated the female physique and/or were featured in sexually suggestive poses (i.e., grinding against a male doll, on hands and knees with legs spread, lifting up their skirts and dresses, laying down in various states of undress—which resembled poses depicted in mainstream print media and hip hop magazines and music videos (Stokes, 2004) (Figures 3.2 through 3.10).

Figures 3.2 through 3.4 *Examples of Cartoon Dolls*

Figures 3.5 through 3.10 *Examples of Cartoon Dolls* continued

It is fascinating that some of the doll graphics referenced popular rap and R&B songs. For instance, a 15-year-old girl (DC) posted an animated doll with jiggling buttocks and the caption "Shake Ya Ass" (Figure 3.11), which is also the name of a rap song by Mystikal (2000):

Figure 3.11

In a similar fashion, she also posted the lyrics to the song, "Milkshake" from the LP, *Tasty* (2003), by the British singer, Kelis—along with an animated image (below) of a cartoon doll with blond hair adorned in a pink camisole and panties (Figure 3.12) (Stokes, 2004):

Figure 3.12

Collectively, these images further demonstrate the ways in which girls align themselves with, and express their sexuality through hip hop and girl culture. Moreover, "Milkshake" was a popular song during the primary data collection period, and many of the girls in NevaEvaLand appropriated images of Kelis and/or made references to the song. Thus, I borrow the metaphor of the "milkshake" bringing "all the boys to the yard" from Kelis to describe girls' attempts to "represent" and stand out (i.e., "n theyre like it's betta than yaz!") among the girls in NevaEvaLand, by using their "milkshakes" to bring the boys (and girls) to their (virtual) yards (profiles) to obtain online popularity and prestige. Ultimately, this phenomenon is problematic because many girls appear to create profiles with the primary motivation of catering to the perceived sexual desires of their audiences (Stokes, 2004). The image with the caption, "Every Ni99az [Niggas] Fantasy" illustrates this phenomenon (Figure 3.13):

Figure 3.13

In light of the well-known findings from the groundbreaking 1930s and 1940s "doll studies" conducted by Kenneth and Mamie Phipps Clark, that demonstrate the "negative effects of racism on Black children's self-concept or what is more often now referred to as their self-esteem" (Chin, 2001, p. 144), the appropriation of cartoon dolls by Black youth in the present study raises interesting questions about whether these pervasive symbols (which have become normalized in NevaEvaLand) influence their self-concept and conceptualizations of sexuality, beauty ideals, sexual self-image, and relationships. Moreover, the selection of dolls also provides unique insights into the individual page author's self-image and attitudes about a range of health and social issues (i.e., friendship, substance use, consumerism, safer sex, sexism, etc.), including sexuality and relationships.

Photographs

Given that Black adolescent girls' lived experiences are deeply impacted by their multiple (embodied) identities—it is not surprising that Black girls' bodies and appearance are extremely important in social networking sites and NevaEvaLand profiles. To this end, the girls in the present study expressed their gender and racial markers in their profiles, and often constructed their identities through their bodies. While only a few of the girls in the pilot study included pictures of themselves, slightly more than one-third (36.6%) of the girls included a photograph(s) of themselves in their profiles. The photographs included close-up shots of girls' faces, photographs that included friends, family, and romantic partners, and (a few) shots of girls holding their middle fingers up or striking sexually suggestive poses. Additionally, many of the girls posted sexually suggestive photographs of themselves wearing bras, panties, swimsuits, and other revealing clothing, which were sometimes deliberately cropped to highlight fragmented and faceless body parts. Interestingly, some of these photographs reminded me of the fragmented versions of women's bodies portrayed in music videos and advertisements—which reflect the overall importance placed on the feminine body in girls' profiles. For instance, "americasnext_topmodel" (15/DC) catered to her audience by posting several pictures of herself striking poses that were intended to be sexy and/or seductive, with captions such as, "Damn . . ." "Plump an Toned" (written on a photograph of her rear end adorned in tight jeans) and "Sexxy Abs" (a close-up shot of her abdominal region)—presumably, the captions were included to assist the audience in interpreting her photographs in accordance with how she wanted to be perceived (Stokes, 2004).

The expert panel commented that girls' with sexually provocative photos probably do not show the photographs or the profiles to their parents, and that girls may be more inclined to experiment or engage in acts on the Web that they would not normally do in person such as "show their body parts." "LD" (17) commented that the girl who created the profile was "nasty" and that some of the girls in NevaEvaLand are probably "strippers or working for somebody . . ." since she had received sexually explicit messages from women associated with pornographic web sites via e-mail and in her guest book. While the expert panel reported that some girls may select pictures because they are readily available, others appear to be more concerned about being perceived as sexually desirable and attractive. Through the process of selecting photographs, the expert panel argued that Black girls carefully construct profiles that represent the selves that they wish to portray to others. Thus, girls who opt to include photographs on their profiles face judgment from others in NevaEvaLand, and those who do not include photographs may do so deliberately, to avoid objectification and criticism. In addition, girls' interpretations of the feedback (solicited and unsolicited) they receive from others in NevaEvaLand influence the photograph selection process.

Girls' Self-Descriptions

The majority (63%) of the girls provided autobiographical information, and some emphasized their non-physical features and attributes more than others. Girls' autobiographical information varied in terms of the level of self-disclosure; however, girls typically included a description of personality traits, as well as information about schools, hobbies, extracurricular activities, families, media, preferences, social activities, and various favorite things (i.e., songs, music, colors, food, designer clothing and shoe labels, etc.). The girls of NevaEvaLand were more likely to provide a description of their physical appearance than to include autobiographical information about their lives, demonstrating the importance of appearance, the physical body, and physical attractiveness in Black online youth culture. Interestingly, many of the girls who provided photograph(s) of themselves also included a written physical self-description. In addition, some of the girls mentioned that they would post pictures soon—apparently, to prove that they were not lying about their appearance. The majority of girls' descriptions emphasized physical features, attractiveness, personal style, and clothing preferences. "Modelchic" (17/GA), wrote, "Fav Clothing Brand: BABY PHAT, Lady Enyce, Ecko Red, Applebottom and JLO." Typical descriptions included height, hair and/or eye color, hair length and/or texture, skin color, and a description of the author's physique. Many of the girls use their profiles to emphasize personal attributes that they perceive to be appealing and/or attractive to potential romantic interests and partners. This practice reflects some girls' desires to measure up to beauty ideals that are valued by other individuals and social institutions such as peers, family members, and the media.

In addition, being "thick in the right places" was a pervasive theme throughout all of the data collection phases that demonstrated girls' resistance to hegemonic beauty ideals. According to the expert panel, in NevaEvaLand, the "right" places refer to girls' breasts, hips, buttocks, and thighs. For example, "Shelly" (16/Oxon Hill, MD) described herself as follows:

> A little about myself: I'm 5'2 (yeah I'm kinda short), Lightskined, brown eyez, shoulder length hair that is brown and gold, have all my teeth, don't smoke but will drink if the party is tight, thick in all the right places, can dress, likes to chill, in 11th grade, a freak when I wanna be, oh and I have a tongue ring but lets kept that between me and you!

Similarly, a few of the girls in NevaEvaLand described themselves as having a "coke bottle" shape or "ghetto booty." In addition, girls uploaded images that illustrated the importance of thickness in Black youth culture, such as the one shown below which was appropriated by many of the girls in NevaEvaLand (Figure 3.14):

Figure 3.14

Similarly, several scholars have reported that Black adolescent boys prefer shapely and "thick girls," which is consistent with the expert panel's testimony (Hernandez, 2005; Stephens & Few, 2007b). The beauty ideals conveyed in girls' profiles are also consistent with those often described in boys' profiles in NevaEvaLand, as well as in popular rap and R&B songs and music videos. In a similar fashion, girls' appro-

priated rap lyrics to express their perceived physical assets. For instance, an extremely common image (illustrated with White blond-haired cartoon dolls) incorporates
references to popular songs by the rap artists, Ja Rule, Juvenile, Master P, and
Fabolous (Stokes, 2004) (Figure 3.15):

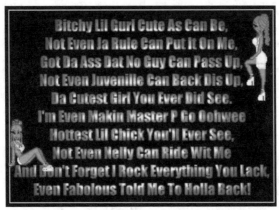

Figure 3.15

By emphasizing "thickness" (which is perceived as "healthy," "positive," and attractive), the girls in NevaEvaLand have overturned the dominant White beauty ideal
in favor of a more realistic view of body image based on cultural ideals of beauty valued in Black youth culture. However, despite the appreciation of the Black female
body expressed through the girls' self-descriptions, some of the portrayals of dominant White beauty ideals appropriated in their profiles are contradictory and suggest that these girls have internalized dominant White beauty ideals. Interestingly,
while some of the dolls had curly hair or Black hairstyles such as corn rows and flat
twists, most of the dolls depicted White girls or girls of color with long, straight hair,
lighter skin complexions, and other features commonly associated with dominant
White standards of beauty—a complex theme that reflects the historical fixation
with skin tone and hair texture in Black communities (Russell, Wilson, & Hall,
1992; Thompson & Keith, 2001), as well as the limited selection of dolls that
resist hegemonic beauty ideals. Many of these dolls also included captions that
emphasized the dolls' perceived attractiveness (i.e., "cute," "Dyme," and "Perfect 10")
(Figures 3.16 through 3.18).

Figures 3.16 through 3.18 *Examples of cartoon dolls that depict dominant beauty ideals*

Moreover, some girls anticipated negative feedback and used dolls to talk back to other girls. For instance, "MsWestside" (17/GA) included an image of a thin, White cartoon doll with long straight brown hair, with the caption, "Hatin' On Me Won't Make YOU Pretty. . . ." Another popular doll included a caption, "Why do hoez hate it's not my fault I look like a model." Interestingly, the girls further reinforced cultural beauty ideals that are unachievable for many girls and policed girls' sexuality through these practices.

Additionally, some girls attempted to generate prestige in NevaEvaLand by posting affiliations with status-boosting "cliques" (similar to groups) that function as web rings (operated by girls and boys), such as those that select girls for membership on the basis of their physical attractiveness (i.e., NevaEvaLand's "finest," "prettiest," "sexy girls," etc.), and attributes valued in Black youth culture (i.e., thickness, "Dimes," "Quarters," "yellow bones," "red bones," "mixed girls," etc.), which is determined by submitting a photograph to the owner(s) of the clique. It is likely that some of these cliques may exacerbate competitiveness and divisiveness among girls in NevaEvaLand.

Collectively, these images and practices suggest that Black girls' beauty ideals are influenced by conceptualizations of female beauty in the media and hip hop culture. However, despite the widespread appropriation of hip hop in girls' profiles described in the present study, with the exception of a handful of studies (Gordon,

2008; Stephens & Few, 2007b), there is a limited body of literature that explores the ways in which hip hop culture shapes Black girls' (and boys') attitudes about body image and standards of beauty (Stokes, 2004).

RECOMMENDATIONS

This chapter highlights the fascinating ways in which Black adolescent girls are creating their own spaces on the Internet to share their daily lives, talk about sexuality and relationships, and navigate the complex process of sexual development by constructing technologically innovative profiles in a social networking Web site. This research also demonstrates that Black adolescent girls are continuing the hip hop tradition of technological innovation by manipulating new media technologies to showcase their creativity, elevate their voices, communicate with a potentially global audience, and express themselves through hip hop culture. While observing the girls' profiles, I found that in the process of constructing identity online, distinguishing their profiles from other girls, and seeking social status and attention from potential romantic interests, many of the girls in NevaEvaLand emphasized their appearance and reinforced hegemonic beauty ideals and internalized racism—often while simultaneously supporting counter-hegemonic cultural ideals of beauty valued in Black youth culture (Stokes, 2004).

In general, I found that the themes in the girls' profiles mirrored dominant themes that pervade hip hop music and culture—including many that have been the subject of critique in the academic and public discourse (Stokes, 2004). As I continue to revisit the girls' profiles and follow their activities in other Web sites, what strikes me most is that although the latest songs, videos, artists, clothing, vernacular, and trends in hip hop and youth culture appropriated in girls' profiles have changed, the themes I observed in girls' profiles in 1999 are still prevalent 10 years later. Whether the girls brag about the power of their "milkshakes" to "bring the boys to the yard" or their enviable "swagg," ultimately, it is troubling that many Black adolescent girls continue to derive their identity, sense of worth, and value from their physical appearance, material possessions, and sexual appeal, which is defined within the constructs of males' desires and fantasies.

Thus, as I argued in my earlier work, parents, educators, girl advocates, girl-serving organizations and programs informed by this research should encourage Black girls to critique media messages and collaborate with them to provide supportive and culturally specific safe spaces for girls to construct their own media that challenges sexualization and hegemonic gender roles and promotes self-worth that encompasses the whole person (Stokes, 2007; Stokes & Gant, 2002). Through my work with HOTGIRLS, I have observed that the Internet has the potential to serve as a space for the cultivation of such transformative resistance strategies among Black girls. Moreover, I argue that curricula should utilize teen-oriented social media as a tool for promoting healthy adolescent development, political awareness, education, and social change. For instance, educational curricula, products, Web sites, social networking applications, and dress-up games informed by hip hop, youth culture, and Black feminist theory have the potential to be effective strategies for reaching Black girls.

Finally, girls' studies scholars need to increase the attention given to Black adolescent girls' cultural productions and they should also diversify their samples to include significant numbers of girls of color. Such studies should also utilize triangulation and rigorous data collection and analysis methodologies such as those employed in this research to address methodological challenges (i.e., the evolving nature of Internet data) and improve the overall quality of online girls' studies. While the research described in this chapter has laid the foundation for future work on Black girls' online performances and cultural productions, the importance of including Black girls in girls' studies research cannot be overemphasized (Stokes, 2004). Finally, more work of this nature should be done to further elucidate the nuances of Black girl culture on- and offline. Future studies should be participatory in nature and include Black girls in meaningful ways that acknowledge their expertise and potential to contribute to the development of liberatory strategies that empower all girls.

Notes

1. Privacy settings were introduced in NevaEvaLand after the primary data collection period, which enabled users to make their profiles private.
2. Profiles constructed by girls younger than 18 are no longer included in the NevaEvaLand member search feature.
3. Quotes are accurate as written. I purposely did not correct grammatical or spelling errors.
4. See (http://auburn_angel1.tripod.com/dollz/id12.html) and Stokes (2004) for an extensive discussion of the origins of cartoon dolls.

References

Altheide, D. L. (1996). *Qualitative media analysis.* Thousand Oaks: Sage Publications.

American Psychological Association (2007). *Report of the APA Task Force on the Sexualization of Girls.* Washington, D.C.

Chin, E. (2001). *Purchasing power: Black kids and American consumer culture.* Minneapolis: University of Minnesota Press.

Emerson, R. A. (2002). African-American teenage girls and the construction of Black womanhood in mass media and popular culture. *African American Research Perspectives, 8*(1), 85–102.

Gordon, M. K. (2008). Media contributions to African American girls' focus on beauty and appearance: Exploring the consequences of sexual objectification. *Psychology of Women Quarterly, 32,* 245–256.

Grisso, A. D., & Weiss, D. (2005). What are gURLS talking about? In S. R. Mazzarella (Ed.), *Girl wide web: Girls, the Internet, and the negotiation of identity* (pp. 31–49). New York: Peter Lang.

Guevara, N. (1996). Women writin' rappin' breakin'. In W. E. Perkins (Ed.), *Droppin' science: Critical essays on rap music and hip hop culture* (pp. 49–82). Philadelphia: Temple University Press.

Hernandez, J. (2005). Male-identified "shorties": Towards a culturally specific understanding of African American girls' self-esteem. In M. Sewell (Ed.), *Growing up girl: An anthology of voices from marginalized spaces* (pp. 273–280). Washington, DC: GirlChild Press.

Kearney, M. C. (2006). *Girls make media.* New York: Routledge.

McCormick, M. (2008). *African American girls on MySpace: Artistic expression, viral marketing and corporate presence.* Tempe, AZ: Arizona State University.

MEE Productions. (2004). *This is my reality—the price of sex: An inside look at Black urban youth sexuality and the role of media.* Philadelphia.

Miles, M. B., & Huberman, A. M. (1994). *Qualitative data analysis: An expanded sourcebook* (2nd ed.). Thousand Oaks, CA: Sage.

Miller, J. (2008). *Getting played: African American girls, urban inequality, and gendered violence.* New York: New York University Press.

Papacharissi, Z. (2002). The presentation of self in virtual life: Characteristics of personal home pages. *Journalism and Mass Communication Quarterly, 79*(3), 643–660.

Rose, T. (1994). A style nobody can deal with: Politics, style and the postindustrial city in hip hop. In A. Ross & T. Rose (Eds.), *Microphone fiends: youth music and youth culture* (pp. 71–88). New York: Routledge.

Russell, K., Wilson, M., & Hall, R. E. (1992). *The color complex: The politics of skin color among African Americans.* New York: Harcourt Brace Jovanovich.

Steele, J. R. (1999). Teenage sexuality and media practice: Factoring in the influences of family, friends, and school. *The Journal of Sex Research, 36*(4), 331–341.

Stephens, D. P., & Few, A. L. (2007a). Hip hop honey or video ho: African American preadolescents' understanding of female sexual scripts in hip hop culture. *Sex Cult, 11,* 48–69.

Stephens, D. P., & Few, A. L. (2007b). The effects of images of African American women in hip hop on early adolescents' attitudes toward physical attractiveness and interpersonal relationships. *Sex Roles, 56,* 251–264.

Stern, S. (1999). Adolescent girls' expression on web home pages: Spirited, sombre and self-conscious sites. *Convergence, 5*(4), 22–41.

Stern, S. (2000a). Adolescent girls' home pages as sites for sexual self-expression. *SIECUS Report, 28*(5), 6–15.

Stern, S. (2000b). *Making themselves known: Girls WWW home pages as virtual vehicles for self-disclosure.* Unpublished Dissertation, University of North Carolina at Chapel Hill, Chapel Hill.

Stern, S. (2002a). Sexual selves on the World Wide Web: Adolescent girls' home pages as sites for sexual self-expression. In J. D. Brown, J. R. Steele, & K. Walsh-Childers (Eds.), *Sexual teens, sexual media: investigating media's influence on adolescent sexuality* (pp. 265–285). Mahwah, N.J.: L. Erlbaum.

Stern, S. (2002b). Virtually speaking: Girls' self-disclosure on the WWW. *Women's Studies in Communication, 25*(2), 223–253.

Stern, S. (2008). Producing sites, exploring identities: Youth online authorship. In D. Buckingham (Ed.), *The John D. and Catherine T. MacArthur foundation series on digital media and learning* (pp. 95–118). Cambridge, MA: MIT Press.

Stern, S. T. (2007). *Instant identity: Adolescent girls and the word of instant messaging.* New York: Peter Lang.

Stokes, C. E. (2004). *Representin' in cyberspace: Sexuality, hip hop, and self-definition in home pages constructed by Black adolescent girls in the hip hop era.* Unpublished PhD dissertation, University of Michigan, Ann Arbor.

Stokes, C. E. (2007). Representin' in cyberspace: Sexual scripts, self-definition, and hip hop culture in Black American adolescent girls' home pages. *Culture, Health & Sexuality, 9*(2), 169–184.

Stokes, C. E., & Gant, L. M. (2002). Turning the tables on the HIV/AIDS epidemic: Hip hop as a tool for reaching African-American adolescent girls. *African American Research Perspectives*, 70–81.

Strauss, A. L., & Corbin, J. M. (1990). *Basics of qualitative research: Grounded theory procedures and techniques.* Newbury Park, CA: Sage Publications.

Takayoshi, P., Huot, E., & Huot, M. (1999). No boys allowed: The World Wide Web as a clubhouse for girls. *Computers and Composition, 16*, 89–106.

Thiel, S. (2005). "IM Me": Identity construction and gender negotiation in the world of adolescent girls and instant messaging. In S. R. Mazzarella (Ed.), *Girl wide web: Girls, the Internet, and the negotiation of identity* (pp. 179–201). New York: Peter Lang.

Thompson, M. S., & Keith, V. (2001). The blacker the berry: Gender, skin tone, self-esteem, and self-efficacy. *Gender & Society, 15*(3), 336–357.

Willett, R. (2008). Consumer citizens online: Structure, agency, and gender in online participation. In D. Buckingham (Ed.), *The John D. and Catherine T. MacArthur foundation series on digital media and learning* (pp. 49–70). Cambridge, MA: MIT Press.

CHAPTER FOUR

East Meets West

Is There a Difference Between Thai and American Girls' Use of the Internet and Negotiation of Identity?

NARISSA MARIA PUNYANUNT-CARTER &
JASON M. SMITH

Past research concerning cross-cultural issues in communication studies has shown that there are several unique similarities and differences between the U.S. and other countries (Olaniran & Roach, 1994; Rubin, Fernandez-Collado, & Hernandez-Sampieri, 1992). Initial studies on cross-cultural issues tried to focus on the differences or similarities between the different cultures (Rubin et al., 1992). Gudykunst (1987) suggested that cross-cultural research should be grounded in theory to obtain more detailed research. The objective of this chapter is to examine cross-cultural differences in Internet use and negotiation of identity by the girls in Thailand and the U.S. Because of the dissimilarity in the cultural perspectives of these two countries/cultures, it is predicted that there will be differences in Thai and American girls' use of the Internet as a means of identity negotiation.

McCann, Ota, Giles, and Caraker (2003) noted that the Southeast Asian cultures have been overlooked in communication studies research. One culture meriting such attention is that of Thailand. Mainly Theravada Buddhist and characterized by collectivism, the culture of Thailand is more likely than that of the U.S. to be private about personal details and to encourage group ideals. On the other hand, the U.S. is mainly Christian and is characterized by individualism (McCann et al., 2003). Hence, one would assume that Americans would be more outspoken about their life and would try to emphasize a person's unique characteristics.

Few research studies have looked at specific Internet behaviors among girls of different cultures (Li & Kirkup, 2007). In addition, little research has looked at the intercultural differences that may exist in the way these girls negotiate their identities online (Thiel, 2004). Hence, the objective of this study is to understand Thai and American girls' Internet behaviors as seen through their personal Web pages.

LITERATURE REVIEW

As the Internet continues to grow into a global phenomenon with the ability to connect all four corners of the earth, it is imperative to understand how Internet users in different countries make use of this medium in particular as it relates to identity development and expression. Researchers have documented Internet use is an influential factor in developing one's self-concept (Dominick, 1999; Foster, 1997; Mazalin & Moore, 2004), such that one can begin with a completely new slate and present a newfound persona to the rest of the world. The ability to e-mail, chat (Foster, 1997), Facebook, MySpace, Twitter, and even own a personal Web site is impacting our social world (Tyler, 2002), especially for young people. Bortree (2005), for example, noted that teenage girls are using the Internet to communicate and express themselves. This leads us to ask how young people choose to portray their identities online, and what social norms are expected in this new dimension? Entering into this new context for communication, researchers are starting to examine the impact it has on human existence.

Young People and the Internet

One of the ways that other researchers have studied identity is the use of self-presentation theories (Bortree, 2005). Goffman (1959) presented his idea that individuals are like actors on a stage and use communication to convey their identities. Oftentimes, the self-presentation is determined by the presenter's goals. According to Tedeschi (1986), self-presentation has mainly been studied when individuals present themselves to strangers. Yet, most of the interpersonal interactions that individuals have with others tend to be with non-strangers, such as friends and family.

In his study of self-presentation on the Internet, Dominick (1999) analyzed 500 different Web sites and used five strategies for categorizing self-presentation: integration, competence, intimidation, exemplification, and supplication. After analyzing all the home pages, Dominick discovered that the most frequent self-presentation goal was ingratiation—the goal of having others admire and/or appreciate you. Oftentimes, ingratiation techniques involve communicating favorable things about others, offering humor, and mild self-deprecating statements. It was mentioned that ingratiation was the most prevalent goal in home pages, because most individuals have a longing to be liked by others. Thus, it could be possible that young adolescent girls may use their home pages as a means of ingratiation.

Turow (1999) noted that the Internet for adolescents can be a place to alleviate social isolation and depression. At the same time, the Internet can promote antisocial behavior. However, research has shown that the Internet has allowed adolescents another way to communicate with their friends and family. Moreover, it allows them a more convenient way of maintaining their relationships. In addition, there is an increase in adolescents creating home pages and using the Internet for computer mediated communication.

Chandler and Roberts-Young (1998) found that the majority of home page owners tend to create their pages only for their families and friends to view. They discovered that some students were embarrassed to find out that other people, such as their teachers, were able to access their personal Web pages. All in all, the Internet provides an unseen audience that adolescents may not be used to when presenting information about themselves. On the other hand, Befring (1997) believed that home pages were created to express the individual and to build relationships with others. He also noted that some enjoy creating their own home page because it gives them a sense of accomplishment; hence, he believed that there are extrinsic motivators toward having a home page on the Internet.

Lenhart and Madden (2005) noted that more than half of the teen population in the U.S. uses the Internet. Moreover, these Internet users often have their own Web page and/or post their personal creations. They discovered that girls (ages 15–17) were more likely than boys to participate in social activities online. Similarly, Dominick (1999) found that, while males and females tend to communicate similar things online (e.g., humor, quotes, and statements), that there were gender specific styles of self-expression on the Internet. Females were more likely than males to build relationships with others, incorporate floral designs, use feminine colors (such as pink and lavender), provide more information about themselves, and offer simple user-friendly technology. Males were more likely than females to use fancier technology, be briefer in their information, and emphasize their status.

In her study of identity expression on the web, Stern (2004) noted differences in the projection of identity through adolescent home pages. She found that most adolescents included mentions of family and friends and hobbies along with descriptions of themselves on their web sites. Moreover, she documented differences between males and females with males evidencing elevated social anxiety and interruption in their identity development when there was much Internet usage which did not show up in the female sample.

Bortree (2005) noted that adolescents may often struggle with self-presentation, because at their stage of life, they are still trying to figure out their personalities and still learning how to communicate themselves. This is particularly true for girls. Shil'shtein (2001) noted that adolescents often try to make themselves more desirable for relationships with others. Moreover, adolescents will often identify themselves as a member of a particular group. In these specific groups, the girls discover ways of developing and expressing their identities without the fear of rejection (Shil'shtein, 2001).

Offer, Schonert-Reichl, and Boxer (1996) noted that adolescence is a difficult time for girls who often have a lot of developmental issues to deal with such as physical development and emotional development. Oftentimes, these developments cause unrealistic expectations and poor self-esteem. Sutton (1999) found that many girls' identities are influenced from popular media. In turn, these media images affect how many girls process the values and standards of femininity in this society. Further, adolescence is a period when attracting boys becomes a motivator. Hence, the main source for validation and socialization comes from their friends. Lueker-Harrington (2001) stated that adolescent girls are "more susceptible to the opinions of friends than to traditional media messages" (p. 13A). The authors observed that friendships are so important to girls that sometimes they might avoid communicating things about themselves to avoid conflict and preserve their relationships, something they can do through their web pages.

Home Page

According to Dominick (1999) a home page or personal Web page is a site that is created and maintained by an individual. The personal home pages can be ascertained by the title of the page, such as "My Page" or "The Carter Website." Sometimes these Web sites can be accessed by the public, while at other times they can be private, meaning that only limited individuals have access to the page. Personal Web pages allow individuals the ability to present themselves in an unrestricted fashion. Creators of personal Web pages often do not know how their communications on these pages may be perceived.

Tyler (2002) writes about computer mediated communication (CMC) in the global village that presents itself on the Internet. He contends that the Internet becomes not only a place where all voices can be heard but also a place where communities arise and are generated into collective identities. He states, "Community, then, is built by a sufficient flow of 'we-relevant' information. The 'we' or the collective identity that results is structured around others who are seen as similar to the 'me'" (Tyler, 2002, p. 25). Of course when one generates a community one must carry characteristics that have been connected to through nurtured experiences in life. CMC is also set up to be low-priced, fast, and independent in nature so its popularity grows more and more every day generating differences in how one communicates and experiences life (Herring, 2004). Some current new trends that form persona are music downloads, role-playing games like World of Warcraft, self-post videos such as YouTube, and search engines like Google. Forming persona does not stop there; there are chat rooms, games, and info sites such as Ask.com. There are so many areas to derive and cumulate together to adjust and solidify anyone's idea of what identity should be.

Media and Community

Jankowski (2002) examines Merton (1949) and Janowitz's (1952) studies on community developed around newspapers as the beginning examples of media generating communities and then moves on to describe two more "waves" of media and community development. The second is electronic media, such as the television and radio broadcasting, and the third is the Internet. The Internet has heralded and generated a new era of community generation because of its openness to messages. Instead of being a one-way street, the Internet is seen as huge multistructure with roads leading everywhere on which anyone with the resources can drive. As a result, a new form of community can be developed.

Community is dependent upon agreement of norms, but the social exchange available on the Internet is generating more and more ideas of what community can be. For instance, Tencent QQ, one of the largest instant messaging programs in mainland China, is a tool set up for the Chinese community to instantly communicate with each other over the Internet. It has grown in popularity to other areas in Asia and has even made its way into the U.S. Facebook, a global online social network, generates the same idea of communication but, furthers this idea by adding search engines, group invitations, comparative quizzes, applications, and so much more. It has never been easier to define your persona and find a community as in the Internet age.

ASIAN VERSUS AMERICAN IDENTITY

Interesting differences arise when comparing the understandings of Eastern and Western cultures. Many scholars believe that identity is formed from the nurturing aspect of one's participation in the society s/he was born into. For instance, Pye (1985) writes on the power relationships and political development in Asia. He notes the presence of the collectivistic culture influencing the perceptions of power and governmental control saying,

> In the West it seemed natural and inevitable to have persistent conflicts in the political realm between demands for greater popular participation and assertions of sovereign authority. In Asia the masses of the people are more respectful of authority. Their

leaders are concerned about questions of dignity, the need to uphold national pride, and other highly symbolic matters. Those in power want above all to be seen as protecting the prestige of the collectivity. (p. vii)

He uses authority to show how identity and power relationships are built around collectivity in Asia versus the individualistic nature of Western thought. This is specifically relevant in the Thai population. Callister and Wall (2004) examine this power relationship and how it setup thorough the Buddhist ideals of most Thai cultures. The focus on harmony and goodness to one another is the focus of most Thai cultures. A life cycle of karma and rebirth is what stabilizes interactions and respect. Living in a culture of thinking of higher ways encourages systematic agreement on lower issues such as personal willfulness, pride, and ambition.

The Buddhist cultural background influences Thai individuals to have a low tolerance for conflict, even to the point of conforming to hostile persuaders (Callister & Wall, 2004). American culture is almost the opposite in their determination of conflict. Conflict is felt to be helpful when it exposes negative ideas and generates solutions to problems. As the previous paragraph implies, Thai cultures are more likely to save "face" or a display of good image to public (Phillips, 1966; Roongrengsuke & Chansuthus, 1998).With an identity surrounded by how to keep a good image generates an orientation to be accommodating with others and even to the point of apologizing for conflict they might have generated.

Values are another large section differentiating Eastern and Western thought. The Asian Values Scale (AVS) by Kim, Atkinson, and Yang (1999) was developed to measure the ethnic cultural values held by Asians to view differences between them and European American values. In the initial development of the AVS, 112 Asian cultural values were rated by 303 Asian American and 63 European American participants. A total of 36 items were depicted as issues with importance differing between the two cultures. Follow-up studies were conducted for validity, internal consistency, and reliability (Kim et al., 1999). Findings reveal that Eastern ideals are mainly in the aspect of conformity to norms, family recognition through achievement, emotional self-control, humility, and familial piety.

In opposition to the depiction of Eastern thought is the setup of the Western culture. It has already been depicted as a strong individualistic culture with power enacted through rights and privileges given on basis of cultural rights, but it has also been seen as very distinct in its social setup of values. In the book *American Cultural Values* (Stewart & Bennett, 1992) the authors note this value setup when they say, " . . . generally, in American society, social background, money, or power bestow perhaps fewer advantages than in any other major society. Lacking obligations to class and social position, Americans move easily from one group to another as they shift position or residence" (p. 89). Perhaps this arises from the American perceptions of individuality but it is an important factor when acknowledging the different norms present in westernized thought. Having the option to easily move in between social classes and positions generates, according to Stewart and Bennett, both good and bad effects. Americans are more adaptive and can easily achieve social interaction. Unfortunately, this comes at the cost of an underdeveloped permanence and depth within social life. Thailand's specific social construction although democratic with a monarchy, amount to a hieratical government (Callister & Wall, 2004). With the norms and practices of superiors and subordinates and the karma-centered culture, power is given to those with seen wisdom and conflict management skills. In many cases the monks serve as a "social institution," or higher authority on how to live life. The value setup is generated from the perspective of keeping the peace at all costs.

The different value setups and how a culture is more collectivistic or individualistic in nature can depict how one might understand global social norms and can setup different identities in Eastern and Western depictions of identity rationale. But how does this affect the Thai girl and her online persona? For this answer we will have to identify how females, in both Thai and American setups, portray themselves on the Internet and then draw correlations from the values, relationships, and cultural depictions.

RATIONALE

Overall, previous research provides insights regarding identity and cultural differences. However, only a few studies have researched adolescent girls' home pages, but no information exists about the differences between Thai and American adolescent girls' home pages. It is believed that researchers will be able to better understand the unique perspectives that may exist among cultures.

Cultures vary in their values and their behaviors. The Thai culture has been shown to have different values from the American culture (Komin, 1991). For example, Roongrensuke and Chansuthus (1998) discovered that Thai children are expected to give their parents a high amount of respect. Moreover, Thai children are not allowed to freely express their opinions or feelings to their parents, because of the rigid Thai family authority structure. It is considered very improper for Thai children to criticize or condemn their parents. Even when Thai children become young adults, these individuals will maintain respectful communication behaviors with their parents. It is evident that Thai daughters communicate differently from American girls. It would be interesting to investigate the differences between American and Thai girls' communication behaviors online. If research suggests that there are differences face-to-face, it is highly likely there are differences online. Thus, one research question for this study is:

RQ1:   Is there a difference between American and Thai girls' use of the
         Internet to negotiate their identity?

Stern (1999, 2002a, 2002b, 2004) studied several American girls' home pages and
investigated their narratives. She discovered that they were filled with "stories of self,
of developing personalities, of loneliness and depression, of disappointment with
reality, but also of hopefulness about love and their futures" (p. 224). Moreover, she
noted that some of the home pages provide a way for girls to reveal themselves.
Hence, the second research question for this study is posited:

RQ2:   Is there a difference in the way that American and Thai girls dis-
         play themselves on the Internet?

METHODS

Since the objective of this study was to look at the characteristics of how adolescent girls communicate their identities online, a content analysis was used. Berelson
(1952) noted that this method is used to explain patterns and evaluate large amounts
of data. Content has been used for various studies understanding personal Web pages
(Haas & Grams, 2000; Papacharissi, 2002a, 2002b; Stern, 2004). Stern (2004)
mentioned

> it is worth noting here the frequently-voiced concern that home page authors can poten-
> tially misrepresent their age and gender on their homepages, thus compromising the
> integrity of the study such as the one described here. Although the possibility for such
> fabrications certainly exists, it is wise for us to remember that the possibility for this type
> of misrepresentation exists in many types of traditional data collections as well (e.g., mail
> surveys, phone interviews).

In this study, the main unit for analysis was the personal Web page. In addition, the
girls were e-mailed and asked a few questions about their Web page. The researchers
asked for institutional review board approval for asking questions to the girls as well
as parental permission. The questions were (1) why they chose to display themselves
in this way, (2) how they determine what to display on their page, and (3) what
makes their page so special.

Sample

The participants were gathered using a snowball sample. For the Asian sample, consisting of Thai girls, the main author did a Google search with a popular Thai name.

Results revealed a 15-year-old girl with that name in Thailand. Her friends were contacted and then other friends were contacted. Most of the Web pages were in English. If the page was in Thai, there was a link to translate the entire Web page from Thai to English.

For the American sample, a similar search was done on MySpace.com. The main author did another search for a common American name. This searched resulted in a 14-year-old girl. She was contacted and then her friends were contacted. All girls for this study had to be between the ages of 14–18. If any of the girls did not meet this requirement and or no information regarding their age was obtained, then their data was excluded.

For the Asian sample, 112 home pages were analyzed and for the American sample, 130 home pages were analyzed. In total, 242 home pages were included for this study. All the girls were contacted via e-mail, but only 19.6% (n = 22) of the Thai girls and 23.8% (n =31) of the American girls actually answered all three of the questions asked. It was deemed that 53 girls was a reasonable number of a qualitative analysis of their answers.

Coding Instrument

The coding instrument in this study mirrored Stern's 2004 study. The home pages were categorized into two sets: content features and stylistic features. Content features include four aspects: descriptions, relationships, interests, and intimate topics.

First, description involves diaries, journals, blogs, tweets, and recordings that explain the owner of the page. Second, intimate topics were communication behaviors about sex, intoxicants, depression, and/or anxiety. Third, relationships were variables that describe social associations of family, friends, and significant others. Fourth, interests were analyzed by looking at other outlets or associations, such as sports, news, hobbies, and extracurricular activities.

On the other hand, stylistic features included four subcategories: organization, visual, feedback, and responsiveness to audience. First, organization involves aspects of how the Web page is laid out, the links, and navigation tools. Second, feedback aspects include places where friends and other visitors can contact the owner of the Web page (e.g., guest books, pokes, messages). Third, visual aspects were measured by the amount of images, music, and colors that the page provided. Fourth, responsiveness is how the Web page owner provides communication to the viewers.

Coders and Reliability

One graduate and one undergraduate student coded all the content on the Web pages. The coders spent over 15 hours in training sessions. The coders were trained on sample Web pages that were not used in this study. They were trained until they had an acceptable level of inter-coder reliability. Coding was completed during April 2009. Using one-tenth of the study sample, reported inter-coder reliabilities were obtained. Again similar to Stern's 2004 study, Scott's pi, reliabilities were determined for every variable (Potter & Levine-Donnerstein, 1999). Coders obtained reliabilities of .80 and higher for all variables.

RESULTS AND DISCUSSION

Content Features

Description

Table 4.1 displays the frequency of the variables dealing with description of the girls. Several of these Web pages included biographies and personal information about the owner of the Web page. Of the American sample, 93% (n = 120) included biographies compared to 71% (n = 80) of the Thai sample. Chi-square analyses revealed significant cultural differences regarding expression, specifically regarding their descriptive biographies, 2 (1, N = 240) = 24.33, p < .001. On other categories under description items, the Thai and American participants were very similar to each other and there were no other significant differences.

Table 4.1: Percentage of Adolescents' Personal Home Pages with Description Items

Participants:	Thai (N = 112)	American (N = 130)
Descriptive biography	71.1%	93.4% *
Photographs of author	39.2%	42.1%
References to appearance	31.8%	33.3%
Quotes	10.7%	12.1%
Discussion of plans for future	28.2%	27.9%
Original essays	19.1%	21.9%
Original poetry	11.3%	13.2%
Likes/Dislikes	26.5%	27.2%
Diaries/Journals	3.2%	5.6%

Note: Chi–square significant results
* x^2 = 24.33, df = 1, p < .001

Results from this study found that communication regarding specific interests such as cartoons, school, and media (e.g., Abercrombie & Fitch clothes) were present. Table 4.2 displays the most cited interest variables. Similar to Stern's 2004 study, music sites were popular with both cultures. Researchers have noted the importance of music in adolescent lives (Main & Fowers, 2009).

Table 4.2: Percentage of Adolescents' Personal Home Pages with References to Specific Interests

Participants:	Thai (N = 112)	American (N = 130)
Links to hobbies	72.1%	75.0%
References to media use	23.8%	67.3% [a]
References to school	4.2%	66.7% [b]
Links to music or music sites	31.2%	39.0%
References to video games	12.2%	22.2%
Links to school sites	2.0%	25.3% [c]
Links to film clips, trailers or film sites	19.0%	27.2% [d]
Links to sports	10.0%	15.5%
Links to social cause cites	8.2%	12.3%
Links to news sites	3.2%	9.0% [e]
Links to magazine sites	4.2%	5.7%
Links to retail product service sites	9.1%	67.8% [f]

Note: Chi –square significant results
[a] $x^2 = 7.66$, df = 1, p < .001
[b] $x^2 = 3.42$, df = 1, p < .05
[c] $x^2 = 4.78$, df = 1, p < .05
[d] $x^2 = 2.22$, df = 1, p < .05
[e] $x^2 = 2.45$, df = 1, p < .05
[f] $x^2 = 8.54$, df = 1, p < .05

At the same time, references to media use were significantly higher for American girls (67.3%) than for Thai girls (23.8%). American girls (27.2%) were significantly more likely than Thai girls (19%) to provide links to film clips, trailers, or film sites. Moreover, the American girls (9.0%) were significantly more likely to provide links to news sites (especially entertainment news sites, like TMZ and Access Hollywood) than the Thai girls (3.2%). In this sample, a large portion of the American girls (66.7%) noted that school was a noteworthy interest. However, Thai girls (4.2%) were significantly less likely to denote school as much. A significant higher number of American girls (25.3%) provided links to their school sites compared to only 2% of the Thai girls. Branding, or naming brands and providing links

to popular brands was significantly more apparent in the American sample than in
the Thai sample. In this sample, 67.8% (*n* = 88) of the American girls linked to popular brands, such as Gap, Abercrombie & Fitch, American Eagle, while only 9% (*n*
= 10) of Thai girls did so.

Intimate Topics

While few Web pages revealed intimate topics, there were two statistically significant differences between the intimate content found on the Web sites of Thai and
American girls (see Table 4.3). One-fourth of the American sample noted a reference to spiritual being/God/creator/religious influence. However, none of the girls
in the Thai sample mentioned a religious influence. It is worth mentioning that 20%
(*n* = 26) of the American sample has some reference to sex. Yet, sex was only referenced in 5% (*n* = 6) of the Thai sample.

Table 4.3: Percentage of Adolescents' Personal Home Pages with Intimate Topics

Participants:	Thai (N = 112)	American (N = 130)
Religion/God	0.0%	24.4% [a]
Drugs/alcohol	0.0%	5.4%
Sex	5.2%	20.2% [b]
Depression	1.2%	2.3%
Loneliness	2.8%	2.9%
Violence	0.0%	1.1%
Self-destructive behaviors	0.0%	0.0%

Note: Chi–square significant results
a $x^2 = 33.75$, df = 1, $p < .05$.
b $x^2 = 14.22$, df = 1, $p < .05$

Relationships

Table 4.4 displays the type of interpersonal relationships implied through the adolescent girls' Web pages. Relationships were determined if the girls referred to an
association with another person either in picture format or text. Similar to Stern's
2004 results, just under half of the Web pages and three-quarters referenced their
friends for both the Thai and American girls overall. In the Asian sample, romantic relationships were only discussed in 5% (*n* = 6) of the Web pages. On the contrary, 22% (*n* = 29) of the American girls referred to a romantic relationship, a

Table 4.4: Percentage of Adolescents' Personal Home Pages with References to Relationships

Participants:	Thai (N = 112)	American (N = 130)
References to friends	77.8%	74.3%
References to family	48.2%	44.9%
Links to friends' home pages	49.3%	49.3%
References to romantic relationships	5.0%	22.0%[a]
Reference to participation in IRC or chat	2.0%	3.0%
Links to family members' home pages	0.0%	18.2%[b]
Icon signaling Web ring membership	5.6%	6.7%

Note. $^* p <.05$.

Chi –square significant results:

a $x^2 = 23.44$, df = 1, p < .05
b $x^2 = 21.33$, df = 1, p < .05

difference that was statistically significant. It is hard to determine if this low number is due to the risk of revealing this information in a public forum or that many adolescents are not involved in a romantic relationship at this age. There were no differences in girls' references to family and friends on their home pages. Three-quarters of both Thai and American girls (77.8%, $n = 87$ and 74.3%, $n = 93$, respectively) referenced their friends and nearly half (48.2%, $n = 54$ of Thai girls and 44.9%, $n = 58$ of American girls) referenced their families on their home pages. In regard to their interpersonal relationships, the two samples were very similar. However, the American girls (18.2%) were significantly more likely than the Thai girls (0%) to provide links to family members' home pages.

Stylistic Features

Organization

It was apparent that the creators of the Web pages have spent a lot of time creating and maintaining their Web pages. A large portion of the Web pages had several links and were well organized. Table 4.5 displays the organizational features of the Web pages posted by these girls. These Web pages mainly had about 5–10 Web pages that were connected to other pages. The links provided more profundity and variety to the Web pages. There were no cultural differences in the ways that the girls organized their personal home pages. This suggests that the organizational aspects of a home page are not defined by culture, but more so the conformity of how most home pages are laid out. It could also be due to the home page server, there may be confinements to how home pages are structured and created.

Table 4.5: Percentage of Adolescents' Personal Home Pages with Specific Stylistic Features

Item Participants:	Thai (N = 112)	American (N = 130)
Organizational	89.2%	88.3%
Table of contents	67.2%	68.1%
Navigational features	60.2%	60.3%
Welcome page	92.0%	94.0%
Visual	69.0%	73.0%
Graphics/clip art	58.0%	59.0%
All dark or white background	34.0%	35.0%
Flashing/moving images	20.1%	22.0%
Under construction icons	12.0%	15.0%
Downloadable sounds, images, or games	67.0%	72.0%
E-mail address	78.0%	83.0%
Hot-linked e-mail address	46.4%	47.8%
Guest book	36.1%	38.4%
Counter	12.2%	16.7%
Alternative online alias	39.8%	42.3%
User survey	18.2%	19.3%
Other feedback mechanisms	8.2%	9.0%

Responsiveness

It is apparent that these girls are catering to their audience. This was displayed in the way that they communicated to others in their home pages. In this study, 100% (*n* = 112) of Thai girls and 94% (*n* = 122) of American girls were categorized by coders as friendly/casual—meaning the page conveyed warmth and affability, Although, the coders did not have any preconceived notions that home pages would be friendly or casual, the vast majority used this language.

Visual

A majority of these Web pages provided items to share with their friends, such as pictures, links, games, music, and coupons. All of the Web pages used colors. Half of both the Thai (42%, n = 47) and American (48%, n = 55) samples used the color pink in their pages.

Feedback Mechanisms

Several of these Web pages offered a way to contact the owner of the Web page, such as providing e-mail addresses. Some of the Web pages offered ways for the viewers to contact the creator of the Web page and/or provide a comment for the owner of the Web page. It is worth noting that less than half of these Web pages had a guest book—Thai (36.1%, n = 41) and American (38.4%, n = 49).

Content Features

When contacted directly about their home pages, only a small percentage (n = 53) of the participants actually answered all three questions asked. Table 4.6 reveals the results of answers.

Many of the answers were grouped into the same category, because they were very similar. For instance, when asked why the girls chose their Web pages to display themselves, some of the statements from the Thai girls were as follows,

V, age 14: I think creating my own home page is a fun way to let other people see who I am.

N, age 15: A couple of my friends showed me their pages and I thought if they have one, I would like to have one.

C, age 15: The Internet is now new and I like to post information that I think will be interesting to my friends.

B, age 16: Having my own Web page allows me to express myself.

When asked why the girls chose their Web pages to display themselves, some of the statements from the American girls were as follows,

A, age 15: All my other friends were doing it. And I wanted to do it too.

B, age 15: It is a great way to keep in touch with my friends.

C, age 16: It is a fun way to keep tabs on my peeps.

When asked who determines what to display on their homepages, some of the statements from the Thai girls were as follows,

> V, age 14:   Me. My Web page shows me.
> B, age 16:   My friends and I share pictures and we like to show our friend ship online.
> N, age 15:   Sometimes, I get ideas from other Web sites and I want to make
> my   page the same way.

When the same question was asked to American girls, some of the statements were as follows,

> H, age 15:   Me! Me! Me! It's mine!
> B, age 16:   My girlz and I like to post the same things, cuz we all like the same things.
> J, age 14:   My rents' are really strict about what I post. They double check everything, because they are so scared about Internet predators.

When asked why the girls think their page is so special, some of the statements from the Thai girls were as follows:

> N, age 16:   The page represents me. Everything about the page is about me.
> K, age 17:   Because it has everything that I love. It has my friends and my passions.
> I, age 15:   I made this page by myself and I take pride in knowing that it is something that I did all by myself.

For the same question, the American girls answered:

> O, age 18:   I know it is special because other people tell me all the time how great it is.
> Y, age 15:   This page gives me a way to showcase myself. To let others know me.
> C, age 14:   becuz I created this page all on my own. No help from anyone.

Chi-square results are also shown in Table 4.6. Some of the statements were significantly different between the Thai and American girls, notably the fact that Thai girls were significantly more likely to say they chose to display themselves as they did in the home pages "because it is fun," while American girls said they did so because "my friends do it."

Table 4.6: Percentages of E-mailed Responses to the Three Questions

Participants:	Thai (N = 22)	American (N = 31)
Display themselves in this way....		
Because it is fun	78%	32%[a]
My friends do it	12%	67%[b]
I like posting things online	5%	0%
Self-expression	4.5%	1%
Determine what to display ...		
My parents	0%	5%
My friends	12%	22%
What other people do	18%	8%[c]
My personal tastes	70%	65%
Siblings	0%	5%
Page so special...because		
It showcases me	44%	51%
Because I made it	19%	16%
It has everything I love	25%	0%[d]
I spent a lot of time	10%	0%[e]
Other people tell me	2%	33%[f]

Note: Chi–square significant results

a	$x^2 = 2.11$, df = 1, p < .05
b	$x^2 = 2.43$, df = 1, p < .05
c	$x^2 = 2.56$, df = 1, p < .05
d	$x^2 = 3.12$, df = 1, p < .05
e	$x^2 = 8.43$, df = 1, p < .05
f	$x^2 = 6.24$, df = 1, p < .05

DISCUSSION

All in all, research has shown that adolescents use home pages to communicate with others about themselves (Stern, 1999). However, very little research looked at the cultural differences that may exist between Thai and American adolescent girls' self-expression on the Internet. The results from this study reveal that, while there are differences between the two cultures, at the same time, Thai and American girls exhibit many similarities in their online expression.

Stern (2004) mentioned that girls want to provide a way to express themselves and to present themselves to others on the Internet. Hence, a Web page allows girls the means and creativity to do so. Yet, Stern's sample was also an American sample. Results from this study revealed that Thai girls do not typically provide that much information about themselves. It appears that the American adolescent girls have much to share with others and would be more inclined to seek approval from others. Stern (2004) noted that this discrepancy may be accounted for by the heightened need at adolescence for social validation. Although adults also are desirous of social validation and construct guest books on their home pages for that purpose (Papacharissi, 2002b), adolescents, in particular, often elicit feedback from others in hopes of validating their emerging self-concept (p. 239).

The findings from this study suggest that these personal Web pages offer a means for the girls to communicate their identities. The differences between cultures suggest that the impact of individualistic and collectivistic influences affects the ways the girls portray themselves online. For instance, in the collectivistic cultures, there are fewer media influences than in the individualistic cultures. The Thai girls did not report as many fashion icons or big name advertisers in their home pages compared to the American girls.

Stern (2004) described that:

> References to self abounded on the home pages, demonstrating that home pages can provide a new opportunity for adults (as well as other young people) to learn about how adolescents choose to represent themselves in a public forum when given the means to do so. Such re-presentations may inform or even contradict the often stereotypical images of young people that abound in the mass media, and which are typically produced by adults. They can also provide information about the extent to which young people construct themselves out of cultural materials at hand. (p. 240)

Moreover, collectivistic cultures, like the Thai culture, rarely communicate intimate topics, such as sex and depression compared to the American culture, which displays a great deal of self-disclosure on these intimate topics on television. In this study, the individualistic girls, or American girls, were just as likely to discuss such matters via a virtual context, their Web pages compared to Thai girls. The American girls' Web pages allowed them a stronger ability to express themselves. It was interesting to see that Thai girls were less likely than American girls to engage in this type of behavior. It could be due to the fact that American girls are more influenced by the media than Asian girls. Moreover, there are different marketing campaigns and ease of obtaining merchandise in each country which influence its popularity.

Thai girls also did not mention school as much as did their American counterparts. This could be due to the fact that Thai girls spend more time in school than their American counterparts. Hence, Thai girls may not want to talk about school in this type of domain. In addition, Thai girls did not provide as many links to other families' home pages as the American girls. This could be due to the fact that Internet technology is more difficult for adults in Thailand. Also, the access to the Internet for adults is more challenging than for these adolescents, who may be able to access the Internet at school or at an Internet computer store.

It was interesting to see that many of the participants in this study used similar organization and visual aspects. Less than half in both cultures used the color pink in their home pages. This suggests that pink is perceived as a feminine color and both cultures like the color. It also suggests that many adolescents may regard layout, organization, and visuals for their Web page in a similar fashion. Results from this study support Agosto's (2004) study that found adolescent girls tend to want their Web pages in a certain manner compared to boys.

Findings on such similarities among the cultures are noteworthy for advertisers, because it shows that adolescent females may also perceive visual content in the same fashion.

Future research might investigate the ways in which girls communicate their intimate thoughts and the words they choose to use. Also, another avenue for future research is to look at the ways in which girls form their identities online. It would be interesting to see if there are cultural differences among boys.

As with most studies, this study has some limitations. First, this study only used girls from Thailand and the U.S. It would be interesting to see if girls from China, Japan, or even India are different. Second, there were only 53 respondents to the open-ended questions. It would have been more fruitful if there were more participants. Perhaps, some of the participants were afraid, because they did not know if this was a true study or if the researchers were Internet predators. The researchers told them the purpose of the study and their true identities, but some girls might have felt that it was unsafe to communicate with someone they did not know. Third, the home pages looked at in this study only included ones that were public or that the researchers were granted access. A large majority of the pages were private. Hence, some of the material posted on those Web pages might be very revealing and/or informative compared to the pages studied in this research.

Overall, this study revealed that there were more similarities than differences in the ways that Thai and American adolescent girls communicate via their personal Web pages. The only area in which there were many significant differences was in terms of "specific interests." For all the other categories, such as "description items," "intimate topics," "relationships," and "stylistic features," there are few significant differences. The significant differences regarding specific interests may be due to culture, but they could also be due to the differences of media influences, parental influences, and environmental influences. Overall, this study revealed that girls are more similar on the Internet than different. Results suggested that girls, regardless of culture, are more alike than unlike. Moreover, results suggested that American girls are very peer focused. In other words, American girls are displaying themselves in a certain way because their friends do it and feel their page is special because others have told them so. On the other hand, the Thai girls are displaying themselves in a certain way because it's fun and not because of any kind of peer influence. More investigations into this area would provide higher reliability, validity, and generalization. Yet, understanding the results presented in this study provides a strong framework for future studies in this area.

Conclusion: Girls and the Internet

Adolescence has been shown as the primary stage for developing the identities (Mazalin & Moore, 2004). It is also a stage in life when many have access to the Internet and its tools. As a young girl this could be the primary source to define personality, values, and beliefs about the world. Unfortunately, there is little research on how girls with different ethnicities differ in their expression of identity on the Internet. There is much to be investigated when determining how females are affected in organizing a new persona in a place that has little constraints. The Internet is a wide open field with many new tools for increasing how we perceive it. Cultures differ on values, motives, beliefs, and cultural understandings. Eastern and Western concepts of power, community, and norms develop separate nurtured understandings. With all of these factors and an investigation of the differences between Thai and American girls online, one can see how identities are expressed on the Internet. Findings from this study revealed that the girls from these two cultures were more similar than different, but did have distinct characteristics of cultural values and norms. One can only assume that the built in ethnic cognitive structure carries over and mixes with other cultural assumptions derived from a media generated community. This process of negotiating identity through media and technology is a predominant and growing activity in which young people are engaged.

References

Agosto, D. E. (2004). Design vs. content: A study of adolescent girls' website design preferences. *International Journal of Technology and Design Education, 14,* 245–260.

Befring, E. (1997). *Analysis of Web pages emphasizing gender.* Telenor Forskningsnotat/Scientific Document, FoU N16/97. Retrieved October 4, 2009, from http://www.telenor.no/fou/publisering/publ97.shtml

Berelson, B. (1952). *Content analysis in communication research.* Glencoe, IL: Free Press.

Bortree, D. S. (2005). Presentation of self on the Web: An ethnographic study of teenage girls' weblogs. *Education, Communication, & Information, 5*(1), 25–40.

Callister, R. R., & Wall, J. A., Jr. (2004). Thai and U.S. community mediation. *The Journal of Conflict Resolution, 48*(4), 573–598.

Chandler, D., & Roberts-Young, D. (1998). *The construction of identity in the personal home pages of adolescents.* Retrieved October 4, 2009, from http://www.users.aber.ac.uk/dgc/strasbourg.html

Dominick, J. (1999). Who do you think you are? Personal home pages and self-presentation on the World Wide Web. *Journalism and Mass Communication Quarterly, 76*(4), 646–658.

Foster, D. (1997). Community and identity in the electronic village. In D. Porter (Ed.), *Internet culture* (pp. 23–37). New York: Routledge.

Goffman, E. (1959). *The presentation of self in everyday life.* New York: Doubleday.

Gudykunst, W. B. (1987). *Bridging differences: Effective intergroup communication.* New York: Sage.

Haas, S., & Grams, E. (2000). Readers, authors, and page structure: A discussion of four questions arising from a content analysis of Web pages. *Journal of the American Society for Information Science, 57*(2), 181–192.

Herring, S. C. (2004). Slouching toward the ordinary: Current trends in computer-mediated communication. *New Media Society, 6*(26), 26–36.

Janowitz, M. (1952). *The Community Press in an Urban Setting.* Glencoe, IL: Free Press.

Jankowski, N. (2002). Creating community with media: History, theories and scientific investigations. In L. Lievrouw & S. Livingstone (Eds.), *The handbook of new media* (pp. 34–49). London: Sage.

Kim, B. S. K., Atkinson, D. R., & Yang P. H. (1999). The Asian values scale: Development, factor analysis, validation, and reliability. *Journal of Counseling Psychology, 46*(3), 342–352.

Komin, S. (1991). *Psychology of the Thai people: Values and behavioral patterns.* Bangkok: National Institute of Developmental Administration.

Lenhart, A., & Madden, M. (2005). *Teen content creators and consumers.* Washington, DC: Pew Internet & American Life Project. Retrieved October 2, 2009, from http://www.pewInternet.org/PPF/r/166/report_display.asp

Li, N., & Kirkup, G. (2007). Gender and cultural differences in Internet use: A study of China and the U.K. *Computers and Education, 48*(2), 301–317.

Lueker-Harrington, D. (2001, July 10). Marketers. *USA Today*, p. 13A.

Main, J., & Fowers, B. J. (2009). Adolescent self control and music and movie piracy. *Computers in Human Behavior, 25*(3), 718–722.

Mazalin D., & Moore, S. (2004). Internet use, identity development and social anxiety among young adults. *Behavior Change, 21*(2), 90–102.

McCann, R., Ota, H., Giles, H., & Caraker, R. (2003). Accommodation and nonaccommodation across the lifespan: Perspectives from Thailand, Japan, and the United States of America. *Communication Reports, 16*(2), 69–91.

Merton, R. K. (1949). Patterns of influence: A study of interpersonal influence and communications behavior in a local community. In P. F. Lazarsfeld & F. N. Stanton (Eds.), *Communication research 1948–49* (pp. 180–219). New York: Arnold.

Offer, D., Schonert-Reichl, K. A., & Boxer, A. M. (1996). Normal adolescent development: Empirical research findings. In M. Lewis (Ed.), *Child and adolescent psychiatry: A comprehensive textbook* (pp. 280–290). Baltimore, MD: Williams & Wilkins.

Olaniran, B. A., & Roach, K. D. (1994). Communication apprehension and classroom apprehension in Nigerian classrooms. *Communication Quarterly, 42*, 379–389.

Papacharissi, Z. (2002a). The presentation of self in virtual life: Characteristics of personal home pages. *Journalism & Mass Communication Quarterly, 79*(3), 643–660.

Papacharissi, Z. (2002b). The self online: The utility of personal home pages. *Journal of Broadcasting & Electronic Media. 46*(3), 346–368.

Phillips, H. P. (1966) *Thai peasant personality: The patterning of interpersonal behavior in the village of Bang Chan.* Berkeley: University of California Press.

Potter, W., & Levine-Donnerstein, D. (1999). Rethinking validity and reliability in content analysis. *Journal of Applied Communication Research, 27*, 258–284.

Pye, L. W. (1985). *Asian power and politics: The cultural dimensions of authority.* Cambridge, MA: Belknap Press of Harvard University Press.

Roongrengsuke, S., & Chansuthus, D. (1998). Conflict management in Thailand, In K. Leung & D. Tjosvold, (Eds.), *Conflict management in the Asia Pacific* (pp. 167–222). Singapore: John Wiley.

Rubin, R. B., Fernandez-Collado, C., & Hernandez-Sampieri, R. (1992). A cross-cultural examination of interpersonal communication motive in Mexico and United States. *International Journal of Intercultural Relations, 16*, 145–157.

Shil'shtein, E. S. (2001). Characteristics of the presentation of self during adolescence. *Russian Education and Society, 43*(6), 35–51.

Stern, S. (1999). Adolescent girls' expression on www home pages: A qualitative analysis. *Convergence: The Journal of Research into New Media Technologies, 5*(4), 22–41.

Stern, S. (2002a). Sexual selves on the World Wide Web: Adolescent girls' homepages as sites for sexual self-expression. In J. Brown, J. Steele, & K. Walsh-Childers (Eds.), *Sexual teen/sexual media: Investigating media's influence on adolescent sexuality* (pp. 265–286). Mahwah, NJ: Lawrence Erlbaum.

Stern, S. (2002b). Virtually speaking: Girls' self-disclosure on the WWW. *Women's Studies in Communication, 25(2)*, 223–253.

Stern, S. R. (2004). Expressions of identity online: Prominent features and gender differences in adolescents' World Wide Web home pages. *Journal of Broadcasting and Electronic Media, 48*(2), 218–243.

Stewart, E. C., & Bennett M. J. (1992). *American cultural patterns: A cross-cultural perspective.* Yarmouth, ME: Intercultural Press.

Sutton, L. A. (1999). All media are created equal: Do-it-yourself identity in alternative publishing. In M. Bucholtz, A. C. Liang, & L.A. Sutton (Eds.), *Reinventing identities: The gendered self in discourse* (pp. 163–180). New York: Oxford University Press.

Tedeschi, J. T. (1986). Private and public experiences of the self. In R. Baumeister (Ed.), *Public and private self.* (pp. 1–17). New York: Springer-Verlag.

Thiel, S. M. (2004). *IM me: Adolescent girls and identity negotiation in the world of instant messaging.* Unpublished dissertation. University of Iowa. Retrieved October 3, 2009, from http://www.proquest.umi.com/theil2004

Turow, J. (1999). The Internet and the family: The view from the family, the view from the press. Philadelphia, PA: Annenberg Public Policy Center. Retrieved October 4, 2009, from http://www.annenbergpublicpolicycenter.org/04_info_society/family/rep27.pdf

Tyler, T. R. (2002). Is the Internet changing social life? It seems the more things change, the more they stay the same. *Journal of Social Issues, 50*(1), 195–205.

CHAPTER FIVE

Go Cyworld!

Korean Diasporic Girls Producing New Korean Femininity

MICHELLE S. BAE

Contemporary girls' social and cultural dimensions have been greatly expanded by advances in digital technology and high-speed Web communication. New technological configurations that allow information to move across previously impervious boundaries provide these girls with experiences beyond the physical zones of daily living, such as school, home, and local communities. As a result, girls' lived experiences on the Internet are culturally and geographically crossed as well as bounded. Hence, my ethnographic study on contemporary diasporic[1] Korean girls' active use of Cyworld[2] focuses on identifying how the girls cyberculture functions as an ideological yet counterhegemonic Web site and how the girls recreate their ethnic femininities, albeit in a culturally hybrid form.

By examining this issue, this small ethnographic study follows a current trend in the discourse of girl studies; namely, the search for a girls' agency and production that the previous dominant discourse, centralized on consumer-oriented girls' culture and White Western girls, too long ignored (Budgeon, 1998; Inness, 1998; Kearney, 2006; Sato, 1998; Suzuki, 1998). In that earlier metanarrative discourse, girls of color were invisible and voiceless. That is, claims of what it means to be a girl generalized from the experiences of White girls undermined the "differences" in identity of girls of color. Besides confronting this challenge, this study challenges conventional methodological approaches[3] to understanding girls' culture by using dialogic interplay[4] between myself and three teenage girl participants[5] to uncover the lives of Korean diasporic girls' active production in the Cyworld culture. The methodological approach for this study with the girls allowed my interaction with them to constantly shift to make our understanding of each other both familiar and unfamiliar. Although I was researching fellow Korean immigrants, differences such as generational gaps and different emigration experiences also greatly influenced our understanding of each other. In the process of understanding each other, the girls and I went through an ongoing series of conflicts, agreements, and negotiations. This dialogic interplay involved in-depth interviews[6] in informal settings, both on-line and off-line, as well as a content analysis of their Cy *hompis*.[7]

This approach echoes the study assumption that diasporic Korean girls' active engagement in production is tightly connected to both their consumption and their agentic roles while using this ethnic online social networking site. Hence, the discussion begins with a brief sketch of the context in which the diasporic Korean girls were situated and actively began using Cy. This context forms the backdrop for an analysis of how and what meanings the girls produce in this imagined cultural space as they reinvent their identities through popular gestures and Precura[8] photographs. The results of the analysis are then complemented by the girls' critical views and the voices that played an agentic role on the Web site.

KOREAN DIASPORIC GIRLS AND CYWORLD

Since the late 1990s, South Korea's movement toward globalization has propelled the unprecedented immigration to the U.S. of middle-class Korean girls, many of whom desire a better education, future professional success, and the cosmopolitan urban lifestyle encouraged by popular media. Regardless of their desire to become global citizens—an idea reinforced by mainstream Korean social discourses—in the U.S. they are essentially labeled outsiders or underrepresented minorities. After their relocation, race and ethnicity become new identity domains to be confronted and coped within daily life. Hence, ironically, for these girls, becoming a global citizen demands exclusion from U.S. mainstream society. In this context, the girls' active use of Cyworld implies an activity essential to supporting an emotional niche that demands pleasurable consumption of Korean popular culture and thus leads to production.

KOREAN DIASPORIC GIRLS' CREATION OF AN IMAGINED CULTURAL SPACE

Cyworld is my small world [in which] I feel connected to South Korea. Since I moved to the U.S., Cy is more meaningful than when I was in Korea. I feel sorry for my White friends who cannot enjoy this fun site. Hee hee. Facebook and Myspace are plain, while Cy is fun and sophisticated. I feel proud to be a Korean. (Lauren, age 15, a comment on her Cy *hompi*)

Cyworld, a cultural arena within which diasporic Korean girls actively engage in their daily lives, has become particularly necessary and more meaningful to them since their migration to the U.S. More specifically, their engagement with Korean contemporary popular culture during their stay in the U.S. is predicated on their willingness to maintain the ethnic culture that makes them feel cultural pride. However, such national pride is also on a par with their nostalgia for a lost Korean girlhood. As Eunbi, a 16-year-old girl, wrote to her friends in South Korea:

> Since moving to the U.S., I feel I have lost my Korean girlhood. When visiting your *hompi*s, I have found so much fun in your everyday lives whether in school or after school. I miss the time with you, my dear friends. If I were there, we could have lots of fun. When I look at your Cy, your photos tell me that you have many fun experiences. You guys go out to eat Korean rice cakes [*duk-bok-kki*] from street vendors or in cafes. Many cafes offer delicious foods like Korean sushi [*kim-bob*], sweet potato pizza, or pork cutlets wrapped in kimchi and cheese. You also go to karaoke [*no-rah-bang*] to sing, and you can walk any place you like. Shopping must be so exciting! Korea has so many places to go with friends after school and during the weekend. I miss being there. I envy you guys. (Eunbi, a response on her *hompi*)

As Eunbi's writing shows, the diasporic Korean girls' longing for Korean girlhood has motivated them to create an imagined world that can best be characterized as a zone in between reality and fiction. Apparaduri (2006), locating imagination in social practice, defined such imagined worlds as new global sociocultural spaces constructed from the "historically situated imagination of persons and groups spread around the globe" (p. 589) through the ethnoscape, mediascape, technoscape, financescape, and ideoscape. This imagined world, he suggested, is produced from concatenations of an unprecedented nomadic lifestyle, new advanced technological configurations, and complex repertoires of image and text linked to commodification, political ideologies, and global capital. From this perspective, the Cy *hompi*, the imagined world produced by the diasporic Korean girls, is a sociocultural space in which fiction and reality become blurred and direct experiences are replaced by mediated ones. In other words, the girls' creation of imagined Korean girlhood is no longer based purely on direct cultural experiences of Korean reality. Rather, it consists of "protonarratives of possible lives" and to a considerable extent is filled with chimerical fantasies to meet their "desire for acquisition" of a Korean girlhood (Apparaduri, 2006, p. 591).

The diasporic girls' production of this imagined cyberworld combines playful mimicry with alternative meaning-making through hand gestures, photography, and

Precura snapshots. Their active creation of this imagined world involves learning and updating contemporary Korean culture, which helps them recover their lost Korean girlhood in the areas of friendship, language, attitude, and behavior. Yet this process is culturally hybrid. That is, it is not an expression of subordination to either U.S. or Korean culture but a reenactment of both cultures, a reenactment into which they project their voices. They present this imagined world primarily through photographed gestures and the Precura snapshots that make up their Cy *hompi*s.

THE GIRLS' PRODUCTION OF ETHNICALLY CROSSED AND BOUNDED PHOTOGRAPHIC GESTURES

Korean diasporic girls' Cy culture emerged as a significant new ethnic cultural production in the U.S., not simply because their stay in America leads them to create an alternative mode of ethnic production, but because it is an outcome of interplay with their ethnic cultural consumption and therefore reflects their ambivalent cultural positioning. Through Cyworld, the diasporic girls actively consume and conform to the dominant contemporary Korean culture and femininity. However, this conformist mode of consumption is tightly connected to their own production, which is in turn marked by a critical yet playful aspect of new ethnic culture and femininity.

One example of the Korean cultural consumption that leads to the girls' production are the extremely popular hand gestures in the self-photographs that ubiquitously decorate their Cy *hompi*s. Such hand gestures typically consist of their hands covering their own mouths or chins and/or V-shaped fingers placed around their faces. These unique cultural behaviors convey both "cuteness" and an ideal of Korean female beauty, a small face. Such ethnically defined cultural behavior creates the photographic culture that is a major part of the girls' subculture on their Cy *hompi*s and that is consumed obsessively by the diasporic Korean girl participant in this study. However, in so accommodating Korean femininity, the girls have recreated meanings that challenge the original ethnic meanings through Cy blogs and texts. Such recreation is exemplified by Jooyoung's visual narratives on her personal *hompi*.

Jooyoung's Narrative

At the time of the study, Jooyoung's Cy *hompi* was filled with her photographs of the Korean gestures popular among Korean girls; most particularly, covering her mouth with both hands. Yet, while her frequent portrayal of this gesture seems to reflect her indulgence in it, the text under one photograph (see Figure 5.1) sends a different message: "These days it is a trend among Korean youths to take this kind of posture, so I imitated; I feel really absurd; I have only exposed my face to people since I was born; I cannot do this, ha, ha, ha, ha." These words suggest that while playfully imitating this gesture popular with Korean girls, Jooyoung realizes it is not for her. Thus, even though her bodily experience of imitating the Korean popular cultural code has seemingly been pleasurable, she ridicules the motif of Korean culture and in so doing unidentifies herself as a typical Korean girl and crosses her Korean ethnic boundaries. Hence, her gestural mimicry goes beyond her conformity to Korean ethnic femininity. Rather, the statement accompanying her image hints at her ambivalent position as she juggles Korean and U.S. culture. Such juggling revolves around the ideas of beauty and body image through gesture.

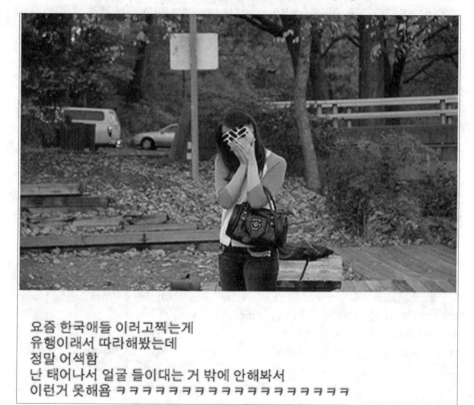

요즘 한국애들 이러고찍는게
유행이래서 따라해봤는데
정말 어색함
난 태어나서 얼굴 들이대는 거 밖에 안해봐서
이런거 못해욤 ㅋㅋㅋㅋㅋㅋㅋㅋㅋㅋㅋㅋㅋㅋㅋㅋㅋ

Figure 5.1 *Jooyoung,* untitled,[9] *September 2008 (digital photograph).*

This hand gesture has been so popular nationwide that every Korean girl knows and imitates it. Most of all, Jooyoung explained to me somewhat sarcastically but with a chuckle, "They try so hard to make small faces, and their faces look relatively small when hidden with a hand." Not identifying herself with the typical Korean girl, she added that all young Korean women desperately desire to have a small face and that this ideal is projected through this gesture in their *sel-ca* (a type of self-photography) images posted on the Cy *hompi*. Hence, this gesture[10] has been revived in the contemporary Korean cultural context but attached to the new meaning of a desirably small face and an image of cuteness. This alternative construct, strongly encouraged by *sel-ca* and the Cy *hompi*, has driven the girls to actively practice a self-image production based on awareness of their appearance; a major feminine practice that continues to be savored by girls coming of age. This attention to appearance and the resulting projects of self-creation reflect a typical manifestation of postfeminist girls celebrating feminine practice (McRobbie, 2007). However, Jooyoung has critically distanced herself from this gesture, saying, "many Korean girls spontaneously make the gesture as if it were natural. It is a Korean thing. But when I do it, it is just for fun, for imitating and mocking. I know that seems cheesy, though." Nevertheless, despite disparaging the Korean gesture, she admitted during our conversation that her self-conscious performance of it in the form of play is linked to Koreanness and is apparently a symbolic Korean act by which she explores herself as a Korean.

I therefore challenged her by asking, "Aren't you Korean?" She showed no emotion: "I am Korean, but it is pretty strange to me to use this gesture to present myself as a Korean."

Her answer implies double layers of resistance. Even though she had imitated the gesture, she told me directly that she was also boldly resisting by not identifying herself with other Korean girls. Yet she asserted her Korean identity. This complicated play on the meaning of Korean ethnic femininity blurs the boundaries of resistance to versus accommodation of Korean ethnic femininity and gives the gesture a new meaning—a refusal to identify with Korean femininity while claiming to be a Korean.

Later, when asked about her motivation to perform this gesture during photo taking, she laughed without hiding her mouth with her hands: "I just did the gesture for fun. But I do not usually do this. That gesture is not for me." She was thus resisting the gesture and preferred to pursue her own path. Exposing her face, she told me, was her real self when taking self-snapshots. Thus, her gestural mimicry gave her an opportunity to explore Korean femininity, one that led her to choose and create her own femininity. In this process, she consciously doubted her sense of Korean belongingness yet asserted herself to be a Korean girl, thereby indicating a "conformist mode of resistance" (Driscoll, 2002, p. 279). This ethnically ambivalent mode of resistance manifested continually on her Cy site through images and blog text, especially the conversational threads from friends commenting on the images she had uploaded and the accompanying text.

BOY1: 헐!!!!!!

BOY2: 들이대야 산다 (You can survive by exposing your face)

GIRL 1: 숨이나 쉬겠냐? (Can you breathe?)

GIRL 2: 유행은 지났다! ㅋㅋㅋㅋㅋ (This fashion has already gone!!!)

BOY3: -_- you, 따라하네... (You imitate it too)

JOOYOUNG: 나도 한쿡에서 유행하는 거 한번쯤은 해보고싶었뜸
          (I also wanted to do what is popular in Korea at least once).

GIRL 2: ㅋㅋㅋㅋㅋㅋㅋㅋㅋㅋ한국은 이제 어머나가 대세야
        (Ha, ha, ha, ha. In Korea, *u-mu-na* is the most popular one)

GIRL 2: 원걸 소희 (Won-Girl So-Hee)

GIRL 3: 엄머나 다시한번말해봐아아(*U-mu-na*, tell me again)

GIRL 2: 오늘 뮤뱅 예은이 결국은 삑사리 내버렸어 ㅋㅋㅋ
        의례적인 삑사리ㅋㅋㅋ (Today, Yae-Eun made a weird
        sound on Music Bank, ha, ha, ha, a ritual-like sound)

JOOYOUNG: 테테테테테테텔미 (Te-te-te-te-te-tell me [she sings
          along in imitation of the song])

BOY 4: Y'all doing it wrong. U need to be like 2mm in front of the
       camera.

BOY 4: Ur eyes like this O_O. C'mon, even I know how to do it
       the Korean way, lol.

JOOYOUNG: Um, when did you decide to be so Korean?

This blog conversation began when Jooyoung's Korean male friends teased her about her Korean gesture of hiding her mouth with her hands in the image. They jokingly suggested that Jooyoung had better expose her face for survival, meaning that they did not recommend her hand gesture. They then followed her Korean girlfriends' teasing by sarcastically suggesting that Jooyoung's mouth-covered hand gesture was suffocating her and was out of date. Responding to such teasing, Jooyoung retorted that her gesture was simply an imitation of the popular Korean one, after which her girlfriends in Korea introduced her to the most recent popular gesture and its correspondence to a rhyme from a popular song. Jooyoung then imitated this latter gesture. Subsequently, in answer to a Korean American boy who had viewed this conversational thread and ridiculed Jooyoung and her girlfriends' play on Koreaness, Jooyoung sarcastically challenged his Americanized bent, which denigrated Koreaness. Her cynical response to the boy is also a subversive act against conventional Korean femininity, in which women are expected to be voiceless and subordinate to men. Her spontaneous, assertive reaction characterizes a multilayered resistance, one that intersects gender with ethnicity in a complex manner.

My initial viewing of her conversational performance on the blog demanded an explanation of a recent neologism in Korean popular culture with which I was initially unfamiliar. At a meeting with Jooyoung after the initial viewing, I asked her, "What is u-mu-na?"

"Like this," she gestured. "You put both hands on the chin and at the same time you must say "*u-mu-na*." She laughed briefly and continued, "My friends told me that this gesture is the most recent popular gesture. They said that my gesture in the photo, hiding my mouth with both hands, is already out of date. I am already quite outdated compared to them."

I then asked about the other new phrase: "So what does Won-Girl-So-Hee mean?"

Surprised, she said, "Don't you know Wonder Girl? Haven't you heard the song *Tell Me*? This is a recently famous dance song that all Koreans know and imitate. So-Hee is a girl singer in a Korean teenage dance group called Wonder Girl. There are five girls, but she is the cutest one. She does this gesture all the time during her dance." She opened a new window to show me an online clip of the Wonder Girls' video performance. The girl singer's gesture is a significant representation of "cuteness" among Korean girls, one that, together with the song's lyrics, has spread rapidly across the entire country and created an ideal image of the cute girl. Hence, the gesture has become a trademark of this girl singer, who almost every Korean girl imitates fanatically.

As a result, the blog exchanges included sarcastic comments from Jooyoung's friends about her imitation of the gesture and her being culturally outdated because of her presence in the U.S. Nevertheless, surprisingly, she did not resist such sarcasm; instead, she showed them that she was learning about current Korean trends. In fact, she seemed to respond modestly to her friends by singing the rhyme with which this currently popular gesture originated. Thus, although she disputed the meaning and form of the Korean gesture in her own text, she did not challenge her friends' updates. Rather, her imitation of the dance group's lyrics was a play on Korean femininity in which she explored what Korean girls currently do and pursue. Her imitation, she told me, is not serious but for fun. That is, her playful accommodation does not mean naively immersing herself in an image of cuteness informed by popular Korean trends. On the contrary, it is rather a conscious exploration of Korean femininity.

For example, pointing to a comment on the page, she added, "The thread of conversation in my *hompi* does not include much serious talk. But sometimes I talk back very boldly, especially when guys tease me or leave obnoxious comments like this one." She pointed to an entry by Boy 4, who had jumped into the exchange last: "He teased our play. He is kinda twinkie.[11] He doesn't understand the Korean culture or girls at all. I cannot help but tease him back." Hence, ironically, she is resisting imitation of the Korean ethnic cultural code of femininity informed by Korean popular culture. On the other hand, she is also overtly resisting the Americanized Korean boy who mocks Korean girls' imitation of Korean popular cultural femininity. In fact, her assertive reaction to the boy suggests a feminist mindset that resists not only the fact of a boy ridiculing her but also the American cultural hegemony he embodies. This double entanglement was the trigger for her explicitly resistant words. Therefore, her imitation of the Korean ethnic gesture does not denote her naïve conformity to the Korean cultural motif, but rather is a vehicle for spontaneously exploring herself and figuring out her identity. However, her imitation played out ambivalently because while resisting Korean femininity, she maintained Korean ethnic cultural pride. Such an ambivalent mode of cultural hybridity in ethnic cultural production is also projected, but in a different manner, in the visual narratives of Eunbi.

Eunbi's Narrative

On her Cy *hompi*, Eunbi frequently displays a variety of hand gesture patterns. On her journey of self-making, she has tried out each popular gesture and even developed her own (see Figure 5.2). In fact, since knowing her, I had assumed that the primary purpose for her making that gesture was desire for a small face. Like those of other Korean girls, her *hompi* was full of chat about appearance, and her friends' opinions about her own appearance in the photographs included both humorous compliments and criticisms. Thus, bluntness and indirectness were blurred.

While examining both photographs and text, my eyes were fixed on a series of sel-ca photos in which her conscious gestures were like those in other photos (see Figure 5.3). Her friends had boldly thrown their opinions into the conversation text with caustic humor (reproduced under Figure 5.3), commenting that the gestures did not help her face look small. In response to such ridicule, Eunbi excused this attempt and her intention to show cuteness through gestures. However, her invention and imitation of the gestures eventually affirmed that the gesture of cuteness did not fit her nor did she identify with it. Rather, in the dialogue, she consciously dissociated herself from the cuteness ubiquitously promoted as representing young Korean femininity in Korean popular media.

Figure 5.2 *Eunbi*, How to Make Your Face Look Small, *February 2008 (digital photograph)*.

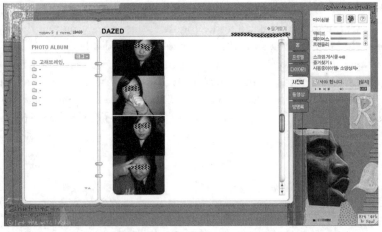

Figure 5.3 *Eunbi*, Unidentified Girl, *February 2008 (digital photographs)*.

GIRL 1: 고루고루 찌겼삼ㅋㅋㅋ. (You took photos in various ways).

GIRL 2: Take hands off ㅋㅋㅋㅋ. 그런다고 얼구리 작아지낭 (Take your hands off, ha, ha, ha; it doesn't make your face small).

Eunbi: Do not put me down. Cute 한거 try해 볼라는 데ㅠㅠㅠㅠ (Do not put me down. I tried to look cute).

GIRL 2: 새 camera가 좋긴 조쿠먼, 빨이 밨는 거시 ㅎㅎㅎㅎ (New camera gave a great result. It made you look great. Ha, ha, ha).

EUNBI: 태클 걸지마라. 후안이 좀.... (Do not get on my nerves. There will be some consequences).

GIRL 2: Cute 하긴 해. Anyway, 퍼감~~~~. (You look cute. Anyway, I would take a photo with you).

EUNBI: Cute 은 내 theme 이 아닌데. (Cuteness is not my style).

GIRL 1: 두번쩨 photo, 저 손은 좀 아닌 듯 ㅋㅋㅋㅋ. (In the second photo, the hand is funny looking. Ha, ha, ha).

EUNBI: 헉...내가 개발한 것임. (I invented it).

GIRL 1: 어떠케 찍겼쌈? 두 손이 다보이는데. (How did you take the *sel-ca*? I can see both hands).

EUNBI: ㅎㅎㅎㅎ tripod 의 힘!!! (It is the power of the tripod!!).

BOY 1: 왕 쌍. 너 말구 카메라 ㅋㅋㅋㅋㅋㅋㅋ (Cool, not you but the camera. Ha, ha, ha).

EUNBI: Shut up. 환경 오염 시키지 마라 ㅎㅎㅎㅎ(Shut up. Do not pollute this environment. Ha, ha, ha).

GIRL 3: 이뽀ㅋㅋㅋㅋ. 나퍼감 ㅋㅋㅋㅋㅋ (You look pretty. I will take it. Ha, ha, ha).

EUNBI: 쌩유 ㅋㅋㅋㅋ. (Thank you. Ha, ha, ha, ha).

GIRL 4: How cute looking!!!

EUNBI: 고마버유~~~~~~, but 제발 cute 하다는 말은 좀 삼가... (Thank you, but do not call me cute, please)

Since my first contact with the Cy *hompis*, I have observed that such cuteness—which I perceive as a young, uncontaminated, pure image that still has a hint of the mischievous—is frequently re-created by Korean girls on their sites. Above all, I have noted that this image of young Korean femininity is different from the dominant image of femininity in U.S. popular culture, which emphasizes sexually empowered women.

"What kind of style do you pursue?" I asked Eunbi.

"I like a stylish, mature, and sophisticated look. Feminine chic is a basic."

"On your *hompi*, you have tried to look cute, using Korean gestures," I teased

"Aha," she replied, not in the least embarrassed by my comment, "on the *hompi*, I did it on purpose because it is a Korean site and I wanted to act like a cute girl as I did in Korea in the past. So that I can still share with my friends in Korea.

It is just for fun."

"You mean the image of a cute girl is not your concept in real life?"

She nodded: "Right. That is not my style; only on the *hompi* and with Korean friends."

Obviously, Eunbi knew what can be "cool" and what she was doing. She was thus aware that cuteness as a symbol of Korean girlness can be played out on a Korean ethnic site but must be replaced in her everyday pursuits outside the site by an alternative image, a more mature look of contemporary feminine chic. Hence, although her efforts to make her face small fit the contemporary standard of Korean beauty, the gestures presented on her *hompi* indicate her playful imitation of cuteness.

"Eunbi, I saw your imitation and re-creation of the hand gestures in the photos on your *hompi*. You seemed to be trying hard to make your face small using hand gestures."

"I did not try hard to do it," she responded quickly with a laugh, "I just experimented in several ways. See, I have a big round face like the moon. I wanted to resize it into a small face."

"I think you are pretty with the size and shape you have," I commented. "I have seen lots of Korean girls on their *hompis* trying so hard to make their faces small using hand gestures. I have learnt that a small face is one of the essential ideal images that Korean girls desire. Where do you think this ideal came from?"

"It might be wrong," she replied, "but I guess we [Korean girls] see many female models and actresses in the U.S. entertainment media. All of them have small faces that make them look photogenic and well proportioned. And lots of Korean models and actresses also pursue this goal on the screen and in photos. I have heard producers and photographers say that a small face looks beautiful on screen… So I guess my desire for a small face is a Korean influence," she reflected, giggling. "Although I live in the U.S., I still want to have one. Compared to my American girlfriends, I have a big chubby face."

"Particularly on the *hompi*," I added, "you keep showing gestures that meet the Korean standard of beauty. Do you still make a gesture to deemphasize your facial size when taking a photo with a White American friend?"

"I am conscious about it," she replied, "but I do not make any hand gestures with them. But with Korean friends and for the *hompi* I do."

"Why do you do it with Korean friends?"

"Because we Korean girls know and play with this gesture. This gesture confirms that we are Korean girls. I want to connect to my Korean friends and culture, which makes me comfortable and feels enjoyable."

I rephrased her remark: "So the gestures conveying your desire for a small face can be a mark of your Koreaness. Is that what you mean?" She nodded in assent.

Thus, it seems, her refusal to look cute is an indication of resistance to a Korean femininity since moving to the U.S., although she still acts this femininity out on her *hompi*. Her performance can therefore be viewed as an ambivalent mode between conformity and resistance. Ironically, her desire for a small face, shaped by the Korean cultural standard for girls, remains regardless of the context in which she finds herself. Hence, those meanings attached to her (re)creation of gestures are an ambivalent ethnic play that represents both her eagerness to fit the standard of Korean culture and her rejection of popular Korean girl femininity. In other words, Eunbi's imitative play on the Korean gestures is an exploration of the boundaries of Korean ethnic femininity that she wants to accept or reject in her creation of herself. Such imitative performance eventually provides an arena in which her resistance to an image of Korean young femininity occurs freely. Yet simultaneously, within this context, her young Korean femininity has been preserved on a conscious level. Thus, her selection of what she would like to be from among available ethnic motifs of femininity is marked by ambivalence and paradox.

Lauren's Narrative

As I then moved on to Lauren's *hompi*, I also began to realize that her ethnic play might have an implicit meaning of resistance. That is, while scanning her pictures, I noticed that she performed differently with Korean friends than with non-Korean friends. Not surprisingly, almost every photograph with Korean friends included V-shaped finger gestures or hands wrapped around chins or covering mouths. In contrast, the photographs with non-Korean friends, including both White and other Asian friends, lacked this distinguishing aspect. One other characteristic of these portraits particularly caught my attention: her gesturing with non-Korean Asian male friends, who were making the same gesture (see Figure 5.4). I suspected that they must have learned and copied the gesture from her.

In the exchanges on her *hompi*, her Korean girlfriends ragged her about her coquettish behavior, including her playful coaching of the gesture. Yet the requests from her girlfriends for Lauren to be a good girl were a mischievous warning that also seemingly showed an envious desire for her play with the boys. Throughout various conversations, Lauren emphasized Korean girls' distinctive beauty in a manner that suggested her confidence as a Korean girl distinguishing herself through playfulness and appearance. Such confidence revealed her power of control over the Asian boys through her appearance. I therefore deemed the girls' position in this conversational thread to be synonymous with the postfeminist definition of the girl as a subject who favors the practice of conventional femininity and gravitates to feminine behavior (McRobbie, 2007; Roberts, 2007). By such enactment of feminine behaviors, girls attain empowerment.

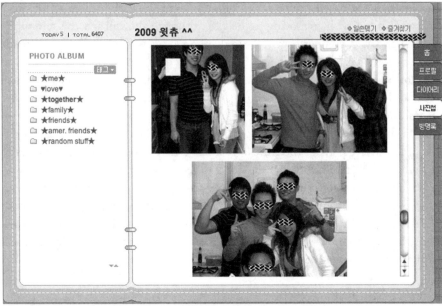

Figure 5.4. *Lauren*, Party Time, *January 2008 (digital photograph and blog).*

LAUREN: 역시 꼬리안들이 젤튀는군 ㅎㅎ funny boyzzz. (Korean looks standing-out fabulously, haha, funny boyzzz)

GIRL 1: lol. J 오빠포정대박, 얼굴가려줘서 쌩유우 ㅋㅋㅋ. (J bro looks great. Thank you for hiding my face with a white box.)

GIRL1: 사진에 니 얼굴만 안나와 ㅋㅋ 저 바나나..기억나니??ㅋ (Only your face is hidden in the photo. Haha, Do you remember that banana?? Ha)

LAUREN: 내가 저러고 놀지말랫지. 너2008자제좀하자. 착하게살자 .기억해라좀. (I told you not to play like that. You need to control yourself in 2008, Remember let's be good.)

GIRL 1: 저하늘색옷입은분오는거면당연히불렀어야쥐 ㅋㅋㅋㅋ이러 (You should've invited me if the guy with a blue shirt would come to the party, hahahaha).

LAUREN: ㅋㅋㅋ나 착하게 살꺼야!!! 그리고 저분 울오빠서... 막이래?ㅋㅋ키딩맨. (hahaha I will be good!!! That guy is my brother...I am making it? Haha I am kidding, Man).

GIRL 1: ㅋㅋㅋ Lauren, 난 자제했다. 홋홋. (hahaha, I already controlled myself. Haha)

LAUREN: 우리 거짓말 안하는착한아이되자.(Let's be honest and good girls).

However, the girls' attention to beauty did not simply mean being the object of the male gaze: it also meant taking pleasure in narcissistically gazing at themselves and enjoying the admiring gaze of friends regardless of gender. Therefore, the legacy of feminist visual culture, the view of woman as the object of the male gaze, has become antiquated and been replaced by the viewing practices of these girls for whom bodily representations are meant to give pleasure to themselves as well as others. That is, placing themselves in a flexible position between subject and object is an empowering act that transverses the gender system. This repositioning of a new ethnic femininity in the image and text thwarts conventional feminist expectations of a transcendent masculine girl subject that freely and boldly plays, gazes, and talks about herself using her own judgment. Rather, the new Korean femininity embraces an ambiguous mode between conventional feminine and feminist qualities.

As my eyes moved through the photos on the *hompi*, I suddenly noticed Lauren's different behavior when taking photos with White girls. Her proud gesturing, which appeared so frequently in other photos, was absent from these images (see Figure 5.5). Rather, she seemed to perform as if she were the same as the other American girls. Such performance, which did not show the Korean popular gesture, initially obscured my understanding and led me to ask whether this act was merely an unresisting accommodation to the U.S.

However, the photos at the homecoming party on Cy (re)presented an alternative meaning through the blog text:

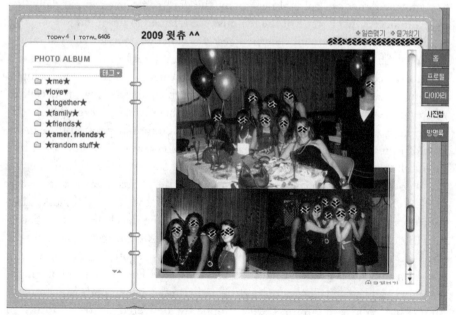

Figure 5.5 *Lauren*, Party Time!, *July 2008 (digital photograph and blog).*

GIRL 1: 너가 저 백인보다 더이뻐이뻐 ㅋㅋ (You look much, much prettier than those Whites)

LAUREN: 오우! 생유 베리마치!! 근데 니가 나보다 더 이쁘다는거??! (Wow, thank you so much!! Do you know that you are prettier than me?)

Instead of apparent accommodation to U.S. behaviors, in these blog conversations, Lauren's Korean friends praised her superior external beauty among the White girls. As Korean girls, they equated this praise with Korean national pride, a proud assent of being Korean that, in this text, is an act of challenge against U.S. images of femininity. Hence, this practice brings to light a major irony: whereas her photographs without Korean feminine gestures seemingly represent her cultural accommodation of the U.S., her words emphasize cultural pride by stressing the superiority of Korean beauty. I thus consider this aspect to be an ambivalent mode of resistance that contradicts a conventional feminist mindset that does not subscribe to women's admission of the traditional femininity structured by the phallocentric world. In reality, Lauren's admission of traditional femininity manifests frequently in her various accommodations of feminine behaviors in both cultures. For instance, her hand gestures and behaviors differ according to varying ideals of self-adornment, heterosexuality, and consumer practices. However, her employment of ethnic cultural pride to overcome American cultural hegemony, the dominant power in her daily life, clearly indicates that a sense of the feminist is engrained in her mind.

Overall, her contextually delivered gestures generate complex cultural meanings in which she playfully accommodates Korean gestures to stress her Koreaness in a Korean context while also conforming to the American context. For example, her contextual accommodation of mimicry—in which she flexibly fits herself to whatever the context demands—was recreated on her Cy *hompi* through the conversation text. Here, she resisted White American culture by praising the superiority of Korean beauty over White beauty. Doing so boosted Korean pride. More specifically, she and her Korean girlfriends viewed the sophistication of Korean beauty as a powerful tool for challenging U.S. culture in the U.S. context. However, this form of challenge was not overt and combative but rather mild and pleasurable. Moreover, the display of mimicry in the photographs and the challenge to U.S. culture through Korean cultural pride not only provides evidence of her multiple identities but can be read as negotiation. However, this negotiating process in turn reveals an ambiguous mode of conformity and resistance. That is, in her photographic mimicry and the challenges on her *hompi*, her resistance to both Korean femininity and White femininity were implicitly delivered as overt forms of accommodation of the ideals of femininity in both cultures.

One day after perusing her *hompi*, I asked Lauren on the phone for her opinion on the Korean gestures. "It's a Korean thing," she replied with a chuckle. "I know it looks funny. When I surfed the *hompi* of my cousins in Korea, [I thought] it looked funny. Cute though. Girls try to look cute using this gesture. But I can recognize right away it is Korean."

"But I did not see this gesture in the photos of the homecoming party with your American friends."

She paused a little at my question: "They do not know the gesture. Also, I did not want to do it with my American friends. It is pretty boring with them. It is not fun at all. Honestly, it looks a little bit sissy and unnatural. An artificial plastic posture. It is fun though with Korean friends." In this way, she brought up a criticism of the gesture, affirming her awareness of its nature. Nonetheless, despite such criticism, the gesture seemed bearable enough to take pleasure in.

I asked her again, "What makes you keep doing it?"

"For fun," she answered. "And by doing this, I see myself as a Korean girl. I want to be a part of the Cy community."

The conversation redirected me to thinking about her imitation of the gesture, which was her conscious performance of belonging to the Cy community. The display of Korean femininity through this gesture was an ironic statement of her practice; that is, although the gesture reveals her accommodation of Korean ethnic femininity and her desire to belong to the Korean community, her personal reluctance about its unnaturalness reflects an ambiguous resistance. Nonetheless, her ethnic play through this gesture has seemingly brought her a sense of belonging. However, I was suspicious about whether she had achieved this sense through mere imitation. In my own dislocating experience, my search for a sense of belonging to the Korean community drew upon a self-realization that I did not belong to it. Hence, I interpreted her ethnic play on the *hompi* as a search for belongingness to her original culture while still re-creating an alternative identity and culture that were different.

For Jooyoung, Eunbi, and Lauren, such parodies of ethnic-specific gender practice in their self-making projects offer opportunities to "play with the range of identities that are available to them and reflect on their contradictory possibilities and consequences" (Buckingham, 2003, p. 10). In this sense, their ethnic gesture can be seen as a form of transgression and subversion of dominant Korean femininity in the face of U.S. culture, yet one that retains Korean cultural pride. That is, their accommodating yet challenging mode is a unique and complex display of hybridity that reflects a juggling between Korean and U.S. cultures. Such an ambivalent mode of Korean cultural production, as recreated by these girls, is derived from their obsessive consumption of Korean culture tempered with critical observation. Thus, their search for what it means to be a Korean girl on their *hompis* is an endeavor of cultural production that includes a self-reflective reinterpretation of hybrid femininity, that is not fixed but fluid.

RECOVERING LOST GIRLHOOD THROUGH PRECURA PHOTOS

> Taking Precura photos at a street Photoshop was so much fun to me. My friends and I acted and posed in whatever body position we wanted in front of the camera and created the background in a cute and humorous way. We acted like a super model, comedian, or whoever you think is famous. We cracked up. That is what I miss a lot when looking at other friends' *hompi*. I feel I am a Korean girl. (Lauren, on her Cy *hompi*)

> When we take the Precura photo, we share the moments that make us feel closer to each other. It is very memorable. It is a Korean thing, so I wanted to do it. It is a substitute for my girlhood in Korea. (Eunbi, on her Cy *hompi*)

One distinctive feature of these girls' search for Korean girlhood is the display on their *hompis* of Precura photographs, picture collections flamboyantly decorated with diverse graphics and letters inserted using computer graphics tools (see, Figure 5.6). This Precura activity is recognized as a highly popular activity among Korean girls and is distinctive in that it takes place in shops on many streets in South Korea. These photo-generating stores provide a camera and a stage equipped with many customized background images and features, as well as the computer graphics software, Photoshop. Therefore, girls go there to take pictures of them with a camera installed in a cubicle in which they can posture freely. They then recreate the photographs themselves using the available graphics tools. What attracts them most is the collaborative creation of performance and decoration, which cements their friendships as specifically Korean. Hence, this activity is not only both a promise and a celebration of their friendship but also a source of memorabilia. As a result, Precura is a major part of Korean girls' street culture and for most, the photographs are a necessary signifier of their identity as Korean girls.

Figure 5.6 *Collection of images, Sticker Photos, March 2008 (digital images in Photoshop).*

Such Precura photos appear frequently on the hompis of the diasporic girls in my study. When they visit Korea, this activity is a core of the trip, one that offers them a partial experience of what Korean girlhood means. Jooyoung explained the activity as follows: "Precura is a fun activity that makes me feel I am a Korean girl. The U.S. doesn't have this. I can enjoy this only in Korea. Through this activity, I partially experience Korean girls' lives." Jooyoung's *hompi*, particularly, showed her excessive uploading of Precura photos with Korean friends taken during her short stay in Korea. These photographs portrayed their friendship in terms of mutual resolution and encouragement for college entrance tests and their successful futures. In the blog text under the Precura images, Jooyoung's best friend had left a mischievous comment, teasing her about her obsessive snapping of Precura photos whenever she met someone during her Korean visit. Yet despite her Korean friends' teasing that Precura is outmoded, Jooyoung did not take such criticism at all seriously. In reality, her continuous photo taking was a playful expression of nostalgia for Korean girlhood and culture, one in which she explored what it means to be a Korean girl. Thus, it was a playful act of both exploring and recovering her lost girlhood in Korea.

Not only the photo-taking activity per se, but the photographic content was saturated by the traits of Korean friendship, the close-knit relationships among girls. Such content often portrayed deep emotional attachment that could almost be misinterpreted as homosexual. In other words, the ethnic tenets of girl friendship, albeit heterosexual, are portrayed in an outwardly homosexual form. For example, in one photograph (see Figure 5.7), Jooyoung had glued her body to her friend by holding the friend's arm as if in an attempt to kiss her. In some other photos, Jooyoung and her friend also display such a loving relationship, calling each other "babe" or "sweetie."

Yet, ironically, such ethnically bounded forms of girl friendship are also marked by ambivalence. For example, the Korean dialogue next to one of Jooyoung's images reads "우린 당당하고 멋진 여자," which translates to "we are confident and wonderful girls!" To stress these words, Jooyoung has colored the Korean adjective in red and yellow against a bubbled light blue background. In the lower portion of the center background, the English word "sexy" is colored a strong crimson with several pink lines surrounding it like a beacon. Such visual effects make the word conspicuous. Hence, such images, designed by the girls, convey the meaning of girl power in a way that associates sexy with being confident and wonderful.

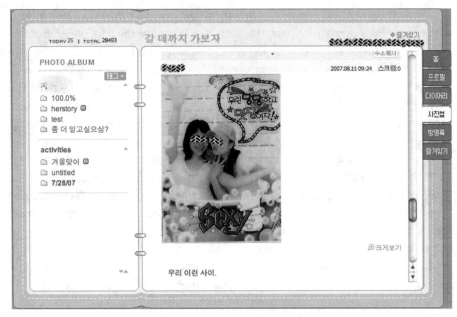

Figure 5.7 *Jooyoung*, Our Friendship, *August 2007 (digital images in Photoshop).*

This pursuit of sexiness captured my attention because it is unusual in the Korean girls I observed in Korea, for whom sexiness is superseded by cuteness, a fantasy of girliness that represents Korean girl femininity. In this photo, Jooyoung and her friend are attempting to perform the alternative feminine attribute of sexiness, more of a U.S. feminine ideal. Nonetheless, the photo conveys no sexually suggestive images or meaning. Rather, sexiness in the form of cuteness is seemingly a sign of the hybrid tendency, a mixture of both Korean and U.S. cultural experiences and a playful mimicry of the cultural identity embodied in the Korean cultural context.

Hence, from school culture to street culture, imagined daily lives are engraved in the minds of the diasporic Korean girls based on their short experiences of girl-hood in Korea and continuous connections with Korean friends through Cy. To them, the meaning of Korean girlhood is partially embodied in taking Precura photographs with friends during their stays in South Korea. Indeed, doing so is seemingly a required activity when visiting the country, a ritual to confirm friendships in a Korean manner yet through hybrid tenets. This hybridity reveals itself in the remix of language accompanying the photographs and the meaning that romanticizing and longing for Korean girlhood attaches to the photos and texts on the Cy *hompis*. Hence, the Cy *hompi*, a collection of these photos, is a culturally hybrid reproduction of the imagined life by a diasporic Korean girl.

CONCLUSION

These diasporic Korean girls, who moved to the U.S for higher education as part of South Korea's globalization movement, now find themselves positioned as a marginalized minority, an unfamiliar label to those accustomed to racially monocultural South Korea. As relief from the social pressures from both Korean and mainstream U.S. culture, the Korean girls have sought a safe place in which to speak out. This search for a safe place as a sense of agency that shapes identity is a framework through which many feminist scholars have examined minority girls' performance of racial identity. Some such scholars, however, have argued that minority girls seem constantly to belong to the U.S., a presumably multicultural society that pretends to be racially integrated but remains racially profiled (Maira, 2002; Pastor, McCormick, & Fine, 1996; Pyke & Johnson, 2003). In my study, this safe place is the Cy *hompi*, on which the diasporic Korean girls share their challenges from both U.S. and South Korean society and shape their sense of agency.

Through this ethnographic study, I found that the diasporic Korean girls' Cy *hompis* are nostalgic expressions of their playful (re-)creation of an imagined world recovered from a lost Korean girlhood. Such Korean ethnic play on the *hompi* comprises photographic production that reflects their mimicry of popular Korean girls' bodily gestures and Precura photography. This taking and uploading of photos creates further meaning-making in the form of blogs, which clearly illustrates that these girls, far from being invisible and voiceless, are well in charge. In this imagined cyber world, their mimicry of Korean ethnic femininity signals a partially embodied fantasy that shows a desire to achieve ethnic femininity yet simultaneously resist it. Ironically, their conscious awareness of being a Korean girl also leads them to resist U.S. culture. More specifically, this imagined world of the diasporic Korean girls reveals an ambivalent agency that takes up the hybrid tenets of new Korean ethnic femininity. Hence, the girls' initiative in exploring their own femininities and agency through the Cy *hompi* is a continuous individual journey, one that is playful yet critical, culturally bounded yet crossed, accommodating yet challenging.

NOTES

1. This term, as used here, refers to a particular type of dispersion of middle-class South Korean youth to the U.S. and other English-speaking nations at remarkable rates since the 1990s in order to seek a prestigious education and English proficiency, and to meet the desire for a cosmopolitan lifestyle. Hence, it often refers to an educational exodus. That many Korean youths come alone and others with only one parent (most often a mother) is a prominent demographic phenomenon that is particularly distinguishable from historical diaspora in other nations by its widespread middle-class participation. It is thus a complex convergence of Korean middle-class

citizens' desire to reject Korea's educational system and seek high quality education abroad in order to achieve both social mobility and global citizenship.

2. Cyworld is an Internet social networking service hosted in South Korea by Sun-Kyoung.

3. This reference is to an objectivist-oriented method that undermines the value of the researcher's subjectivity, including background, experiences, and bias in the process of interpretation. As a result of this approach, the participants are not present in the research process, particularly in representation.

4. This term refers to a methodological approach that fosters negotiated meaning making between the researcher and participants. This understanding necessitated not my sole endeavor to define or describe the girl participants, but the mutual engagement between myself and the girl participants through dialogue. Such collaborative knowledge production led to equal power relations between myself and the participants in research contexts, such as interviews, observations, and writing. Data in the dialogic encounter is no longer treated as an independent object waiting for us to interpret, but rather as a negotiated source of meaning.

5. The girl participants in this study are Lauren (15 years old), Jooyoung (15 years old), and Eunbi (16 years old). The names used in this chapter are pseudonyms.

6. These interviews are the main source of data collection where the participants and I often sat next to each other in front of their *hompis* and have conversation about their sites. The girls specifically agreed to let me use all of the images and quoted text used in this chapter.

7. This refers to an individual home page provided by Cyworld.

8. The term "Precura," sticker-like photos, originated from "print club," which the Japanese changed for ease of pronunciation.

9. The titles of the figures throughout this chapter came from the participants' Web sites.

10. This gesture was originally a sign of innocence signifying ideal Korean traditional femininity, a traditional meaning that became a deep-rooted regulation of female behavior that women should not laugh aloud with an open mouth because a woman's mouth is a symbol of the female reproduction organ, so revealing it is disgraceful.

11. This derogatory slang word refers to Koreans born and raised in the U.S., who are viewed as Korean looking but Americanized.

REFERENCES

Apparaduri, A. (2006). Disjuncture and difference in the global cultural economy. In M. G. Durham & D. M. Kellner (Eds.), *Media and cultural studies: Key works* (pp. 584–603). Malden, MA: Blackwell.

Buckingham, D. (2003). Media education and the end of the critical consumer. *Harvard Educational Review, 73*(3), 1–15.

Budgeon, S. (1998). "I'll tell you what I really, really want": Girl power and self-identity in Britain. In S. A. Inness (Ed.), *Millennium girls: Today's girls around the world* (pp. 115–144). Lanham, MD: Rowman & Littlefield.

Driscoll, C. (2002). *Girls: Feminine adolescence in popular culture & cultural theory.* New York: Columbia University Press.

Inness, S. A. (1998). *Millennium girls: Today's girls around the world.* Boston, MA: Rowman & Littlefield.

Kearney, M. C. (2006). *Girls make media.* New York: Routledge.

Maira, S. M. (2002). *Desis in the house: Indian American youth culture in New York City.* Philadelphia, PA: Temple University Press.

McRobbie, A. (2007). Postfeminism and popular culture: Bridget Jones and the new gender regime. In Y. Tasker & D. Negra (Eds.), *Interrogating postfeminism* (pp. 27–39). Durham, NC: Duke University Press.

Pastor, J., McCormick, J., & Fine, M. (1996). Makin' homes: An urban girl thing. In B. J. R. Leadbeater & N. Way (Eds.), *Urban girls: Resisting stereotypes, creating identities* (pp. 15–34). New York: New York University Press.

Pyke, K. D., & Johnson, D. L. (2003). Asian American women and racialized femininities: "Doing" gender across cultural worlds. *Gender and Society, 17*(1), 33–53.

Roberts, M. (2007). The fashion police: Governing the self in what not to wear. In Y. Tasker & D. Negra (Eds.), *Interrogating postfeminism* (pp. 227–248). Durham, NC: Duke University Press.

Sato, R. K. (1998). What are girls made of? Exploring the symbolic boundaries of femininity in two cultures. In S. A. Inness (Ed.), *Millennium girls: Today's girls around the world* (pp. 15–44). Lanham, MD: Rowman & Littlefield.

Suzuki, K. (1998). Pornography or therapy? Japanese girls creating the Yaoi phenomenon. In S. A. Inness (Ed.), *Millennium girls: Today's girls around the world* (pp. 243–268). Lanham, MD: Rowman & Littlefield.

SECTION TWO

Girls as Cultural Producers

CHAPTER SIX

Me/Her/Draco Malfoy

Fangirl Communities and Their Fictions

JAIME WARBURTON

Fan fiction, specifically slash and shipper fiction, came into its own as the domain of adult female *Star Trek* fans. In 2008, however, the fastest growing group of slash and shipper writers was adolescent girls, who had been helped along on their journey by the popularity of the *Harry Potter* and, more recently, *Twilight* series (*Harry Potter* and *Twilight* are, respectively, numbers one and three on the list of most populated fandoms on FanFiction.Net, with 407,208 and 93,193 posted stories [last accessed July 6, 2009]). Specific writing communities on FanFiction.Net, LiveJournal.com, and Facebook.com have presented fan girls from around the globe with the opportunity to create relationships with each other at the same time as they create relationships between their favorite characters. Because this demographic tends, more so than others, to write themselves into their fics as characters, teenage female authors begin to literally create themselves. How does writing fan fiction in a possibly anonymous forum allow girls to write their own identities? This chapter will address the importance of community to the identities/identity formation of young female fans in a context of gender/sexuality performance, nationality, and ethnic background; it will also encompass brief analysis of the fics themselves in order to shed light on their communities and relationships with each other—as well as with their texts.

FANFICTION

I love the world of Harry Potter...writing in it is like coming home.
—KRISTI, 21, OHIO, USA

Fanfiction (FF), or stories written using, in part, the characters, basic plotlines, or settings of another author, has exploded into popular consciousness since self-styled aca-fan (his term for a person engaged with fandom in both an academic and a pleasurable sense) Henry Jenkins (n.d.) first began to write about *Star Trek* fan writers in the early 1990s (2006b). A now Internet-based phenomenon born in the 1930s magazine *Fanzines*, FF continues to grow side by side with the World Wide Web (Jenkins 2006b, Thomas 2006). Particularly championed by the scholarship of Angela Thomas and Rebecca W. Black, FF is slowly being viewed as more acceptable than pure "poaching" (Jenkins, 2006b), copyright infringement, or laziness, as it was first treated by educators and academics. Of course, what academics have to say on the subject is interesting, but what the authors have to say is perhaps more meaningful. Fic writer Cryogenia,[1] a young American woman, describes fanfiction as something that touches even people who may not think of themselves as involved with any fan community:

> "Fan fiction" to me is short for a more general category, "derivative fiction." Derivative fiction is somewhat hard to pin down, but in general, I define it as the act of writing a work of fiction expressly incorporating characters or settings from a previous work of fiction that the author did not create. By this definition, if you have ever written a story about modern-day Sherlock Holmes? You've written fanfiction. If you have written a story in which Darth Vader and Luke Skywalker rematch? You've rewritten fanfiction. If you write a story in which *Gone With the Wind* is redone from a slave's point of view? You've written fanfiction. (Warburton, 2007)

By that definition, Geraldine Brooks' Pulitzer-winning novel *March* is certainly FF, but the last bit of explanation is that FF by that name is self-published, mostly on the Internet, and not for profit. So if that's what FF is, why read it instead of the "original"? Furthermore, why write it yourself?

Seelah, another young adult female American writer, explains that FF "expands our understanding of the author's universe":

> People have said—I can't remember who off the top of my head—that a story isn't a story until readers see it, and after that it's no longer in the author's control. It's the readers who understand it in their own unique ways. Each person who reads something sees it differently, and fan fiction allows that creativity to be heard. In J. K. Rowling's *Harry Potter* series, specifically, the world and characters are so rich that they get in your head, and the only way to get them out is to write about them. Once you've read the books you know the world inside and out, you almost feel like you're in it, and writing fanfic lets you explore. With fan fic-

tion, I can focus on the story, on the actual act of molding it into what I want it to be, without worrying about worldbuilding because it's all there for me to play with. It's like writing about the real world, only better! I also think the greatest form of appreciation for an author is loving their world and characters so much that you spend your time and energy writing about them yourself, for no personal gain except for the joy of spending more time in that world.

As Cryogenia points out, FF is accessible to anyone with an imagination and a favorite story, and Seelah emphasizes the accompanying reading and writing process' interactivity along with the pleasure it can give author/audience and the respect that most FF authors have for the creators of their explorable universes. As FF authors immerse themselves in their favored universes—picking up the characters, putting them down, experimenting with their surroundings and reactions—they show a marked desire both to make an imagined world more real and to prove themselves experts on the human (or vampire, or wizard) psyche. Grossberg (1992) and Thomas (2006) have both established that pleasure, or more specifically affect, is an integral part of fandom in general and FF in particular, and many FF readers and writers have explained their involvement as fun, amusing, interesting, sexually satisfying, or a natural expansion of a love of reading (Warburton, 2009).

FAN COMMUNITIES

While in the mid- to late 1990s usenet groups/lists (such as alt.tv.x-files.creative for *X-Files* fics) or personal and universe-specific sites (such as xenafan.com/fiction for *Xena: Warrior Princess*) were the foremost places to find fics, in 2009 the surfer is more likely to visit the veritable warehouses FanFiction.Net or LiveJournal.com. To find a wider audience or perhaps proclaim an affinity for fics and connect with others of like mind, one might also join a group on Facebook.com. FanFiction.Net and LiveJournal.com host the more active communities, as their platforms exist in order to share writing, and authors often ask for and receive detailed feedback on their posted stories, as well as support each other's work through community challenges and contests. Writers may be connected through themed groups/communities or on forums as well as having a personal page hosting a story archive, information about reading/writing tastes, and, sometimes, personal information.

Oft-cited figures place girls and women as approximately 90% of FF authors (Jenkins, 2006a). FF site users are, however, of all genders, faiths, and ethnicities. FanFiction.Net has banned fics rated NC-17, meaning that droves off fans who prefer more sexually explicit writing have posted their work on LiveJournal.com or AdultFanFiction.net either instead or as a supplement. Although FanFiction.Net, LiveJournal.com, and Facebook.com began in the U.S. (FanFiction.Net in Los

Angeles in 1998, LiveJournal.com in 1999 in San Francisco, and Facebook.com in Cambridge in 2004), they are all accessible globally.

METHODS

Data was collected from May 28, 2009 to June 15, 2009 by means of a 23-question survey including rating scales, multiple choice questions, and short answers. The survey covered basic demographic information and also asked for volunteers' opinions on fanfiction, their friends, favorite characters, and communities. A link to a survey with a request for volunteers was posted in 11 communities that focused on *Harry Potter* (HP) or *Twilight* fics and two wide-spectrum writing sites: on FanFiction.Net, the Writers Anonymous forum; on Facebook.com, in the groups "Addicted to Twlight Fan Fiction," "Admit it, You Read Harry Potter Fan Fiction," "Fanfiction," "Harry Potter will not be over as long as there is fan fiction," "I'm a Harry Potter Fan Fiction Writer!!," "Twilight Fan Fic," and "Twilight Fan Fiction"; and on LiveJournal.com, within the communities "hp_slash," "hp_girlslash," "hp_fics," "dissendiumff," and "twilight_fics." Venues were chosen for their openness to non-story solicitations, their likelihood of providing both "gen" or "het" writers (those who write stories about heterosexual pairings, often those who are involved in the "original," canon texts) and slash/femslash writers (those who write about same-sex pairings), and their spectrum of represented fandoms in addition to their focus on HP and *Twilight*. Although this study will focus on females aged 21 and under, there was no stipulation preventing males or older women from participating.

In addition to this survey, three qualitative interviews were conducted with randomly chosen young adult female FF writers, and the researcher read randomly chosen samples of fan writer bios and fan writing posted online along with a sample of stories volunteered by survey participants.

RESULTS

The survey garnered 103 respondents in 19 days; two survey responses were omitted for inadequate completion. Of the remaining 101 participants, four (4%) identified as transgender, eight (7.8%) as male, and 89 (88.1%) as female,[2] comparable to the rough figure of 90% female fan fiction participants (Jenkins, 2006a). Responses from those who self-identified as male or transgender were omitted; the remaining set of 89 females formed the basis for this study.

Although some particpants chose to supply their exact ages, all were invited to choose from sets under 10, 10–12, 13–15, 16–18, 19–21, and over 21. Fifty-one, or 57.3%, of the female participants were 21 or under at the time they took the survey, and 78 of the 89 girls and women (87.6%) had begun writing or reading fanfiction at or before age 21; 39.3% (n = 35) of them had begun reading/writing FF between the ages of 13–15.

Quantitative data presented from this point forward has been drawn from the set of 51 females aged 21 or under, with information provided by women over 21 used (when noted) for further perspective. The intended focus of this study is adolescent girls, but as Arnett and Taber (1994) point out, "in the contemporary West…a culture that allows individuals great latitude in when and how to make the transitions to adulthood, it is difficult to designate a particular age or even age range that signifies the end of adolescence and the beginning of adulthood" (p. 518). Therefore, while those who chose "over 21" will be referred to as "adults," it is recognized that adolesence is more than a marked time period, and the reflections of those in their early twenties are a valuable part of addressing adolescent identity.

Of the 44 (86.3%) girls 21 and under who choose to supply their favored fandoms, 90% (n = 40) identified the *Harry Potter* universe; 20.5% (n = 9) identified anime/manga; and 15.9% (n = 7) identified *Twilight*, following the HP, Naruto, *Twilight* hierarchy on FanFiction.Net. (Participants were allowed to choose more than one answer, so numbers may not add to 100.) The most popular genres among the 21 and under set were heterosexual/general romance (shipper), Alternate Universe (AU), slash (male/male romance), and femslash (female/female romance). The numbers showed a heavily female and mainly adolescent population focused primarily on relationships and recasting relationships.

Demographics

Of the 51 girls under age 21, 72.5% (n = 37) identified as White, 11.8% (n = 6) as mixed race, 7.9% (n = 4) as Asian, and 1.9% (n = 1) each as Black, Latina, East Asian, and Middle Eastern.[3] In terms of sexuality, the category with the highest response (37.2 %, or 19 out of 51) was bi- or pansexual; 13 respondents (25.5%) identified as gay or lesbian. Ten (19.6%) girls identified as straight—9 (90%) of the straight-identified girls noting that they had friends who were not straight—and the remaining nine (17.6%) said they were unsure of their sexual identity. A plurality of girls aged 21 and under who volunteered religious information identified as spiritual but not religious (27.5%, n = 14), closely followed by atheist and Christian (25.5%, n = 13, and 21.6%, n = 11). In recognition of mixed-faith families, girls were allowed to choose more than one religious identification if necessary; 10 girls chose to do so, most often to combine "spiritual but not religious" with their family of origin's religion or to denote cultural Judaism (see Table 6.1). That non-religiosity and atheism both outranked any stated religion is of note, as the countries majorly represented in these numbers are Christian-majority countries. However, religious demographic numbers tend to be based on people over age 18 and rarely reflect teens. It is possible that these numbers reflect a trend in youth at large, but it is also possible that FF communities, with their support of identity experimentation and trangressing of cannon, either encourage or invite those who question establishment-based faith.

Table 6.1: Percentages of Religious Identification: 51 Girls Age 21 and Younger

Religious Category	Percent Self-Identified	Number Self-Identified
Spiritual but not religious	27.5	14
Atheist	25.5	13
Christian	21.6	11
Wiccan/Pagan	7.8	4
Agnostic	5.9	3
Buddhist	5.9	3
Jewish	3.9	2
Muslim	2.0	1

Location and Language

The Internet offers the opportunity for people to come together regardless of physical distance, and participants in this survey represented 15 countries and territories and at least 23 states within the U.S. (see Table 6.2). Most of them were from English-speaking countries, and 45.1% (*n* = 23) of respondents were from the U.S., a number which may in part reflect current worldwide Internet usage statistics—in 2009, 74.4% of North Americans had Internet accessed compared with only 23.8% worldwide (Internet World Stats, n.d.). Additionally, as Harrington and

Bielby (2007) pointed out, another barrier to addressing a global fandom is language, and that particularly pertains to written FF. The survey was posted in English in venues titled in English that showcase English-language work, and fandoms of particular interest to this researcher are originally English-language stories, one British and one American. Yet at the time of this writing, the *Harry Potter* books have been translated into 67 languages (Dammann, 2008) and the *Twilight* books into 20 (Meyer, n.d.). Respondents were not limited to native speakers: a fan whose native tongue is Latvian may still participate in the Potterverse in English, gaining fluency along the way. While this survey was affected by its focus on English-language texts, it represented global Internet usage and included those for whom English is a second language.

Table 6.2: Location of Participants: 51 Girls Age 21 and Younger

Country/Territory	Percent	Number
U.S.	45.1	23
United Kingdom	17.6	9
Australia	13.7	7
Canada	7.8	4
Latvia	3.9	2
Finland	2.0	1
Germany	2.0	1
Indonesia	2.0	1
Luxembourg	2.0	1
Norway	2.0	1
Singapore	2.0	1

Black (2005) has identified FanFiction.Net, in particular, as a safe place for English language learners (ELLs) to improve their language skills in a social yet nearly academic environment. Beta readers (select persons who will read a pre-published draft for line edits and story suggestions) or audience critiques encourage young writers to further develop their language skills so that they might receive more positive feed-back, thereby increasing the pleasurable affect of belonging to FF communities. Several survey participants commented on the benefits of FF to ELL:

~ Fan fiction helps to better my english. (Rauna, 16, The Netherlands. Began writing between ages 13 and 15.)
~ I find it improves my language skills, too (I'm not a native English speak-er, but I write in English). (Froggy, adult, Norway. Began writing at 13.)[4]
~ I'm not a native English speaker, and writing fanfiction has improved my English a lot. (Lena, 19–21, Luxembourg. Began writing between ages 16 and 18.)

While not every person who writes in English is a native speaker, the sample did remain primarily Northern and Western. ELLs seem to feel comfortable in "trying on" English in a safe space where their readers can understand that their language acquisition is a process.

ANALYSIS

Relationships/Community

Stated demographics highlight a community where most respondents (1) are friends with those of the same gender; (2) are about evenly split between being close to the same age and far apart in age from their friends; (3) live far away from each other; (4) don't identify with the *same* sexuality as their friends; and (5) don't pay much attention to race or religion (are either different or don't know/don't care).

Thirty-two girls under 21 (62.7%) chose to answer questions about the demo-graphics of friends they had made through fanfiction. Participants could chose between "the same," "close or similar," "dissimilar or far," "very dissimilar or far," or "not applicable" in the following categories: age, gender, race, religion, sexuality, loca-tion, and reading/writing interests. The most respondents to any one category was 19 (37.2%), possibly denoting that some girls were friendly with other writers/read-ers on a partially anonymous basis that would leave them without knowledge of their friends' religion, race, and so on, as those are topics that may not come up in dis-cussions about stories and can be easily hidden in the faceless medium of the Internet. However, this sample was 72% ($n = 37$) White: perhaps White authors/readers, especially those writing within fandoms whose characters are mostly White, take for granted that the race of those around them is also White.

The most striking trends emerged around location, where 63.2% ($n = 12$ of 19) of respondents answered that their friends' locations were "very far or dissimilar," and gender, where 88.2% (n = 15 of 17) claimed their friends' genders were the same; 47.4% (n = 9 of 19) were similar or close in age to their friends, but 42.1% (n = 8 of 19) were dissimilar or far, a nearly equal split; 47.1% (n = 8 of 17) were similar or close in sexuality, with no other answer coming close. Interestingly, none of the nine people who chose to comment on race noted that their race was the same as their friends, and five (55.6%) of those nine chose some degree of dissimilarity. Another three (33%) of the nine respondents marked N/A, meaning either that they do not know about their friends' races or that it is not important to them. The pattern that emerged in regard to religion was similar but even more marked: eight (61.5%) of the 13 respondents to that question marked N/A, and while other responses were split, none were "same."

These numbers reinforce the idea that FF communities are female-majority communities whose members' *understood* differences are mostly between age and location. While this survey did tap into two large, general FF communities, the emphasis was clearly on the *Harry Potter* (seven groups approached) and *Twilight* (four groups approached) fandoms, areas which might be expected to yield a high female readership. Yet as *Twilight* has been recognized as a "femme franchise" (Keegan, 2009, p. 8), more male adolescents and pre-adolescents seem to read the *Harry Potter* books than do females (Stotsky, 2009). It therefore seems reasonable to recognize the discrepancy as a part of FF itself, not of fandom. To study the involvement of males in FF, it may be more appropriate to address a fandom such as *Star Trek*: according to the *Star Trek* Fan Fiction page of the Fan History Wiki, in "January 2008, males made up 52% of the visitors" to TrekFanFiction.net, a catlog of between three and 400 stories (2009). There is no data, however, on the age of those visitors or which of them read versus write FF.

It seems that few writers disclose their race or religion, nor do they ask for another's, but since this sample heavily preferred romantic fics, whether het, slash, or femslash, an understanding of each other's sexuality may not be surprising. The nearly all-female space presented by FF communities may contribute to creating a safe space for sexuality play wherein teen girls have the freedom to express and experiment without the threat of the judgment of males, who are *typically* viewed as those who take an active role in intiating sexual/romantic relationships The importance young readers/writers themselves have placed upon their identities as young, sexual females calls for further analysis of such.

Friends and Relationship

They can get me through anything and help me with my mental illness.

—FAIRY, 20, U.K.

Just how important is the "community" aspect of a FF community? Thirty-nine girls answered questions about their friends, and of those 39, only 1 (2.6%) said she had not made friends through FF. Twenty-one (53.8%) said yes, and that they talked frequently online, another 15 (38.5%) replied that they commented on others' stories but did not necessarily consider their authors friends, and the last two (5.1%) replied that they had even met their FF friends in real life (RL). It seems that, by joining a FF community, a girl can expect to either give and receive "acquaintance-level" support or, more likely, friendship.

Entrance isn't automatic, though. Jade47, a self-described "girl/woman" (age 20 at time of posting), placed the following warning on her LiveJournal in December of 2007:

> I'm gonna admit though, that I'm a leery re-friend-er. This is because I'm paranoid. I've been around the internet for, oh, about nine years now. I've spent the bulk of that time on some pretty great message boards. But in that time I've also run into some not very nice people who really don't like me and my friends. Also the internet can be a scary place. Look no further than the kid who committed suicide because of MySpace bullying or a dozen other incidents.
>
> Now I'm not saying anyone who's friended me is a scary psycho. Ya'll all seem to be pretty nice. But in general, if someone friends me that I don't know from else where, I'm not gonna friend them back. If you wanna get to know me, comment in my LJ a few times, and let me know you're friending me, odds are I'll friend you back.

Jade47 is not alone, judging from the affirmative comments on her post (sprinkled with a few hurt remarks from those unreciprocated frienders who were the post's catalyst). She mentions wanting to keep safe from both people who don't actually like her and her friends, seeming to indicate people who already know her in RL, and the *Dateline*-esque "scariness" of the Internet, indicating strangers. Jade47 will be "friends" with people only after they have passed through an acquaintance stage through commenting.

It is during this commenting that a girl has a chance to present, through written words alone, an identity that, hopefully, the girl she wants to friend will find attractive. Disembodied, girls have a chance to connect with people without the baggage of their looks or their classroom social standing (Stern, 2007). While common understanding of "fans" entails the socially inept, a faceless fandom can protect those whose social capital is high, too. Older teens and women in their early twenties bring an element of perspective to how FF communities have affected, and continue to affect, their social identities. "Jax," an American adult woman who began writing FF between the ages of 13 and 15, admitted, "i work in the music industry, i'm an ex model, i have to constantly 'be cool.' it's nice to kind of be a dork. walk into a comic book shop and people look at me like i'm lost. but online people dont see me and i'm able to sort of let lose to to speak." Bergit, a 22-year-old woman in Norway who began writing in English and Norwegian during her late teens, says of her FF friends, "They only know the internett 'me' and that goves me freedom to show them me in another way than my other friends." Bergit's use of the word "show" implies a purposeful, conscious identity construction: She is aware of the person she presents both online and in real life (RL). "Letting loose" and feeling free appeared with regularity in survey answers, along with the explanation that FF friends are "often more similar [...] than your 'RL' friends" (Mary, 17, England). A common underpinning of girls' responses tended to be a feeling that they simply felt supported, never judged, inside the community. Perhaps more important than calling FF communities places where girls can "be themselves" is recognizing them as places where girls can be *any* selves.

If wider community support can lead to a sense of freedom and support, what interactions characterize individual friendships? FF authors surveyed here indicated a progression from talking about work, to fandom, to each other's lives. Many indicated that they had met their best friend, boyfriend, or girlfriend through their fandoms, and that weekly or daily messenger interactions, including advice from sometimes thousands of miles away and talk about "regular life things" on top of fandom/writing discussions, were a valued part of their lives.

Sexual Identity

There is heavy emphasis on romantic pairings in FF, perhaps as a natural extension of the wish fulfillment that stories can grant their audiences/authors. These romantic stories may pair a "canon" couple such as HP's Harry/Ginny or *Twilight*'s Bella/Edward, or they may (and often do) venture outside of canon. When pairings remain heterosexual (Harry/Hermione) the relationship or "ship" is called het, short for heterosexual. But not all pairings are het; when considering FF, an inevitable pathway is slash. Named for the symbol between two names that denotes romantic paring (Kirk/Spock), slash grew from *Star Trek* pairings of Kirk and Spock to encompass all male-male stories. "Femslash" is the name given to female-female stories (MacDonald, 2006). Draco Malfoy is a popular lead in HP slash stories, often paired with Harry or another character with whom Draco experiences animosity, and fans of Fred and George Weasley can venture into a more outre slash called "twincest" (Fan Fiction Terms, 2008). Femslash, a more recent phenomenon, helped along greatly by subtext in *Xena: Warrior Princess*, might explore Hermione/Fleur (Tosenberger, 2008). Until around 2005, slash was mainly viewed, in the academic community, as "normal female interest in men bonking," the title of a 1998 Henry Jenkins essay that focuses on adult women writing about sex between two men who were not gay (Jenkins, 2006a). Driscoll (2006) pointed out the intertwining of romantic gratification and sexual gratification in fan fiction, opening the discussion to include the emotional appeal of particular pairings whether male/female, male/male, or female/female.

Various scholars have made the case that slash is feminist and anti-feminist, political and apolitical, resistant and merely as transgressive as other FF. Scodari (2003) wrote that slash merely replicated hegemonic structures, while Woledge (2006) described the attitude of slashers as "homoindifferent." On the other hand, MacDonald (2006)[5] pointed out that HP slash writers were somewhat less straight than scholars had previously thought, and Lackner, Lucas, and Reid (2006) agreed: "The too-easy identification of slash as *straight women writing gay men* has served to mask the extent to which the sexual pleasure is created by women (of all genders/sexual identities) for women (of all genders/sexual identities)" (p. 201). Busse, also in 2006, kept the "woman" and lost the "straight" when she wrote that

> within slash fandom in particular, issues of homosexuality are central, and fandom, with its greater tolerance, has often been a place for women to explore and negotiate issues of sexuality by reading and writing their desires, by acknowledging and sharing sexual preferences…slash in particular raises particular issues of identity and sexualities: women writing fantasies with and for one another projected through and by same-sex desires suggests that fandom may be a queer female space. (p. 208)

Two years later, Tosenberg (2008) included young adults in the debate, claiming that "Potter slash readers and writers have access to a space where queer sexuality, whether teen or adult, can be depicted in its full, messy, exuberant glory, and the emphasis is on *jouissance*" (p. 201). And, in an age where pop stars like Katy Perry and Lady Gaga capitalize on bicuriousity, why not?

The authors of fics themselves may be as split, but are they also so indifferent to politics? Besides talking about fics as pornography ("Porn with characters I know well, so personality actually happens," from Cory, 16–18, Connecticut, U.S., and "I love it and it's better than watching porn," from Estela, 19–21, Colorado, U.S.), young female authors also say that they write FF because there is "too little representation of LGBT characters in media" (Ann, 19–21, Canada). Others agree:

~ "As I'm lesbian myself, it's really enjoyable to write something between two girls." (Maili, 16–18, Finland)
~ "I also enjoy femmeslash pairings because I"m a bisexual girl in a monogamous relationship (with a man) and no longer get to enjoy relationships with other women." (Jess, 21, U.S.)
~ "Slash makes everything better. I also like how being gay in the wizarding world can present a lot of social problems for the characters, and I like to see how they deal with them." (Emma, 13–15, California, U.S.)
~ "I like to read mainly femslash because I see chemistry between characters that isn't explored or is flat out ignored in books. Plus I just like to imagine." (Rebel, 19–21, Texas, U.S.)

Besides interest in story, girls are seeming to write slash because of their own lives. In this sample of 51 girls, aged 21 and under, only 10 (20%) described their sexuality as "straight," and nine (90%) indicated that they did have friends who are not heterosexual. An 84% (n = 43) selection of women identifying as other than heterosexual is overwhelming. Even if one were to assume that, contrary to previous belief, only non-heterosexual people were writing slash, the inclusion of one slash and one femslash community in the 13 posting locations is unlikely to have tilted the results so dramatically.[6] The number of girls who admitted that they were unsure about their sexuality (17.6%, n = 9) may also suggest that fanfiction communities may be safe havens for not only differing sexualities, but for a non-physical exploration of the possibilities of sexuality. The recognition of sexuality as a spectrum rather than points bolsters such exploration. In FF, an author can try on as many different genders and sexualities as she pleases through her characters, whether voyeuristically or identificatorily, and is no way bound to them. While Busse remarks that some female fans "acknowledge their queerness often is restricted to the virutal realm as they live their 'real' heteronormative live" (2006, p. 209), it remains to be seen if this generation of young fan writers leave their broader sexuality online or bring it into their homes.

Character Identification as a Means to Identity

Identity

Thomas has found that "it is common for fan fiction writers to insert versions of themselves into their characters" (2007, p. 158), and claims that "the fictional characters are also a means for the girls to fashion new and emerging identities for themselves…a rehearsal of who they want to become" (p. 160). Identification with a character, whether through perceived similarities or a desire for those similarities, will result in greater reading pleasure (Jose & Brewer, 1984). Remembering that affect is one of the main forces behind fandom (Grossberg, 1992) and therefore FF, it seems reasonable to say that people will write/read characters they find pleasurable, or with whom they can identify, and most likely with characters they might desire, even if the stated goal is to explore "interesting" relationships within a text. The identification and "wishful identification" that Greenwood (2007) brings up in her study of girls' relationships to female action heroes combined with Thomas's assertion leads us to believe that when a person describes the characteristics of her favored narrators or leads, it follows that they are likely describing characteristics that they either believe they have or wish to have.

Authors may deny, however, that they insert or reflect themselves in their stories, due in part to community disdain for "Mary Sue," a practice wherein an author inserts a thinly (if at all) veiled version of him- or herself into a story for the express purpose of, say, seeing herself marry Edward. In real person fiction (RPF), stories featuring celebrities or other real "characters" from a person's life are viewed unfavorably in most communities; Emily (19–21, Minnesota, U.S.) explained, "I write RPF, which is considered quite taboo and even disrespectful in some communities. I defend myself by saying that people are just characters to me—it's the same as writing an autobiography and just changing the names. By recognizing that what I'm writing has never happened and I maintain that I don't know the people, I (attempt) to respect the people I write." Of the 40 under-21-year-old girls who chose to supply information about versions of themselves in their story, 19 (48%) claimed never to base characters on themselves, 13 (32%) said they did, and eight (20%) reported that they may have, although not purposefully. When asked about favored pairing or narrators, however, several answered that they wrote or read about certain characters because they could identify with them. Luz, a 25-year-old in Mexico who has been writing since she was between 16 and 18, said of her favored stories, "I can identify myself with the characters. If I don't feel identified, I simply don't read or write anything about them."

The girls were eager to describe the narrators of characters they liked best, some representative samples of which follow:

~ "Sarcastic, uncool, gay or bi, from a dysfunctional family, imperfect" (Emma)
~ "calculating, logical, surprised by the intensity of their/others emotions" (Cory, 16–18, Connecticut, U.S.)
~ "Easy-going, vivacious; the more they laugh, the better" (Beatrise, 19–21, Latvia)
~ "Beauty + brains, insecurity + defensiveness, a good knowledge of other peoples' thoughts or feelings" (Emily)
~ "outgoing, kinda shy sometimes, artsy in some way" (Tacy, 16–18, Canada)
~ "Girls who aren't perfect. Not model-ish and curvy. And maybe a little cynical and sarcastic" (Willa, 19–21, Florida, U.S.)
~ "Smart, independent, willful" (Estela)
~ "funny, quirky, flawed but fundamentally good; charming, flirty, light-hearted. The best narrators are usually when a genuinely entertaining writer just lets go and rolls with what comes to them" (Saari, 16–18, Australia)
~ "Intelligent, dark, troubled, curious, fiery" (Devorah, 19, Australia)
~ "awkward, nerdy types" (Barb, 16–18, Canada)

There is an emphasis in these answers on intelligence, independence, realistic body types, and honesty. These characters (often female but sometimes male), are creat-

ed by girls and for girls; even when the characters are used in part for sexual satisfaction via explicit stories, it remains important to the authors and audience that they
are *people*, true to themselves whether awkward or self-confident.

I asked Beth, a 25-year-old scientist who was very active in FF communities
between the time she was 14 and 18, about the identities she had as a young writer
and those she observed in others:

> I knew that no matter where I was or who I was with, I was constructing, consciously, a face
> to present to the world, so it wasn't an idea that 'here I can really be myself,' but rather, 'I
> enjoy THIS performance more.' sort of trying on faces, seeing how people react to the com-
> bination of the performance and whatever authentic non-performance is shining through,
> seeing if they can pull it off convincingly. And from the perspective of what they're writing,
> I think the most obvious thing one could say is that these kids are exploring their desires and
> what they think about sex and relationships, but by actually writing it out into a story, they're
> sort of exploring the line between what they 'want' in the deep recesses of their mind and
> what they would actually want to experience and whether, on page 50 of their relationship
> with Harry Potter or Buffy, they're still interested in that or ready to move on, so I think it's
> a lot of processing of cultural narratives through their own desire, and spending some time
> fixating on one specific scenario to see if that's going to be the thing, the combination, that
> makes them comfortable in this world.

Beth's perspective helps to solidify the idea that identity remains an integral part of
FF writing, whether it is formed through friendships with a diverse group or
through the recasting of canon situations and pairings.

Writing

Many 21 and under authors I communicated with disparaged their own writing, saying it wasn't good, or wasn't beta'ed, or wasn't recent, recalling the discussions of
teenage girls' self-esteem that Mary Pipher (1995) brought to American consciousness with *Reviving Ophelia*. But they present their work anyway, perhaps like
the girl who moans "I'm so fat!" so her friends will assure her that she isn't. It seems
that as girls get older and more experienced within the FF community, the effect
of a community of like-minded, same-gendered people who are comfortable with
(and identify with) their issues/identities contributing to low self-esteem is a shed-
ding of their pre-packaged disclaimers.

Sophie, a Canadian girl between the ages of 19 and 21 who began writing
between 13 and 15, describes herself on her bio: "I'm fairly shy, like to keep to myself,
but I am trying to open up. I write fanfiction, mainly Fleur/Hermione femslash
that's fairly heavy on plot. I like to explore myself and my writing so I try to avoid
typical romance templates. I love controversy. You'll find I'm really laid back and easy
going but I certainly do not back down from a debate, in fact I love and thrive on
it."

Her story "Walking a Mile," a Hermione/Fleur fic Sophie offered in her survey responses, often reflects the uncomfortable relationship between being a girl and being smart (Warburton, 2008). Sophie's Hermione thinks,

> Ever since she was little, even in muggle schools, no one liked her. She was too smart. But her greatest sin was that her intelligence was obvious, blatantly loud for the whole world to hear. "I know," "I understand," "you only need say it once, or you may never need say it at all because I will find out anyway." Hermione Granger was a prodigy in her own right. They had hated her for it. Naturally, she built barriers around herself. She would be the genius they all hated, she buried herself in knowledge of the world to avoid actively dealing with it, until eventually she could no longer pinpoint any other characteristic in herself.

Sophie spends a notable amount of time both fleshing out her characters and working on plot as well as sensuality, and her characters reflect this sample's consensus on preferred narrators. Her commentary on the way noticeably intelligent girls are treated could have been lifted from the pages of a feminist journal, whether or not the author would describe herself as a feminist.

On the younger end of the spectrum, writer Glitterz, a 12-year-old American who writes in the *Twilight* fandom using primarily canon, het pairings, changes Bella into a girl who fits in better with the boys in her class. Her version of Bella muses,

> I've never really been considered a normal girl at my school. I didn't have many friends…that were girls. I've always had guys as friends. I'm not sure why, I guess I just can relate to them more. I've been more of the sporty type, not the snobby kind. I shudder at the mere thought of skirts and dresses. I like to wear just simple jeans or basketball shorts. Mostly jeans. I'll only wear shorts if its way too hot (ha! If possible in Forks) or if I'm playing some sport with my friends.

Glitterz separates Bella from the shopping-friends that she makes in canon, and recreates her as a tomboy, a casual, confident girl who is unaware of Edward's interest and is a far cry from the fainter portrayed in Meyer's books. Glitterz also breaks the fourth wall in her stories, stopping the narration to say, "Okay, well I don't know about detention, cuz ive never gotten it but I think you have it right after your last class or something. I don't know." While she writes about characters who are sent to detention, a recognizable trope of young adult literature, she needs to let her audience know that *she* isn't the kind of girl who makes decisions that end up in punishment. In the author notes at the end of her first chapter, Glitterz also abases herself in a way that seemed typical of younger authors, saying, "I'm sorry it's so long. I just really loved writing it. This is probably the only story I liked writing of mine. Please review.!!" Glitterz received positive affect from the act of writing the story, but seems to not want to believe that her work is worthy of praise at the same time that she asks for responses. The responses she received were favorable, however, and encouraged her to continue writing: "Hey, I'm really loving your story so far! It's so good and I love how Bella had no idea that Edward liked her the entire time. I hope you write more for the story!" As Glitterz's reviewers draw her further out, she may, through this support and mentorship, begin to present her work with more confidence as older teen writers as Sophie can.

Mentorship

Sometimes a personal friend and sometimes solely a writing partner is the beta reader, the person who reads critically and makes suggestions for revisions to a first, unpublished draft. As Karpovich (2006) pointed out, the author and beta reader enter into a kind of contract, and it is expected that an author thank her beta when she does post a story. It can also be seen as disresepctful to a community if an author posts her story without having had it read by a beta, as that might cause an audience to have to wade through sentence-level confusion. Beta readers can be grown organically, but on sites such as fanfiction.net, there are searchable listings where a person can find a beta. Those who register as readers will fill out a profile that lists their strengths and weaknesses, any kinds of stories they won't read, and estimated response times.

The "gentle critiques" (Black, 2007, p. 125) and encouragement that beta readers provide young authors follow the standard procedure of in-person conferences used in writing centers. Sentence-level issues come along with global concerns (story, structure, character), and do not drive the conversation unless these issues are sense-hampering, and suggestions, rather than corrections, are made, thereby emphasizing the partnership of a community writing project (Black, 2007; Thomas, 2007). When writing about their FF friends, 44% (n = 11 of the 25 girls who chose to supply this information) referenced their "betas" or the fact that they "beta'd" for other friends.

While a beta reader can be a partner, she can also be a mentor. Emily, who began writing between ages 10 and 12 and has been a part of with FF communities for nearly a decade, explains her long involvement by saying, "I started out dissatisfied with the way my favourite books ended—Now I read it mostly as a beta to provide young authors with feedback. And it's hella amazing." Having received encouragement from older writers at the beginning of her FF career, Emily takes pleasure in passing on her knowledge through mentorship. As Spencer and Liang (2009) reported in their work on formal mentoring relationships between girls and women, an emotional rather than situational connection can provide a girl with meaningful support; the Internet, with its cross-spectrum accessibility, is a natural match. Mentoring allows FF writers/readers to stay involved with their communities perhaps longer than they stay involved with writing FF itself, moving from a connection with characters to a connection with other girls behind keyboards.

CONCLUSIONS

Fanfiction communities are heavily female and youthful, particularly the audience for *Harry Potter* and *Twilight*, making them natural places to observe groups of girls. As the communities tend to be organized around love for a particular universe, character, or pairing, they put emphasis on the life of the mind and imagination (and often literature) over body, social standing, race, religion, or sexuality—although the groups are fairly diverse in those ways. Within these like-minded, supportive groups, girls teach each other about writing, reading source material, and about identity: in similar-aged and mentoring relationships, these girls from across the U.S. and around the world become people for each other, but ultimately for themselves.

"Fangirl" has become an identity of its own, yet not one that comes with any requirements other than love for a fandom. When following through the progression of acceptance, from commenting on others' stories to making a profile and acquaintances, writing her own stories, developing friendships, and perhaps becoming a beta reader, a girl can develop confidence that comes from a supportive community. At the same time, she has the freedom to try on a variety of identities and test-drive them, as it were, in the social settings that she has observed in her favored stories. She can create characters that reflect her own hurdles (intelligence, for example) and, perhaps, as her characters assert and explain themselves in fiction, begin to believe that she can assert herself in RL as well.

FF stories tend to emphasize sexuality of all sorts, and the prevalence of femslash is more recent than male-male slash. While in popular culture girl-on-girl action tends to be for a male gaze, in fan fiction those writing femslash are overwhelmingly female—and, although they *may* be heterosexual, tend rather to be girls who want to be with girls writing about girls with girls. They aren't unaware of their recasting of canon, either, as seen in girls' comments on the lack of LGBT characters and the importance of their favored narrators having a broad-spectrum sexuality.

It is this fluidity of identity including and beyond sexuality and a developing confidence in each liquid stage that sets FF communities apart from RL, where a girl can hear about it if she starts or stops wearing chandelier earrings. And when it comes to femslash PWP might stand for porn without plot, but not porn without politics. In fact, fanfiction communities throw the term "identity politics" into new light—their members may not view themselves or their created identities as oppressed, but they may begin to view them as worthwhile.

Notes

1. All names have been created for anonymous individuals or changed unless an of-age author has chosen to use her own.
2. The net total result of 88.1% (n = 89 of 101) female fan fiction participants is statistically comparable to the oft-cited 90% as transgender respondents historically haven't been given a between-the-boxes choice before; two of the four (50%) of the transgender respondents here were FTM and the other two (50%) were MTF. An inclusion of female-born FTMs would have increased the percentage of "females" to 90.1% (n = 91). A later study of young transgender fan fiction participants could shed needed light on transgender involvement in narrative reconstruction.
3. *Harry Potter* and *Twilight* are not only English-language texts in the originals, but are also about predominantly White characters (as Emily pointed out, Jacob from *Twilight* is the "most stereotypical Native American ever"). Anime fandoms such as Naruto (number two on the list of most populous fandoms on fanfiction.net), which is Japanese, may draw a more racially diverse crowd.
4. All quotes from subjects are shown as written, including typos and grammatical or spelling errors.
5. In MacDonald's sample of 10 females, 40% (n = 4) identified as heterosexual, 30% (n = 3) as bisexual, 20% (n = 2) as gay, and 10% (n = 1) as having no sexual preference.
6. 19.6% (n = 10) identified as heterosexual, 25.5% (n = 13) as gay/lesbian, 31.4% (n = 16) as bisexual, 5.9% (n = 3) as pansexual, and 17.7% (n = 9) as unsure. The inclusion of females over age 21 (group of 89 as sample of 101 is adjusted for gender but not for age) in the sample creates a nearly equal split between heterosexuality (28.1%, n = 25), bisexuality (25.8%, n = 23), and gay/lesbian (26.9%, n = 24), but "non-heterosexual" still outpaces "heterosexual" by three to one.

References

Arnett, J. J., & Taber, S. (1994). Adolescence terminable and interminable: When does adolescence end? *Journal of Youth and Adolescence, 23*(5), 517–537.

Black, R. W. (2005). Access and affiliation: The literacy and composition practices of English-language learners in an online fanfiction community. *Journal of Adolescent & Adult Literacy, 49*(2), 118–128.

Black, R. W. (2007). Digital design: English language learners and reader reviews in online fiction. In M. Knobel & C. Lankshear (Eds.), *A new literacies sampler* (pp. 115–136). New York: Peter Lang.

Busse, K. (2006). My life is a WP on my LJ: Slashing the slasher and the reality of celebrity and Internet performances. In K. Hellekson & K. Busse (Eds.), *Fan fiction and fan communities in the age of the Internet* (pp. 207–224). Jefferson, NC: McFarland.

Dammann, G. (2008, June 18). Harry Potter breaks 400m in sales. *Guardian*. Retrieved August 6, 2009, from http://www.guardian.co.uk/business.2008/jun/18/harrypotter.artsandentertainment

Driscoll, C. (2006). One true pairing: The romance of pornography and the pornography of romance. In K. Hellekson & K. Busse (Eds.), *Fan fiction and fan communities in the age of the Internet* (pp. 79–96). Jefferson, NC: McFarland.

Fan Fiction Terms. (2008). Ruby Quills fiction terms database. Retrieved August 6, 2009, from http://www.terms.rqarchive.com

Greenwood, D. N. (2007). Are female action heroes risky role models? Character identification, idealization, and viewer aggression. *Sex Roles, 57*(9/10), 725–732.

Grossberg, L. (1992). Is there a fan in the house?: The affective sensibility of fandom. In L.A. Lewis (Ed.), *The adoring audience: Fan culture and popular media* (pp. 50–66). New York: Routledge.

Harrington, C. L., & Bielby, D. (2007). Global fandom/global fan studies. In J. A. Gray, C. Sandvoss, & C. L. Harrington (Eds.), *Fandom: Identities and communities in a mediated world* (pp. 179–197). New York: New York University Press.

Internet World States: Usage and population statistics. (n.d.). Retrieved July 12, 2009, from http://www.internetworldstats.com/stats.htm

Jenkins, H. (2006a). "Normal female interest in men bonking": Selections from the Terra Nostra Underground. In H. Jenkins (Ed.), *Fans, bloggers, and gamers: exploring participatory culture* (pp. 61–88). New York: New York University Press.

Jenkins, H. (2006b). Star Trek rerun, reread, rewritten: Fan writing as textual poaching. In H. Jenkins (Ed.), *Fans, bloggers, and gamers: Exploring participatory culture* (pp. 37–60). New York: New York University Press.

Jenkins, H. (n.d.). Confessions of an aca-fan. Retrieved May 15, 2009, from http://www.henryjenkins.org/

Jose, P. E., & Brewer, W. F. (1984). Development of story liking: Character identification, suspense, and outcome resolution. *Developmental Psychology, 20*(5), 911–924.

Karpovich, A. I. (2006). The audience as editor: The role of beta readers in online fan fiction communities. In K. Hellekson & K. Busse (Eds.), *Fan fiction and fan communities in the age of the Internet* (pp. 171–188). Jefferson, NC: McFarland.

Keegan, R. W. (2009, Nov. 19). Twilight: The fan girls cometh with cash. *TIME Magazine*. Retrieved July 20, 2010, from http://www.time.com/time/arts/article/0,8599,1860676,00.html

Lackner, E., Lucas, B. L., & Reid, R. A. (2006). Cunning linguists: The bisexual erotics of Words/Silence/Flesh. In K. Hellekson, & K. Busse (Eds.), *Fan fiction and fan communities in the age of the Internet* (pp. 207–224). Jefferson, NC: McFarland.

MacDonald, M. (2006). Harry Potter and the fan fiction phenomenon. *The Gay & Lesbian Review, 13*(1), 28–30.

Meyer, S. (n.d.). *Official bio*. Retrieved May 15, 2009, from http://www.stephaniemeyer.com/bio.html

Pipher, M. (1995). *Reviving Ophelia*. New York: Ballantine Books.

Scodari, C. (2003). Resistance re-examined: Gender, fan practices, and science fiction television. *Popular Communications, 1*(2), 111–120.

Spencer, R., & Liang, B. (2009). "She gives me a break from the world": Formal youth mentoring relationships between adolescent girls and adult women. *The Journal of Primary Prevention, 30*(2), 109–130.

Star Trek Fan Fiction. (2009). In *Fan history wiki*. Retrieved October 14, 2009, from http://www.fan-history.com/wiki/Star_Trek_fan_fiction

Stern. S. T. (2007). *Instant identity: Adolescent girls and the world of instant messaging*. New York: Peter Lang.

Stotsky, S. (2009). What boys are reading. *Education.com*. Retrieved August 14, 2009, from http://www.education.com/reference/article/Ref_What_Boys_Reading/

Thomas, A. (2006). Fan fiction online: Engagement, critical response and affective play through writing. *Australian Journal of Language and Literacy, 29*(3), 226–239.

Thomas, A. (2007). Blurring and breaking through the boundaries of narrative, literacy, and identity in adolescent fan fiction. In M. Knobel & C. Lankshear (Eds.), *A new literacies sampler* (pp.

137–166). New York: Peter Lang.

Tosenberger, C. (2008). Homosexuality at online Hogwarts: Harry Potter slash fanfiction. *Children's Literature, 36*, 185–207.

Warburton, J. (2007, April). *The fandom of Christ: Searching for belief in Christian- and fanfiction.* Paper presented at the National Popular Culture Association/American Culture Association Conference, Boston, MA, U.S.

Warburton, J. (2008, June). *Compulsory heterosexuality, compulsory mediocrity: The queerness of the gifted girl.* Paper presented at the International Children's Literature Association Conference, Bloomington, IN, U.S.

Warburton, J. (2009). Fanfiction survey. *Surveymonkey.* Posted on May 28, 2009: http://www.survey-monkey.com/a.aspx?sm=FT8ilE_2fddLDAn_2faDGWubhw_3d_3d

Woledge, E. (2006). Intimatopia: Genre intersections between slash and the mainstream. In K. Hellekson & K. Busse (Eds.), *Fan fiction and fan communities in the age of the Internet* (pp. 97–114). Jefferson, NC: McFarland.

CHAPTER SEVEN

Looking into the Digital Mirror

Reflections on a Computer Camp for Girls by Girls

KRISTINE BLAIR, ERIN DIETEL-MCLAUGHLIN & MEREDITH GRAUPNER HURLEY

"Hey, Sarah, what color underwear today?" In this version of a recent public service announcement series "Be Careful What You Post," teenager Sarah is increasingly alarmed as men and boys, all strangers, comment on her online activity. As the scenario progresses from high school boys to athletic coaches, to theatre ushers, and finally to the tattooed custodial staff at her own school, the message is clear: "Anything you post online, anyone can see: family, friends, and even not so friendly people. Think before you post." A similar PSA in the series portrays an increasingly distraught teenager repeatedly attempting to remove a sexually provocative image of herself from a hallway bulletin board that keeps reappearing, an analogy to what happens to girls online who do not consider the consequences of their online content. As with the first PSA, this scenario ends with the suspicious male custodial worker surreptitiously removing the image, presumably for future viewing pleasure.

According to the Pew Internet and American Life Project, "the use of social media—from blogging to online social networking to creation of all kings of digital material—is central to many teenagers' lives" (2007, p. 4). Despite the statistics that suggest that girls are an ever-growing presence on the net, particularly with blogging and photo posting (Pew Internet, 2007), there remains a culture of fear where girls are often told that digital spaces are not safe for them. This is the case particularly given the legitimate concerns about cyberstalking and the way the

Internet can become a presumed site of online victimization, as cases such as the 2006 suicide of a Missouri teenage girl bullied by a neighborhood mom clearly suggest (Steinhauer, 2008). Nevertheless, as Stern (1999) suggests, girls must have opportunities to experiment with computer technologies in safe instructional environments and that "the growing number of girls' home pages lends credibility to the notion that the Web may present a new and much-needed forum for girls' 'safe' self expression" (p. 23). Equally important, the American Association of University Women (AAUW) (2001) has also contended that the need to develop and sustain digital literacy initiatives for girls is vital to leveling the technological playing fields within these arenas in order to foster a view of technology as an important form of both academic and professional development.

This chapter profiles our own technology and gender-equity efforts through a four-day residential computer camp for middle school girls titled The Digital Mirror, a space in which girls receive instruction and mentoring in new media literacies such as blogging, Web-authoring, digital imaging, and video and audio editing. During the camp, girls work in a state-of-the-art computer lab housed in the Bowling Green State University School of Art, and they experiment with such software as Adobe Dreamweaver and Photoshop, Apple iMovie, and GarageBand, as well as Web-based technologies such as blogs. In addition to functional literacy skills acquired through experimentation with these and other technologies, the girls receive opportunities to reflect on the role of communication technologies in both school and family life, creating a personal Web portfolio that documents technological growth and reflects the ways technology helps maintain connections with family and friends.

To help prevent the exclusion of girls from lower-income backgrounds, we set the family contribution at just $20 for each girl, which includes meals and materials for the duration of the four-day camp. We recruit girls from a variety of socioeconomic contexts, and girls enter the camp with varying degrees of technological literacy. In an effort to preserve the woman-centered, feminist approach of the camp, all instruction and chaperoning is provided by women, and student-to-student mentoring is encouraged. Funded in part by a national grant from the AAUW and now in its third year, the camp, as its Web site (http://www.bgsu.edu/departments/english/digimir08/USB20FD) details, has evolved into two separate tracks, one for new girls and one for returning girls in order to sustain both the interest and the skill sets obtained the previous year in a team-development model. Returning girls develop a professional Web presence for the camp itself, conducting interviews and writing for various audiences about elements of the camp, including safety concerns as well as curricular benefits and social opportunities. In this sense, the Digital Mirror Camp has aimed to foster positive experiences with technology at a formative age and to provide girl-centered spaces to foreground both the social and educational aspects of computing, particularly for girls from diverse cultural backgrounds or for girls whose access to technology has been limited because of class, gender, ethnicity, or a range of home and school constraints.

Because our overall goal is to help our female participants develop an understanding of the role of technology in their own identity formation as young women in personal, academic, and professional contexts, in this chapter we first articulate the theoretical rationale behind the camp and its emphasis on multimodal literacy narratives in foregrounding technology's role in connecting the girls to friends and family. We then document the important connection among digital media, reflection, and identity formation in adolescent girls through several first-year camper profiles, as well as the migration from a personal to a professional, collaborative form of identity development in our second-year camper curriculum. Finally, we argue that making such technological opportunities more accessible to girls from a range of social and cultural backgrounds aligns with the need for feminist researchers within digital spaces to engage in activities that responsibly blend theory and practice to ultimately benefit the populations we teach and study and to positively impact both the cultural rhetorics and local realities of women and girls' online lives.

REFLECTING ON WOMEN AND TECHNOLOGY: WHY A COMPUTER CAMP FOR GIRLS?

Girls and Computers

In its role as a equity-advocate for women and girls, The AAUW (2001) has called for safe, hospitable instructional environments for women to experiment with technologies the larger culture has often prescribed as male (Kearney, 2006). Such cultural messages are distributed and consumed within both global media and desktop systems that often reinscribe the view of technology as a gendered enterprise—consider, for example, Microsoft PowerPoint clip art under the search topic of "computers" that continues to portray male as opposed to female users. A better known example is the popular Apple Computer advertising campaign featuring a young, hip twenty-something male as "MAC," and a more stodgy male complete with business suit as "PC," notably both White. Such characterizations initially begged the question: Where are the women? In more recent ads, the Mac and PC characters have been joined by a female portraying the Mac Genius device that enables file-transfer between the Mac and the PC, and as such, a symbolically "peripheral" figure with subordinate status. Regardless of the cultural assumptions surrounding women and computers, both Apple and Microsoft have reached out to the female consumer with a number of ads featuring female computer users articulating their preferred technology specifications.

But despite living in an era of mp3 players, texting, and social networking, Twenty-first century girls don't seem to get the same message about technology-based career options within the larger culture, as the gap between women and girls as users of technology versus women and girls as producers of technology continues to be a wide one. For Claudia Herbst (2009), "gender imbalances in coding translate into gender imbalances in the use of the Internet. Those who write code and create virtual spaces inadvertently have a different relationship to cyberspace than those who merely visit it after construction is completed" (p. 138). As Takayoshi (1994) has noted, cyberspace has been imbued with masculine values of sterility, logic, and impersonality; professions and careers in technology marked as "hard" and unfeminine. As a result, it is little surprise that just as adolescent girls are being socialized within the larger culture to adopt specific gender roles, they begin to lose interest in technology around the middle school years, a phenomenon that the AAUW (2009) contends has lead to a range of consequences:

~ By 2010, one in four new jobs will be "technically oriented," or involve computers. However, women still lag far behind in earning computer technology degrees and working in computer technology-related professions.

~ High school girls represent only 17 percent of computer science Advanced Placement (AP) test takers.

~ College-educated women earn only 29.1 percent of bachelor's degrees in mathematics and computer science (down from 39.3 percent in 1984) and 24.7 percent of doctorate degrees in mathematics and computer science.

With these numbers in mind, many academic and corporate institutions have made efforts to increase the female demographic in science, technology, engineering, and math via specific training and mentoring programs. Such concerns about gender equity in computing, however, extend to humanities and social science specialists as well, specifically those of us who embrace feminist theories and pedagogies. As feminist scholar-teachers, we embrace opportunities to theorize the material conditions that impact women's experiences with technology, as well as opportunities to develop action-based research projects designed to benefit those communities in which we are not just teachers and researchers, but also mothers, daughters, sisters, and friends. This latter goal led to a working group of women at BGSU that included representatives from departments of Art, American Studies, Communication, English, and Higher Education. Together, our group recruited middle school girls for Year 1 of the Digital Mirror Camp, its title meant to represent an emphasis on personal reflection about technology's importance in our participants' personal and academic lives.

The need to raise critical awareness of technology's socioeconomic role is certainly not limited to female users, but is perhaps especially relevant to girls and women as they are often defined by and through such technologies and are "typically acculturated to accept discourses that privilege males, often at the expense of females" (Lalik & Oliver, 2007, p. 49). Because the girls in our camp and those of similar age have never known a time without computing, email, streaming video, and instantaneous information, it is virtually impossible for these "digital natives" (Prensky, 2001) to identify the bias, limitations, and even opportunities for boundary blurring available through technology. While many users are aware of the consequences to both safety and reputation resulting from posting private or sensitive information in online forums, many do not realize the ways technology and media help define and delimit self-identity. These definitions and representations of self-made possible by computing are inescapably tied to gender. Judy Wajcman's *Technofeminism* (2004) reminds us of the "mutually shaping relationship between gender and technology" (p. 7), and this awareness of technology as a force contributing to both personal and cultural identity mandates continued outreach to encourage young women like those at the Digital Mirror Camp to take more active, critical positions as technology users and consumers.

Indeed, in our collective roles as technofeminists, we share a similar recognition that, as Wajcman (2004) notes, "the enormous variability in gendering by place, nationality, class, race, ethnicity, sexuality and generation makes a nuanced exploration of the similarities and differences between and across women's and men's experience of technoscience all the more necessary" (p. 8). In the next section, we weave several theoretical strands to articulate the goals behind the Digital Mirror Camp. The resulting tapestry foregrounds a multimodal literacy acquisition that, as we will argue, allows our camp participants see themselves as producers of and composers within new media, as opposed to mere consumers of it. Such a shift in subjectivity ultimately involves an equal emphasis on narrative and story as a form of articulating women and girls' experiences with technology, enabling broader potential for identity construction within digital spaces.

Safe Spaces

Despite this potential, a range of girls studies scholars have acknowledged a dichotomy in the way in which digital spaces are perceived in relation to young women. On one hand is the notion of the Internet as a "safe haven" (Stern, 1999; Thiel, 2005; Tulley & Blair, 2003) for girls to experiment with expressions of identity; on the other is the notion that Internet spaces not only reinscribe traditional assumptions about gender identity (often by mirroring traditional media's emphasis on body image and appearance), but also prey on women and girls' status as consumers of these assumptions. Shayla Thiel (2005) concludes that the result of this dichotomy is "a culture of adolescence that is often confusing for girls who may seek alternative discourses from which to construct alternatives identities or who wish to construct a comfortable identity while still attempting to fit in with peers and attain a media-perfect version of reality" (p. 183). For these reasons, an expanded definition of technological literacy is equally necessary to provide girls with a skills set not only to interrogate the messages about girlhood they encounter online but also to consider the role of audience and purpose as they construct their individual representations of self. Relevant to our discussion is Stuart Selber's (2004) three-point continuum of technologically literate practice: (1) functional—the users of technology; (2) critical—the questioners of technology; and (3) rhetorical—the producers of technology. Speaking of these modes, Selber contends, "the goal is not to endorse one over the others, but to help students learn to exploit the different subjectivities that have become associated with computer technologies" (p. 25).

Certainly, the concept of a safe-haven to develop these important literacies can appear utopic, and within our own discipline of Rhetoric and Writing, various scholars have called for all students, regardless of gender, to experiment with technologies in ways that establish reciprocal mentoring models among students and between students and teachers. At the same time, we have recognized that deploying electronic pedagogies does not guarantee a utopic egalitarianism rhetoric (Hawisher & Selfe, 1991) that presumes each and every student or citizen has a voice and is empowered by sheer virtue of access to online forums. As a result, a major goal of the Digital Mirror Camp has been to develop an educational outreach program in which we might theorize the possibilities and constraints of digital identity development in a range of multimodal spaces where adolescent girls do more than just learn "how" to use digital tools, but to consider how these literacy tools play an important role in developing their stories of personal reflection and interpersonal connection to friends and family, as well as professional connection to external audiences. In many ways, girls are functionally literate users of technology in their daily lives; through their use of texting and instant messaging, along with social networking, many girls across cultures are comfortable communicating online. What they are perhaps less comfortable doing is reflecting upon the possibilities and constraints of technology in their understanding of themselves and their connections to others.

A significant component of this reflective process involves the use of narrative as a rhetorical practice. Thiel (2005) notes that narratives are crucial to "shaping personal and social identity and…shedding light upon the social relations that create and maintain gender norms and power structures" (p. 187). Our own field has valued technological literacy narratives for their potential to foster student reflection "on how their attitudes and beliefs develop, both socially and individually" (Kitalong,

Bridgeford, Moore, & Selfe, 2003, p. 219). But equally significant, narrative aligns with both feminist and technofeminist practices that foreground "women's lived experiences in a respective manner that legitimates women's voices as sources of knowledge" (Campbell & Wasco, 2000). In the context of the Digital Mirror Camp, such practices involve both a "coming together of many diverse voices engaged in dialogue, influencing each other and each being modified in the process" (Wajcman, 2004, p. 8). Thus the following profile of three first-year campers suggests, while we must certainly acknowledge the important work of technofeminist and girls studies scholars, we must not forget the stories girls themselves tell about their technological literacy history. As Henwood, Kennedy, and Miller (2001) conclude in their collection *Cyborg Lives: Women's Technobiographies,* women's stories help us make sense of our experiences with a range of technologies, particularly, in our case, the new media tools that the girls used to represent themselves and the social and material conditions that limit the role of these tools in constructing girls' digital identities.

COMING INTO FOCUS: FUNCTIONAL AND CRITICAL LITERACIES ONLINE

The Digital Mirror camp is designed with the above issues in mind as we work to create a safe, girl-centered, technology-rich environment where girls can develop functional, critical, and rhetorical technoliteracies. We encourage campers to express their individual identities through their Web portfolios, for which the girls make a variety of choices about navigation, color scheme, content, and overall look and feel. Many campers extend this personalization by including pictures of friends and family, links to their personal blogs and favorite Web sites, and audio and video material. Throughout the Web portfolios, a number of themes emerge with respect to how the girls represent their identities visually through their connections to friends and family, their increased sense of audience awareness, and an increased awareness about the visibility of technology. Similar to Stern's analysis of youth online authorship (2008), our emphasis is upon paying "serious attention to youth online expression, as sites of meaning making and identity production" (p. 114). Specifically, we've chosen three Web portfolios to demonstrate how these themes manifest themselves in the expression of an online girlhood identity. Like other campers, these girls receive instruction on the basic fundamentals of Web authoring (utilizing tables, choosing color palettes, creating links, inserting images, and so on) and video creation (storyboarding, filming, and editing), while they are also encouraged through several reflective activities to consider the ways in which their design and content choices reflect certain aspects of their identity.

Marissa[1]

Marissa is an African American 7th grader from a large, blue-collar family in northwest Ohio. Though Marissa comes to the camp with fewer socioeconomic resources and preexisting technological literacies than some of the other campers, her family is a strong source of support and enthusiasm about her participation in the camp. This enthusiasm is particularly evident when Marissa's entire family— including the family dog—drops by midway through the camp to visit Marissa and show their support for her developing technological literacies. Given these strong family ties, it is perhaps not surprising that Marissa maintains a consistent emphasis on family throughout her Web portfolio, evident in both her design and content choices. On her site's index page (see Figure 7.1), for example, under a banner of "What You Should Know About Me," Marissa writes, "I love spending time with my family and my dog!" In keeping with this family-centered expression of her identity, one of the most prominent sections of Marissa's portfolio is the "My Family" section, which contains multiple photos of family members, as well as photos of the family dog. Further, when asked to discuss her favorite technology in a blog entry, Marissa cites texting family and friends as being "THE MOST AWSOME[2] THING IN THE WORLD!!!!!!!!!!!!!!!!!!" before noting that this activity "usually makes a relly big bill, unless you have unlimited texting." Thus, Marissa demonstrates her understanding of technology as a means for maintaining close family connections, while also demonstrating her critical awareness of the economic implications of those technologies.

Marissa finds family connections to other camp experiences, as well. When discussing a painting she viewed during our camp's field trip to the Toledo Museum of Art, Marissa writes in her blog that "[t]he piece called New York 1 reminded me of my past, because every year my family and I go to New York to visit relatives and we always drive on the Brooklyn Bridge!!!" In this way, Marissa used the Web portfolio project as an opportunity to reflect on and critically harness the experiences of the camp for the purposes of reinforcing strong family ties—which, for Marissa, constituted the key aspect of her identity she wished to share with site viewers.

Indeed, throughout Marissa's Web portfolio, the emphasis is placed on foregrounding the individuals she sees as being most significant in her life—from family members to pop star Beyoncé—as opposed to foregrounding specific details about herself. In another blog entry, Marissa touches on this reluctance to reveal details about her personal identity when she writes, "I would not use a real picture of myself, because I do not want my real identity to be revealed EVER!!!!" While the exact motivation for wanting to conceal her identity remains unclear, Marissa nevertheless demonstrates her understanding of the Web portfolio project as being a place where she can control which messages get disseminated, thereby facilitating a sense of agency and rhetorical savvy not always cultivated among girls of her age group. In other words, Marissa's Web portfolio demonstrates what the Pew Internet & American Life Project has termed "self literacy" (Rainie, 2008), as Marissa effectively manages her online identity by choosing which aspects of her life to share and how much personal information to disclose.

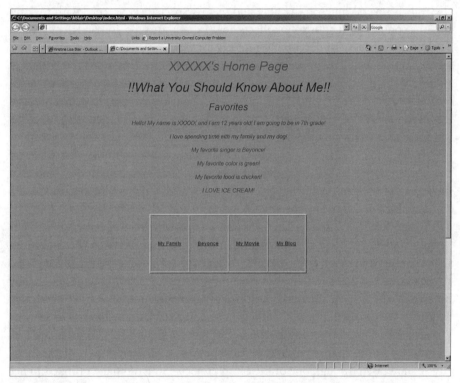

Figure 7.1 *The index page to Marissa's Web portfolio emphasizes family as being key to Marissa's identity.*

Jordan

Jordan is an Asian American 7th grader from northwest Ohio. An only child and the daughter of university employees, Jordan makes it clear throughout her Web portfolio that she is no stranger to using technology for a variety of purposes. In contrast to Marissa, Jordan came to the camp having already acquired much technological literacy, presumably as a result of greater access to technologies throughout her childhood and adolescence. In a blog entry, for instance, Jordan describes her parents giving her opportunities to experiment with technology from the age of three and insists that she "cannot live" without a computer.

While she comes to the camp already possessing some basic HTML skills, Jordan expresses in a blog entry her desire to learn more Web design skills as part of the camp curriculum. Additionally, when asked to discuss what identity she hopes to reflect in her Web portfolio, Jordan writes that she hopes visitors to her site can tell that "I'm more or less a sarcastic person, that I love RENT, and that I enjoy my iPod but have no qualms about making fun of them." Interestingly, Jordan mentions these goals several times in her blog and seems especially concerned with making sure the content of her portfolio reflects her sarcastic attitude. Jordan later expresses her satisfaction with developing projects that she saw as meeting this criterion and makes a specific reference to her video about iPods: "iPods: MP3 technology changing the lives of otherwise apathetic teens. What does that imply to you?" While Jordan's sarcasm may not be immediately apparent to the viewers of her site, it is nevertheless clear that Jordan sees humor as being a means for creating "a speaking space in the crowded World Wide Web" (Killoran, 2001, p. 127). As Jonathan Alexander (2006) has noted, experimentation with satirical strategies also suggest that Jordan understands "the constructedness of self as Web commodity" and uses her attempts at satire "to mock the surrounding world of representations and media constructions or to hold up the self for mockery and self-irony" (p. 119).

In another blog entry, Jordan references her existing technological skill and her desire to reflect her identity with an aesthetically pleasing Web site: "I mostly tried to make everything look nice—like, I have an issue with backgrounds. If the image doesn't flow (like you can tell where the image stops and starts) then I get a teeny bit ticked. So I just tried to make everything look really nice." Consistent with this concern with design aesthetics, Jordan chose a simple, patterned image to serve as a seamless background for her portfolio images (see Figure 7.2). Jordan's site features four sections that seem to each correspond to a different aspect of her identity as showcased through one of the camp projects—the filmmaker (linked to her iMovie), the lawyer (linked to her blog), the song writer (linked to her GarageBand track), and the dancer (linked to a page of external links). The images for each section are taken from promotional materials for the Broadway production, *Rent*, thereby integrating Jordan's identity with that of her favorite play, while also demonstrating a rather sophisticated integration of webbed and offline documents (Alexander, 2006).

Jordan's Web portfolio reflects not only her functional literacy with Web authoring, image manipulation, and multimedia composition, but also her growing capacity to critically reflect on those literacies at the same time that she asserts and executes a specific plan for how she wants her Web portfolio to be received by visitors. Jordan also demonstrates what Cynthia Selfe and others have termed "visual literacy" (2004, p. 69) by creating, combining, and using visual elements (including her choice of background texture, color, and images) to communicate key aspects of her identity—a practice that she reflects on in her blog narratives. Like Marissa, Jordan avoids using specific information about or images of herself in her Web portfolio; rather, Jordan's Web portfolio reflects her desire to express her online identity through text and images related to her interests, as well as her desire to experiment with humor as a means for challenging the very notion of the Web as constructed self-representation.

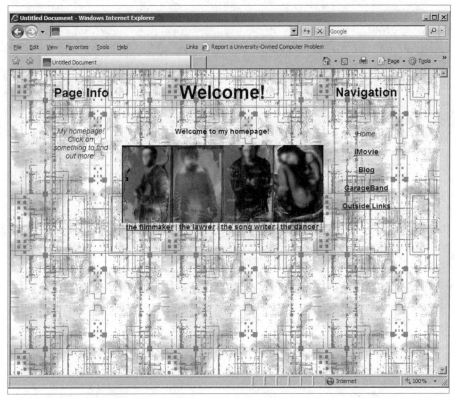

Figure 7.2 *Jordan's Web portfolio utilizes images and color to convey meaning.*

Claire

Claire is a Caucasian 7th grader, also from northwest Ohio. Like Jordan, Claire describes her parents teaching her to use technology from a young age, her earliest memory being interaction with a Barbie computer game. Claire recognizes technology as being a significant component of her daily life, as she admits being able to spend up to four hours on the computer playing games such as The Sims without realizing how much time has passed. In a blog entry, Claire writes that she looks forward to the camp activities as a means for cultivating her own expertise, as well as that of her friends: "I know that I will keep learning new things and hopefully i will be able to pass them onto my friends." In fact, Claire seems keenly aware of her technoliteracies as being situated within her larger community of friends and family, and she perceives technology as being a means for maintaining those relationships. This attention to the use of technology as a communication tool is evident in Claire's video clip, in which she discusses the many technologies she uses on a daily basis to interact with friends and family, including e-mail, instant messenger, her blog, a cellular phone with text messaging capabilities, and social networking sites like YouTube. In this way, Claire seems to be developing a "cyborg literacy" (Inman, 2004, p. 163) by making visible the many real and virtual systems that constitute her meaning-making practices. Interestingly, while Claire's video is composed under the title of "My Favorite Technology," the resulting discussion reflects Claire's recognition that she in fact interacts with multiple, something overlapping technologies on a daily basis—a reality made visible to her through the technology autobiography project.

Claire's growing awareness of the complexity of her relationship with technology, community, and identity can be seen in other parts of her Web portfolio, as well. When asked to discuss plans for her digital identity early in the camp, Claire writes that she sees herself as being "digitally sophisticated"; by the end of the camp, however, Claire expresses a more complicated understanding of her evolving technoliteracy and the rhetorical nature of a Web identity:

> At first, I wasn't really sure what i was getting myself into and why i wanted to be here. When i got here, i realized that there was so much technology that i haven't used and i haven't heard of. It really was a great experience getting familiar with a new computer and new technology. We were on the computers almost all day but it was worth it because we came out with great finished products. When i was putting together my web page and blog, i really had to think how i wanted it to be set up. Like what kind of colors go with each other and what readers could take out of the blog and web page. I also had to think what i wanted to put on the internet because anyone can see what i wrote or what i put out there. Overall it came to be a wonderful experience and i found out that there are many different ways to express yourself through technology.

In this blog entry, Claire recognizes the multifaceted nature of constructing her girlhood identity online—from the overwhelming process of learning to use new technologies in service of a functional literacy, to the critical literacy involved with questioning the ways in which an identity can be expressed through technology, to the rhetorical literacy involved with moving toward the more audience-centered enterprise of content creation.

GIRLHOOD IDENTITY AND THE DIGITAL WEB PORTFOLIO PROJECT

The emphasis on audience awareness as represented in the Web portfolios is demonstrative of the girls' emerging critical and rhetorical literacy skills and further characterizes the representations of those identities with an audience of friends and family in mind. Collectively, these Web portfolios demonstrate each girl's desire to experiment digitally with her identity in a multitude of roles rather than solely as a stereotypical adolescent girl. Further, these examples and other digital artifacts from the camp show how the Web portfolio project functioned as an ideal space for first-time campers to "negotiate and construct their self-representations in purposeful ways" (Alexander, 2006, p. 105) at the same time that they critiqued the role of technology in their lives. These portfolios show girls identifying themselves as friends, sisters, and daughters, which further situates them in communities beyond the online spaces of their Web portfolios. Moreover, their careful choices regarding the use of images speaks volumes as to the ways in which girls are often represented by others, as opposed to how they actually choose to represent themselves, using technology to tell their individual stories. Of the portfolios discussed here, only Claire's includes pictures of the girl herself; even then, Claire is always pictured with friends or family in photos manipulated with Adobe PhotoShop, thereby drawing the focus more to Claire's technological skill than to the presence of her bodily image on the Web. In short, Jordan and Claire's narratives about community and family in their portfolios reflect many trends we see in how girls work in and construct identities in online spaces. Stephanie Rosenbloom (2008) of the *New York Times*, for example, explains how girls create online content to express themselves and to create and maintain social relationships more often than boys.

Yet, as Jane Margolis and Allan Fisher (2002) note in *Unlocking the Clubhouse: Women in Computing*, despite the fact that women "make up a majority of Internet consumers...few women are learning how to invent, create, and design computer technology" (p. 2). As a result, women and girls continue to be left out of the computing loop, which results in considerable personal, professional, and economic ramifications. It is with this reality in mind that we approach extending our camp's initial focus on individual identity construction to a more professional orientation.

CREATING A PROFESSIONAL, COLLABORATIVE IDENTITY

In the second-year curriculum, the shift between developing a personal identity to a professional, collaborative identity takes place as campers create digital materials to publicize the camp. Practicing feminist pedagogy, which includes "the decentering or sharing of authority, the recognition of students as sources of knowledge, and a focus on processes (of writing and teaching) over products" (Jarratt, 2001, p. 115), continues to be a crucial part of the second-year curriculum. Thinking as a team, with the goal of reaching out to potential campers and their parents, the returning girls focus on their critical and rhetorical literacy skills (Selber, 2004) as they develop a professional, collaborative identity. This section discusses the efforts of these nine returning campers, who together develop a Web site and a logo to publicize the Digital Mirror Camp as a camp that is not only *for* girls, but is also designed *by* girls. Working in groups of three for the majority of the camp, each group showcases their collaborative identity through the creation of a single Web page and video—a project that is then presented to parents and campers alike on the final day of the camp.

Use of Color in Identity Construction

Instead of using color to represent their individual identities in the design of the Web site, as they did in the first year of the camp, the returning girls must determine how to use color to represent their collaborative identity as campers from the Digital Mirror Camp. This proves to be a challenge for the girls because their initial thoughts were to borrow a color scheme (orange and brown) from BGSU since that is where the camp is held. This initial choice reflects how the campers associated their collaborative identity with their location. Though location is a component of the camp's collaborative identity, using colors that only represent that component hides the girlhood identities of the campers themselves. To incorporate the BGSU component of the camp, the girls decide to use a pastel orange rather than a bright orange color for the background of the sidebar and the headings on each page of the site (see Figure 7.3).

After maintaining some aspect of BGSU with the collaborative identity the girls were representing online, the returning campers then determine how to represent their identities in response to the traditional colors used to represent girls. Shades of pink and purple are the stereotypically girl colors, so the girls consider these as choices for representing their collaborative identity online. At the same time, the girls do not want to use these colors primarily because, by themselves, those colors do not reflect a girlhood identity that is also tech-savvy and interested in computers—qualities that are still predominantly seen as masculine. To strike a balance between a girlhood identity and the stereotypical masculine identity, the girls ultimately choose to use a light pink color for the background of each Web page and royal blue as the background for the heading. Even more representative of this balance is the choice to include white polka dots in the blue heading and a whimsical font for the camp's name. In the case of color choice, the girls have developed a collaborative identity that feminizes a stereotypically masculine space, thus further shaping their rhetorical literacy skills as they negotiate traditional female and male stereotypes.

Figure 7.3 *Campers use color to convey a collaborative camp identity.*

Use of Audience in Identity Construction

Knowing that the Web site would be viewed by the parents and potential campers, the campers must keep the perspectives of those audiences in mind when deciding how to represent their collaborative identity online. Therefore, the returning girls create two pages in addition to the home page, one for parents and one for potential campers, with corresponding videos to communicate their identity. This choice shows the development of the second-track campers' rhetorical literacy skills and an increased understanding of their collaborative identity. Not only do they have to think about how their own parents and friends would perceive their identity, but they also have to think about how other parents and girls in their age group would perceive that identity.

Information for Parents

On this page (see Figure 7.4), the girls represent their collaborative identity by including the educational and safety components of that identity in response to the perspectives of parents. The embedded video begins with interviews of the campers from each curriculum regarding what they learned. Across these interviews is an emphasis on teamwork and learning new digital literacy skills—both attributes of the camp's identity that are valued by campers' parents and parents of potential campers. At the end of the video is a segment on safety in the dorms where the girls enact a scenario that shows how the dorms are restricted to residents only through the use of keys and personal entry devices (PEDs).

Aside from the embedded video, the girls include images showing the campers hard at work in the computer labs. Showing the campers' work ethic to parents shows their commitment to developing their digital literacy skills and the potential for professional application of those skills. Next to these images is a list of the names and credentials of the camp staff. Though not representative of the girls' identities directly, the names and credentials of the staff reveal how educated, female role models are incorporated as part of the collaborative identity.

Figure 7.4 *The "Information for Parents" page is one of three pages created collaboratively by returning campers to reflect a camp identity.*

Camp Highlights

On this page (see Figure 7.5), the girls have chosen to represent their collaborative identity by including the entertainment value of the camp by appealing to potential campers. As preteens, the prospect of leaving home to stay on a college campus for a few days is an important component of the camp's identity. For this group, it is appealing not only to have the independence of being away from home but also to have the independence of using digital media. In cases where computer access is limited in the home, the perceived identity of the camp can seem less limiting. In addition to the appeal of staying in college dorms, meeting new people and taking field trips to the Toledo Art Museum and the COSI Science Center are also significant components of the girls' collaborative identity formation. Working with other campers and taking field trips, as well as staying in the residence halls, show the community aspect of their collaborative identity as depicted by the camp. These community components challenge the perception that technology is isolating and make the collaborative identity and the camp more appealing to prospective campers. Technology therefore becomes more than just for entertainment, but something that allows girls to make an impression on other girls through the presentation of that collaborative identity.

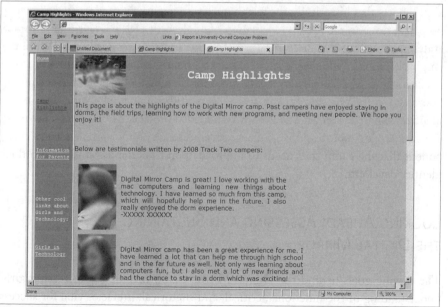

Figure 7.5 *The "Camp Highlights" page features testimonials from campers to convey fun and educational camp experiences to parents and future campers.*

Representing a Collaborative Identity Online and Offline

Part of developing a professional, collaborative identity for the camp involves being able to confidently project that identity to those within and outside the camp. By the end of the camp, the girls have created a Web site that represents their online collaborative identity to a variety of audiences. Offline, however, the girls need more preparation before making an informal presentation of their identity to parents and campers from the first-year curriculum. Without the use and guidance of public speaking strategies and presentation software like PowerPoint, the offline presence of their collaborative identity has not been as reflective of the online presence as it could be. In response to the need for the girls to develop a stronger professional, collaborative identity online and offline, the camp staff has decided to more directly incorporate the use of such strategies and presentation software in the future.

Adopting this component of their collaborative identity will help the girls think more about how they can become more than users of technology—they can be content creators, as well. Though the collaborative identity that the girls created in the second-year curriculum represents a move in the direction of technology creation, there is still evidence of their identities as primarily technology users. One example of this can be seen in the decision to place a cell phone on the camp's logo developed by the second-year campers for use on future camp T-shirts. Kearney (2007) notes that historically, the telephone has frequently been identified as a technological trope in the identify formation of adolescent girls in ways that both liberate and constrain larger cultural constructions of modern girlhood. While the emphasis on cell phone use is attached to technology and to community (i.e., the need to stay in regular contact with family and friends), the image of the cell phone does necessarily represent the creative aspects of technology in their collaborative identity that are evident in the Web site and video projects. Helping the girls more directly develop a professional, collaborative presence online and offline is a component that the camp staff needs to improve upon to better assist girls with their identity development.

LOOKING AHEAD: ASSESSING AND SUSTAINING THE DIGITAL MIRROR

The driving goals behind the Digital Mirror Camp include (1) increasing girls' understanding of the functional, critical, and rhetorical, literacies vital for success and safety in digital environments; (2) fostering a space to reflect on the role of technology in women and girls' personal and professional lives; (3) foregrounding the ways in which experiences with technology impact identity construction; and (4) emphasizing the value of camaraderie and mentorship among women. While the camp's primary focus is on technological experimentation within the girl-centered lab space, the exploration of technological literacy is not limited to work done in the lab. In fact, the success of the camp is largely due to the involvement of individuals and community organizations outside of the core instructional team. During meals, campers meet and talk with several women currently involved in or pursuing careers in technology. The participants stay in campus residence halls with camp facilitators and additional volunteers to enhance the mentoring and training environment, along with the showcase session for parents. The benefits of the intensive community-driven approach to the camp become clear through the reactions from parents. During the final showcase session of our first camp, for example, one father, who previously would not allow a computer in the family home, indicated that he was so impressed with his daughter's work that the family would not only purchase a computer, but would also attempt to send both their daughters to the camp the next year. In fact, several girls and their families contacted us after completing the first camp to inquire about returning the following year, suggesting not only that our pool of campers and camp supporters will continue to grow as the camp thrives but also that family involvement in and responsibility for sustaining technological literacy is vital, particularly in a culture that continues to reinforce stereotypes about women in general and women and technology in particular.

To counteract the perception that technological careers are more male than female, our second track for returning campers builds on the functional and critical literacies cultivated during the previous year. Specifically, the curriculum encourages students to experiment with new technologies of print and digital media (functional literacy) in order to develop a collective camp identity for the purpose of communicating that identity to an audience of their peers (critical literacy), as well as advancing rhetorical literacy by bringing students into the realm of interface design (Selber, 2004). The second track also provides an opportunity to involve campers in a collaborative effort to assess and sustain the camp by facilitating individual and group reflections on camp experiences, benefits, and possibilities. By drawing from their own knowledge and experiences to collaboratively create a useful, meaningful, Web-based resource for a larger community of peers, the returning campers are immersed in a type of service-learning project that prompts "student writing to become both community focused and critically reflective" (Alexander, 2006, pp. 366–367). Additionally, involving campers in efforts to sustain the camp is not only important for emphasizing the relationship between technology, reflection, and girls' identity construction, but also for assessing the degree to which the first camp met its projected goals over an extended period of time in sustaining participants' technological literacy. Because the multimedia artifacts produced by new and returning campers provide opportunities for self-assessment in the form of testimonials as well as design choices and photo selection, they become key documents from which we can continue to assess and develop curriculum that continues to foster our goals.

Our efforts toward creating spaces that encourage girls to maintain an interest in technology use and production are similar to other outreach organizations across the country. Some of the organizations that the second-year campers chose to provide links for on the camp Web site include Girls in Technology (http://girlsintechnology.org/), TechBridge (http://www.techbridgegirls.org/), and Girl Geeks (http://www.girlgeeks.org/). While these organizations are important for many of the reasons we've discussed, they are somewhat limiting for girls if they do not incorporate opportunities for reflecting on identity development. It is equally important for young women to be guided through the process of developing their identities while sustaining an interest in science and technology. Without this guidance, girls will be unprepared for how to challenge stereotypes in higher education and in the workforce. Though these stereotypes are breaking down as women continue to pursue degrees in science and technology, they are still sexualized. For example, *Newsweek's* article titled "Revenge of the Nerdette" describes how young women are challenging the "geek stereotypes" by "being just as proud of their sexuality as they are of their geekiness" (Bennett & Yabroff, 2008, p. 45). Bennett and Yabroff (2008) even refer to successful women, such as "Ellen Spertus, a Mills College professor and research scientist at Google—and the 2001 winner of the Silicon Valley 'Sexiest Geek Alive' pageant" (p. 44) to show how women are challenging these stereotypes.

Certainly, it is important to show young women that they can be feminine and interested in science and technology, but with role models like those discussed above, it seems as if some women are replacing one stereotype with another. For that reason, building a sense of community among girls and women as we individually and collectively construct digital identities is vital to disrupting "the male order of things" on the Internet" (Wilding, 1998, p. 9) through the development of women-centered spaces that enable girls to experiment with technology and to use narrative to reflect on their own use of that technology as they develop online identities in safe, empowering, and sustainable ways. Stern (1999) calls for more research to explore the "potential the Web may hold for granting girls a louder voice" (p. 38). Inevitably, we designed the Digital Mirror Camp with both the theoretical and practical goal of enabling girls to construct counter-narratives to larger cultural assumptions about gender and technology, to foster positive experiences for girls whose technological literacy acquisition, despite our best efforts at gender-equity, will continue to be mediated through inequitable cultural, material, and educational frameworks.

NOTES

1. Pseudonyms are used.
2. Quotes from the Web portfolios are exact. Grammatical and spelling errors were not corrected so as to be true to the exact content written by the girls.

REFERENCES

Alexander, J. (2006). *Digital youth: Emerging literacies on the world wide web*. Cresskill, NJ: Hampton Press.

American Association of University Women. (2001). *Tech savvy*. Washington, DC: AAUW.

American Association of University Women. (2009). Position on science, technology, engineering and mathematics (STEM) education. Retrieved May 26, 2009, from http://www.aauw.org/advocacy/issue_advocacy/actionpages/STEM.cfm

Bennett, J., & Yabroff, J. (2008, June 16). Revenge of the nerdette. *Newsweek, 24*, 44–45.

Campbell, R., & Wasco, S. (2000). Feminist approaches to social science: Epistemological and methodological tenets. *American Journal of Community Psychology, 28*(6), 773–791.

Hawisher, G., & Selfe, C. (1991). The rhetoric of technology and the electronic writing class. *College Composition and Communication, 42*(1), 55–65.

Henwood, F., Kennedy, H., & Miller, N. (2001). *Cyborg lives?: Women's technobiographies*. York, UK: Raw Nerve Press.

Herbst, C. (2009). Masters of the house: Literacy and the claiming of space on the Internet. In K. Blair, R. Gajjala, & C. Tulley (Eds.), *Webbing cyberfeminist practice: Communities, pedagogies and social action* (pp. 135–152). Cresskill, NJ: Hampton Press.

Inman, J. (2004). *Computers and writing: the cyborg era*. Mahwah, NJ: Lawrence Erlbaum.

Jarratt, S.C. (2001). Feminist pedagogy. In G. Tate, A. Rupiper, & K. Schick (Eds.), *A guide to composition pedagogies* (pp. 113–131). Oxford: Oxford University Press.

Kearney, M. C. (2006). *Girls make media*. London: Routledge.

Kearney, M. C. (2007). Birds on the wire: Troping teenage girlhood through telephony in mid-twentieth-century US media culture. *Cultural Studies, 19*(5), 568–601.

Killoran, J. (2001). @ Home among the .coms: Virtual rhetoric in the agora of the web. In L. Gray-Rosendale & S. Gruber (Eds.), *Alternative rhetorics: challenges to the rhetorical tradition* (pp. 127–144). Albany: State University of New York Press.

Kitalong, K., Bridgeford, T., Moore, M., & Selfe, D. (2003). Variations on a theme: The technology autobiography as a versatile writing assignment. In P. Takayoshi & B. Huot (Eds.), *Teaching writing with computers: An introduction* (pp. 219–233). Boston: Houghton Mifflin.

Lalik, R., & Oliver, K.L. (2007). Differences and tensions in implementing a pedagogy of critical literacy with adolescent girls. *Reading Research Quarterly, 42*(1), 46–70.

Margolis, J., & Fisher, A. (2002). *Unlocking the clubhouse: women in computing*. Cambridge, MA: MIT Press.

Pew Internet and American Life Project. (2007). Teens and social media. Retrieved May 26, 2009, from http://www.pewinternet.org/Reports/2007/Teens-and-Social-Media

Prensky, M. (2001). Digital natives, digital immigrants. *On the Horizon, 9*(5), 1–6.

Rainie, L. (2008, June 10). Teenagers' online safety and literacy. Pew Internet & American Life Project. Retrieved June 2, 2009, from http://www.pewinternet.org/Presentations/2008/Online-child-safety-and-literacy.aspx

Rosenbloom, S (2008, February 21). Sorry, boys, this is our domain. *The New York Times*. Retrieved May 2, 2009, from http://www.nytimes.com/2008/02/21/fashion/21 webgirls.html?_r=1

Selber, S. (2004). *Multiliteracies for a digital age*. Carbondale: Southern Illinois University Press.

Selfe, C. (2004). Toward new media texts: Taking up the challenges of visual literacy. In A. Wysocki, J. Johnson-Eilola, C. Selfe, & G. Sirc (Eds.), *Writing new media: Theory and applications for expanding the teaching of composition* (pp. 67–110). Logan: Utah State University Press.

Steinhauer, J. (2008, November 26). Verdict in MySpace suicide case. *New York Times*. Retrieved May 28, 2009, from http://www.nytimes.com/2008/11/27/us/27 myspace.html?_r=1.

Stern, S. (1999). Adolescent girls' expression on web home pages: Spirited, sombre, and self-conscious sites. *Convergence: The International Journal of Research into New Media Technologies, 5*, 22–41.

Stern, S. (2008). Producing sites, exploring identities: Youth online authorship. In D. Buckingham (Ed.), *Youth, identity, and digital media* (pp. 95–118). Cambridge, MA: MIT Press.

Takayoshi, P. (1994). Building new networks from the old: Women's experiences with electronic communications. *Computers and Composition, 11*(1), 21–35.

Thiel, S. (2005). IM me: Identity construction and gender negotiation in the world of adolescent girls and instant messaging. In S. Mazzarella (Ed.), *Girl wide web: Girls, the internet, and the negotiation of identity* (pp. 179–201). New York: Peter Lang.

Tulley, C., & Blair, K. (2003). eWriting spaces as safe, gender-fair havens: Aligning political and pedagogical possibilities. In P. Takayoshi & B. Huot (Eds.), *Teaching writing with computers: An introduction* (pp. 55–66). Boston: Houghton Mifflin.

Wajcman, J. (2004). *Technofeminism*. Cambridge, UK: Polity Press.

Wilding, F. (1998). Where is feminism in cyberfeminism? *n.paradoxa, 2*, 6–12.

CHAPTER EIGHT

We Wanted Other People to Learn from Us

Girls Blogging in Rural South Africa in the Age of AIDS

CLAUDIA MITCHELL, JOHN PASCARELLA,
NAYDENE DE LANGE & JEAN STUART

Adolescent girls' blogs provide one entry point for examining how the activities of girls are renegotiating boundaries: the boundaries of their lives, their relationships, and of public/private space. Given the opportunities that blogs offer girls, to write and share personal experiences and opinions with potential public readers, their importance in the lives of girls needs to be addressed and better understood. (Bell, 2007, p. 108)

Bell's words are particularly relevant to the lives of girls in rural South Africa and to the issues of gender violence and HIV and AIDS that they face. Indeed, one of the most striking statements given by one of the girls in a rural secondary school in the province of KwaZulu-Natal, South Africa, during a focus group discussion after a series of workshops on blogging was the statement "we wanted other people to learn from us." Further, when asked how discussing HIV and AIDS in their blogs was different than talking openly about the subject in class, students in the group commented that they felt as though their words would have an impact on a greater audience, inspiring others to change at-risk habits and views about sexual practices they otherwise felt uncomfortable discussing openly. These comments, we believe, suggest a different way of thinking about the potential uses for new media in a section of South Africa that is regarded as the epicenter of HIV and AIDS infections. They also say something about the ways in which girls and young women, who are three to four times more likely to be infected than males of the same age, and who are a greatest risk in relation to gender violence can be positioned as knowers, rather than as victims, through access to the Internet and new media. In this chapter we look back on a series of workshops on blogging, focusing in particular on the participation of girls, in order to look ahead to mapping out an agenda for the use of new media in addressing sexuality education in an age of AIDS.[1] In so doing we also address the digital divide as a challenge in rural and under-resourced areas of the country, but offer some ideas on ways of addressing these issues through new media as a result of our experiences in engaging young people and teachers, and especially girls and women. Our approach is to draw on what we describe elsewhere as "girl-method" (Mitchell & Reid-Walsh, 2008), where we recognize the need for tools and methods in our work with girls that highlight the significance of girls' voices and that make the work girl-centered. Drawing from the work of Joseph Tobin (2000) and the idea of close readings as an approach to unraveling the words of children and young people, the chapter sets out to unravel the statement "we wanted other people to learn from us."

WHY THE NEED FOR ENGAGEMENT?

Schools in the rural province of KwaZulu-Natal have been hard hit by HIV and AIDS, as AIDS-related morbidity and mortality have an overwhelming impact in the rural areas (MacQueen & Abdool-Karim, 2007). Significantly, in a recent study of the HIV status of pregnant women attending the Mafakatini Clinic in Vulindlela, more than two-thirds tested as HIV positive (CAPRISA, 2006). Within this context, the education sector faces particular challenges in terms of survival and care of children affected by HIV and AIDS. South Africa not only has the largest number of HIV-positive people in the world, namely, between 6.29 and 6.51 million, it also has largest number of AIDS orphans at 2.3 million. This figure is expected to rise to 3.1 million by 2010 (UNAIDS, 2004). Despite the many efforts in South Africa to reduce the rate of transmission of HIV and AIDS, certain populations, particularly the youth—and within this group, young women between the ages of 15 and 19—continue to be the most vulnerable. It is estimated that over 60% of all new infections occur in youth between the ages of 15 and 25, with young women being infected earlier and at higher rates. Young women between the ages of 15 and 19 are acquiring 24% of all new infections (UNAIDS, 2004).

There is no shortage of data that highlights the prevalence of gender-based violence in rural schools and rural contexts in South Africa. Several studies, including the Scared at School report by Human Rights Watch (2001) and a more recent study by South African Human Rights (2006) draw attention to the ways in which gender inequality as experienced by girls and young women results in high levels of gender violence (Mitchell, 2009). In a book edited by Leach and Mitchell (2006), *Combating Gender Violence in and around Schools*, a key point is made about the need for interventions which place young people's voices at the center. Similarly, Moletsane, Mitchell, Smith, and Chisholm (2008) highlight in their book *Methodologies for Mapping a Southern African Girlhood* the significance of interventions that give a voice to girls to talk about and "make public" issues around gender violence. In particular they make reference to a set of video-making workshops in which girls produce documentaries about such issues as incest ("Speaking the Unspeakable"), but also note that in mixed sex groupings of video-making the girls may well end up as re-victimized. Although there are no chapters in either book that specifically address the use of the Internet, it is clear that approaches that engage girls and that promote reflexivity are the keys. Thus, we wondered how blogs could offer girls a medium in which they could have an imaginative, reflexive, and critical discursive space in contexts where they would otherwise have little voice. We also wondered how the idea of public spaces associated with blogs would work.

WHY BLOGGING?

The use of blogs (web logs)[2] dates back to the mid- to late 1990s, although the study of specific users has been more recent. Since 2003, for example, studies have surfaced on the uses of blogs in university settings, teacher preparation programs, and K-12 classrooms, with a range of research questions and objectives at the intersection of instructional design and practices, technological abilities of teacher and learner, and promotion of learner participant reflection (Coutinho, 2007; Stiller & Philleo, 2003; Tan, 2006; Wassell & Crouch, 2008). Perhaps, the most significant contribution to this literature can be seen in Luehmann's (2008) findings in teacher development which determined that "blogging contributed to [a] teacher's development of her vision and dispositions, led to new understandings of content, pedagogy, and her students, and positively affected her practice by helping her in planning and other decision-making processes" (p. 176). These studies offer significant contributions to the understanding and development of the use of blogs among young adults enrolled in teacher preparation programs and the youth they are being prepared to teach. By keeping online journals for which users control who can have access, who can say what, and what gets published, modified, or deleted, youth are empowered to document their lives, provide commentary and opinions, express deeply felt emotions, articulate their ideas through writing, and form and maintain community forums (Harper, 2005; Nardi, Schiano, Gumbrecht, & Swartz, 2004; Pascarella, 2008).

WHY GIRLS AND BLOGGING?

The literature noted above demonstrates the potential uses of blogs as an imaginative, reflexive, and critical discursive space, given adequate access and education. Indeed, the topic of girls and blogging, while somewhat overlooked in the early work on blogs, as Brandi Bell (2007) highlights, suggests some of the ways in which the idea of the private space associated with girls' writing (e.g., through diaries and journals), might be re-invented as a public and safe space for addressing issues that are critical to the lives of girls and young women. Bell in her essay entitled "Private writing in public spaces: Girls' blogs and shifting boundaries," notes that the somewhat dismissive approach to the private writing of girls and women as explored, for example in Cinthia Gannett's (1994) work in the early 1990s, has been reproduced in relation to the blogs of girls and young women, even though as Lenhart and Madden (2005) emphasize, adolescent girls (at least in the North American context) make up a large portion of blog authors. While data on online behavior are constantly changing, in their 2005 study 25% of online girls between the ages of 15 and 17 were bloggers as compared to 15% of boys of the same age (Lenhart & Madden, 2005).

A study by Bortree (2005) of blogs written by North American adolescents (both male and female) found that girls' blogs were often monologues rather than discussions, and more likely to offer intimate details of the girls' lives. She concluded that the girls' blogs were more like paper diaries. Similarly Cadle (2005), who did an in-depth study of four North American girls' blogs, notes the links between blogs and other forms of personal writing such as diaries and journals. Her interest is in deepening the understanding of how blog writing might relate to issues of identity and literacy. What Bell, Bortree, and Cadle all highlight is that, to date, not enough research has been done on the differences between "paper" writing and writing through the use of digital media, and that what is needed is a more nuanced look at the significance of the private space of diaries and journals and the more public space of the blog. As Bell notes, audience is a key feature of this; girls are not just writing about their personal feelings. They are also interacting with friends and in a sense participating in community building. And although none of the authors above link their findings to other social networks through, for example Facebook and Twitter, we see that community is a commonality: girls do not seem to be blogging "just for themselves."

While the bulk of the work on girls' blogs is on their out-of-school "free time" use of blogs, here we were interested in seeing how girls might use blogs within a more structured setting. Our reasons for doing this rest primarily on the fact that the participants generally lacked access to a "free space" for Internet usage and as such had had no exposure to the idea of blogs outside of our work with their school where there was at least a computer laboratory set up.

DOING FIELDWORK WITH YOUNG PEOPLE AND BLOGS IN RURAL KWAZULU-NATAL

The fieldwork described here was all part of a larger project called Youth as Knowledge Producers, a study that seeks to develop arts-based methodologies with young people in rural schools to create a more youth-centered approach to knowledge production and behavior change in the context of HIV and AIDS. While a core group of pre-service teachers at the University of KwaZulu-Natal had already been involved in a number of arts-based activities such as exploring the use of hip hop, drama, photography and video in their work with learners in school, the blogging workshops were meant to involve the learners and their teachers (as well as the pre-service teachers) more directly. The blogging workshops were carried out in May 2008. As a team we hosted a series of digital media workshops for pre-service teachers, rural youth, and their teachers, which incorporated the development of personal blogs. The main participants of the work we describe here were students from one rural secondary school in the province of KwaZulu-Natal, all learners enrolled in a computer science class, although it is important to note that the school itself was only in the process of getting "wired," and the computer teacher had relatively little experience with the Internet. The component of the project described here included a short introductory session at the school, a Friday night-Saturday residential session at the University of the KwaZulu-Natal, a follow-up session back at their school again shortly after the blogging workshop, and then a focus group with three of the girls some months later.

Here we focus on the blogging activities involving the five girls, Thandi, Grace, Pontso, Lindiwe, and Lungile (pseudonyms). They are Zulu girls, one living in the village around the school, one in a nearby village, and others in a nearby town, requiring them to travel to and from school using public transport. They are all IsiZulu speakers, with English being their second language. Two of the girls are in grade 9 and three in grade 10. They are all 14 or 15 years old. As they revealed in our interviews with them, they enjoy many of the same things common to adolescent girls elsewhere in the world: hanging out with their friends, watching television (in one or two cases where they had television), and "going places." In relation to their "dreams for the future" three of the girls who also take Commerce as a subject dream about becoming, respectively, a chartered accountant, a marketing manager, and an entrepreneur. Typical of many girls in their position, they spoke about wanting to earn enough money to drive a fancy car and to "escape" rural life.

Although they all take computer application technology (CAT) as a subject, none of them had been exposed to blogging before the workshops. At the time of the workshops, the school did not have Internet connectivity and the rural community as a whole still does not have easy access to the Internet. As revealed in interviews with the CAT teachers themselves who also participated in the workshops, they too were not experienced with blogging so therefore were not able to introduce blogging to their students.

Blogging Workshops

Though we had little knowledge of the new media practices of the participants prior to conducting the blogging workshops, we continually spoke in the workshops of the role a blog might play in gaining a more nuanced understanding of community and school issues. Emphasized throughout all the workshops was the nature of using blogging as a *tool* or a device that can be accessed, created, and manipulated, along with carefully planned and critically minded questions which challenge learners/participants to reproduce themselves in an online setting. The benefits from the intrinsic qualities of creating this particular form of new media, that is, to create and manipulate their own discursive, interactive media space, are examined further in this chapter. We asked participants to think of a blog as their own personal web site in which they can represent themselves, their informed judgments, and beliefs, and later share this blog with their peers, and foster online affiliations with other concerned groups or individual bloggers. Drawing from the work of Mitchell, Walsh, and Moletsane (2006), this work acknowledged "the importance of participation of children and young people, as well as those who work with them, in mapping out issues and, more significantly, as protagonists in taking action" (p. 103).

Session 1: Getting Started "How many of you have experienced the Internet?"

The first session was held at the learners' high school in rural KwaZulu-Natal, a one-and-a-half-hour drive from the Edgewood Campus of the University of KwaZulu-Natal. The session was designed to first meet the learners, to introduce them to the basic functions of an Internet browser, such as search engines, e-mail communication, YouTube Web videos, and blogs, and of course to "set the stage" for the weekend workshop that would follow. Using a university laptop and "3G Card," we had made repeated attempts to access the Internet at the high school, with minor success. Students were able to view a Web browser, conduct a Web search, and view a personal blog. Having located a YouTube video, *Vulindlela*, students were excited to listen and view the video despite the choppy connection. For most of the participants, this basic tutorial was their first Internet experience. For this reason, basic computer literacy skills were incorporated into our learning objectives for the upcoming workshops.

Session 2: Friday Evening

During the first "hands-on" session with the learners, the youth as knowledge producer group of pre-service teachers assisted in developing the digital media skills necessary to creating e-mail accounts and conducting basic Internet searches. When asked what a blog was, only one student speculated what it might be: "a Web site for writing reflections, like an online journal." Throughout the session, the two grade 10 teachers in attendance participated in all the activities and discussions, and one of the teachers helped to co-create a community blog, organized around the question: "What is it that you would like to improve in the community of [Vulindlela]?" Students spent 15–20 minutes typing responses and learning the posting features of *Blogger* software. Some of their responses are listed here, and give a sense of the diversity of issues that concern young people, but also the central role that the community itself plays in their concerns:

~ "To put Internet in our computers."
~ "I would like to have more computers."
~ "Anything that can make [the] community happy."
~ "What I like in [Vulindlela] is sports, so I would improve its ground."
~ "I would like to teach my community and motivate them [to learn] how the computer works so that they should be proud of what they [are] doing."
~ "I would like more information [on using] the computer and understanding everything [you're] teaching me."
~ "To learn more in our school and get job opportunities."
~ "I [would] like to improve in motivating the people of [Vulindlela] community about how bad teen pregnancy is."
~ "I [would] like to improve [my] confidence and [we] need other people that can help; and [we] need people that clean our school."
~ "I [would] like to improve our community at [Vulindlela] by [constructing] tarred roads."
~ "[Vulindlela] MUST HAVE A WEB SITE."

The comments posted to the community blog provided us with an immediate survey of the very specific objectives participants had in mind for the workshops—the participatory nature of the workshop design facilitated this process in a learner-centered format. Participants chose the question to post and to which to respond. Though the question was directed to addressing change in their home community, many of the responses target the very social issues we sought to address in the form of various problem-posing activities using blogs. Although the purpose of problem-posing activities often differs depending on the context, objectives, and content of particular learning communities, the same basic pedagogical method is employed. As Pascarella (2009, p. 125) notes, "Problem-posing is a strategy rooted in the works of Paulo Freire, Ira Shor, John Dewey, Lev Vygotsky, and Jean Piaget (among others), educational theorists who advocated for a learner-centered or participatory approach to pedagogy that situates students as "critical co-investigators in dialogue with the teacher" (citing Freire, 1971, p. 68). Successful problem-posing activities foster a learner's ability to participate in critical self-engagement or self-reflection that contributes to developing alternatives to a problem that he or she believes she has a stake in solving (Nixon-Ponder, 2008; Pascarella, 2009).

Session 3: Saturday

In the next session, youth were assisted in the creation of personal blogs by using free online blogging software: http://www.blogger.com. They worked together in pairs on laptops. There they responded in their blogs to four questions: (see Figure 8.1) Learners were provided with a handout titled "We are all affected by HIV/AIDS: Blogging about agency and community." The handout was provided to participants in both English and IsiZulu. Below the title, there is an information box containing definitions, which primarily served as a reference list to guide participants' work and included the following keywords: Agency, AIDS, Blogging, and Community. After having established their blog and entered their first posting by introducing themselves and their blog to the blogging community, learners were given this guide sheet, instructions were reviewed, and the activity was demonstrated using an overhead projector. Participants were asked to select a photograph from those taken in earlier photovoice projects that had taken place in their school (Wang, 1999). As Moletsane, De Lange, Mitchell, Stuart, and Buthelezi (2007) note, in these photovoice projects, youth had been given cameras to take pictures of what they saw as "challenges and solutions to addressing stigma in relation to HIV and AIDS." (It is important to note that under the terms of ethical approval, these images were able to be used in follow-up activities with learners from the same school.) After choosing a photo from those preloaded onto a common blog, students downloaded and reloaded the photo onto their own blogs for the purpose of the problem-posing activity that followed.

Youth as Knowledge Producers: Blogging Workshop
Instructor: John Pascarella

We are all affected by HIV/AIDS: Blogging about agency and community

Agency *n*. the action, medium, or means by which something is accomplished
AIDS *n*. a disease of the immune system caused by infection of the retrovirus HIV, which destroys certain white blood cells and is transmitted through blood or bodily secretions such as semen
Blogging *v*. also known as *web-logging* is the practice of creating and posting onto a self-constructed web page that allows users to post written postings and upload images, sounds, music, videos, hyperlinks, and other digital media using blog hosting software such as Blogger.com or by using a mobile phone
Community *n*. a group of people who live in the same area, share a common background, history, economic/social interests or cultural beliefs

INSTRUCTIONS: Today, you have learned how to create your own personal blog. Using the digital file of a photograph you have chosen, please upload the photograph in a new blog posting on your blog. In addition to adding the photograph, respond to the following prompts/questions in your blog posting:

1. <u>What do you see?</u>: Write a clear description of the objects (places, scenery, rooms, buildings, things, etc) and subjects (persons) you notice in the photograph.

2. <u>What do you know?</u>: Do you think that all people are affected by HIV/AIDS? If so, in what ways are the people depicted in the photograph affected?

3. <u>What do you believe?</u>: How might the people in the photograph play a role in raising HIV/AIDS awareness in their own community? Do you believe that adults play a greater or lesser role than teenagers or children? Why or why not?

4. <u>How can we confront challenges?</u>:
   a. What strategies (language, actions, activities, projects, behaviors, etc.) are effective when dealing with people who have difficulties discussing sex, sexuality, and/or sexually transmitted diseases? Create a list of ideas.
   b. Do you believe that the persons depicted in the photographs are willing to discuss these topics directly and openly with one another? Why or why not?
   c. What responsibilities/obligations do individuals have to one another to raise awareness, confront taboos, and discuss preventions of HIV/AIDS in their community? Elaborate your response.

Figure 8.1 *Blogging workshop worksheet: "We are all affected by HIV/AIDS"*

The worksheet was meant to facilitate the participants' voices by introducing a digital medium with which they had never worked, but had openly expressed interest and motivation (creating a blog). Participants affirmed this objective by producing claims to having a vested interest in furthering HIV and AIDS education in and beyond their own community, as later depicted in Thandi's blog excerpts below. When the workshops ended, we were still left with the question: How does the medium of blogging produce distinctly different outcomes from an open discussion of the same topics using the same questions in their traditional classrooms or school community?

Session 4: Follow-Up Interview at the School

Once we arrived at the high school several days later, the students who had participated in the blogging workshops the weekend before were congregated in the school's computer lab. We conducted a small informal focus group discussion with the learners to elicit their ideas, feelings, or questions or concerns about what they had encountered during the various workshops the weekend prior. When asked "what are the benefits of blogging about HIV and AIDS," several participants agreed that they were more comfortable writing about their thoughts specific to sex and sexuality than discussing these thoughts in their traditional classrooms. They were happy that they had been encouraged to write their blogs in their native language, IsiZulu if they so wished. Nearly half of the bloggers had written their postings in IsiZulu. Most notable from the blogging experience for participants was the feeling of having communicated their knowledge and awareness of HIV and AIDS to a broader (possibly global) audience beyond their immediate rural community.

Session 5: Follow-Up Focus Group Interview: Pontso, Lindiwe, and Lungile

Some months later we return to the high school to interview the girls regarding the success (and shortcomings) of the blogging workshops. Here we report on the responses of three of the girls who participated in a "you can say what you think" focus group interview. Since the workshops in May 2008, Internet access had been supplied to the high school. Though accessibility has been limited by radio signal issues and software challenges in the school's lab, bringing access was a much desired and needed improvement to the school's available resources.

FINDINGS

In this section we explore the engagement of the girls who participated in the blogging workshops. We start with the responses of Thandi (not her real name) and the evolution of her blog, and then include an analysis of a focus group interview with three others girls Pontso, Lindiwe, and Lungile some months later.

Thandi's Blog

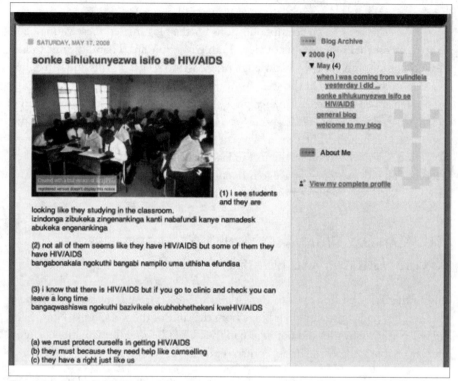

Figure 8.2 *Screen shot of blog*

Considering that this is Thandi's first blog ever, we first recognize the important milestone achieved in creating a blog and then responding to the posted photograph and the questions. We provide a translation of the IsiZulu text below:

> The title, "sonke sihlubkunyezwa isifo se HIV/AIDS," encapsulates the concern of the learner community, "We are all affected by HIV/AIDS."

> (1) I see students looking like they are studying in the classroom. The walls look fine and the learners and the desks have no problem.

> (2) Not all of them seems like they have HIV/AIDS but some of them they have HIV/AIDS. They can be identified by their lack of health when the teacher is teaching.

> (3) I know that there is HIV/AIDS but if you go to clinic and check you can leave [live] a long time. They can be sensitized about how they can protect themselves from HIV /AIDS.

While there is of course a great deal that could be said about each one of Thandi's responses, perhaps what is most critical here is to point to her enthusiasm and engagement, and the statement made in the follow-up session *"We wanted other people to learn from us."* The prompt questions for the blog invited these young people to draw on their own points of view. Framed as they are, Thandi brings to her selected photograph her own knowledge of a classroom such as this and offers her own interpretations of what she sees. As outlined above, her message is that despite the surface appearance of "normality" in a classroom she expects that some learners will have (rather than *could have*) HIV and AIDS, their status suggested in some way by "lack of health." The action of a visit to a clinic, she believes, can offer some protection against or improve life in the face of HIV and AIDS. Even in this her first blog, Thandi assumes a space to influence discourses on HIV and AIDS as she brings forward her own insights for the reflection of herself and others.

"You Can Say What You Think": Reflections from Pontso, Lindiwe, and Lungile

One of the first questions put to the girls in the focus group interview related to whether they had continued their blogs from the time of the workshops. None had, and when asked why they did not maintain their blogs beyond the activities encountered at the blogging workshops, Pontso replied:

> No, we haven't continued. Of course, we didn't have Internet here in our school (then). And, and Internet [*sic*] was installed in our computer late; see, so we haven't got time to…to check our blogs…[…] And also teacher and the others who, who weren't in the project didn't know how to do blogs.

Most notable in Pontso's response is her summation of paying forward the blogging skills she gained from the workshops to others, affirming the very nature of the social purpose of blogging in this context, despite the inactivity on the blogs since. However inactive the blogs now are, the participants' conceptualization of the social purpose of blogging is threaded throughout the girls' responses during this interview when they are asked how they felt about the opportunity to participate:

Lindiwe: Umm…we felt very happy.

Pontso: Excited.

Pontso: Umm…[we were excited] because we never knew about blogging before, and we were just happy that we were going to learn about blogging.

I: Did you think it was going to help you personally?

Lindiwe: It's good to help me communicate with…uh…other people.

Ponsto: And we also learned that you can say what you think about the blog and answer the questions and answer the questions in their blog. I think you can say what you think about their blog. I think that can also help us.

With an understanding of the purpose of the blog, the girls were able to recognize the importance of tapping into this new medium for various reasons including personal ones. The following excerpt taken from the transcripts of the focus group interview provides insight into the material outcomes of the blogging workshops as it affects the lives of the girls since their original participation. Starting with the original purpose of the blogging workshops (addressing social issues adolescent girls face in their rural community), we pose a series of questions about the challenges facing girls today, and move these into an exploration of precisely what role or "how" blogs aid ability to confront those challenges:

I: And what did you think if we now, if we think about today? What do you think are most important challenges that affect your lives here as young girls in this community…today? What are challenges? What are difficulties that you face as young girls today?

The girls include in their responses HIV, teen pregnancy, peer pressure, drugs and alcohol, abuse, and crime in their responses, but also note the nice feeling of living in a familiar place—knowing the people of your community, your family, and school. When asked where the crime, HIV, and violence comes from, Pontso replied, "Most of the people that get affected by HIV are the youth and [most] crime is the youth…teenage pregnancy…teenagers…ja…peer pressure—most of the teenagers get peer pressure from their friends." Lindiwe and Lungile nod in agreement with Ponsto as she makes this claim. We probe Pontso's response, inquiring who the crime happens to, who causes it to happen, and does it happen to people she knows. All girls respond in the affirmative. It does happen to people they know and is carried out by people they know in their community. Lindiwe adds that some crime occurs by their relatives, people she lives with. Noticing Lindiwe's discomfort, Pontso explains: "Because many people are abused by their relatives…and beaten."

I: So thinking about these challenges that you've mentioned, do you think that the questions on that worksheet that you used in the blogging—the ones that you have in front of you now—do you think that those questions on the worksheet actually help you with the challenges that you mentioned? Did you think the blogging helped you?

Lindiwe: Umm…in addressing the challenges?

I: And in what way?…How did the blogging help you to think about and address those challenges?

Pontso: If I think of my community and all, all the challenges that we face like crime and…violence…and other stuff…You see the question [on the worksheet] says 'what do you see?' Like what do I see in the community. And the second question says 'What do you know?' And the third question is 'What do you believe?' And the fourth question 'How can we confront challenges, like how can we confront challenges we face in the community? I think the blogs help us to answer those questions for ourselves.

In Pontso's response, the nature of the problem-posing process is broken down and astutely summarized in her summation, "I think the blogs help us to answer those questions for ourselves." The blogs provided the forum for the problem-posing questions to situate participants as stakeholders in the very problem-solving process for which they were stakeholders in their own communities. Without speaking to other adults who may in fact be abusers or perpetrators of crime, teen pregnancy or the spread of HIV in their community, the blogs offered girls an anonymous forum to explore their thoughts on these topics. In the interview we take note of the nature of the questions examined specific to "confronting challenges."

I: Can you say a little bit more about how it helped?

Pontso: Okay, I think it help us like, to answer the questions like "How can we confront the challenges that we face in our communities?"Like how can we confront, how can we…for example, how can we stop violence in our communities? And how can, how do you believe…like I can say that I believe that…um…[She laughs] the police should arrest all people who commit crime…that's what I believe and I think it help you, it help us to…um… answer the questions for ourselves.

I: Okay, to sort of make your own solutions—

[Girls nodding and agreeing]

Lindiwe:	Ja…the…these questions, it help us a lot because we can… it is easy to answer.
I:	In what way does it help you address the problems, the challenges that you face?
Lindiwe:	It…it helped me to…like…on what do you believe…it helped me on what I believe in…]
Pontso:	I also think it help us in a way that…uh…you can think [for] yourself…If you answer like the fourth question, if you answer the fourth question: "How can we confront challenges?" like I cannot say what Lindiwe thinks but what I think so I think it also help us in that way…so of answering the questions the way you think and how the challenge, how do they challenge you as an individual.

The interviewer goes on to raise questions about the nature of the blog as a forum for expression:

I:	Okay…so some people said during the project that it was easier to talk about issues on HIV on the blog. Was that the case for you?…It's easier to talk about HIV on the blog than to talk about it outside the blog?
Lungile:	Yes. I think…I think many people in our communities still don't understand HIV and still don't understand that we should talk about HIV and AIDS so when you, when you are talking about it in a blog, nobody sees you [laughs a bit along with other girls], knows you, so it is easier to talk about it.
Lindiwe:	Ja, and, it, it, it is easy to talk about HIV on a blog because if you talk to the, to people about it…people do not understand it…
I:	And what do you mean by that?
Lindiwe:	Some, some people do not believe that HIV…ja, HIV kills. So if you talk about AIDS to them they think—
Lungile:	It discriminates you…
Lindiwe:	Ja, they, they…discriminate you like if you have HIV and people know that you are HIV-positive, they, they discriminate you.
I:	So it is easier to talk on the blog?

All girls:	Yes.
I:	...than to talk face-to-face?
All girls:	Yes.
I:	Now who would read the blogs? The people who need to know? About HIV?

Lungile and Lindiwe: Yes.

Lungile:	Most of them. Most of the people who want to know about HIV will obviously read the blog. Um...and also those people who are HIV positive want information on HIV and AIDS, want like —maybe if I want to help someone who is HIV and AIDS, I go to the blog about HIV and find information how to help, how to prevent, how to do anything that involves HIV and AIDS so I go and help the person who is HIV-positive.
I:	I know the English is a little bit tough [Girls laugh] and that you've got the words in Zulu, but you are doing wonderfully, and it doesn't matter if we...struggle with the words...it's fine...I think you are doing wonderful. So I just want to ask another question: Do you think there is a special place or a particular use for blogs in addressing sexuality and HIV and AIDS in schools?...Do you think blogs are good in the school...to get to understanding sexuality and HIV and AIDS?
All girls:	Yes.
I:	Why?
Lungile:	Because...um...I cannot start to—if I am HIV-positive, I cannot tell my friends in school like "Guys, I'm HIV-positive." So if I go to a blog and write about those stuff, other people like...um...other children from school who, who hate people HIV-positive, maybe they can go to the blogs and learn about HIV-positive, HIV and AIDS and...learn that they should not discriminate people that are HIV-positive. They should love them, respect them, treat them as equal people, ja.
Lindiwe:	And so learners can have more information on HIV.
I:	Okay...so it is a source of information. [Girls agreeing] And so who puts the information on the blogs?

Lungile: Um…us. [Girls laugh]

I: So it's your knowledge that you want to put up there—and what if you see something that's incorrect on the blog? What if you see information about HIV that's incorrect? How do you respond to that?

Lungile: I'll try to respond…I'll tell them that what they have written is wrong, and tell them why don't say that.

I: So you can actually begin a debate on the blog…about some issue that is misunderstood?

All girls: Yes.

I: If we look at the bigger picture in the world, the work in other parts of the world—Canada, where you know Claudia comes from—and elsewhere suggests that blogs are good tools especially for girls to talk about their issues. Um…what do you think…about blogs being especially good for girls?

Lungile: Ja…because…um…girls are…the most people who face those challenges, HIV and AIDS [Interviewer agreeing] and they, girls also love talking so . . .

I: So, so you say girls face the biggest challenges? In HIV and AIDS and of course—

Lungile: Teenage pregnancy.

I: And, of course, teenage pregnancy. And you say they like talking…Okay…anything else?…How it's a good tool for girls…

Lungile: I think it is um…it is good for girls because…most of the people don't really see what girls believe in and what they think so…ah…so most of the girls are uh like that thing whereas most of the girls who blogging help them so they can communicate and tell people what they think, what they believe in because many people if they talking face-to-face—like if a girl can tell someone like an old man, 45-year-old man that HIV and AIDS kills, that man won't believe her. So if she, if she goes to a blog and then writes that HIV and AIDS kills then there are people who will read that blog…and maybe…believe her.

I: So you think that the voice will be better heard?

Lungile: Yes.

I: In a blog. The voice of a girl. Because in society girls don't often have a voice?

All girls: Yes. [Smiling]

While we would of course have preferred to have the statement "because in society girls don't have a voice," we acknowledge some of the challenges of posing the questions in English and having the girls respond in English—and of course some of the formality of a focus group interview as opposed to, say, the use of photovoice or some other more participatory approach to data collection (Mitchell, Walsh, & Moletsane, 2006). Our sense, however, is that the girls have offered some clear ideas about why having a voice through blogging has such potential in their setting and for them as girls.

DISCUSSION: REFRAMING SEXUALITY EDUCATION IN A DIGITAL AGE

We want to highlight the idea of girls as resources to themselves (as knowledge producers). While as noted above there is no shortage of literature on the significance of knowledge and information about sexuality as a necessary pre-condition to addressing HIV and AIDS (Mitchell & Pithouse, 2009), there remain few interventions that regard the social functions of technology as part of the solution. It would be difficult to draw too many conclusions from any one of the blogs produced as part of the project we describe here. But one area around which there is a great deal of consensus amongst policy makers in education in South Africa is the need for access to technology. Lessons elsewhere, however, suggest that unless people see a use for technology in their lives, mere access will never be enough. In the case of Thandi and the other girls in her group we see that the communicative functions of blogging are crucial. Mary Celeste Kearney (2009) in her work notes that adolescent girls are some of the most prolific users of social networking tools, and notes that it is the communication component that is the point. Imagine Thandi, Grace, Pontso, Lindiwe, and Lungile as five girls in this small rural school in the middle of the most rural province in South Africa being able to write about how they are seeing issues around sexual violence, stigma, the difficulty of negotiating the use of condoms and so on and in IsiZulu if they should choose to write in their first language.

Working in a rural district in which the HIV and AIDS prevalence rate is high and where gender-based violence is a part of daily life, the need to create a space for discussing such issues is key to addressing them. This ties in with the focus of the Faculty of Education Research Niche Area, "Every voice counts: Rural teacher education in the age of AIDS," drawing in not only the teachers, but also the youth and the community. We have been particularly interested in working with the youth, because of their vulnerability in terms of gender-based violence and HIV and AIDS, and the importance of engaging them directly as a way to explore their understanding of the pandemic. In so doing we see that having them produce their own knowledge, in this instance using the blog, to individually respond to the four questions posed is a critical entry point. The title of the blog, "We are all affected by HIV/AIDS" underscores the urgency of prevention and intervention, with the participant raising the point that many of the learners in the class could be HIV positive and that this would be visible in their unhealthy appearance (showing the symptoms of HIV). A critical point though is that the participant is clearly aware that help is available in the form of antiretrovirals (ARVs). The stigma of HIV however often prevents an HIV positive person from accessing the ARVs, as is the case of the rural community in the Eastern Cape as presented through the story of Sizwe in the *Three Letter Plague* (Steinberg, 2008). Turning to the title of the paper, "we want other people to learn from us," positions these youths in a rural community as able to communicate important messages such as this one.

At the same time, the public spaces of the Internet also offer the girls access to other online information about sexuality and HIV and AIDS. While it is beyond the scope of this chapter to map out the other ways in which the private and public come together in relation to sexuality, clearly there are many possibilities beyond blogs for the uses of digital technology in the age of AIDS (Mitchell & Reid-Walsh, 2007; Mitchell, Reid-Walsh, & Pithouse, 2004; Mitchell & Sokoya, 2007; Weber & Mitchell, 2007). As Jenkins, Clinton, Purushotma, Robinson, and Weigel (2006), Buckingham (2007), and many others point out in terms of convergence, we need to take a more integrated approach to digital culture. More than anything, though, we want to highlight the idea that blogging and other uses of new media can be regarded as girl-centered spaces for girls to both identify the issues that they want to explore but also to find solutions. As noted elsewhere, girlhood studies as an interdisciplinary area of research and activism seek to broaden the agenda for ensuring that girls' voices are heard (Mitchell & Reid-Walsh, 2009). As both a media and pedagogical tool, blogs allowed users to be situated as stakeholders in their classroom and their community. Leach and Mitchell (2006) in their study of interventions related to youth and gender-based violence found that "surprisingly few interventions are driven by young people themselves" (p. 9). While blogging in this instance required the involvement of adults to get started, the possibilities for girls to continue on their own seem likely now that the school actually has Internet connectivity.

CONCLUSIONS AND IMPLICATIONS FOR FURTHER RESEARCH

Some of the scenes described in this chapter may seem quite remote from the experiences of girls growing up online in North America and even in other parts of South Africa where there is likely to be easier access to the Internet and the various forms of new media. Clearly the kind of work we are describing above starts first with a school-based initiative or some structured context. What we have tried to show, however, is that regardless of limited access (even in 2008 and 2009), and regardless of the fact that the girls were participating in a crash course on using the Internet, getting an e-mail address and blogging all at the same time, there is a great deal of potential for youth within a participatory culture framework to express their views and perspectives in relation to key areas of health and sexuality. While we recognize the many challenges, and as noted above acknowledge that there is still a great deal to be done in terms of ensuring that rural schools have access to the Internet, we see that the possibility for girls to interact through their blogs with girls in other social and geographic contexts is there, and suggest several implications for further work in these areas. Their expression of "we wanted others to learn from us" signals a sense of ownership, we think, of the issues, and offers up the idea of blogs as a decolonizing tool for social change. This work needs to be further developed in studies of girls and sexuality. In the broader literature on girls and media making (see, for example, the work on video making by Bloustien, 2003; Kearney, 2006), issues related to girls and identity are critical, and although much of the previous literature on girls and blogging looks at the idea of private writing in public spaces as an overarching idea that reframes the extensive body of work on girls and diary writing, we see that there is a need to re-examine girls blogging "in the age of AIDS" as more than simply private writing and connectedness (though both of those are important to the lives of girls and young women). In so doing it is possible to explore further the idea of girls themselves as knowledge producers.

NOTES

1. The interventions that we report on in this chapter (Youth as Knowledge Producers and Every Voice Counts) are part of the work of the Center for Visual Methodologies for Social Change in the Faculty of Education, University of KwaZulu-Natal, in South Africa. Founded in 2004, the vision of the Center is to promote visual methodologies such as photovoice and participatory video in research for social change in southern Africa.
2. Here we refer to a blog or Web log as a unique online format that has evolved from the more pedantic form of a personal online journal to the interactive form of a Web utility that allows users to create multimodal forms of self-expression.

REFERENCES

Bell, B. (2007) Private writing in public spaces: Girls' blogs and shifting boundaries. In S. Weber & S. Dixon (Eds), *Growing up online: Young people and digital technology* (pp. 95–112). New York: Palgrave Macmillan.

Bloustien, G. (2003). *Girl-making*. New York: Berghahn Press.

Bortree, D. S. (2005). Presentation of self on the web: An ethnographic study of teenage girls Weblogs. *Education, Communication and Information, 5*(1), 25–39.

Buckingham, D. (Ed.) (2007) *Youth, identity, and digital media*. Cambridge, MA: MIT Press

Cadle, L. (2005). *A public view of private writing: Personal Weblogs and adolescent girls*. Unpublished doctoral dissertation, Bowling Green State University, Ohio.

CAPRISA (Centre for the AIDS Programme of Research in South Africa), (2006), Retrieved August 18, 2008, from http://www.caprisa.org/Projects/women_and_aids.html#.

Coutinho, C. (2007). Infusing technology in pre-service teacher education programs in Portugal: An experience with weblogs. In R. Craslen et al. (Eds.), *Proceedings of the 18th International Conference of the Society of Information Technology and Teacher Education*, SITE 2007 (pp. 2027–2034), Chesapeake, VA: AACE.

Freire, P. (1971). *Pedagogy of the oppressed*. New York: Seabury.

Gannett, C. (1994). *Gender and the journal: Diaries and academic discourse*. Albany, NY: State University of New York.

Harper, Jr., V. B. (2005, The new student-teacher channel. *T. H. E. Journal, 33*(3) 30–32.

Human Rights Watch. (2001). *Scared at school: Sexual violence against girls in South African schools*. New York: Human Rights Watch.

Jenkins, H., Clinton, K., Purushotma, R., Robinson, A., & Weigel. M. (2006). Confronting the challenges of participatory culture: Media education for the 21st century. *Building the field of digital media and learning: An occasional paper on digital media and learning*. MacArthur Foundation. http://www.digitallearning.macfound.org/atf/cf/%7B7E45C7E0-A3E0-4B89-AC9C-E807E1B0AE4E%7D/JENKINS_WHITE_PAPER.PDF

Kearney, M. C. (2009), Malina Obama, girl photographer. Retrieved August 7, 2009, from http://flowtv.org/?p=2360

Kearney, M. C. (2006). *Girls make media*. New York: Routledge.

Leach, F., & Mitchell, C. (2006). Situating the study of gender violence in and around schools. In F. Leach & C. Mitchell (Eds.), *Combating gender violence in and around schools* (pp. 3–12). London: Trentham Books.

Lenhart, A., & Madden, M. (2005). *Teen content creators and consumers*. Washington, DC Pew Internet and American Life Project.

Luehmann, A. L. (2008). Blogs' affordances for identity work: Insights gained from an urban teacher's blog. *The New Educator, 4*, 175–198.

MacQueen, K., & Abdool Karim, Q. (2007). Adolescents and HIV clinical trials: ethics, culture, and context. *Journal of the Association of Nurses in AIDS Care, 18*(2), 78–82.

Mitchell, C. (2009). Geographies of danger: School toilets in sub-Saharan Africa. In O. Gershoern & B. Penner (Eds.), *Ladies and gents* (pp. 62–74). Philadelphia: Temple University Press.

Mitchell, C., & Pithouse, K. (2009). *Teaching and HIV&AIDS*. Johannesburg: Macmillan.

Mitchell, C., & Reid-Walsh, J. (2007). Culture and digital technologies in the age of AIDS. In S. Weber & S. Dixon (Eds.), *Growing up on line* (pp. 195–210). New York: Palgrave Macmillan.

Mitchell, C., & Reid-Walsh. J. (2008). Girl method: Placing girl-centred research methodologies on the map of Girlhood Studies. In J. Klaehn (Ed.), *Roadblocks to equality: Women challenging boundaries* (pp. 214–233). Montreal: Black Rose Books.

Mitchell, C., & Reid-Walsh, J. (2009). Editorial. *Girlhood Studies, 1*(2), 2–3.

Mitchell, C., Reid-Walsh, J., & Pithouse, K. (2004). "And what are you reading, Miss? Oh, it is only a website." Digital technology as a South African teen's guide to HIV/AIDS. *Convergence, 10*(1), 191–202.

Mitchell, C., & Sokoya, G. (2007). New girl (and boy) at the Internet café: Digital divides, digital futures. In S. Weber & S. Dixon (Eds.), *Growing up on line* (pp. 211–225). New York: Palgrave Macmillan.

Mitchell, C., Walsh, S., & Moletsane, R. (2006). Speaking for ourselves: A case for visual arts-based and other participatory methodologies in working with young people to address sexual violence. In F. Leach & C. Mitchell (Eds.) *Combating gender violence in and around schools* (pp. 103–112). London: Trentham Books.

Moletsane, R., De Lange, N., Mitchell, C., Stuart, J., & Buthelezi, T. (2007). Photo voice as an analytical and activist tool in the fight against HIV and AIDS stigma in a rural KwaZulu-Natal school. *South African Journal of Child and Adolescent Mental Health, 19*, 19–28.

Moletsane, R., Mitchell, C., Smith, A., & Chisholm, L. (2008). *Methodologies for mapping a Southern African girlhood*. Rotterdam: Sense.

Nardi, B. A., Schiano, D. J., Gumbrecht, M., & Swartz, L. (2004). Why we blog. *Communications of the ACM, 47*(2), 41–46.

Nixon-Ponder, S. (2008, November 18). Teacher to teacher: Using problem-posing dialogue in adult literacy education. *Ohio literacy resource center*. Retrieved February 2, 2009, from http://literacy.kent.edu/Oasis/Pubs/0300–8.htm

Pascarella, J. (2008). Confronting the challenges of critical digital literacy: An essay review. *Educational Studies, 43*(3), 246–255.

Pascarella, J. (2009). *Blogging as critical praxis: Becoming a critical teacher educator in the age of participatory culture*. Unpublished doctoral dissertation, McGill University.

Steinberg, J. (2008). *Three letter plague*. Jeppestown, Johannesburg: Johnathan Ball.

Stiller, G. M., & Philleo, T. (2003). Blogging and blogspots: An alternative format for encouraging teacher reflective practice among preservice teachers. *Education, 123*(4), 789–798.

Tan, A. (2006). *Does scaffolded blogging promote preservice teacher reflection? Examining the relationships between learning tool and scaffolding in a blended learning environment*. Unpublished doctoral dissertation, Indiana University.

Tobin, J. (2000). *Good guys don't wear hats: Children's talk about the media*. New York: Teachers College Press.

UNAIDS (2004). *Facing the future together: Report of the Secretary General's task force on women, girls, and HIV/AIDS in Southern Africa*. Geneva: Joint United Nations Programme on HIV/AIDS.

Wang, C. (1999). Photovoice: A participatory action research strategy applied to women's health. *Journal of Women's Health, 8*(2), 185–192.

Wassell, B., & Crouch, C. (2008). Fostering connections between multicultural education and technology: Incorporating weblogs into preservice teacher education. *Journal of Technology and Teacher Education, 16*(2), 211–232.

Weber, S., & Mitchell, C. (2007). Imaging, keyboarding, and posting identities: Young people and new media technologies. In D. Buckingham (Ed.), *Youth, identity, and digital media*, (pp. 25–48). Cambridge, MA: MIT Press.

CHAPTER NINE

Blogrings as Virtual Communities for Adolescent Girls

JACQUELINE RYAN VICKERY

Girls' blogs provide just one entry point into analyzing the creation of communities in online spaces. Deciphering what constitutes a blogging community can be challenging for many reasons, primarily because of the fluid nature of blogs which do not have clear boundaries, shared space, or clear membership. Additionally the disembodied identities and audiences complicate traditional notions of community, thus begging the question: How are blogs enabling a sense of community? Assuming girls create communities via blogs my next question is why do these communities matter? More specifically, what are the social and/or cultural implications of these online blogging communities for adolescent girls, specifically with relation to their sense of identity?

Arguably, blogging and online communities have the potential to be particularly significant for adolescent girls. Psychologists have noted that during adolescence girls often experience a loss of voice and support (Brown & Gilligan, 1992; Gilligan, 1982; Iglesias & Cormier, 2002), but journaling has been cited as a potentially positive intervention for combating the silencing effects of girlhood (Belenky, Clinchy, Goldberger, & Tarule, 1986). In many ways blogging can be viewed as an evolution of journal writing, although, unlike journaling, blogging has the potential to offer a community space for girls to find support beyond the limitations of a journal. However, a reoccurring question is to what extent do blogs just provide girls a space to dump their emotions thus reinforcing their silence? Or can this space take the shape of a supportive and empowering discursive community that transcends their loss of voice? In other words, girls are speaking but is anyone listening?

To answer these questions I conducted a discursive analysis of three girls' blogs. I primarily considered the community building aspects of the blogs and also recognize that identity and community coexist in a symbiotic relationship. Erikson (1968) argued identity is formulated and constructed by individuals, but must also be confirmed by others—the community. While I was primarily concerned with community this is not to suggest that identity and community are mutually exclusive; instead I recognize the two emerge and develop in tandem with each other, but for the purpose of recognizing community in its own right, I tended to avoid much identity discussion except as a basis for discussing community aspects.

CONCEPTUALIZING ONLINE COMMUNITIES

As part of analyzing online communities, I turn to Benedict Anderson's (1991) *Imagined Communities*. For Anderson, modern day communities do not consist of quotidian face-to-face interactions; instead members hold an imagined affinity for the community. Although he was writing before the rise of the Internet, his recognition and definition of communities as imagined is significant not only because it redefines a modern day understanding of community, but also because this understanding opens up a space for analyzing disembodied communities as they exist in virtual spaces as well.

Howard Rheingold's definition of community is strikingly similar to Anderson's in that community is "a group of people who may or may not meet one another face to face, and who exchange words and ideas through the mediation of computer bulletin boards and networks" (1996, p. 414). Here again, community is not defined by the physicality of embodied interactions, but through affinity and disembodied communications. Rheingold takes an optimistic and hopeful approach to virtual communities in ways that do not necessarily problematize some of the inherent difficulties that emerge in disembodied communities. For example, how does limited access to the Internet shape and define who is able to participate in virtual communities? And how do virtual communities define their identities and borders? Undoubtedly, the nature and significance of virtual communities is still a rather contested subject.

Very early computer-mediated communication research (Beniger, 1987; Healy, 1997; Peck, 1987) suggested that virtual communities were somehow less "authentic" than "real" (i.e., face-to-face) communities. For example, Healy (1997) says, "real" community entails more than the "voluntary association of like-minded individuals" (p. 61). Additionally, some early computer-mediated communication research

(Doheny-Farina, 1996) suggested "real" communities were bound by the containment of place. As Dohney-Farina state:

> A community is bound by place, which always includes complex social and environmental necessities. It is not something you can easily join. You can't subscribe to a community as you subscribe to a discussion group on the net. It must be lived. It is entwined, contradictory, and involves all our senses. (p. 37)

While I agree with Doheny-Farina's argument that communities are "complex," and must be "lived," I posit that certain virtual experiences, such as blogging, transcend the necessity for place as an indicator of community. While not all bloggers would consider their blogging experience to necessarily be a "community experience," some blogging communities can occupy a shared space that opens up the possibilities for "real" community experiences to emerge.

Thus, recognizing that communities—both virtual and offline—can transcend the boundaries of place, I turn to Nancy Baym (1998) in order to further define what constitutes a community. She argues that virtual communities develop around a shared cultural text, experience, discourse, and identity, all of which create a sense of belonging. This sense of belonging becomes a vital component of community, and this belonging comes from shared discursive practices and constructs as defined by the community. Shared bonds within virtual communities are created through the evolution and maintenance of functional communicative spaces. In the words of Baym (1998), "it is these stable patterns of social meaning, manifested through a group's ongoing discourse that enables participants to imagine themselves part of a community" (p. 62). Because blogs are primarily text-based, discursive practices, girls are able to create communicative spaces to share experiences and identities. As Lister, Dovey, Giddings, Grant, and Kelly (2003) state, "If it is assumed that discourse shapes social reality then particular discursive practices shared by a group may be said to construct a social reality, and that reality, it can be argued, would constitute a community" (p. 174). Through the discourses of girlhood and adolescence, some girls in blogging communities create a sense identity and belonging, and thus community.

Efimova and Hendrick (2005) have also found that virtual communities do not necessarily form around cultural artifacts, but as Baym has noted, they form around discursive constructs such as age or gender. "In comparison with many other types of online communities (e.g. those forming around forums or chat rooms), weblog communities emerge from connections between weblogs and their authors, and not around a single shared space" (Efimova & Hendrick, 2005, pp. 2–3). Additionally, they also note the simultaneity of blogs as both public and private spaces. Bloggers reveal private information by telling their stories but they often go to great lengths to guard their embodied identities (name, location, age, etc.). Scheidt (2006) agrees that the "writers elevate the private into the public sphere by their choice to [write] on the weblog" (p. 207). By occupying a public space, girls have opportunities to construct identities and communities in a more visible manner. This is significant because, historically speaking, girls have often been socialized to be "seen and not heard" (Brown, 1991; Kearney, 2006). Moreover, adolescents have had few opportunities to speak in such a public manner (Stern, 2008). The hybrid public and private spaces in which girls choose to publish their blogs are a testimony to their insistence upon being heard.

With all of this research as the foundation for analyzing girls' blogs, it becomes evident that girls' blogs are at least, in theory, virtual communities. However, practical analysis becomes a little more difficult to pinpoint tangible evidence that would suggest that girls feel they belong to a blogging community. Scholars (Bortree, 2005; Huffaker & Calvert, 2005; Stern, 1999) tend to focus on blogs and their precursor personal webpages as places for identity formation. Susannah Stern's (1999) work on girls' homepages is to a certain degree applicable to blogging communities and thus worth addressing. She found that, similar to blogs, girls use home pages as a space to negotiate their identities and, through the experience of identity construction, the girls also form communities. Home pages, like blogs provide girls with an audience and offer a place for their voices to be heard. Because of the shared experiences and the presence of an audience, I argue that blogrings also facilitate the creation of community structures. In a later study Stern (2008) analyzed girls' blogs which included a discussion of the audience. After taking down her blog, one girl Stern interviewed said, "I felt like as long as I had the blog, I had an audience—and having an audience made me feel as if what I was saying was important. Without it, I don't feel anyone is listening to what I say anymore" (p. 104). Thus Stern's study supports the argument that, in part, girls choose to blog because they desire an audience (i.e., they want to be heard).

Another useful approach to understanding the hybrid space blogs occupy is Denise Bortree's (2005) argument that moves beyond the notion of public/private spheres, but rather argues that blogs exist as interpersonal communication within the confines of mass communication. She notes girls' awareness of the dual nature of their audience—targeted both to friends (interpersonal communication) as well as to a larger unknown audience (mass communication). This recognition of the dual audience is significant in understanding how bloggers present and perform their identities while negotiating the private and public self. The acknowledgment of the visible and invisible, or perhaps known and unknown, audience also contributes to the emerging community-building aspect of blogs. Thus, I would like to extend the conversation by analyzing the content of girls' blogs to move beyond mere recognition of an audience, but rather I intend to explicitly identify indicators of a community. Little research has explicitly addressed the community building aspects of girls' blogs and the ways in which girls police and regulate the boundaries of the communities. Perhaps one reason for placing identity negotiation at the forefront of blog research is because it is so difficult to define the actual parameters of blogging communities, but certainly the community aspects of blogs warrant careful consideration in their own right.

Girls' Cultural Production

Lastly, it is important to situate girls' blogs within a larger body of research devoted to girls' media and cultural production. As previously noted, blogs as a form of personal narrative have a lot in common with journaling, however, unlike journaling blogs provide opportunities for girls to create communities. Zine culture serves as a more applicable comparison to blogs and blogging communities by acknowledges girls' media production and community formations prior to digital technologies. Zine culture is part of a counterhegemonic do-it-yourself culture in which girls create, publish, and distribute their own mini-magazines known as zines (Kearney, 2006). Girls often create zines as part of punk-feminist youth culture, Riot Grrrl being one of the most well known. These zines are often handwritten or type-written, hand-drawn, and often incorporate images from commercial media texts. They are often distributed in local bookstores, at concerts, amongst groups of friends, and through mail-based subscriptions.

I would like to suggest that blogs are similar to zines in many ways. For one, girls use both zines and blogs as discursive spaces to negotiate identities and represent themselves in ways that often challenge mainstream representations of girlhood (Kearney, 2006). Second, zines and blogs are both voluntarily self-authored and operate outside of educational or authoritative spaces, and in many ways serve to challenge hegemonic and capitalistic society. Finally, like blogs and blogging communities, zines provide a space for girls to form supportive communities through the negotiation of identities. As Mary Celeste Kearney (2006) writes in her book, *Girls Make Media*, "though female identity is a dominant discursive framework within grrrl zines, many female youth who produce these texts reveal their savvy about zinemaking as a mechanism for experimentations with, rather than simply reflections and thus reproductions of, identity" (p. 154). Thus, unlike journaling which might contribute to the further silencing of girls' voices by providing a pseudo-empowering space in which nobody is actually listening, zine culture, and its successor blogging culture, embrace the notion of the audience and construct a community based solely on the textual practices of writing. Through textual practices, self-authorization, and community, blogs function in a similar manner to earlier zine cultures.

METHODOLOGY

In an attempt to heed Kearney's (2006) call of more attention to girls' media production, combined with an analytical lens focused on community formations, my goal is to apply specific concepts of community and virtual community to girls' blogs in order to identify the specific components of a blogging community and the implications of the communities within girls' lives. I spent countless hours navigating the blogosphere from April 2007 until March 2008 in search of my carefully selected participants. Because the intent of this research was to gain an in-depth understanding of girls' blogs, my sample was not intended to be representative of the girl blogging population writ large, but rather to provide more in-depth insight into a few girls' blogs.

I found the girls' blogs through blog search engines such as Blogarama, AOL RED Blogs (a teen-only blog server), and Google Blog Search. To be considered for selection the blogs had to be authored by girls, and gender had to be explicitly stated or strongly implied (blogs in which gender was unclear were not considered). The girls had to be in high school or could have recently graduated only if it was evident they had maintained their blogs while in high school. Age had to be explicitly stated or strongly implied, and I considered blogs authored by girls aged 14–19 years. All blogs had to be written only in English and had to be written in a style that was easy to read and decipher (as opposed to blogs written in more than one language or blogs that used codes and excessive abbreviations that required exclusive knowledge to read). Race and ethnicity were not considered as criteria for selection because this information was not often disclosed. Additionally, the blogs had to have been maintained for at least six months, had to be updated at least three times a month, and had to include comments from readers.

This chapter is part of a larger project for which I gathered an initial sample of nine blogs which met the criteria and which I felt provided meaningful insight into girls' blogging communities. In the interest of space, however, I have only included three girls and their respective blogs in this chapter. These three were chosen for the richness of their blogs and the visibility of their blogging communities. I used Google Reader to archive the girls' blogs so I could read all of their entries dating back to the beginning of the blog. While analyzing the blogs and blogging communities I paid particular attention to instances in which the girls explicitly addressed their audiences and/or the blogging communities. I also read the comments left by other bloggers, and when possible I read the commenters' blogs in order to determine if the correspondence was mutual. Additionally I analyzed the links girls provided on their blogs as further evidence of a community. I have included several quotes from the girls' blogs and in order to preserve their voices I did not correct grammar or spelling; all quotes are exactly as they appeared on the girls' blogs. In order to protect the girls' privacy and identities, all the names in this study are pseudonyms.

Defining Terms

While reading girls' blogs I noticed an important distinction between what I call blogs written to a *circle of friends* and what I refer to as blogs written to an *audience of strangers*. I chose to only focus on girls who wrote to an audience of strangers and thus included this as an additional criterion for selection. These girls deliberately write to an audience they do not know in their offline lives, and some girls go to great lengths to keep their offline embodied identities anonymous. While they generally still post links to other blogs and receive comments from their readers, it is strikingly evident that they only know their readers via their online lives. I make this distinction for a very important reason: I believe girls who write to an audience of strangers are afforded greater opportunities to negotiate identity, express themselves, and present an identity that is different from their offline identity, therefore, these blogs serve as a potentially more candid platform for analyzing girlhood, girl culture, and represented (online) identities. Likewise, the communities that evolve around these blogs differ from their face-to-face offline communities and provide new opportunities for interpersonal relationships and support. Thus all of the girls included in this study write to an audience of strangers and go to great lengths to hide their embodied offline identities.

One additional term which ought to be defined and explained is blogring. In their earliest form, prior to push button publishing, blogs were essentially a medium whose "currency was links" (Blood, 2004, p. 55). That is, the blog was not so much about content, but rather a way to share links to other common interest sites. Today the sidebar of a blog is still full of links to other blogs of common interest, which makes blogs unique in both form and content. The original intent of blogs often gets ignored, as researchers tend to only focus on their content (daily entries). Understandably, at first glance, the content of blogs appears to be the most significant feature. One cannot even begin to interpret a blog without analyzing the content; however, to truly gain an understanding of a blog's function, the linking aspects must also be taken into consideration. Links connect blogs with other blogs, writers with readers, and knit together the blogging community, that has come to be known as a blogring (Blood, 2004).

Since Blogger (now owned by Google) introduced push-button publishing in late 1999, user-friendly blog interfaces allow for commenting, permalinks, linking to other sites (without having to hand-code the links), private messaging, and tag boards, thus more easily facilitating the creation of blogrings. Only recently have blogrings become officially sanctioned and organized by servers (primarily Xanga and LiveJournal), but still, the majority of blogrings are informally created and discovered by following the links from one blog to another. While navigating through the different blogs it was easy to recognize the common interests connecting them. Blogs written to an audience of strangers, like the blogs in my sample, tended to link to other blogs that remained very similar in theme and tone, and it was evident that the girls did not know each other offline. However, there was an unspoken understanding that a girl should provide links to other blogs she reads, and in turn girls would provide a link to her blog. In his research on girls' websites, Walsh (2006) noted that, "for a community of practice to operate, it must generate and appropriate a shared repertoire of ideas, practices, and loyalty" (p. 7). Informal blogrings serve that very purpose by creating a navigable community of like-minded bloggers who get to know one another by reading each other's blogs. It is imperative to take these features into account when interpreting the community aspect of blogs.

JASMINE'S BLOGGING COMMUNITY

The first blog I analyzed was written by a 16-year-old African American girl in California, named Jasmine. Her blog had over 27,000 visits in a year, and her entries tended to average about two comments each. It was not uncommon for Jasmine to specifically address her audience and/or reference specific comments that she has received. For example, on February 10, 2007, her blog had received over 300 hits (visits) in one day. In response Jasmine wondered "who the hell reads her blog" and then followed this up with a statement which assured her readers she meant no offense, she was just surprised people wanted to read what she had to say. She went on to say she worried someone from school would read her blog and then know all her "hopes and dreams and that would suck." Jasmine acknowledged that she had a lot of readers, and in this same post she asked her readers to comment more, "If you people actually like my writing, why don't you comment? It makes me feel better about what I write and it motivates me to write more!" Thus, while Jasmine was pleased to have an audience, she also made it clear she desired feedback. Despite her request for more comments, this post only elicited two comments from readers, both of which were encouraging and praised her for her writing. However, a couple of weeks later on February 26, 2007, a girl who referred to herself as jen210 left a comment on an entry that actually referenced the February 10th post. The comment read:

> I like your formats in writing; for the most part you stay on topic, and sh*t girl! You really know how to say what you think...Your blog is awesome. And don't find it "mildly shocking" for me to be reading this, because hell, some people do actually take the time to read about your life (not that I am a stalker or anything haha...) I don't judge people, (but if you

do count this as judging you, so be it;) you seem like a down-to-earth, outspoken, strong-hearted chica who knows her stuff! Keep it up.

Jasmine's blog received a lot of comments similar to this one; comments telling her she was a good writer and that they enjoyed reading her blog.

In other instances readers left her advice, for instance, on January 30, 2008, Jasmine wrote an entry she titled, "life is an awful, ugly place not to have a best friend." She discussed the fact that her friends have always helped her get through life, but now she felt she no longer had the support of her friends. "My friends were my foundation, the one thing that I could look forward to in my otherwise piece of sh*t life. But now? My foundation is kind of non-existent." It could be argued in part that Jasmine was blogging because she had lost the support of her friends; she often mentioned that she felt she had nobody to talk to anymore. Additionally, Jasmine felt all of her friends were changing and she was often conflicted about her own morals, which further complicated her friendships. By discussing these moral dilemmas and feelings of loneliness, her blogging community, at least to a certain degree, was compensating for a loss of support in her offline community. In this same post a reader told Jasmine that perhaps she should try to talk to her friends because maybe they felt the same way:

> As hard as it is, I think you either need to a) talk to your current friends about how you feel. It'd be an awkward conversation, but maybe they don't realize you feel that way, or maybe they feel that way too and you guys could work it out. I mean, what's the worse [sic] that could happen? They go on ignoring you? …It couldn't hurt [to try]. Cuz you're right, everyone needs friends to survive!"

A week later on February 7, 2008, Jasmine brought her blog readers up to date and announced that she talked to one of her friends about her recent dilemmas and she felt much better. I do not want to suggest that Jasmine only talked to her friend because a reader suggested it, however, Jasmine obviously used her blog as a space to identify her own emotions and in so doing, worked through problems. And so it is possible that through writing out her feelings on her blog and receiving support and encouragement from her blogging community, Jasmine found the motivation she needed to confront her friend about their recent problems.

However, regardless of the potential offline benefits, it was clear that Jasmine felt a part of her blogging community which was significant in its own right. She thanked readers for comments, asked them to comment more often, apologized to them when she was in a bad mood, and apologized when she went a long time without updating. Apologizing to her readers revealed a sense of loyalty that Jasmine felt toward the community. One girl who commented on Jasmine's blog lamented the fact she lost all her readers because she did not update for over a month. Therefore, frequent updates were an expected aspect of this blogging community. I found further evidence of this on Jasmine's blog with relation to the links; I noticed Jasmine removed links if the blogs were not frequently updated. In other words, if a blog remained "silent" (referring to a blog that had not been updated in a long time) or went "dead" (a blog that was completely abandoned), then Jasmine removed the link from her blog.

At the time of data collection, Jasmine provided links to eight other blogs. Because the comments on the blog allowed me to see a brief profile of who the commenter was, I was able to conclude that Jasmine's blogging was mostly comprised of other adolescent girls. This is not to suggest that males and/or adults were not reading her blog, however, if they were they were not leaving comments, and so my analysis was limited to the visible community—those who leave comments. Likewise, I did not want to presume that Jasmine did not read male or adult blogs; however, she chose to only provide links to other adolescent female blogs on her site, which is further evidence of her blogging community. I also want to note that Jasmine did not link a blog simply because someone had left a comment on her blog. There were plenty of commenters whose blogs Jasmine chose not to link on her own, and while I do not know for sure why Jasmine chose to link a particular blog and not another, I noted that gender, age, anonymity, and frequent updates were common denominators in all of the blogs on her blogroll. And while I did not read all of the blogs in her blogging community as closely as I followed Jasmine's, I noticed the other girls' blogs appear similar to Jasmine's in that they were spaces for girls to negotiate their identities as adolescent girls. Additionally, Jasmine's community provided positive and supportive feedback. It appeared that the bonds in her community revolved around discourses of age and gender (adolescence and female), and the bloggers identified with each other because of and through affinity spaces, as Gee (2004) would refer to them.

Additionally through the course of reading Jasmine's blog I discovered very late into the study that she was the only African American in her grade and one of eight African Americans in her entire school. She often alluded to the fact that she felt socially isolated not only because her friends were changing (as previously mentioned), but also because she did not fit in with the White community of her school. Thus in many ways Jasmine was isolated from her offline embodied community and was seeking a supportive online community via her blog.

For Jasmine, her blogging community gave her the encouragement to take her online voice to her offline community. While she often expressed feelings of frustration, isolation, and marginalization at school and with her friends, she used her blog as a space to identify her emotions and find a sense of belonging. She explicitly sought out advice from her blogging community and acknowledged the importance of her online relationships which she had made via her blog. Furthermore, her blog readers provided assurance that she was not alone in her experiences, but rather others were also going through similar situations and empathized with her. The ways in which Jasmine interacted with her readers demonstrated her desire for a community and not just an audience.

LIZ'S BLOGGING COMMUNITY

The next girl in this study was Liz who started her blog in November 2005, at the age of 13. As of February 2008, she had over 300 entries and was then 16 years old. While my discussion of the blogging community has been positive thus far, I do not want to give the impression that blogging communities are always positive or harmonious. As Liz's blog demonstrates, the community can misinterpret information and cause frustration for its members. The blogging community on Liz's blog was active and visible, which provided a lot of valuable insight into both her view of the community, as well as the function of the community. In 2005, when Liz was only 14 years old, her blog was featured on the home page of AOL RED blog, which helped attract a lot of readers to her blog. In response to the increased readers Liz wrote, "O my gosh. I am so shocked. I really haven't smiled this big all day. I can't even believe that my blog was chosen. AOL you made my day: D" (November 29, 2005). During the immediate months following AOL's promotion of her blog Liz received a lot of comments, sometimes as many as 10 or more per entry; in later updates she averaged about two comments per entry. Because of the increase in comments (and readers), I was afforded more insight into the nature of the blogging community because it was a lot more active during this time than the other blogs I address.

During this time period Liz was going through some painful experiences and had begun to question the idea of love. In her own words:

> i just want to say. its not that I don't love. It's not that I don't want to love. I am afraid to love. I afraid of getting hurt again. Boys and crushes. They didn't break my heart they didn't make me scared to love. My parents. family and friends. they made me afraid to love. afraid to get hurt. and somehow I keep falling in love with these things over and over. and every time I end up hurting. with a broken heart. when I give something everything I am and everything I have I always end up in tears. (November 28, 2005)

Her emotional post elicited a lot of feedback from readers who offered her support and advice. Over the next few entries she continued to use her blog as a place to express her pain and negotiate what she wanted to do about it. At first she was grateful for the comments and made a point to thank her readers for caring about what she had to say and for offering support. Liz tended to write in a poetic and often vague way and although the quote above specifies to whom she was referring (her friends and family), a lot of her entries were more elusive; this led readers to assume that her broken heart must have been about a boyfriend or a crush. She got a lot of comments offering romantic advice as well as readers who shared their personal breakup stories. Despite Liz's attempts to clarify the source of her hurt, many readers did not pay attention. On December 1, she wrote, "I'd really like for the comments about some crush that I guess I seem to have to stop. down there I explained why I don't trust love. please I am really tired of reading about things I never even said." However, the comments about her "crush" or "ex" did not stop. I speculate this was most likely because people came to her blog, read only one entry, and assumed her heartache was caused by a boy (which of course reveals the romantic and heteronormative nature of this particular blogging community). Eventually she was frustrated enough to turn on the community in a very emotional and passionate plea for the "boyfriend" comments to stop. It was long but to preserve the intent of the post and to provide Liz with a voice in this paper, I include it in its entirety:

> ok. that's the last time I hope to ever get a comment about me being crushed by some guy. HOW MANY TIMES DO I HAVE TO SAY THIS IS NOTHING TO DO WITH A GUY. OPEN UP YOUR MINDS LOVE ISNT ALWAYS ABOUT GUYS. YOU GUYS MAKE ME REDICULOUSLY ANGRY WITH THESE COMMENTS THAT HAVE NOTHING TO DO WITH ANYTHING TO BE HONEST I DONT WANT YOUR ADVICE ON LOVE. YOU DON'T UNDERSTAND ME AND YOU HAVE NO IDEA WHAT MY LIFE IS LIKE. SO JUST STOP. STOP .STOP WITH ALL THESE LOVING GUYS COMMENTS I DONT EVEN NO WHERE U PEOPLE GOT THE IDEA THAT I WAS DYING TO TALK ABOUT LOVE. MY LORD BACK OFF. go ahead AOL take me of featured blogs I really don't care just stop those comments! and please hate me. go ahead and hate me. i am fed up with this and stop leaving comments for me to go to your blog i can't look at 40 peoples blogs and please if you want me to look at your blog make it so i can comment you. (December 3, 2005) (emphasis original)

Not so surprisingly, some members of the community did not respond well to Liz's angry post. A lot of people left comments defending themselves saying they were "only trying to help" and "why is she posting if she doesn't want help?" Although others defended her rant as a justified reaction and agreed with her because they "know how she feels." A couple of readers told her that they have deleted comments they do not like (which is a way to prevent other people from posting similar comments). This was an interesting example of bloggers actually policing and controlling others' voices; thus while some girls exerted a voice via blogs, they were also subject to control from other bloggers.

It can be argued that a community does not really bond until it is forced to defend and thus define itself. Within this particular blogging community the boundaries were defined only when members began to behave in ways that were not approved of by Liz. Similarly, the dialogue within the comments revealed differing viewpoints regarding the nature of the blogging community. For some members of the community the agreement seemed to be that if you were posting an entry online then you opened yourself up to feedback and therefore you had no right to complain if you did not like the feedback the entry elicited. For others in the community, the consensus was that you should only comment if you were familiar with the blogger's situation (by reading an appropriate number of entries), and therefore these members deemed many of the comments on Liz's blog to be "inappropriate" because the readers were unfamiliar with her blog. Additionally, for other members of the community there appeared to be an assumption that it was generally acceptable to ask someone to read your blog. However, general blogging norms have often deemed it bad etiquette to ask someone to link you to their blog. Likewise, Liz was annoyed with the requests and instead asked readers to just send her an e-mail if they wanted to tell her something.

After her rant the number of comments decreased significantly, however, Liz made a point to note that she would delete any comments related to "guy problems" or "guy advice." I do not know if fewer people were commenting, or if Liz was just deleting them, though it was clear that she was still receiving some "guy" comments because she still had to make the occasional plea for them to stop. Also, with relation to this particular blogging community, age surfaced as a discursive indicator of belonging. While Liz was only 14 years old at the time, it appeared that many of her readers were younger (around 11 or 12 years old). Liz was rather dismissive of their advice as well as their blogs because she felt they were "too young" to understand life and love. However, she countered this with an acknowledgment that she was also very young, but her point was that she "did not want advice from 6th graders." Again, the community only regulated its borders when the borders were threatened. To what degree of success the community was able to regulate itself was hard to decipher, but it was clear it attempted to dismiss members who were either "too young" or "too obsessed with guys."

Over two years after these occurrences Liz still had to reestablish the fact that her blog was not about a break up or boy problems, however, she was a little calmer about it in her later posts. She still made an effort to thank her readers and let them know she appreciated their comments. It was quite common for her to respond to a comment on an entry and either offer advice or just reflect upon what has been said. Additionally, she acknowledged that many of her readers helped her through difficult situations. For Liz, her blog was a place to voice feelings she could not express offline, and the online community offered her the support she was seeking. In February 2008, she announced she was going to leave the blogging world, she ended her intended final entry with an apology to her readers as well as advice. She wished her readers good luck and said, "i hope somewhere in these years and pages i have helped you that i still can help you, in here are all my secrets, dreams and troubles how i survived through ending friendships, began new friendships, brought God into my life and so much more" (February 11, 2008). At the very end of her post she told readers they had helped her "find her home." For Liz the blogging community was not just a place to rant, but through the outpouring of emotions, it helped her make sense of who she was. Liz returned to the blog less than three weeks later, and I argue, her writing and the blogging community helped her find a voice—both online and in her offline identities. Thus in many ways her blogging community functioned as a support group for Liz and her readers. Liz's role within the community appeared to be symbiotic in that she sought help while simultaneously attempted to help others. By sharing unique experiences related to both age and gender, the girls created a supportive community for each other.

Liz used her blog as a space to find validation, identify emotions, seek support, offer advice, and make sense of her experiences. Liz clearly valued her blogging community and bonded with other bloggers via shared discourses of femininity and adolescence. Perhaps in a more explicit manner than the other two girls, Liz acknowledged the extent to which she relied on her blogging community to help her through problems. Sometimes this help was in the form of advice, but often this support was found simply in the assurance that Liz knew her blogging community was listening to her; in other words, she knew she had a safe space to share her story. While there were times her community deviated from her desires of what the community should be, the disruptions were indicative of the way the blogging community attempted to define and regulate its boundaries. Again, she explicitly desired her readers to be more than a mere audience, but rather she explicitly acknowledged and addressed her readers as a community.

KRYSTAL'S BLOGGING COMMUNITY

My final participant is 18-year-old Krystal who lived in England; she started her blog in March 2007 and it included over 50 entries as of December 2007. She explicitly stated that she started her blog as a place to discuss her relationship with her girlfriend; a relationship her mother did not approve of, and which, therefore, Krystal kept private. Additionally, Krystal attended an all-girls high school and also kept her relationship with J (the only way she ever referred to her girlfriend) a secret from the girls at her school. Clearly sexuality was the discursive construct through which Krystal's online blogging community was formed. Even the title of her blog was indicative of the fact that she could not discuss her sexuality in her offline life and therefore her blog was a space for her to express her identity in ways not afforded her in offline situations. Krystal provided links to about 15 other blogs and the majority of them were related to Gay, Lesbian, Bi, Trans, and Queer (GLBTQ) communities. For example, they were either links to other personal blogs maintained by self-identifying queer authors, or links to professional blogs which focused on the GLBTQ community (primarily in Western cultures). Because many of the blogs were professional blogs (bloggers who make a living from blogging) they were less likely to be linked back to Krystal's blog or to leave a comment (as compared to Jasmine and Liz's blogging communities). Nonetheless, Krystal had a loyal fan base of readers and her entries averaged ten or more comments each. However, despite providing links to many GLBTQ blogs and websites, Krystal did not include other signifiers that would link her to the GLBTQ culture, such as queer icons. It was only through reading her blog and/or following the links she listed that her queer identity was visible.

Because Krystal's blog followed a narrative format, many of the comments were predictions about the future of Krystal and J's relationship or questions that asked for clarification about something she had discussed on the blog. Overall the comments did not tend to offer advice; likewise, Krystal rarely sought advice. However, her readers were definitely supportive of Krystal and J's relationship. Similar to Liz, the true community surfaced when it was threatened. However, unlike Liz's community which was threatened from the outside. Krystal herself threatened to discontinue the blog. At one point she and J broke up and Krystal took an extended leave of absence from the blogging world. Upon her return her readers enthusiastically welcomed her back, many of whom had been leaving comments inquiring of her whereabouts (virtually speaking). Krystal apologized to her readers for not updating, which was indicative of her loyalty to her readers. One reader who was the fifth to comment on her return entry remarked, "You know, I think the blogging community here should have been more responsive to your royal return. But perhaps they thought you fell off the face of the earth during that brief hiatus" (October 10, 2007). Here a reader explicitly referenced the blogging community and expressed her disappointment in their lack of response. However, given time the number of comments increased. Unfortunately Krystal's return was short-lived (only four more entries appeared) and her relationship with J remained uncertain, although in her final post (at the time of writing) on December 29, 2007, she and J were still together.

For Krystal, the community building aspect of her blog came from just having someone to whom she could tell her story. Per a reader's request, Krystal disclosed more information about her parental situation and the secret nature of her relationship with J. Her parents were suspicious of their relationship and disapproved of homosexual life styles. However, this was not the only reason Krystal hid her relationship from her parents; it was also because she was still unsure of her own sexuality. As she put it:

Most people know when they've "come out", but for me, it's all a bit confusing. I don't quite identify with being a lesbian or bisexual, at least not yet so there has been no need to make any kind of "I'm here and queer" statement to my parents. Except...there's one minor thing—*J*, my girlfriend. (May 7, 2007)

Krystal frequently questioned her own sexuality and acknowledged that her blog was the only place she could discuss her identity. Yet, while she did not elicit advice per se, she appreciated the support she received from the blogging community and felt a sense of obligation to inform the community of her relationship. Other young readers validated Krystal's confusion by relaying their own experiences and (sexual) identities as well.

For Krystal, issues of identity and community were inextricably linked; the blogging community was the only place for Krystal to express her sexual identity (other than with her girlfriend). Thus what was important was not necessarily the comments and feedback that her blog generated, although they were also important, but rather the presence of an audience at all (just knowing someone was "listening" regardless of the feedback). Perhaps equally important was the presence of an online GLBTQ community for Krystal. Not only did she find a place to express herself, but she was also able to read other blogs related to adolescent sexuality and uncertainty. The blogging community (as defined by links not comments) provided Krystal access to information and dialogue she otherwise did not have access to in her offline life. By participating in the GLBTQ community, Krystal found a community through which she could express her identity; a community she was lacking in her offline life. In this way Krystal's blogging identity and community were in many ways more "authentic" than her offline embodied identity and community in which she had to hide her sexuality. It could be argued that Krystal's blog and respective blogging community was the only space she could safely and freely express her sexual identity, which is demonstrative of the significance of her blogging community.

CONCLUSION

In conclusion, the three girls in this study illustrate the significance of online blogging communities. Jasmine, Liz, and Krystal all explicitly addressed their online communities and explicitly acknowledged the import of their respective communities. For these three girls the online blogging communities provided spaces for safe expression and the girls created online communities that differed from their offline communities. For Jasmine, her online community provided the encouragement to take her online voice and express it in an offline community. For Liz, her blogging community provided a safe space to discuss personal issues and find supportive advice. And for Krystal the community provided the only outlet for sexual expressions and identities. Just as identity is fluid, so too are the communities. The nature of the communities appeared to be temporal and always evolving; always redefining themselves.

This study demonstrates the ways in which some girls actively produce media, find their voices, and create communities—communities not often afforded girls in their offline lives. Similar to Stern (1999) and Bortree (2005), I found that the girls in this study used their blogs as spaces of identity negotiation and community building. While their online blogging communities certainly did not replace their need for offline communities, the girls in this study demonstrated the significance of blogs and blogging communities as well as the influence their blogs had on their lives. Their blogs also illustrate the ways in which the girls defined and regulated the discursive boundaries of their respective communities.

All three of the girls expressed feelings of social isolation or marginalization which could be mere coincidence. However, it is also important to consider that the girls in this study all wrote to an audience of strangers and were therefore granted greater opportunities to express identities and form communities which differed from their offline communities. Future research would benefit from knowing the extent to which socially isolated girls choose to blog (to an audience of strangers) and the ways in which blogging communities could be particularly meaningful for otherwise socially isolated girls.

REFERENCES

Anderson, B. (1991). *Imagined communities: Reflections on the origin and spread of nationalism*. New York: Verso.

Baym, N. (1998). The emergence of on-line communities. In S. G. Jones (Ed.), *Cybersociety 2.0: Revisiting computer-mediated communication and community* (pp. 35–68). Thousand Oaks, CA: Sage.

Belenky, M., Clinchy, B., Goldberger, N., & Tarule, J. (1986). *Women's ways of knowing: The development of self, voice, and mind*. New York: Basic Books.

Beniger, J. (1987). Personalization of mass media and the growth of pseudo-community. *Communication Research, 14*(3), 352–371.

Blood, R. (2004). How blogging software reshapes the online community. *Communications of the ACM, 47*(12), 53–55.

Bortree, D. S. (2005). Presentation of self on the web: An ethnographic study on teenage girls' weblogs. *Education, Communication & Information, 5*(1), 25–39.

Brown, L. M. (1991). Telling a girl's life: Self-authorization as a form of resistance. In C. Gilligan, A. G. Rogers, & D. L. Tolman (Eds.), *Women, girls, and psychotherapy: Reframing resistance* (pp. 71–86). New York: Harrington Park.

Brown, L. M., & Gilligan, C. (1992). *Meeting at the crossroads: Women's psychology and girls' development*. Cambridge, MA: Harvard University Press.

Doheny-Farina, S. (1996). *The wired neighborhood*. New Haven, CT: Yale University Press.

Efimova, L., & Hendrick, S. (2005). In search of virtual settlement: A exploration of weblog community boundaries. *Communities and Technologies*. Retrieved February, 20, 2008, from https://doc.telin.nl/dsweb/Get/Document-46041/

Erikson, E. (1968). *Identity: youth, and crisis*. New York: Norton.

Gee, J. (2004). *Situated language and learning: A critique of traditional schooling*. New York: Routledge.

Gilligan, C. (1982). *In a different voice: Psychological theory and women's development*. Cambridge, MA: Harvard University Press.

Healy, D. (1997). Cyberspace and place: The Internet as middle landscape on the electronic frontier. In D. Porter (Ed.), *Internet culture* (pp. 55–72). New York: Routledge.

Huffaker, D. A., & Calvert, S. L. (2005). Gender, identity, and language use in teenage blogs. *Journal of Computer-Mediated Communication, 10*(2). Retrieved November 20, 2007, from http://jcmc.indiana.edu/vol10/issue2/huffaker.html

Iglesias, E., & Cormier, S. (2002). The transformation of girls to women: Finding voice and developing strategies for liberation. *Journal of Multicultural Counseling and Development, 30*, 259–271.

Kearney, M. C. (2006). *Girls make media*. New York: Routledge.

Lister, M., Dovey, J., Giddings, S., Grant, I., & Kelly, K. (Eds.). (2003). *New media: A critical introduction*. New York: Routledge.

Peck, M. S. (1987). *The different drum: Community-making and peace*. New York: Simon & Schuster.

Rheingold, H. (1996). A slice of my life in my virtual community. In P. Ludlow (Ed.), *High noon on the electronic frontier: Conceptual issues in cyberspace* (pp. 413–436). Cambridge, MA: MIT Press.

Scheidt, L. A. (2006). Adolescent diary weblogs and the unseen audience. In D. Buckingham & R. Willett (Eds.), *Digital generations: Children, young people, and new media* (pp. 193–210). Mahwah, NJ: Lawrence Erlbaum.

Stern, S. R. (1999). Adolescent girls' expressions on web home pages: Spirited, sombre, and self-conscious sites. *Convergence: The International Journal of Research into New Media Technologies, 5*(4), 22–41.

Stern, S. R. (2008). Producing sites, exploring identities: Youth online authorship. In D. Buckingham (Ed.), *Youth, identity, and digital media* (pp. 95–118). Cambridge, MA: MIT Press.

Walsh, C. S. (2006). Disrupting girls in virtual communities of practice: Discursive performativity as agency. Retrieved October 21, 2007, from http://www.aare.edu.au/06pap/ wal06500.pdf

SECTION THREE
Online "Spaces" for Girls

CHAPTER TEN

Whyville versus MySpace

How Girls Negotiate Identities Online

JILL DENNER & JACOB MARTINEZ

The best thing is myspace, youtube, & txting. Those are my favorite things about technology.

—PATRICIA, AGE 13

My favorite thing about technology is iphones, DS, computer, MV2, Ipod, Zunes, TV, cars, whyville, youtube, Google, Yahoo.

—ELSA, AGE 12

For Patricia and Elsa (not their real names) technology is invisible—it is not *what* they do…it is woven throughout their lives (Herring, 2004; Lewis & Fabos, 2005). Many in their generation focus less on what they can do with technology, and more on who they are and how to express their identity through technology (Turkle, 1984). In this chapter, we look at the different ways technology is used, and the role of relational and cultural contexts in the negotiation of identity. To this end, we focus on a group of girls whose online experiences are usually absent from discussions of the girl wide web.

The two girls quoted above, Patricia and Elsa, live in a rural, Latino community where most teens have a cell phone, but only half have Internet-connected computers at home. The two girls described liking similar things about technology, but there were some key differences such as the type and range of their interest in technology. As shown in the quotes above, Patricia stated a preference for social networking on the web site called MySpace, as well as texting others—both examples of how she used the technology to connect with friends, and how she actively shaped the technology. In contrast, Elsa's quote offered a broader range of interests and use of technology. Like Patricia, Elsa is also involved in social networking sites where she can actively create technology (Whyville), and in this chapter we will discuss the ways this community offers different opportunities than MySpace. Those differences, and what they can tell us about the range of ways that girls negotiate growing up in online spaces, are the focus of this chapter.

CONCEPTUAL FRAMEWORK

We know more about where youth go online than we do about why or what they do there. For example, a national survey of teens found that 51% check social networking sites more than once a day (Common Sense Media, 2009), but our understanding of how these spaces are used is limited to small studies of (mostly) privileged youth. This is increasingly important as a broader range of youth move from being consumers to being authors and producers of technology (Guzzetti, Elliott, & Welsch, 2010; Lenhart et al., 2008). Feminist scholars have been anticipating this change. More than 10 years ago, Kearney (1998) challenged us to shift our focus away from how girls consume culture to look at the ways in which girls produce culture. She writes that many girls are involved in "the subversion and resistance of privileged notions of gender, generation, race, class, and sexuality" (p. 298). Online spaces allow but also limit these opportunities.

The shift away from a focus on youth as consumers has also led to a shift away from an image of individuals alone at their computer. Indeed, computing takes place within virtual and real social contexts. To understand how youth negotiate the developmental tasks of adolescence online, we must also consider their real world social and cultural contexts, such as the offline relationships that are part of everyday life. For example, the reason youth become involved in certain online communities has less to do with the content of those communities, and more to do with their offline social networks. Teens join networks like MySpace to maintain connections with friends (boyd, 2007). In fact, when teens play online games, they are more likely to play with people from their offline lives than with people they met online (Lenhart et al., 2008). Thus, it is important to view youth participation online in terms of active engagement, but also within the dynamic context of their relationships.

The relational nature of computing has led to a growing body of research on how the Internet has become a space for identity exploration. Much of this research builds on situated identity theory (Alexander & Lauderdale, 1977), which focuses on how behaviors are enacted in order to claim particular identities. That is, behaviors are chosen because they define for others who we are, or at least how we would like to be identified in the situation. For example, Pelletier (2008) shows that how girls and boys talk about gaming and online play varies, depending on the social context. Their responses were as much about who was listening as they were about how they play. Some have debated which of these presentations constitute the "real" self, but Stern (2008) argues that youth do not see these shifting identities as any less "real," but rather see them as an opportunity for feedback as they try to capture who they are. Indeed, this feedback can take the form of suppressing the identity exploration of peers. In middle school, girls use instant messaging to construct their social status with peers, but also to create exclusive spaces by blocking messages from certain peers (Thiel, 2005).

Ito et al. (2008) also described variation in the way that youth engage with digital media. In a large, ethnographic study of U.S. youth, they identified two genres of participation. On the one hand, youth who engage in friendship-driven participation are more likely to focus on the social aspects of the Internet, and to develop social networks that are the focus of their romantic interests. On the other hand, in interest-driven participation, engagement is also self-motivated, but based on connecting with others who have similar interests, and who are engaged in the same struggles for status and recognition that they are (Ito et al., 2008). These two genres of participation highlight the different motivations that youth have to participate in online communities.

There is a third genre of participation, one with more political motivations for engaging in online communities. Educational research provides some insights into what those motivations might be for Latina girls. A well-known educational study describes the practice of "subtractive schooling," as the way schools are organized that "fracture students' cultural and ethnic identities, creating linguistic and cultural divisions among the students and the staff" (Valenzuela, 1999, p. 5). Students who respond with resistance do so because they experience a sense of powerlessness. Taking this perspective online, Merskin (2005) described the way that some girls use blogging and other forms of technology production in order to challenge existing narratives of girlhood. These "culture jammers" use the media to challenge the media, a subversive act that suggests a deep understanding of and skill with technology. But little is known about how youth, particularly youth from certain minority groups in the U.S., engage in online culture jamming. As Harewood and Valdivia (2005) show in their analysis of the animated character Dora—the only popular "Latina" image available for U.S. girls—racial and ethnic politics are an important but understudied context in which girls experience the web.

There is a growing body of research that shows how children are actively making meaning and negotiating gender as part of an interplay between the technology and the relational setting. Guzzetti (2008) describes how the gendered nature of most virtual communities can put constraints on girls' identity exploration and expression. Similarly, in a study of Asian and White Canadian girls, Kelly, Pomerantz, and Currie (2006) described how girls learned what is expected of them in virtual spaces, and the way that girls "enacted, contested, or parodied conventional femininity" (p. 9). Their study shows that, like offline communities, there are "rules" of interaction, and consequences to challenging those rules. However, these rules did not stop, and in some cases enticed, the girls to challenge these expectations.

In summary, this chapter contributes to research on how gendered identities are negotiated by middle school girls in online spaces. We focus on two distinct groups of girls from a Latino community in order to highlight the interplay between virtual and real-world relational contexts.

THE REAL-WORLD SETTING

Our data come from 16 girls who attend middle school in a rural, agricultural town in California. In 2000, the town's per capita income was $13,205 (half the U.S. per capita income), 75% of the population was Latino (primarily Mexican migrants and immigrants), and almost 53% of residents had no high school diploma. The schools receive NCLB Title I support, despite significant increases in academic performance in the last 5 years. In the two middle schools in this study, there are high numbers of English language learners (39% and 72%), the majority of families are low income (77% and 83%), and few parents have graduated from college (28% and 27%). Data we collected from over 150 students suggest that the digital divide still exists in this town—only half the students had a computer at home, and fewer had a computer that worked or had Internet access.

The girls were voluntary participants in the Girl Game Company (GGC), an after school and summer program for middle school girls who have limited access to online technology (Denner, Bean, & Martinez, 2009). The classes met two days a week for 1.5 hours after school, and during the summer every day for 5 hours/day for 3–4 weeks. Students participated for up to 272 hours over 16 months. The GGC program was designed to strengthen students' computing skills, concepts, and capacities. It built on recommendations by the Association for Computing Machinery K-12 Task Force (2003) that students need to "be prepared to be knowledgeable users and critics of computers, as well as designers and builders of computing applications that will affect every aspect of life in the 21st century." GGC activities also addressed the national educational standards (International Society for Technology in Education, 2007) which emphasize the importance of creative thinking and innovation—using technology to learn rather than learning to use technology—as well as communication, critical thinking, and digital citizenship.

GGC strategies are based on research in developmental psychology, education, and computer science, resulting in strategies that aim to overcome individual, relational, and institutional challenges to girls' participation in IT.

During their participation in GGC, girls spent most of their time creating digital games, often with a partner. Students used Creator by Stagecast, Inc., which is a child-friendly, visual programming language (i.e., uses picture-based rules) that employs a movie metaphor. Although the Creator interface is simple to use, it incorporates some key programming concepts, like conditional execution, subroutines, iteration, and variables. Students created characters and programmed them to move and interact within a range of game genres (e.g., mazes, trivia games, and action games where a character dodges moving objects). As they got comfortable with the software, they drew their own characters (e.g., animals, people, and monsters), and downloaded background images from the Internet. Because students were not required to learn complicated syntax, they quickly learned the basics of making games and how to personalize them. Over time, the students learned to create increasingly more complex games, starting with a simple maze game, and ending with adventure games where the main character moves through a sequence of events. For example, a girl gets transported to an imaginary planet and she must find her way home by communicating with the aliens. In another adventure game, the player must help a chef travel through town to look for ingredients to his recipe, but he only gets the ingredients if he correctly solves math equations.

As part of GGC, students also spent time in their online offices. This was a private space where girls could decorate using images from the Internet, write messages to their partner and other friends, respond to questions from the researcher, and save their game files. About halfway through the program, each girl was assigned to a virtual mentor—a female who was either employed in the information technology industry or studying in a computing field. The mentor and mentee interacted via the online office, which allowed them to post and respond to messages, but not to chat in real time. The frequency with which each pair exchanged messages varied greatly, and was dependent on how often the mentee initiated contact, and how responsive the mentor was.

The girls also completed an online questionnaire upon entry to the program, and when they exited. Several scales were created: confidence with computers (10 items, alpha=.69), their attitudes toward computers and computer careers (10 items, alpha=.73), computer use (11 items, alpha=.85), and interest in computers (3 items, alpha=.63), support from parents to attend college and to pursue a science or IT career (8 items, alpha=.68), and higher levels of support from friends and teachers for their interest in computers (8 items, alpha=.57). These multiple sources of data are used to understand how two online communities offer and constrain opportunities for gender identity exploration.

THE VIRTUAL-WORLD SETTINGS

The two online communities mentioned in the introduction of this chapter played a major role in the lives of Girl Game Company participants. In the remainder of this section, we describe each.

MySpace.com

In this social networking Web site, users post images, music, self-made videos, and information about themselves. Friends post and respond to messages via message boards, and this space is often used as a mechanism to coordinate offline social networks. Youth use MySpace home pages to express who they are, how they feel, what they are interested in, and who they know. Most home pages feature a picture of the whole person, although faces are not always visible. There are options to customize a home page by using HTML to change fonts and colors. Although users are supposed to be 14 years old, when people sign up they are asked for, but do not need to verify, gender, and age. In recent years, enrollment on MySpace has slowed, but boyd (2007) found that Latinos, more than any other group, have embraced MySpace as their social networking site.

MySpace was blocked by school district-imposed firewalls. Regardless, throughout the program, many girls found ways to subvert the firewall and get onto MySpace. During the sessions, girls often looked at or updated their MySpace page, keeping it hidden, but open in another window. They waited for teachers to move away from their computers before opening the page and checking for messages. These girls also sought out strategic locations where their computer monitors were the least visible to the teachers. They also gained access to MySpace through other sites that had been specifically designed to subvert the firewall. These sites were not yet blocked by the schools, and allowed them to send updated content and images to their MySpace account without having to be logged on. When asked how they found these sites, the two most common answers were that they learned about the sites from friends who know someone in high school, or they figured it out themselves by searching for "Myspace school," which would take them to pages and steps to gain access.

Whyville.net

This virtual world is aimed at teen and preteen girls and boys and has over 5 million registered members. It was launched in 1999 by Numedeon, Inc. Avatars move freely across locations, which include a food court, mountains, beaches, a NASA space center, and the Getty Museum. When they first join, players have a "newbie" face—a blue oval with eyes, nose, and a smile. Over time, more committed players create elaborate avatars and get their license to chat. Players can design, buy, sell, or trade "face parts" or clothing for their avatars; they can also write articles for the Whyville paper and serve in leadership roles on what is called the "Street Team." Members earn virtual money by playing games focused on science and mathematics, and they use that money to create and dress their avatar, and to earn privileges, such as riding in virtual cars. Numedeon asks for (but does not verify) gender and age, and requires written parent permission and successful completion of a safety test to chat.

There are many hidden places within Whyville that only the most dedicated Whyvillians know about. Research by Kafai (2008) on users of Whyville shows the ways that youth interacted offline to learn about secret commands and places. The youth were motivated by the opportunity to customize their avatars, and obtain "insider knowledge" that gave them privileged access to virtual spaces that few know about. However, players in Whyville had few choices if they wanted to create an avatar that appears Latina (Kafai, Cook, & Fields, 2007).

The two virtual spaces described offer very different kinds of online experiences and opportunities. To better understand the similarities and differences in these settings, we took a closer look at 16 girls in the Girl Game Company that could be clearly identified as a MySpace girl or a Whyville girl at the beginning of the school year. We describe these two groups in more detail next.

Negotiating Identities across Contexts

MySpace

The eight girls in this category were identified using several criteria. First, each girl had a MySpace account and had lied about her age on her home page, which stated that they were three to four years older than they actually were. Second, they were not actively involved in Whyville; they either had newbie faces, or had logged into Whyville less than 10 days in the last year, and were not making a salary (the virtual money is called clams). Finally, they resisted participating in program activities that involved interacting with girls outside their immediate social group.

The MySpace girls were also identified by the teacher as students who were disruptive in the classroom. Conflicts with the teacher were a result of several factors. For example, the MySpace girls were more likely to arrive late to class, and to complain that they were not having fun. When asked to participate in group cohesion activities, they were often resistant to the activity and asked the teacher whether they had to participate. Their focus was on being with friends, rather than on being part of the class. Both students and teacher expressed frustration about the relationship.

Whyville

The eight girls in this category all had active accounts in Whyville. They logged on between 54–251 days over the course of the program and earned a regular virtual salary—at least 14 clams a day. Many were members of the Street Team, which means they volunteered to recruit others to join Whyville, resulting in rewards and special recognition for each recruit. These girls had elaborate avatars, which included accessories such as pets and jewelry, but none of the avatars resembled the girl in real life—many had white faces, and a few had blonde hair. Most had completed a variety of optional activities (e.g., filling out information about themselves, writing for the virtual paper) on Whyville.

The Whyville girls were also identified by the teacher as being consistently on task during the class. They spent more time interacting with the teacher and volunteering to help with demonstrations or taking attendance. They were enthusiastic about group cohesion activities, and told the teachers that they enjoyed getting to know people outside their immediate social clique. They enjoyed going outside and being active or playing games with the whole group. These girls also spent a great deal of time playing cooperative games on Whyville, such as Chinese checkers, and trading avatar parts with others in the classroom.

COMPARING MYSPACE GIRLS AND WHYVILLE GIRLS

We used several sources of data to help us understand the differences in how these two groups engaged with online technology. As shown in Table 10.1, the groups were similar in many ways, but there were two statistically significant differences. MySpace girls reported greater interest in staying in their hometown, and fewer visits to Whyville. Several other differences were notable (Whyville girls had higher program attendance and spoke more English at home), but were not statistically significant due to the large variance and small sample size.

Data from the online questionnaire they completed in their last class also showed that, in many ways, the two groups were more similar than different. For example, there were no differences in their reported level of confidence with the computer, their stereotypes about people who work with computers, their attitudes toward computers, or their computer use or interest. However, there were statistically significant differences in a few areas. For example, Whyville girls reported higher levels of computer skills, such as searching the Internet to find information, and communicating with others. Whyville girls also reported higher levels of support from parents for them to attend college and to pursue a science or IT career, and higher levels of support from friends and teachers for their interest in computers. These findings are used to interpret the variation in the types of games they created.

Table 10.1

	MySpace n=8	Whyville n=8
Average number of hours attending Girl Game Co	166	201
Average of percent of possible hours in attendance	75%	84%
Average age at program end	12.37	12.12
Race/ethnicity	All Latina	5 Latina, 2 White, 1 Filipina
Percent who speak all or mostly English at home	25%	62%
Percent who hope to remain in their home town	50%	0%
Average number of visits to Whyville in the past year	19	93

Girls in both groups created several games over the course of the program. However, the MySpace girls were less likely to complete their games, due in part to lower rates of attendance, but also to their primary focus being the social aspects of the program. MySpace girls reported lower skill levels with computers, and their games were less likely to have any advanced programming that went beyond moving a character through a maze, a quiz, or a series of challenges.

The games by Whyville girls were more complex, and involved more technical programming, due in part to higher attendance, but also to their high level of involvement in Whyville, which has a more gamelike and animated interface than MySpace. For example, in the Chef Baker game, the player can "talk" to people by pressing the space bar, and responding to multiple choice questions about math. The player gets feedback on right and wrong answers.

Computer game design offered an opportunity for girls to express their creativity, and to explore real world issues and concerns. Each game was required to have an Introduction page that described the rules and goals of the game, and Tables 10.2 and 10.3 include descriptions of some of their games, as written by the girls.

Overall, the MySpace girls were more likely to use their games to explore real life, particularly social and emotional issues. Two of the games (Miss Sunshine and Samurai Zombie Attack) had female heroines, both of whom were trying to rescue loved ones (their family or a dog). One game (Diabetes) had a female character that had to answer health questions correctly. Two of the games depicted children that were alone and lost. In New Girl, New School, the girl negotiates a challenge in a familiar place, while in The Great Adventure, which took place on a camping trip, the main character was a boy. The girl in that situation was worried, while the boy must watch out for monsters. Finally, two games took place in historical context (Working Hard to Make Things Better and Samurai Zombie Attack), but only one game (Working Hard to Make Things Better) incorporated the girls' home culture, as it explored the challenges of César Chávez, a Mexican American civil rights activist. The focus on real-life situations was consistent with this group's higher level of interest in staying in their home town.

The Whyville girls were more likely to imagine games that took place in far-away lands, and that depicted more traditional gender roles for their characters. For example, in Princess and Dragon, the princess must be rescued, and in the Adventure of Jacob Black, the hero searching for treasure was male. Two games had female characters. In one (Locos) the female character went on an adventure, but her goal was to try and find her way home to her daddy. In the other, the female character must correctly answer questions about diabetes. Two of the games challenged traditional gender roles for males. In the game about Osiris, the hero was male, but he was searching for his mother, in an effort to keep the family together, and in Chef Baker, the person making cookies was male. Finally, in Japan! the main character was a male vampire, and in the Multiplication and Division game, the main character was a male student who must solve the math problems to win the game. Although the Whyville girls' games include more traditional gender roles, they also reflected a spirit of adventure, which is consistent with their reported higher levels of support from family and friends to pursue education and careers that would take them out of their home town.

Table 10.2: Games by MySpace Girls

Title	Introduction Page
Working Hard to Make Things Better	You are Cesar Chavez, a farm worker that made the world better. Also you work at night and all of a sudden you start missing things. For example your sweater, lunch box and your shovel. In 2nd stage you have to find out which row is correct to become famous. In 3rd stage you found your crowd.
New Girl, New School	This game is about a girl named Annie. She is a new girl in a new school and she has no friendz. She is lost and really worried so she tries to find her classes and new friends. Help her find her classes.
The Great Adventure	There was a boy named Fred. He and his three friends went camping. Then his friends ditched him in the middle of nowhere!! Can you help him find his way home? But you'd better watch out, there are monsters who eat people.
Miss Sunshine	You are the doll (Miss Sunshine). You have lost your dog (Star). You are in the bottom and the ghost is shooting pumpkins at you. If they shoot you, you die. In the second stage the ghost and some flowers are going to be shooting you. In the last stage you will find Star in the forest. Then you will be really happy.
Samurai Zombie Attack!	This game takes place in medieval Japan. You must help Ai-Chan get her family back from the samurai zombies. And after you kill all of them you can go back home. If the zombies kill you well you lose and die.
Do u know diabetes well?	Hey welcome to "Do you know diabetes well?" Good luck and enjoy the game.

Table 10.3: Games by Whyville Girls

Title	Introduction Page
Princess and Dragon	Once upon a time there was a princess and a dragon came and took her to his castle. All you have to do is use the arrow keys and save the princess.
Chef Baker	Chef Baker has a problem. He ran out of ingredients and needs to make his delicious sugar cookies in time for his bakery's grand opening at 8:00! He already has butter, vanilla, and salt but he needs eggs, flour, and sugar. Help Chef Baker ask the neighbors for ingredients. But BEWARE! They might ask you to do favors for them.
Adventure of Jacob Black	One night Jacob was dreaming about a treasure that is buried in a place that he has never been before. Help Jacob find the place and get the treasure. Obstacles are in the way so be very careful.
Try to Find Osiris's Mom	The main characters are Horus, Isis, some pharaohs. The problem is that Osiris's mom has died and Osiris was looking for her because she was sick and Horus wanted to have the family together. The story takes place in Philae Egypt in a temple.
Japan! (dza-pon)	Use the arrow keys to move around and dodge the spears that have been thrown to Japan the vampire. You must also solve mysteries. So enjoy yourself!
Locos	Your two best friends dared you to go into a haunted house…you then somehow transported to a strange planet. In this game you will be trying to find a way out. This planet has a normal point of gravity and air. This little guy is called a loco. They inhabit most of this planet. PS-have fun!
Multiplication and Division Adventure Game	You are a student trying to pass his multiplication and division math test. If you get all the answers right you pass the test. If you get one wrong you fail so try your best to pass!

Kearney (1998) argues that girls become producers of culture in order to subvert or challenge expectations tied to gender and race/ethnicity. We found this to be true in an earlier study of girls creating games (Denner & Campe, 2008). But in the current study, while some of the MySpace girls used their games as an opportunity to explore real-life struggles, most from both groups did not use their games to explore or challenge traditional notions of girlhood having to do with romance and finding a boy. Instead, the girls did what Walkerdine (2007) calls the "work" of femininity, which often requires managing competing positions, such as balancing competition with cooperation. Indeed, she suggests that girls who are too independent run the risk of being seen as too masculine, so they must find ways to appear feminine while maintaining a legitimate place in whatever world they are negotiating.

CASE STUDY: ELSA

Elsa's[1] experiences highlight how online spaces are used to understand, negotiate, and resist cultural expectations about what it means to be a girl. Although we initially characterized her as a Whyville girl, over time her real-world and virtual social interactions, as well as her games, gradually incorporated elements that were more similar to those found in the MySpace group. We used a variety of data to provide a narrative of how (from her perspective) her movement between the virtual and real-world social networks related to Whyville and MySpace, can be viewed as challenging cultural norms and expectations.

Elsa began the program in the spring of 5th grade, and graduated after 16 months, during the summer between sixth and 7th grade. She was dedicated to the program—she attended 245 of the possible 272 hours, but the nature of her participation shifted over time from being one of the first to answer the teacher's questions to focusing more on her peers. Elsa had access to a computer at home. Her mother and father were born in Mexico, and each had attended some college. Both parents worked in dentistry, and Elsa's early career interest was to be a dermatologist, because the daughter of her mother's boss inspired her to pursue that path. But throughout the program, she described other career goals, including being a dentist and being a computer game designer. In her writings to her mentor, she said that what might keep her from reaching her dream career was not getting into the university she wants, or having to attend one that is far from her home.

The way that Elsa portrayed herself to the world evolved over time, as her identity shifted depending on when and with whom she was interacting. For example, Elsa created a screen name when she entered the program, which included the word "kitten." Although her name didn't change over 16 months, she changed the decorations in her office from photos of cute, real-life kittens, to images of a cartoon-like cat from "Skelanimals," with the logo "Dead & Cuddly." She also posted photos of kittens on her MySpace page, next to an image of herself in a pose that reveals her legs in a short skirt, with her face obscured. The shift over time from cute to "dead & cuddly" kittens and from innocent to sexy is an example of what Brown (2003) describes as "girls' complex and often contradictory realities" (p. 2). In this case, Elsa chose to present her identity using images that work the boundaries of the multiple worlds (Whyville and MySpace, real and virtual) that she straddles.

Elsa's games were also indicative of her identity negotiation over 16 months. In her first game, a princess had to find her way through a maze and avoid several different monsters in order to get home. This game employed the skills the whole class learned in the beginning, which was to make a character move through a maze and avoid challenges. However, Elsa added additional features, which included a hand-drawn character that she called a "loco" and an option for the player to click on a banana and make it fall off the tree. In her last required game, Elsa revisited her earlier idea about the loco, but in this game, the princess was transported to another planet after her friends challenged her to enter a haunted house. In that game, although the main princess character remained the same, the additional challenge by peers was reflective of her real-life challenges, described in more detail in her blogging below.

Elsa's last game also employed additional programming complexity. It was still a maze game, but the player had to figure out that they need to "talk" to the monster in order to find out that they first need to retrieve a gold coin (which doesn't appear until you talk to the monster). After retrieving the coin, a bridge appears across the river, and then the player can access the door to the next stage. The winner finds her daddy at the end, an element that was in her original game. This was one of the most technical games created by any of the girls, and the new elements shifted the focus from a girl fighting off monsters to one that can confront these monsters and gather resources on her journey of self-exploration. However, the goal was to return to the familiarity of home.

Elsa's interactions with her virtual mentor over 8 months were another way that she used online communication for identity exploration. The communication was steady over time, with messages exchanged almost every week. The conversations began with Elsa asking her mentor questions about her family and where she lives. Over time, she wrote about her own life, including her on and off relationship with a boy at school, her attendance at school events like dances, and her performances in school plays. In the spring of her second year in the program, Elsa wrote "Do you think it is bad for a kid to have a myspace?" The mentor responded by cautioning her to not reveal identifying information on her page. In a subsequent entry, Elsa wrote "I have a photo of me but I want to change it 'cause I got a haircut. It's blocked so people can['t] find me on it; I have to friend request them." In her last messages to her mentor she talked about getting into trouble at school for fighting with a boy, and working with her friends to advocate for the school to not cancel the band class. These events, both on and offline, show her experimenting with resistance in response to what Valenzuela (1999) identifies as challenges to her identity.

Halfway into the relationship with her mentor, Elsa wrote a long message that described her efforts to understand who she was, and where she fit in. "Hey, I feel I've changed. Well at first i didn't want anyone to know the real me and now it's harder than ever 2 be the real me, it's just the friends i like 2 hang out with are r all emo's and rockers, and i'm one 2, but i also have friends that are all girly and want me to hang out with them i like to be with them but i like to be with my rocker and emo friends because i one of them."[2] While social groups have been a presence in U.S. schools for decades, their translation to virtual worlds is evident in Elsa's attempts to negotiate where she fit in at school and online.

These themes about identity and inclusion/exclusion were also found in Elsa's blogging interactions with her peers. The online office provided a space for girls to collaborate and connect in a way that they believed was unregulated by adults (although they were told that the research staff, not the teacher, had access to what they wrote). Blogging was used most often by MySpace girls. In the example below, the girls tried to keep the messages away from prying teacher eyes by speaking in Spanish and posting only to one or two other girls. Note the following comment from a MySpace girl: "Manda me mesajes en espanol pa que no entendan las teachers" ("Write me messages in Spanish so the teachers can't understand").

The way in which Elsa negotiated and struggled with her transformation is captured in her blog interactions with other girls in Girl Game Company. These included sending messages to her new MySpace friends, as well as communication with a Whyville girl (Isabella) with whom she used to be close friends. Themes of connection and exclusion were pervasive, which is similar to findings by Thiel (2005), who found that girls used messaging to make social plans, which provided both a form of connection, and exclusion (of those not invited). The messages show how Elsa attempted to negotiate a place with the MySpace girls by outwardly rejecting her previous friend. These online interactions were similar to what Brown (2003) described as the ways that girls express their confusion and resistance to institutional and relational systems of oppression, which sometimes involve girlfighting. The following are direct quotes from the girls' blogs written during the Girl Game Company program.

Karina, a MySpace girl, asks Elsa: "ARE U REALLY GOING TO THE MOVIES WITH ISABELLA?"

Elsa responds: "NO WAY!!!!!! SHE ACKS ALL WIRED IN PUBLIC SHE'S ALWAYS SCREAMING AND RUNNING AND TELLING ON ME!!!! LET'S JUST GO ME YOU AND SOME OTHER FRIENDS. YA SHE CAN GO ONLY IF SHE STOPS ACKING LIKE THAT."

Then in another message, Elsa writes to Isabella: "OMG ISABELLA!!!!! Y CAN'T YOU GET YOUR OWN FRIENDS!!!! I NEEDED [ANOTHER GIRL]. IT WAS AN EMERGENCE (SIC)!!! CAN'T BELIEVE U!!!! YOU CAN SO FORGET ABOUT THE MOVIES ON SUNDAY I HAVE OTHER PLANS. BYE."

In summary, we have described how Elsa moved in between identifying with the Whyville and MySpace groups, and how this negotiation across virtual and real worlds shaped her developing identity. The online interactions with her virtual mentor and her peers showed a girl searching for her place in the world by exploring what it means to be a good girl or a bad girl. In the section below, we interpret these findings within the context of prior research.

DISCUSSION

In this chapter, we have highlighted two groups of girls who participated in an after-school technology program. In this section, we discuss the implications of our findings for educators and researchers who want to understand and promote girls' active participation in shaping the culture and content of online worlds.

This chapter fits within a genre of studies of identity negotiation among youth growing up in a digital age. Large-scale studies of girls and technology typically talk about them as one homogenous group, although Harris (2004) described the dichotomy that the popular press makes between "can do" girls and "at risk" girls, and the ways that these two categories of young womanhood shape the experiences and identities of girls in the U.S. But these two categories of girls are typically thought of as existing in different communities, or at least at different types of schools; a pseudonym for the suburban-urban dichotomy. As we showed in this chapter, these two groups can coexist, and they are not only interdependent, but girls move between them in a process of constructing identities in virtual and real worlds.

We initially identified two groups of girls, and differentiated them by their level of connection to school, and the extent to which they are viewed by their teachers as troublemakers. Girls in both groups joined the program in order to belong to something, but stayed for different reasons. The Whyville girls were motivated by spending time on the computer and learning to do new things, or what Ito et al (2008) called interest-driven participation. The MySpace girls were characterized by friendship-driven participation. However, girls in both groups were typically not involved in sports or other extracurricular activities, so Girl Game Company provided a place for them to belong.

The two groups had different experiences at their schools, where Latinos were the majority of students but the minority of teachers. The teachers expressed high academic expectations for the Whyville girls, but low expectations for the MySpace girls. Indeed, the survey data completed by the girls suggested that the Whyville girls perceived higher levels of support to attend college and pursue computing from their parents and their teachers, and also reported higher levels of skill with computers. The MySpace girls felt less confident academically, and were more likely to get reprimanded and to be viewed as troublemakers by the teachers. Regardless, both groups of girls had similar attendance records and built a strong identification with the afterschool program. Their different experiences may be due, in part to different orientations to their Latina identity. To the girls who spent more time on Whyville, having an avatar that looked like their real world self was not a top priority, since few avatar parts appeared to be Latina. However, MySpace allowed the use of real photographs, so girls who chose to spend their time on this site appeared to place greater value on making their ethnicity a visible part of their online identity.

The findings showed the ways that online identities are dynamic and responsive to real world relational contexts. For example, some girls used the online chat function in their office to create an online social world that overlapped with their offline world, and allowed them to reflect, try out, and get affirmation or rejection by peers, a finding that is similar to Guzzetti's (2006) study of older girls. Both Whyville and MySpace girls used technologies to express their creativity, and to grapple with real world questions and issues. As shown in the summary of their games, MySpace girls' games were more socially conscious, while the Whyville girls created more fantasy-based games. Only one girl used game production to address issues of culture and inequity, a finding that is consistent with Hurtado's (2003) study of adult Latinas; their social identity as Latinas became more apparent as they spent more time with non-Latinas.

The MySpace girls preferred online spaces that they saw as unregulated by adults, such as the online chat feature of their office. In fact, this feature was used almost exclusively by the MySpace girls, and it provided an unregulated space for Elsa to negotiate her development as she moved from elementary school into middle school, which included navigating the cultures of two different social groups. What was unique about Elsa was that she used both Whyville and MySpace, but she also sought out adult input about what it meant to be a part of a community like MySpace. In particular, Elsa's messages to her virtual mentor about MySpace show the ways she used that space to both explore and hide her identity. Harris (2004) wrote about how the Internet created a space that is both public and private, allowing girls to voice their opinions and concerns, while keeping dimensions of who they are hidden from view, except by certain friends.

The case study of Elsa provided some insight into how girls use online spaces for their own purposes. As we stated earlier, Elsa's user name included the word "kitten." Walkerdine (2007) described how some girls choose cute and cuddly characters "to divert attention away from power and aggression—we see cuddly kittens not dangerous tigers. Or perhaps being cute and cuddly is a way of tolerating oppression and powerlessness and making it into a virtue" (p. 52). We did not see a similar transformation in the content of her games, which suggests she did not use game creation as a site for identity exploration. Elsa did have a lot of pride in her games, and was one of the first girls to personalize her game with unique features. Her technical skills grew over time, as she made increasingly complex games, but the lack of a local audience for her game probably limited it as a site for self-exploration.

CONCLUSION

The two groups described in this chapter are recognizable in every school across the U.S. Like others (Brown, 2003) have suggested in their own research, it is our hope that the findings from this research will help educators change the way they think about and interact with "bad" girls. As we indicate, the MySpace girls are the ones that are often dismissed as disruptive or uncaring about school. As a result, the Whyville girls typically get the most attention and resources from key people like teachers and counselors. In the computing fields, where men vastly outnumber women, we cannot afford to disregard the MySpace girls. Although these girls' interest in the afterschool technology program was driven by friendship, they also developed notable skills (e.g., learning to subvert a firewall) that will prepare them well for future computing careers. In fact, it may be even more important to focus on MySpace girls, because efforts to connect these girls to more formal opportunities to become technology producers would likely have a lasting impact on who shapes future online communities and who creates the future of technology.

ACKNOWLEDGMENTS

The authors are grateful for the contributions of Steve Bean to this work. This material is based on work funded by the National Science Foundation under grant number 0624549. Any opinions, findings, and conclusions or recommendations expressed in this material are those of the author(s) and do not necessarily reflect the views of the National Science Foundation.

NOTES

1. All names are pseudonyms.
2. Emo is a subset of youth culture that derives from "emotional hardcore," a type of alternative music that is associated with both and punk rock, as well as confessional lyrics. According to Wikipedia (2009), emos have a reputation for being anti-establishment, and for acting as though they don't care about anything.

REFERENCES

Association for Computing Machinery K-12 Task Force (2003). *A model curriculum for K-12 computer science, 2nd edition*. Computer Science Teachers Association. Retrieved on November 12, 2008, from http://www.csta.acm.org/Curriculum/sub/CurrFiles/K-12ModelCurr2ndEd.pdf

Alexander, C. N., Jr., & Lauderdale, P. (1977). Situated identities and social influence. *Sociometry, 40*, 225–233.

boyd, d. (2007). Why youth (heart) social network sites: The role of networked publics in teenage social life. In D. Buckingham (Ed.), *MacArthur Foundation series on digital learning—Youth, identity, and digital media volume*. Cambridge, MA: MIT Press.

Brown, L. M. (2003). *Girlfighting: Betrayal and rejection among girls*. New York: NYU Press.

Common Sense Media (2009). *Is social networking changing childhood? Results of a national poll*. Retrieved on August 17, 2009, from http://www.commonsensemedia.org/sites/default/files/Social%20Networking%20Poll%20Summary%20Results.pdf

Denner, J., Bean, S., & Martinez, J. (2009). Girl game company: Engaging Latina girls in information technology. *Afterschool Matters, 8*, 26–35.

Denner, J., & Campe, S. (2008). What games made by girls can tell us. In Y. B. Kafai, C. Heeter, J. Denner, & J. Sun (Eds.), *Beyond Barbie and Mortal Kombat: New perspectives on gender and gaming* (pp. 129–144). Cambridge, MA: MIT Press.

Guzzetti, B. J. (2006). Cybergirls: Negotiating social identities on cybersites. *E-Learning, 3*, 158–169.

Guzzetti, B. J. (2008). Identities in online communities: A young woman's critique of cyberculture. *E-Learning, 5*, 457–474.

Guzzetti, B., Elliott, K., & Welsch, D. (2010). *DYI media in the classroom: New literacies across content areas*. New York: Teachers College Press.

Harewood, S. J., & Valdivia, A. N. (2005). Exploring Dora: Re-embodied Latinidad on the web. In S. R. Mazzarella (Ed.), *Girl wide web: Girls, the Internet, and the negotiation of identity* (pp. 85–103). New York: Peter Lang.

Harris, A. (2004). *Future girl: Young women in the twenty-first century*. New York: Routledge.

Herring, S. C. (2004). Slouching toward the ordinary: Current trends in computer-mediated communication. *New Media & Society, 6*(1), 26–36.

Hurtado, A. (2003). *Voicing Chicana feminisms: Young women speak out on sexuality and identity*. New York: New York University Press.

International Society for Technology in Education (2007). *National educational technology standards and* *performance indicators for students (NETS*S), second edition.* International Society for Technology in Education.

Ito, M. et al. (2008). *Living and learning with new media: Summary of findings from the digital youth project.* John D. & Catherine T. MacArthur Foundation. Retrieved May 16, 2009, from http://digitalyouth.ischool.berkeley.edu/files/report/digitalyouth-WhitePaper.pdf

Kafai, Y. B. (2008). Gender play in an online tween community. In Y. B. Kafai, C. Heeter, J. Denner, & J. Sun (Eds.), *Beyond Barbie and Mortal Kombat: New perspectives on gender and gaming* (pp. 111–124). Cambridge, MA: MIT Press.

Kafai, Y. B., Cook, M., & Fields, D. A. (2007). "Blacks deserve bodies too!" Design and discussion about diversity and race in a teen virtual world. *Situated play: Proceedings of DiGRA 2007 conference.* Retrieved April 7, 2010, from http://www.digra.org/dl/db/07312.14099.pdf

Kearney, M. C. (1998). Producing girls: Rethinking the study of female youth culture. In S. A. Inness (Ed.), *Delinquents & debutantes: Twentieth-century American girls' cultures* (pp. 285–310). New York: New York University Press.

Kelly, D. M., Pomerantz, S., & Currie, D. H. (2006). "No boundaries?" Girls' interactive, online learning about femininities. *Youth & Society, 38*(1), 3–28.

Lenhart, A., Kahne, J., Middaugh, E., Macgill, A., Evans, C., & Vitak, J. (2008). *Teens, video games, and civics.* Retrieved January 12, 2009, from http://www.pewInternet.org

Lewis, C., & Fabos, B. (2005). Instant messaging, literacies, and social identities. *Reading Research Quarterly, 40*(4), 470–501.

Merskin, D. (2005). Making and about-face: Jammer girls and the World Wide Web. In S. R. Mazzarella (Ed.), *Girl wide web: Girls, the Internet, and the negotiation of identity* (pp. 51–67). New York: Peter Lang.

Pelletier, C. (2008). Gaming in context: How young people construct their gendered identities in playing and making games. In Y. B. Kafai, C. Heeter, J. Denner, & J. Sun (Eds.), *Beyond Barbie and Mortal Kombat: New perspectives on gender and gaming* (pp. 145–159). Cambridge, MA: MIT Press.

Stern, S. (2008). Producing sites, exploring identities: Youth online authorship. In D. Buckingham (Ed.), *Youth, identity, and digital media* (pp. 95–118). John D. & Catherine T. MacArthur Foundation Series on Digital Media and Learning. Cambridge, MA: MIT Press.

Thiel, S.M. (2005). "IM me": Identity construction and gender negotiation in the world of adolescent girls and instant messaging. In S. R. Mazzarella (Ed.), *Girl wide web: Girls, the Internet, and the negotiation of identity* (pp. 179–201). New York: Peter Lang.

Turkle, S. (1984). *The second self: Computers and the human spirits.* Cambridge, MA: MIT Press.

Valenzuela, A. (1999). *Subtractive schooling: U.S.-Mexican youth and the politics of caring.* Albany: State University of New York Press.

Walkerdine, V. (2007). *Children, gender, video games: Toward a relational approach to multimedia.* New York: Palgrave Macmillan.

Wikipedia (2009). Emo. Retrieved August 4, 2009, from http://en.wikipedia.org/wiki/Emo

CHAPTER ELEVEN

When Girls Go Online To Play

Measuring and Assessing Play and Learning at Commercial Websites

Lillian Spina-Caza

In *The Practice of Everyday Life* (1984), de Certeau turns attention away from producers of popular culture to consumers and what consumers *make* or *do* with media artifacts. He argues for the illumination of everyday practices or ways of doing things often embedded in the obscure background of social activity to reveal "the secondary production hidden in the process of [sic] utilization" (p. xiii). Accordingly, de Certeau maintains the importance of formulating theory, research questions, methods, and perspectives that make it possible to articulate these types of interactions.

The popularity of commercially produced Web worlds appealing to girls, such as Barbie Girls, Club Penguin, Habbo, Stardoll, and Webkinz, suggests the same sorts of careful analyses de Certeau proposes be given to the study of online play. What do girls do when interacting with these sites? What do they create or make when playing online? These questions are particularly important in light of claims made by commercial sites (usually found on parent information pages) that they are educational, can teach girls to think creatively, build language and technological skills, or promote social development.

Research on children's Internet use frequently examines issues of access, identity, literacy, and safety, often emphasizing the need for critical analyses of Web content (Cross, 2009; Gee, 2007a, 2007b; Lankshear & Knobel, 2006; Livingstone, 2003b; Turkle, 1995; Willett, 2009). The Internet is also identified as both a place for cultural and democratic participation, a space for creative self expression (Center for Media Literacy, 2008; Cordes & Miller, 2000; Kellner & Share, 2005; Livingstone, 2003a; 2006; Mazzarella, 2005). Equally, the Internet is viewed by marketers as a location for product placement in games and, as Jenkins and Cassell (2008) point out, one where "advertisers [push] for games that will attract female consumers" (p. 15). Undeniably, virtual worlds offer marketing opportunities for real-world brands (KZERO, 2009) and, as Grimes and Shade (2005) argue, are imposing consumer culture on children, thus "denying children a degree of autonomy and agency in creating their own spaces" (p. 195).

Marsh (2005), on the other hand, like de Certeau, maintains culture is produced, not just consumed, and "[a]lthough children's culture is often shaped by adults and taken up by children (or not, as the case may be), [sic] children also create their own, child-centered cultural practices" (p. 3). Livingstone (2003b) writes, "…children themselves play a key role in establishing emerging internet-related practices" (p. 159). She suggests by taking a child-centered rather than a technology-centered approach, children can be viewed as agents in their own right.

Identifying what children are doing, making, or learning at popular commercial websites is essential for gaining a better understanding of what happens when young people go online to play. As de Certeau (1984) suggests, it is important to make explicit the systems which compose a culture and illuminate the "model of action characteristic of users whose status as the dominated element in society [as children often are], is concealed by the term 'consumers'" (p. xi).

Across disciplines there is agreement a need exists for empirical research demonstrating what occurs when children play in digital spaces. Roussou, Oliver, and Slater (2008), who use activity theory as a tool for analysis of user interaction in virtual environments comment, "To date, very few efforts exist that explore the value of interactive virtual environments and applications, especially the added value that these can bring to children's learning" (p. 141). Livingstone (2006) points out, future studies need to identify the potential educational benefits of Internet use by young people. She notes "much work has tracked the diffusion of Internet-based technologies into the home and classroom, but little work has examined, let alone demonstrated unequivocally, the positive benefits this has for educational achievement" (p. 220).

Several vital questions can shape research concerning everyday practices of children who go online to play. For example, what recognizable patterns of engagement emerge in the process of play at popular commercial websites? What do these patterns tell us about literacy or technology practices and skills that might be acquired during online play? Do play patterns support claims made about the "educational" benefits of web play? What kinds of site tools afford children opportunities to be creative—to direct their own play activities, or make something new or imaginative as they play? How accessible or robust are such affordances?

In this chapter I address some of the questions regarding patterns of play in virtual worlds. I explore the appeal pet adoption and dress-up doll websites have for girls, and compare the interactions of two girls, ages 8 and 10, across two websites to develop ways to measure and assess what happens when girls play online. The goal of this early study is threefold: (1) to formulate approaches for assessing play at popular commercial websites in order to identify what young girls might learn, do, or make when playing online; (2) to present data collection and coding methods to support scholarly research about how play unfolds in Web environments; and (3) to suggest ways to enrich play online overall.

VIRTUAL PLAY COMMUNITIES: FEMALE-CENTRIC, EDUCATIONAL, SOCIAL, AND SAFE

Thorne (1993) partitioned the landscape of childhood into three major sites: families, neighborhoods, and schools, and chose to examine the organizational features of schools as "they bear upon, and get worked out through the daily gender relations of kids" (p. 29). More than 16 years later, the Internet has altered the landscape of childhood, creating another major site where new organizational features and forms of play are only just emerging.

Popular commercial pet adoption sites such as Neopets, Club Penguin, and Webkinz, and virtual communities like Habbo, Gaia Online, and Millsberry, are attracting young people to the Internet in large numbers. Most of these commercially produced sites are touted as "safe" environments, where children can adopt and care for pets, learn new things, create customizable characters (i.e., virtual dress-up dolls), and explore virtual towns or cities. Many provide communication tools that enable site users to chat with others while playing at these sites.

Significantly, commercially popular websites frequently emphasize safety and educational opportunities, and appear to attract more girls than boys online to play. Quantcast, which tracks website traffic, shows both popular pet adoption and virtual communities have "slightly female centric" audiences. Many of these sites seem to be targeting tween-age girls. For example, Whyville.net, a corporate-sponsored, educational website that came online in 1999, tells potential sponsors on its *Whyville for Sponsors* page it appeals to children from ages 8 to 15 years. On the *Whyville for Parents* page, however, the site clearly addresses parents of tween girls:

> Researchers have identified the middle school years as a time when children, especially girls, lose their interest in math and science. Studies suggest that exposure to engaging educational, and in particular scientific, activities during this critical period can substantially influence future academic and career choices. (¶2)

This is a claim frequently made in the literature on gender and gaming, which suggests computer games hold the key to attracting and keeping girls interested in engineering and science from an early age. Jenkins and Cassell (2008) call it, "a sort of head start program for technological literacy" (p. 10). The authors note, however, that the number of girls and women in computer science has actually gone down over the past 10 years, and argue "without a more general cultural sense of the diversity of gendered experience, girl games are just another tool with which to construct a gender divide" (p. 14).

Just as commercial video games seem to be the predominant playgrounds for boys, commercial Web environments, like the ones explored here, may turn out to be girls' turf. A gender split along the lines of play environments is not surprising. Heath (1983), who conducted communication ethnographies between 1969 and 1978 in two communities in the Piedmont Carolinas, found games to be sharply differentiated for boys and girls, noting divisions along gender lines begins early. She observes in one community:

> Girls are given metal tea sets, while boys get plastic soldiers. Girls are given dollhouses and doll furniture; boys are given trucks, tractors, campers and jeeps. Girls are given books about little girls, babies, and baby animals living in a human family-like setting; boys are given books about trucks, ballgames, and boys and their animals. (p. 132)

Heath's study looks at how the ecology of a community and its practices—including children's toys and play habits—can impact learning beyond the boundaries of formal schooling. Similar ecologies can be identified in play communities on the Internet, and might also impact learning outside of school settings.

Thorne (1993), who studied the interactions of boys and girls in school settings, observed playgrounds are sites of extensive separation by gender. She found boys controlled the larger fixed spaces reserved for team sports, while girls dominated jungle gyms and smaller cement areas closer to school buildings, "taking up perhaps a tenth of the territory that boys controlled" (p. 44). According to Thorne, the physical ecology or characteristics of different spaces have a significant impact on gender interaction or separation.

Jenkins (2006) argues the attraction of video games for boys at the turn of this century parallels outdoor games of the 19th and early 20th centuries. He equates video game play to the "active exploration and spontaneous engagement with their physical surroundings" boys were accustomed to in the past (p. 335). According to Jenkins, girls played closer to home, confined to safe, domestic, or educational activities that prepared them to be mothers. He suggests, the types of video games appealing to girls "adopt a slower pace, are less filled with dangers, [and] invite gradual investigation and discovery . . ." (p. 357).

Cassell (1998) writes, "Many games for girls are educational [sic], many entail play situations that have traditionally been associated with girls such as those involving dolls, horoscopes, clothing, and make-up" (p. 301). Since the debut of games such as Barbie Fashion Designer in the 1990s, girls have been attracted online to play with games that have, as Denner and Campe (2008) point out, "creative components, puzzle elements, tips, positive unsolicited feedback, a slow or variable pace, clear and predictable rules, and the absence of violence of killings" (p. 130).

Popular pet adoption and dress-up doll Web-based communities can best be understood then as the types of gendered play spaces associated with so-called girl games. In effect, these sorts of commercially produced sites transfer offline and video game practices typically (or stereotypically) identified as "girls' play" to virtual environments. Not surprisingly, the types of commercially-produced sites discussed in this chapter are promoted as "fun" and "safe" domains where girls feel at home (playing in the confines of their own homes), and where they can be creative or learn something new.

While there is precedent for informal learning and creative practices situated in popular culture, there is also a need to test the claims made by commercial sites to determine their validity. The next section takes a look at some of the claims popular websites make about the educational value of site content, pointing out these claims are more often than not directed to the parents of girls rather than boys.

LEARNING AND CREATIVE PRACTICES SITUATED IN POPULAR CULTURE

Popular Commercial Websites Claim Educational Value

Commercial Web environments appealing to children, and increasingly girls, are routinely described as virtual communities; as such these spaces can be explored and compared in ways that are similar to how physical communities might be explored and appraised. Like a real community, a virtual community has its own ecology, and offers various opportunities for play and learning (Heath, 1983).

Features of architecture, settings, and material variables associated with indoor play environments are known to influence or enhance the value of play in children's development (Neuman & Roskos, 1992). Web environments can be likened to indoor play environments and, arguably, have features embedded in them that may or may not enrich learning and development. Popular commercial websites, to greater or lesser extents, promote site content as "educational" and, for marketing purposes, point to features designed to enhance the value of play. For example, under the heading "What are the benefits of Club Penguin?," Disney's Club Penguin's *Parent's Guide* states:

… Club Penguin is a great place to learn and grow. On Club Penguin, children practice read-ing, develop keyboarding skills and participate in creative role playing. By accumulating and spending virtual coins earned through game play kids practice math and learn about money management. The cooperative nature of the Club Penguin environment, along with initia-tives such as our secret agent and tour guide programs, also help children develop impor-tant social skills while gaining a deeper understanding of their role as members of a community (¶1)

On the "Powerpets Difference" page of the Powerpets *Parent Center* guide (2009), the website is identified as "a fun environment for players of all ages with many edu-cational aspects" (¶2). The site declares, "your child will have to learn something if they want to be successful in the game."

Moshi Monsters—a "monster adoption" site—asserts children will learn to think creatively, hypothesize, strategize, manage scarce resources, and learn new vocabularies. According to its *Parents* page, "Education is right at the heart of the Moshi Monsters experience. Every day your child's monster will create a series of fun puzzles that test everything from vocabulary and arithmetic to logic and spa-tial skills" (¶1).

The two Web environments examined in greater detail later in this chapter make similar claims to educational content. At Webkinz.com, the "Webkinz World and Learning" page tells parents: "Your child can learn lots of fun facts at Quizzy's. The questions at Quizzy's are age-appropriate, and most are educationally based" (¶1). Site activities such as *Webkinz Newz* and the *W Tales* are alleged to encourage reading, and site contests "encourage writing, creativity, and problem-solving" (¶3).

Interestingly, Millsberry.com, the other web environment explored in this study, does not actively promote learning opportunities to parents. This site is mar-keted to tweens and teens as a fun, virtual community that can be explored through the eyes of a customizable avatar character or "Buddy." It is only near the bottom of the "Ask Us" page—accessed by clicking on the "Help" button on the site's main page—that site navigators (i.e., children or curious adults) gain an understanding of the site's potential learning activities. Here, a site user can learn more about the statistic bars which are always located below her "Buddy." For example, the green "Buddy" stats bar measures a character's participation in activities that keep the city safe and clean, while the yellow bar measures intelligence and demonstrates a char-acter's ability to think, and solve problems. Intelligence is said to improve when a character reads a book or plays puzzle games; a high level of intelligence helps a vir-tual character find secrets and bargains.

While informal types of learning activities may be found at popular commer-cial websites, the pursuits girls find most engaging may not be the ones that encour-age the acquisition of new vocabulary words or logical thinking skills. Examining site content for the existence of "educational" activities may not provide an accurate picture of what young people actually do, make, or learn as they play in virtual spaces.

In order to better understand how informal learning or creative practices unfold on the Web, it is useful to consider how these practices have evolved over time in popular culture. Literacy and games studies provide useful insights into learning that happens outside of formal classrooms, and can help illuminate the everyday practices of girls who go online to play.

Informal Learning and Creative Practices Shaped by Culture

Hutchins (1996) observes human cognition is a phenomenon that "is not just influenced by culture and society but that it is in a very fundamental sense a cultural and social practice" (p. xiv). He writes, "Humans create their cognitive powers by creating the environments in which they exercise those powers" (p. xvi).

Literacy theory and research links environment to learning practices. Literacy studies that take an ecological approach to understanding how play influences cognition make it possible to identify informal learning occurring in environments located outside of formal educational settings (Barton & Hamilton, 1998; Brandt, 2001; Heath, 1983; Neuman & Roskos, 1992; Vincent, 1989).

Barton and Hamilton (1998) consider socially situated learning to be informal sorts of learning and sense making, and suggest different literacies are associated with different domains of life. They describe informal literacy practices as vernacular practices that are free from institutional control. Consequently, these practices are more likely to be "a source of creativity, invention and originality, and [sic] can give rise to new practices—improvised and spontaneous—which embody different sets of values from dominant literacies" (p. 253).

Vincent (1989), referring to mass print literacy, recognizes the "exercise of the imagination [as] one of the greatest and most persistent incentive for gaining command of the tools of literacy, and their first and most satisfying application" (p. 226). The Internet has provided similar impetus for understanding how to both navigate and use new digital technologies to gain expertise in support of creative pursuits.

Theory and research in video game and Internet studies also provide useful ways for understanding how informal learning and everyday creative practices are situated within the context of popular culture (Braun, 2007; Gee, 2004, 2007a, 2007b; Marsh, 2005; Selfe & Hawisher, 2007; Squire, 2008). For example, Squire (2008) notes research comparing video game play to traditional academic literacy suggests "gaming *is* thoroughly a literacy practice, requiring players to produce meaning with texts and become expressive with technology in multiple forms . . ." (p. 636).

Gee (2007b) argues when people learn to play video games they are in fact learning a new, multimodal literacy, thus we need to "think of literacy more broadly" (p. 17). He writes, "...language is not the only important communication system. Images, symbols, graphs, diagrams, artifacts, and many other visual symbols are significant, more so today than ever" (p. 17). Young people who navigate and play in online spaces are acquiring new skills and practices that are altering the way they think about and interact with the world.

Williams (2007), in the "Afterword" to Selfe and Hawisher's *Gaming Lives in the Twenty-First Century*, remarks that the meaning and use of games begin with the game developers, but is refashioned and recoded by the player in a rich, complex process" (p. 257). He suggests open-ended, less linear play encourages more creativity and digital literacy.

Braun (2007), who examines the online literacy practices of teens, suggests educators harness what is good about new technologies and explore the different ways these technologies might be used in support of content creation. She points out literacy skills are enhanced when teens collaborate with others to build content; read, write, produce, and/or respond to content; and create something new.

Like commercial video games, commercial Web play communities on the Internet are semiotic domains where new social and cultural practices are only just emerging. Empirical research is needed to identify and measure how play and learning unfold online, and how various types of commercial sites or domains (e.g., pet adoption or virtual character-driven communities) might support opportunities for both informal learning and creative sorts of play.

The remainder of this chapter looks briefly at research methods and practices currently employed to develop a better understanding of everyday Internet practices, and presents exploratory research methods which might prove useful for gaining new insights into play and learning at two popular children's websites.

METHODS AND PRACTICES FOR CONDUCTING WEB RESEARCH

Methodologies for studying Internet use include research practices associated with literacy and media studies. Internet research presents new challenges because, as Livingstone (2003a) points out, "...the lack of a shelf of books or video tapes, means that new media researchers must characterise the texts, genres and forms of their medium without any easy way of capturing their materials" (p. 9). She emphasizes the importance of learning from users themselves.

Livingstone's (2006) UK Children Go Online project, which examines the Internet practices of young people, produced qualitative and quantitative findings for guiding future studies on "new media access, use, and consequences within the social, cultural, and political parameters of young people's lives" (p. 219). Data were collected using a variety of methods, including "in-home, face-to-face, computer-assisted interviews with 1511 children and young people aged 9–19 years, plus a self-completion survey of their parents, and a series of focus group and family observations" (p. 220).

Selfe and Hawisher (2007), in a large-scale, seven-year study of digital literacy practices in the U.S. and abroad, use life-history interviews conducted with more than 350 participants to identify "literacies acquired, practiced, and valued within the digital environments of computer games" (p. 2). According to the authors, literacy and learning are understood as a set of practices only when situated in "a particular historical period, cultural milieu, or cluster of material conditions" (p. 32).

Leander (2008) suggests one of the best ways to examine the "everydayness" of Internet practices is to confront these as lived experiences in the everyday lives of youth. He views digital literacies as social practices and argues for ethnographic studies that build knowledge based on the situated evaluation of technology in use. Leander explains an ethnographic approach does three things: insists that understanding phenomena requires empirical observation; remains open to new data and new codes for interpreting data; and grounds observations in a specific field.

Offline literacy studies can also be useful for exploring online environments. For example, research conducted by Neuman and Roskos (1992) comparing activities at two daycare centers—one that was enriched with literacy objects and one that was not—explores the "organizational dimensions that might influence children's opportunities to actively engage in literacy learning" (p. 203). Data collection techniques used for this study included videotaped observations of children in specific play areas, samples of play activities, individual play behavior and literacy demonstrations, and the coding of play frames or behavioral units bound by location with a particular focus or interaction. The authors found the confluence of spatial organization, play materials, classroom organization, and familiarity with play contexts all influence the quality and complexity of play.

The various research methods mentioned here suggest valuable ways to approach the study of Web environments designed for young people. However, an ecological perspective, like that taken by Neuman and Roskos, seems particularly useful for examining *technology in use* to identify opportunities for learning through play. This sort of study, particularly the analysis of play frames or behavioral units attached to locations, can readily be adapted for the study and enrichment of online environments—commercial or otherwise.

ASSESSING ONLINE PLAY: TALE OF TWO WEBSITES

Millsberry.com and Webkinz.com

Two children's websites mentioned earlier in this chapter were analyzed and compared as part of a preliminary research study exploring methods for measuring and assessing play at commercial websites: Webkinz.com, a popular online pet adoption website, and Millsberry.com, a virtual community with customizable avatars or "Buddies." These sites were chosen because they are the first online environments where my own children, daughters ages 8, 10, and 13 asked to play, and both are typical in quality and design to other popular pet adoption and dress-up doll websites (i.e., Neopets, Club Penguin, Habbo, etc.).

According to unofficial or estimated demographic data available at Quantcast.com (October, 2009), Webkinz.com is a virtual pet adoption site visited by an estimated 2.4 million people in the U.S. monthly, and is favored more by Caucasian youth between the ages 3 and 17, who make up 62 percent of the traffic at this site. The site is slightly female centric (56 percent female to 44 percent male), and is accessible to anyone who purchases a Webkinz stuffed animal from the Canadian-based Ganz Company. Stuffed animals come with codes that provide access to "Webkinz World" for one year; new animals must be purchased in order to continue playing at the site.

Millsberry.com is a General Mills Company website advertised on the boxes of cereal products. Quantcast's unofficial demographic data as of October 2009 shows Millsberry.com is estimated to reach 553.9 thousand people in the U.S. monthly, 58 percent of who are female and 42 percent male. It is visited more frequently than Webkinz.com by African American, Asian, and Hispanic girls (29 percent versus compared to just 7 percent), also between the ages 3 and 17. Unlike Webkinz.com, Millsberry.com is a free site that can be accessed without any requisite product codes or purchases beyond the initial purchase of a box of cereal.

At Millsberry.com, a child customizes her "Buddy" character, and can participate in activities such as selecting a neighborhood to live in, decorating a home, having a yard sale, or playing at a game arcade. In order to purchase clothing, food, pets, and other items, a player accumulates "Millsbucks" every time she logs into the site, takes part in certain site activities like taking the weekly poll, or plays arcade games.

Both Webkinz.com and Millsberry.com are considered virtual communities and offer similar activities (i.e., designing rooms, adopting pets, playing dress up and arcade games), and both share qualities which have often been identified with games designed to appeal to girls.

Background Information

To gain a better understanding of what happens when girls go online to play at commercially popular websites, I developed a preliminary, exploratory study to examine and compare activities across two websites. Since I would be examining play behavior comprised largely of visual data, I had to establish ways to measure what I was analyzing. Video screen capture technology and basic video editing software were useful for collecting visual data and segmenting it into units for coding and analysis.

As my children first brought Webkinz.com and Millsberry.com to my attention, I invited them to be active participants in the research process. The 8 year old and the 10 year old both agreed to allow the recording of several online play sessions using video screen capture technology.[1] All three girls responded to questions about what they did, what they liked to do, and what they would like to be able do at the two sites, but could not do at the present time. Video capturing online play activities, informal discussions, and written responses to questions about site interactions, were the main data collection methods employed for this early study.

Analyzing Streams of Play

Research methods used to examine how play unfolds online derive from methods associated with the collection, coding, and analysis of verbal streams of data (Geisler, 2004). According to Geisler, verbal data analysis is a methodology for exploring and describing streams of language with the goal of "building a descriptive analysis that can be articulated, makes sense, and is reliable" (p. xiii). It is also a method consistent with media content analysis used to determine, for example, the relative frequency of television violence. Once data are collected, they are segmented into units appropriate for analysis that help identify the level at which the phenomena of interest occurs.

The research method used for the preliminary study analyzes streams of activity data captured as children interact in real-time with commercial websites. This type of analysis requires children's play sessions be recorded in real-time to gather both visual and aural information. The recorded data are viewed and segmented into discrete activity units or *a–units* for coding, based on how long a child engages in a particular activity. A-units are similar to the "play frames" described by Neuman and Roskos (1992), insomuch as these are used to segment "play that is bound by location and a particular focus of interaction" (p. 213).

Four out of seven play sessions recorded at Webkinz.com and Millsberry.com were randomly selected for coding, with sessions times ranging between 17 and 24 minutes. Play sessions were segmented into video clips using Windows Movie Maker; the discrete clips represented complete activities or *a–units*. After all of the screen-capture video clips were reviewed, three coding schemes were created to better understand how play unfolds within Web environments.

Coding Schemes

According to Druin, Bederson, Boltman, Miura, Knotts-Callahan, and Platt (1999) children want three things when they interact with technology. First, they want to feel in control of an environment, to make choices about what they do and when they do it, and to be able to choose from a variety of activities. Second, they want to interact socially, to "share, show, and use technologies with others" (p. 65). Finally, they want expressive tools that enable them to tell stories or build things. "Children enjoy many different forms of expression: sound, visuals, movement, and physical appearance. They want all of these [sic] in the technologies they use" (p.66).

The coding schemes developed for this exploratory study take into account the types of interactions Druin et al. (1999) have identified as being most important to young people: a variety of play options, an ability to interact with others, and a means for self-expression. The three schemes—*Coding for Range of Activities, Coding for Social Activities*, and *Coding for Engaging Activities*—are designed to:

1. Calculate the number of activities a child chooses during play and/or the *menu bar items* or number of activities available to a child in a specific web environment (categorized as *high, medium*, or *low* depending on the number of activities selected or offered);
2. Identify opportunities to contact and socially interact with other players using site-based communication tools (coded as *social-responsive, social-unresponsive,* or *non-social,* respectively, if a child makes contact, attempts to contact, or cannot contact another player on a website); and
3. Classify the different types play activities available at popular websites, using the coding terms *search, select, design,* and *direct* to describe which types of activities children find most engaging, and which allow for more imaginative or self-directed play.

More information on each coding scheme, and how data collected using these schemes might help in assessing play at popular websites, is included in the discussions of preliminary research findings that follow.

Range of Activities

Coding for "Range of Activities" illustrates individual differences in the way children play online, and also play variations occurring across websites. "Range" refers to both the number of activities a child chooses to engage in while playing at a particular site, and also reflects the number of *possible* activities a child can choose from within a specific Web environment. If a child chooses to play only one or two games or spends most of her time trying clothes on her virtual "Buddy," then the range of activities she participates in will be lower than a child who chooses more options (see Figure 11.1).

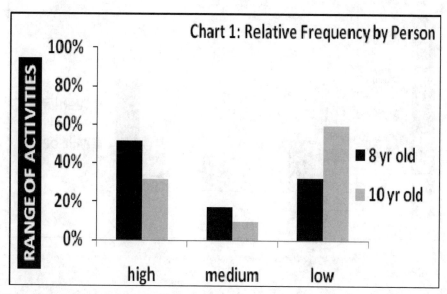

Figure 11.1 *Relative frequency by person chart shows a marked difference in range of activities chosen by 8- and 10-year-old girls.*

The "Relative Frequency by Person" chart reveals the number of activities selected was higher (51 percent) for the 8-year-old than the 10-year-old (31 percent). A review of the video capture data shows the 10-year-old chose to play arcade games, while the 8-year-old engaged in a greater number of activities that included, but were not limited to, playing games. Used in a larger study, coding for range could be useful for identifying different patterns of play by gender or age. Connections might be made, for example, between age and attention span or gender and play preferences, using this type of coded data.

Coding for "Range of Activities" also shows that different websites offer more or less activities or options for play, which might impact on both the quality of interactions and opportunities for informal learning or imaginative sorts of play. For example, the "Relative Frequency by Website" chart (Figure 11.2) indicates the children in this study engaged in a higher range of activities at Webkinz.com than at Millsberry.com (60 percent versus 26 percent). The results are not surprising, however, because of the two sites, Webkinz has a more accessible and robust, pop-up "Things to Do" menu.

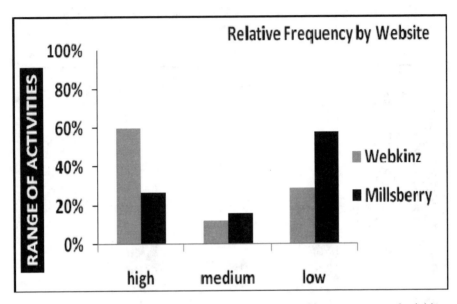

Figure 11.2 *Relative frequency across websites shows children engaged in a greater range of activities at Webkinz.com.*

Social Activities

The second coding scheme identifies opportunities for social or collaborative play. For example, if a child challenges another site user to a game, or communicates with a friend using site-defined chat tools, interactions are coded "social-responsive." When a child attempts to contact someone, but is unable to make a connection, activities are coded as "social-unresponsive." If no social interactions occur and/or there are no tools readily available to make social connections within an activity, interactions are coded "non-social."

Interestingly, in the preliminary study, no social interactions occurred during play at Millsberry.com. Although children are able to go to the Millsberry Post Office and send notes or gifts to other friends who also play at Millsberry.com—provided they have a username or a "Buddy's" home address—neither the 8- or 10-year-old opted to do this in the play sessions recorded.

As the "Frequency by Website" data (Figure 11.3) shows, there were a total of 16 social-responsive and two social-unresponsive activities recorded at Webkinz.com. The corresponding video capture data shows that most social-responsive activities occurred within the context of game play, when the children invited other online players to compete in arcade games.

Frequency By Website:				
	social-responsive	social-unresponsive	non-social	Total
Webkinz	16	2	17	35
Millsberry	0	0	38	38
	16	2	55	73

Figure 11.3 *Frequency of social types of interactions across websites.*

Engaging Activities

Definitions of activity in virtual environments suggested by Parés and Parés (2001) were useful for the development of the third coding scheme, or coding those activities children found most engaging. The authors describe activity in virtual worlds as explorative, manipulative, and contributive. *Explorative* refers to the ability to navigate within a virtual environment, *manipulative* indicates an ability to influence or control elements within that environment, and *contributive* suggests the ability to add to or modify the environment as a whole.

Building on Parés and Parés, I use the terms *search, select, design*, and *direct* to describe activity or a-units representing the ways in which children engage in online play. For example, when a child is exploring or looking for something to do at a website, it is coded *search*. If she chooses an arcade-like game to play, or picks out clothing or food items for a virtual pet, activity is coded *select*. The video data captured for this early study show activities associated with *search* and *select* are inherently more repetitive than creative.

The third coding scheme was particularly useful for understanding how interactions in web environments occur over time. For example, as shown in the temporal charts for "Engaging Activities" (Figures 11.4 and 11.5), when children played only at arcade games, activities were coded as "search" and "select" with greater frequency because interactions associated with these types of games typically involve *searching* for a game to play and *selecting* or making choices in the game that eventually result in wins or losses.

When a child manipulates site tools to customize objects, that is, decorates a tee shirt or a living room, activities are coded *design*. If she contributes something new to the environment, activities are coded *direct*. For example, at Webkinz.com—with 1000 in KinzCash—a child can purchase "Webkinz Studio," and write and direct movies; at Millsberry.com children can log in to a "Recording Studio," sample music, layer sounds, and record "original" songs. Affordances like these provide opportunities for self-directed play, which result in the creation of new content. Activities coded *design* or *direct* correspond to creative practices that are both imaginative and/or self-expressive.

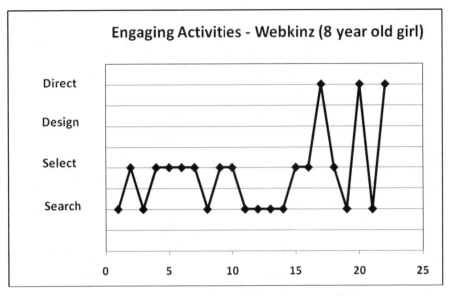

Figure 11.4 *Temporal chart shows an 8-year-old girl engaged in 22 activities at Webkinz.com during a play session lasting 17:22 minutes. No activities are coded as design, and only three are coded direct.*

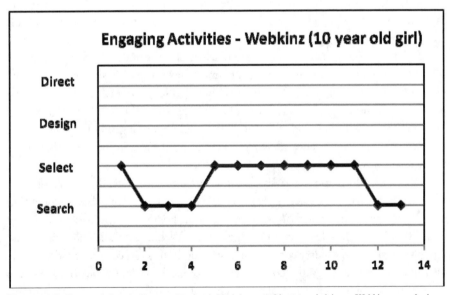

Figure 11.5 *Temporal chart indicates a 10-year-old girl engaged in 14 activities at Webkinz.com during a play session that lasted 17:53 minutes. No activities are coded as design or direct.*

Overall, the three coding schemes developed for this study suggest useful ways for exploring patterns of online play. Used in a larger study, these coding schemes might tell us more about:

~ what children like to do most when they visit popular commercial sites
~ whether similar patterns of play occur across websites
~ which sites offer children more affordances or robust tools for self-directed or creative sorts of play
~ whether or not play supports informal learning

Most importantly, capturing and coding play enables researchers to look at the trajectories young people take as they wind their way through Web spaces. As Squire (2008) suggests, "scholars might benefit by examining how participants learn through participation in these structures" (p. 655).

Discussion

Recording and coding the segmented video screen capture data for this exploratory study helped identify methods for classifying activities two girls engaged in when playing at two popular commercial web environments. This approach to understanding online play underscores the fact that what someone says they do and what they do can be very different things. Not surprisingly, conversations with the girls about which activities they like to play at Webkinz.com or Millsberry.com do not always reflect what they did when play sessions were recorded. For example, the types of *design* and *direct* activities they claim to enjoy most—making a movie, recording music tracks, directing a virtual pet's actions—did not occur during any of the four sessions coded for this study. Activities the girls frequently engaged in were those that paid off in "KinzCash" or "Millsbucks," and allowed them to purchase things for their virtual pets and avatars.

The recorded play data reveals Webkinz.com has a more robust menu bar and thus offers a greater number of activities than Millsberry.com. At Webkinz there are more opportunities for social interactions between players. Players can use simple chat tools in the KinzChat area, choosing pre-selected words and phrases, to communicate with friends who are online or to invite others online to participate in game play. Millsberry.com does not offer real-time communication with other players, though players can send postcards and gifts to each other, and are able to visit other players' virtual homes.

Both sites are text heavy, requiring well-developed language skills in order to take full advantage of site activities without adult assistance. Both use newspaper formats to convey information to site users: Millsberry has the "Millsberry Gazette" and Webkinz the "Kinzville Times." The emphasis on text also indicates the sites are designed to appeal to girls who, according to Calvert, Mahler, Zehnder, Jenkins, and Lee (2003), prefer to interact with "words and dialogue," and who are viewed in some of the research as "more likely to engage in verbal, symbolic styles of interaction and representation" (p. 630).

Due to the limited data collected for this early study, no significant results can be reported concerning the kinds of activities girls prefer to engage in when they go online to play. A controlled study involving more participants and the recording of longer play sessions is necessary to obtain results that can be used to draw inferences about the types of activities young people engage in most at popular websites, and whether these activities support imaginative, self-directed play and/or informal learning.

CONCLUSION

The exploratory study discussed in this chapter provides a useful methodological framework for the study of commercial websites as play environments. As Neuman and Roskos (1992) point out, different play settings constrain certain behaviors and permit others (p. 220). Commercial Web environments can enrich or inhibit learning through play, thus it is important site producers consider whether creative affordances or educational features are at least—if not more—robust than the consumptive play practices these sites seem to privilege. Taking an ecological approach to the design of commercial sites aimed at young people is one way this might be accomplished.

While preliminary data shows the attraction of making and spending money eclipses learning or creative sorts of play, there may be several possible explanations why someone spends a good deal of time playing games to earn money that go beyond the obvious. First, creative sorts of activities may not be as compelling or rewarding as playing games in arcades. Take the "Recording Studio," at Millsberry.com. To gain access to this area, a child must sign up for the CTC Music Mixer, create a DJ name, and a new password to remember. Sometimes this feature is unavailable or "temporarily down," which can be frustrating.

Second, site affordances that support creative play activities may not permit certain types of play young people want to engage in. A child who wants to direct her adopted virtual pet in a movie using Webkinz Studio, but is forced to use stock pets or characters other than her own, may choose not to engage in this activity. Creating easy-to-access and dynamic affordances that reinforce imaginative or self-directed activity would certainly go a long way toward enriching online play environments.

A third hypothesis for why playing arcade games was the predominant activity could be attributed to the fact that the play sessions coded for this study lasted less than 25 minutes. Subsequent discussions with all three of my children reveal when they first log onto Webkinz and Millsberry they take part in daily activities and games to earn KinzCash or Millsbucks so they can shop and buy things for their pets and avatars. For example, the 13-year-old explains some of the typical every-day activities she does when she goes to Webkinz.com include:

> . . . spinning the "Wheel of Wow" for a prize, going to the employment office to get paid for doing a job, searching for gems for a "Webkinz Crown of Wonder," playing "Wacky Bingoz" for a chance to win the jackpot, playing "Wishing Well" to win free money, and click-ing on the "I Love My Webkinz" heart to fill in the heart at the end of the week to win prizes [food and money].

If longer sessions had been recorded, evidence of educational and creative play prac-tices might have been observed at both Webkinz.com and Millsberry.com. While I do not want to diminish either the addictive or consumptive nature of online game play, pinpointing what types of activities resonate with girls in virtual pet adoption and avatar or character-based communities is critical for identifying the types of play that support—or do not support—informal learning, creativity, and self-directed play. Research capturing play activity on the Internet, as it happens in real time, is critical to understanding what young people might learn, make, or do with newly acquired digital literacies. As Hayes (2008) observes about girls and video game play:

> We have little specific or systematic documentation of individual players' trajectories of learn-ing and development of expertise—which games are more likely to trigger such learning, which players engage in such practices, or what conditions seem to be important in support-ing this trajectory of expertise. The literature on out-of-school learning [sic] can be a start-ing point for identifying what factors might be important. (p. 222)

The same holds true for how play unfolds at commercial websites. We know little about site users' trajectories of learning, and we need to know more. Literacy stud-ies are useful for identifying "out-of-school" learning and creative practices in pop-ular culture, including those situated in video games and web environments. Methods for capturing and coding play presented in this chapter may be useful for securing the kinds of systematic documentation Hayes proposes. Knowledge gained from this type of research can also be used to enrich the design of online environ-ments created with girls in mind, as well as improve learning opportunities for young people overall—girls and boys alike—available on the Internet.

NOTES

1. As the participants in this exploratory study were my own children, and the research was con-ducted for a research methods course, IRB approval was not obtained. However, all three chil-

dren have read and signed an "Assent/Consent to the Use of Research Data" form, co-signed by their father, giving permission for the data collected to be used for academic publications (print or electronic), books, journals, and presentations at conferences or workshops. The form makes explicit the children will not be identified by name, only by the age they were at the time of the study.

REFERENCES

Ask us: Questions about my character/buddy. (2009). Retrieved July 22, 2009, from http://consumer-contacts.generalmills.com/ConsolidatedContact.aspx?page=FAQ-http://www.millsberry.com#TOP

Barton, D., & Hamilton, H. (1998). *Local literacies*. New York: Routledge.

Brandt, D. (2001). *Literacy in American lives*. Cambridge, UK: Cambridge University Press.

Braun, L. (2007). *Teens, technology, and literacy, or why bad grammar isn't always bad.* Westport, CT: Libraries Unlimited.

Calvert, S., Mahler, B., Zehnder, S., Jenkins, A., & Lee, M. (2003). Gender differences in preadolescent children's online interactions: Symbolic modes of self-presentation and self expression. *Applied Developmental Psychology, 24,* 627–644.

Cassell, J. (1998). Storytelling as a nexus of change in the relationship between gender and technology: A feminist approach to software design. In J. Cassell & H. Jenkins (Eds.), *From Barbie to Mortal Kombat: Gender and computer games* (pp. 298–326). Cambridge, MA: MIT Press.

Center for Media Literacy. (2008). Literacy for the 21st century. Second edition. Retrieved March 7, 2009, from http://www.medialit.org/pdf/mlk/01a_mlkorientation_rev2.pdf

Cordes, C., & Miller, E. (Eds.). (2000). Technology literacy. *Fool's gold: A critical look at computers in childhood*. Alliance for Childhood, College Park, Maryland.   Retrieved October 19, 2009, from http://www.eric.ed.gov/ERICDocs/data/ericdocs2sql/ content_ storage_01/0000019b/80/23/07/fa.pdf

Cross, B. (2009). Mimesis and the spatial economy of children's play across digital divides: What consequences for creativity and agency? In R. Willett, M. Robinson, & J. Marsh (Eds.), *Play, creativity and digital cultures* (pp. 125–142). New York: Routledge.

de Certeau, M. (1984). *The practice of everyday life*. Berkley: University of California Press.

Denner, J., & Campe, S. (2008). What games made by girls can tell us. In Y. Kafai, C. Heeter, J. Denner & J. Sun (Eds.), *Beyond Barbie and Mortal Kombat: New perspectives on gender and gaming* (pp. 129–144). Cambridge, MA: MIT Press.

Druin, A., Bederson, B., Boltman, A., Miura, A., Knotts-Callahan, D., & Platt, M. (1999). Children as our technology design partners. In A. Druin, (Ed.), *The design of children's technology* (pp. 51–72). San Francisco, CA: Morgan Kauffman.

Gee, J. (2004). *Situated language and learning: A critique of traditional schooling*. New York: Routledge.

Gee, J. (2007a). *Good video games + Good learning: Collected essays on video games, learning and literacy.* New York: Peter Lang.

Gee, J. (2007b). *What video games have to teach us about learning and literacy. Revised and updated edition*. New York: Palgrave Macmillan.

Geisler, C. (2004). *Analyzing streams of language: Twelve steps to the systematic coding of text, talk, and other verbal data*. New York: Pearson Longman.

Grimes, S., & Shade, L. (2005). Neopian economics of play: Children's cyberpets and online communities as immersive advertising in NeoPets.com. *International Journal of Media and Cultural Politics 1*(2), 182–198. doi: 10.1386/macp.1.2.181/1

Hayes, E. (2008). Girls, gaming, and trajectories of IT expertise. In Y. Kafai, C. Heeter, J. Denner, & J. Sun (Eds.), *Beyond Barbie and Mortal Kombat: New perspectives on gender and gaming* (pp. 217–230). Cambridge, MA: MIT Press.

Heath, S. (1983). *Ways with Words: Language, life, and work in communities and classrooms.* New York: Cambridge University Press.

Hutchins, E. (1996). *Cognition in the wild.* Cambridge, MA: MIT Press.

Jenkins, H. (2006). Complete freedom of movement: Video games as gendered play spaces. In K. Salen & E. Zimmerman (Eds.), *The game design reader: A rules of play anthology* (pp. 330–363). Cambridge, MA: MIT Press.

Jenkins, H., & Cassell, J. (2008). From Quake Girls to Desperate Housewives: A decade of gender and computer games. In Y. Kafai, C. Heeter, J. Denner, & J. Sun (Eds.), *Beyond Barbie and Mortal Kombat: New perspectives on gender and gaming* (pp. 5–20). Cambridge, MA: MIT Press.

Kellner, D., & Share, J. (2005). Toward critical media literacy: Core concepts, debates, organizations, and Policy. *Discourse: Studies in the cultural politics of education 26*(3), 369–386.

KZERO Worldwide. (2009). Kids, tweens and teens in virtual worlds: Leading players, new companies and key strategies for success in the KT&T market place. Retrieved October 29, 2009, from http://www.kzero.co.uk/research-reports.php

Lankshear, C., & Knobel, M. (2006). *New literacies: Everyday practices and classroom learning. Second edition.* New York: McGraw-Hill Education Open University Press.

Leander, K. (2008). Toward a connective ethnography of online/offline literacy networks. In J. Coiro, M. Knobel, C. Lankshear, & D. Leu (Eds.), *Handbook of research on new literacies* (pp. 33–65). New York: Lawrence Erlbaum.

Livingstone, S. (2003a). The Changing nature and uses of media literacy. Retrieved June 6, 2009, from http://www.lse.ac.uk/collections/media@lse/pdf/Media@lseEWP4_july03.pdf

Livingstone, S. (2003b). Children's use of the internet: Reflections on the emerging research agenda. *New Media & Society, 5*(2), 147–166. DOI: 10.1177/1461444803005002001.

Livingstone, S. (2006). Drawing conclusions from new media research: Reflections and puzzles regarding children's experience of the internet. *The Information Society, 22*, 219–230.

Marsh, J. (2005). Introduction: Children of the digital age. In J. Marsh (Ed.), *Popular culture, new media and digital literacy in early childhood.* New York: RoutledgeFalmer.

Mazzarella, S. (2005). Introduction: It's a girl wide web. In S. Mazzarella (Ed.), *Girl wide web: Girls, the Internet, and the negotiation of identity* (pp. 1–12). New York: Peter Lang.

Neuman, S., & Roskos, K. (1992). Literacy objects as cultural tools: Effects in children's literacy behaviors in play. *Reading Research Quarterly, 27*(3), 202–225. Retrieved July 19, 2009, from http://www-personal.umich.edu/~sbneuman/pdf/LiteracyObjects.pdf

Parent Center: Powerpets Difference. (2009). Retrieved July 22, 2009, from http://www.powerpets.com/parents/welcome.asp?s=1&nocache=676.571

Parents: Education. (2009). Retrieved July 22, 2009, from http://www.moshimonsters.com/parents

Parent's Guide. What are the benefits of Club Penguin? (2009). Retrieved July 22, 2009, from http://www.clubpenguin.com/parents/club_penguin_guide.htm#benefits

Parés, N., & Parés, R. (2001). Interaction-driven virtual reality application design a particular case: El ball del fanalet or lightpools. *Presence, 10*(2), 236–245.

Quantcast: Millsberry.com. (2009). Retrieved October 31, 2009, from http://www.quantcast.com/millsberry.com#summary

Quantcast: Webkinz.com. (2009). Retrieved October 31, 2009, from http://www.quantcast.com/webkinz.com#summary

Roussou, M., Oliver, M., & Slater, M. (2008). Exploring activity theory as a tool for evaluating interactivity and learning in virtual environments for children. *Cognition, Technology and Work 10*(2), 141–153.

Selfe, C., & Hawisher, G. (2007). *Gaming lives in the twenty-first century: Literate connections.* New York: Palgrave Macmillan.

Squire, K. (2008). Video game literacy: A literacy of expertise. In J. Coiro, M. Knobel, C. Lankshear, & D. Leu (Eds.), *Handbook of research on new literacies* (pp. 635–669). New York: Lawrence Erlbaum

Thorne, B. (1993). *Gender play: Boys and girls in school.* New Brunswick, NJ: Rutgers University Press.

Turkle, S. (1995). Life on the screen: Identity in the age of the Internet. New York: Simon & Schuster.

Vincent, D. (1989). *Literacy and popular culture: England 1750–1914.* Cambridge, UK: Cambridge University Press.

Webkinz World and Learning. (2009). Retrieved July 21, 2009, from http://www.webkinz.com/us_en/pa_webkinz_learning.html

Whyville for Parents. (2009). Retrieved July 21, 2009, from http://b.whyville.net/smmk/top/gatesInfo?topic=whyville_for_parents

Whyville for Sponsors. (2009). Retrieved July 22, 2009, from http://b.whyville.net/smmk/top/gatesInfo?topic=whyville_for_sponsors

Willett, R. (2009). Consumption, production, and online identities: Amateur spoofs on YouTube. In R. Willett, M. Robinson, & J. Marsh (Eds.), *Play, creativity and digital cultures* (pp. 54–67). New York: Routledge.

Williams, D. (2007). Afterword. In C. Selfe & G. Hawisher (Eds.), *Gaming lives in the twenty-first century: Literate connections* (p. 257). New York: Palgrave Macmillan.

CHAPTER TWELVE

Talking Pink and Green

Exploring Teen Girls' Online Discussions of Environmental Issues

DENISE SEVICK BORTREE

In January 2008 a 14-year-old U.K. girl chained herself to the Japanese Embassy in protest of the whaling activities of Japanese fishing vessels. In an article in the *Birmingham Post* (UK), Sophie Wyness is quoted as saying, "It's a very important subject at the moment. They're such amazing creatures and they deserve rights and love and a bit of respect." This extraordinary act of a young girl drew international attention to an important issue. Her activism generated media coverage that challenged the typical media portrayal of young girls as self-interested with overwhelming concern for beauty and fashion (Kelly, 2006). Rather, she demonstrated that young girls can be strong and courageous activists, in this case, for animal rights. This type of bold action on the part of Wyness represents the vision that many feminists, educators, and parents offer as a model for young women's behavior and empowerment. Scholars have suggested that the road to empowerment for young women lies in part with the media with which young women engage (Potts, 2001; Kelly, Pomerantz, & Currie, 2006; de Vreese, 2007). According to Wyness, the impetus for her action was a movie distributed by activist organization Greenpeace International on the fishing practices of Japanese fishing vessels. Her revelation suggests that media can play a role in empowering young women and moving them to action. This chapter explores the current dialogue about environmental issues in an online media forum for young girls. It finds that young girls are interested in learning about and discussing substantive topics, such as environmental issues, when given the medium to do so. However, the source of the information and the way the content is framed plays a key role in engaging girls.

Prior research has suggested that the content of media for teen girls can have destructive outcomes, leading young girls to misconceptions of body image as well as a limited view of their role in society (Ballentine & Ogle, 2005; Botta, 2003; Clark & Tiggemann, 2006). At the same time media can be used to help young girls gain personal competence, knowledge, and a sense of social responsibility as illustrated by Sophie Wyness's actions.

One important media outlet for young girls is the teen magazine. With millions of readers, these magazines—*Cosmo Girl, Seventeen, Girl Friend, Girl's Life*, etc.—act as sources of socialization for young girls and a way for them to learn about femininity and the expectations of gender (Hess-Bibber, 1996; McRobbie, 1991; Currie, 1999). Writing in 1995, Steiner argued that women's media are responsible to move beyond the trivial and begin empowering women to take control of their lives. According to Steiner, media should encourage women to act as agents for social change. To explore how this could be happening in teen girl magazines, this chapter looks not only at media-generated content but also the dialogue that is occurring online by teen girls who respond to one area of political and social debate—environmental issues.

LITERATURE REVIEW

According to Pew Internet & American Life Project (Lenhart, Madden, Smith, & Macgill, 2007), 93% of teens are online, with girls leading in some types of new media use, such as blogging, and boys leading in others, such as video use and uploads. An earlier study found that teen girls are "power communicators and information seekers" (Lenhart et al., 2005, p. 9), engaging in many types of information seeking and Internet use. Kelly et al. (2006) found that teen girls use communication technology to explore gender limits by experimenting with atypical gender behaviors such as playing a more aggressive role in a relationship as well as by fighting back against sexual harassment.

One popular use of new media among girls is reading online magazine content by girls and for girls (Sarkio, 2003; Bayerl, 2000). Accessing magazine content in this format allows girls to read content for free but also to create content and respond to content created by others. Through comments and postings, girls are able to voice their opinions about the content of magazines, and they are able to read other's comments and respond to them. A quick review of the online versions of teen girl magazines pulled from multiple lists[1] revealed that some online magazines allow for comments and even create a moderated discussion of the topic that teen girls can use to dialogue about the issue. Others simply repurpose content from the traditional source, providing the reader with identical copy to the offline magazine and no opportunity to interact with it. This chapter will examine the content of those who provide an opportunity for teen girls to discuss magazine content.

Teen Girl Magazines

Teen girl magazines have traditionally played a key role in educating young girls about their role in society, their role within their peer groups, and in romantic relationships (Hess-Bibber, 1996; McRobbie, 1991; Currie, 1999). The magazines are written to be appropriate for the developmental stage of early adolescents. The content provided covers key developmental and social issues that trouble young girls at this age (Pattee, 2004). However, the content that is frequently absent is content that educates and encourages young girls to become active on social and political issues (Budgeon, 1994). One study of women's magazine content found that discussions of environmental issues are fairly rare; however, encouragingly, the number had increased between 1971 and 1991 (Budgeon & Currie, 1995). If teen girl magazines are to act as valuable sources of information that can lead to empowerment of young girls, then the content should include reasoned discussions of political and social issues. For environmental issues, this would mean addressing knowledge gaps that young girls experience about environmental topics (Arcury, Scollay, & Johnson, 1987; Schahn & Holzer, 1990) and framing issues in a way that empowers girls to take action on the issues.

Online versions of teen girl magazine content offer two avenues to empowerment of teen girls. The first way that new media format can empower teen girls is by moving beyond the traditional topics covered by girls' magazines, including celebrity, beauty, and fashion (Guzzetti & Gamboa, 2004). Rather, online versions of magazines for young girls have fewer space limits and could create a space for teens to talk about more "weighty" issues and as a result educate young girls about topics of larger significance. Second, by allowing girls to interact with content that has traditionally been static, they become contributors to the dialogue on important issues (Zobl, 2004). They can engage in a debate and try out arguments for their beliefs while participating in a safe, relatively anonymous environment. This experimentation allows them to build confidence in their own stance on issues, and may lead to more initiative in offline discussions and debate about topics such as environmental issues.

Teen Girls and Environmental Issues

Research has linked exposure to environmental issues in magazines and the formation of attitudes toward environmental issue in teens (Eagles & Demare, 1999).

However, teen girls lag behind boys in their knowledge about some environmental issues (Lyons & Breakwell, 1994). Through exposure to environmental topics and the opportunity to dialogue about those topics, online magazines can encourage a more sophisticated understanding of environmental issues among teen girls.

Prior research has found an excessive amount of consumer messaging in teen girls' magazines (McRobbie, 2008; Labre & Walsh-Childers, 2003) suggesting that "action" or activism may take the form of consumption for teen girls. McRobbie (2008) explains that media focus on consumption and products encourages "instant gratification through access to consumer goods" (p. 545). In the case of political and social issues, the solution is not instant, and the idea that purchasing can lead to a better world is deceptive. Offering a commodified strategy for environmental issues is to oversimplify the issues. Simply purchasing "environmentally friendly" products does not address the broader impact of consumption on the environment.

Adolescence has been noted as a time of loss of self-esteem and self-confidence among young girls (Brown & Gilligan, 1992). However, young girls who become active on environmental issues and other social and political issues experience more empowerment in their lives (Fry & Lousley, 2001). For young girls it is important that they see themselves as powerful and able to enact change in their world. This helps to balance power between genders and gives them a voice in their community and society.

The focus of the study is the conversations of the teen girls in response to online magazine articles. Scholars have argued that new media offer power to those who are traditionally excluded from dialogue and gives them a voice in the ongoing debate around important political and social issues (de Vreese, 2007). In this case, comments made by teen girls in response to magazine articles are analyzed to help illuminate how teen girls perceive environmental issues and the types of strategies they use to learn about and engage with the issues. The key questions addressed in this study are:

~ How do online magazine forums engage young girls in discussion of environmental issues?
~ How do gender and identity play a role in teen girls' conversations about and understanding of environmental issues?
~ In what ways are online discussions of environmental problems empowering teen girls to address environmental issues?

METHOD

This study examined the comments that teen girls made on online environmental articles. The commenting function is meant for readers to give feedback to the writer or magazine, but also it allows readers to interact with one another. An exhaustive list of online versions of teen girl magazines was constructed through a Web search in late 2008.[2] See Table 12.1 for the complete list of online magazines reviewed in this study.

Table 12.1 Full list of teen girls online magazines.

Online Magazine	Website address
American Cheerleader	http://www.americancheerleader.com/
Brio	http://www.briomag.com/
CosmoGirl	http://www.cosmogirl.com/
Dolly	http://dolly.ninemsn.com.au/
ElleGirl	http://ellegirl.elle.com/
Girlfriend	http://au.youth.yahoo.com/girlfriend/
Girl's Life	http://www.girlslife.com/
J-14	http://www.j-14.com/
New Moon	http://www.newmoon.com/
Seventeen	http://www.seventeen.com/
Teen	http://www.teenmag.com/
Verve Girl	http://vervegirl.com

The online content of the magazines was searched with keywords "environmental" and "green." All results were reviewed and only those that met two conditions were considered. First, the articles needed to be on an environmentally related topic. Second, the article needed to have comments from readers. In the end, 45 articles with a total of 573 posts were considered in the analysis process.[3] All articles were dated 2007 and 2008. After reading the posts, the author of this chapter eliminated an additional seven articles because they did not have any posts on environmental issues. These tended to be articles on green celebrity activities, and the posts related to the celebrity rather than environmental issues. After reading through all posts, only those posts that related to the story or to environmental issues were retained. In the final count, 38 articles and 573 posts were considered in the analysis of this study. These articles appeared in five magazines—*CosmoGIRL!*, *Dolly*, *GirlFriend*, *Girl's Life*, *Seventeen*, and *ElleGirl*.[4] See Table 12.2 for the total number of articles and comments identified in each magazine. Possibly, some of the posts were not written by teen girls, but the researcher was not able to discern the difference; therefore, all posts were analyzed as if they were produced by teen girls. Identities are often obscured in an online setting, and that was the case in this study. Because these magazines are explicitly written for a teen girl audience, the assumption was made that most visitors are girls and most comments are made by girls. Any comment that identified the writer as male or as falling outside the teen audience target (12–19) was eliminated from the study. Authors of comments in one of the online magazines, *Girl's Life*, created avatars that accompanied their posts. If the avatar was male, the comments were eliminated. This happened in only two cases.

Table 12.2 Article counts and comment counts by magazine.

Story Type	Number of Articles	Number of Comments
CosmoGirl	11	114
Dolly	4	27
ElleGirl	2	6
Girlfriend	8	130
Girl's Life	6	158
Seventeen	7	138

The analysis process for this study combined a top down and bottom up qualitative approach. The researcher first approached the data with the three research questions in a top down manner, hoping to find answers to the questions. Second, the author considered the content of the girls' posts and comments for any other themes that they might suggest. The results of the analysis are reported here.

FINDINGS

The online magazine content were categorized into six different types of articles: an "event article" written on a specific event, such as Earth Day; a "product article" which featured an eco-friendly product to be purchased; "issue feature" which typically covered an environmental issue in some depth; a "how-to" or "tips article" that would offer a list of behaviors that one could adopt or a list of products that one could purchase to be more environmentally responsible; a "quiz" which asked readers to respond to questions about environmental products or behaviors; and a "product for a cause" article which featured a product that could be purchased with proceeds going to a worthy environmental cause. The most common type of article was the how-to article with 13 articles (34%) falling into that category. The issue feature made a strong showing too, with 11 articles (29%) in that category. The least common was the purchase for a cause article type (5%), but it was the one that drew the most posts with an average of 32 posts per article. See Table 12.3 for a complete list of the number of articles in each category, the number of comments each category received, and the average number of comments per article in the categories.

Table 12.3 Number of relevant comments for each story type.

Story Type	Number of Articles	Number of Comments	Mean	SD
Issue Feature	11	115	10.45	8.57
How-To or Tips	13	229	17.62	16.76
Product Article	5	90	18.00	16.81
Event Article	6	54	9.00	3.69
Quizzes	1	21	21.00	0.00
Purchase for Cause	2	64	32.00	41.01
Total	38	573	15.08	14.87

Both the how-to articles and the product articles frequently featured "green" products and linked being environmentally responsible with purchasing behaviors. Combined, these articles totaled nearly half of the articles in the study suggesting that the magazines are offering consumption as a valid solution to environmental issues. In some cases these articles read like advertisements, promoting a product, providing price, and even ways to purchase. Content of the issue feature articles and the event articles (environmental events) offered more empowering solutions to girls. The issue feature articles often covered environmental topic in depth and offered solutions such as writing to a political leader, using less electricity or water, and visiting an environmental organization's website. Event articles recommended, as the name suggests, that readers participate in environmental events, giving teen girls the opportunity to act on their beliefs and participate in activism in a public context. Although quizzes are frequently found in teen girl magazines (and online magazines), only one quiz on environmental issues received comments in the magazines. It rated respondents' environmental responsibility based on their answers to questions about their current behaviors. An article type that blends both purchasing and activism is the product for a cause article. These articles share information about a product whose purchase results in a contribution to a cause. For example, in the article "Save the Earth with Cute Flip Flops" (*Seventeen*), girls learned that for every pair of shoes purchased, a contribution would be made to an environmental organization. This article type garnered the most comments, suggesting that teen girls see contribution toward an environmental issue as important and enjoy the direct link between their purchases and donations to a cause.

In general, the magazines were presenting environmental issues to young girls, either in the context of consumerism or in the context of minimizing one's impact on the environment. More importantly, when responding, the girls seemed to be offering their own strategies for addressing environmental issues. These too ranged from consumerism to conservation, with some gender related strategies emerging in their discussions.

"hey i totally agree with you"[5]

A dialogue between readers of environmental articles appeared to happen in most of the magazines, some more than others. Girls asked questions of each other and solicited advice, for example, asking for advice on starting an environmental club or asking where to purchase a certain environmentally friendly item. When one girl asked about Earth Day, "is there a certain time that we have t do this 60 hr thing or can we do this anytime of the day?" (*Girlfriend*) another answered "yes there is a special time its like 7:30 or something close to that." However most posts about environmental behaviors offered advice rather than solicited it. As an example, one girl recommended that others should "pick up trash around you're neighborhood, help to clean local lakes, rivers and ponds of pollution . . ." (*CosmoGIRL!*).

Interestingly, in the case of one magazine, *Girl's Life*, a moderated discussion forum was created for responses to the articles. What resulted were many girls directing questions to the moderator rather than to other girls. For example, girls posted "hey MOD where do you get the moose lip stuff" and ""***mod*** do you know if pantene products were tested on animals?" While there was still dialogue between the girls, many more comments were directed to the moderator, in a way defeating the goal of creating community and spurring interactions between the girls.

Interactions that moved beyond simple questions and answers or the offering of advice appeared in response to one type of article—the issue feature article. These articles covered topics such as global warming ("What Do McCain and Obama Think about Global Warming?" *Seventeen Magazine*), offshore drilling ("So, What's the Big Deal About 'Offshore Drilling'" *Seventeen Magazine*), and recycling ("Face Off: Should Recycling Be Mandatory?" *CosmoGIRL! Magazine*). In response to these articles, the girls offered arguments to defend their opinions and beliefs on the issues. Some comments sounded a lot like media sound bites, but others were well-reasoned arguments. On the issue of offshore drilling, the girls offered arguments on both sides of the issue:

> i believe that offshore drilling is completely out of the question. it would only be 3% of the oil we need, and it would not affect gas prices for another 10–15 years! We need results NOW. (*Seventeen*)

> i am for offshore drilling, i am sick and tired of giving my money to extremists in the middle eastand Shavez in South America. (*Seventeen*)

The same was true for recycling. An article in *CosmoGIRL!* on whether or not recycling should be mandatory received 24 comments. The quality of the comments suggested that the girls had given some thought to the issue, and were testing out arguments to defend their opinions.

> recycling helps the enviroment so much! Why would cost madder? its weird how the U.S. can afford war but cant affort to make the enviroment better. There is so much that we can do to make things better not just for us but for the ecosystem. Recycling saves trees and production. And yes you may have to use a truck to pick up recycling but what about changing to alternative fuels...or electricity which would help even more. Recycling should deffietly be mandatory. (*CosmoGIRL!*)

> . . . i think that we should reduseand reuse more than we recycle. recycling is good, but we wouldn't have to do it if we just used less of things and reuse scrap sheets of paper. (*CosmoGIRL!*)

"i'm a greenie and proud of it"

In the comments the girls not only talked about environmental issues, but some presented an identity that included the concept of environmentalist. A number of the girls labeled themselves as green or as vegetarians (for environmental reasons), incorporating these aspects of environmentalism into their identity. Statements of

254 | GIRL WIDE WEB 2.0

identity from the girls ranged from "i am a green person" to "i personally am a recycling fanatic . . ." In about 15 posts, girls specifically labeled themselves as "vegetarians" or "tree huggers" or "green"—yet in only one instance was the label gendered
"i am a green girl." It's admirable that they take on these identities and feel empowered to make changes in their lives. At the same time it was interesting that they
did not overtly link their environmental identity to gender. This was true in discussions of their preferences or their strongly held beliefs about the environment as well.
The word "girl" appeared only this one time except in reference to a girlfriend. It
appears that the girls do not think of being environmentally responsible as a gendered thing, but simply as an important thing to do. Prior research has suggested
that the genders are conceptualized differently in their relationship to nature
(Hunter, Hatch, & Johnson, 2004; Dryzek, 2005; Lee, 2008), with females being
"closer to nature," raising the possibility that teen girls see a link between their femininity and their environmental behaviors and beliefs, but that does not appear to
be the case in this sample.

Some girls linked their religious identities to their beliefs and opinions about
environmental issues, invoking God and the Bible on both sides of the global
warming issue. Girls arguing against the reality of global warming often pointed to
a Biblical passage promising that the earth would never be destroyed by flood
again. They used this to dispute the facts around climate change, arguing that
polar ice caps will not melt and flood the earth.

> i totally disagree with everyone worrying about global warming it's not true at all. God said
> he would never flood the earth again. If global warming too effect the whole earth would
> flood and according to God it cant. He promised he would never flood the earth again. He
> wouldnt go against his word. (*Girl's Life*)

On the other side of the argument, girls argued that believing in God does not pre-
clude one from believing in global warming.

> ya. i do believe in god. but, i believe in science as well, it explains a lot more. if you don't
> believe in global warming than you should watch **AN INCONVENIENT TRUTH**. It
> will tell you non-global warming believers the truth about what is happening to our plan-
> et. A truth that you 'non believers' just might not be able to handle. . really watch the movie,
> then you'll be eco-friendly, trust me. (*CosmoGIRL!*)

"i love all this stuff, especially the shoes."

Though there appeared to be little influence of gender in the way the girls identified themselves, gender played a role in the way the girls assigned value to environmental issues and in the strategies that they preferred to use to address issues. Some

of the most popular articles, those that received the most comments, were on topics of green consumerism of gendered products—eco-friendly hair care products, environmentally friendly beauty products, and green fashion. The responses to these articles suggested that the girls thought of eco-friendliness as a benefit that made products more appealing; however, the primary motivation for purchasing the products was still fashion, beauty or health. One girl wrote "It's so nice to be chic and eco-friendly at the same time! This is a great article . . ." (*ElleGirl*) and another said "ya i love my spritz hair spray. it makes me feel better knowing i am helpin the earth and looking pretty" (*Girl's Life*).

Young girls are socialized to be consumers of beauty and fashion products (McRobbie, 2008; Labre & Walsh-Childers, 2003), and it appears that this is happening around environmental issues too, with a large number of comments appearing on green product articles. Girls may be drawn to these products and feel that through purchasing them they are addressing environmental issues while also improving themselves. On one hand, the girls seemed to be genuinely interested in becoming more environmentally responsible, as two of the girls write "i am trying to go green, maybe i'll check out one of these hairsprays!" and "coolie! i've been trying it find some hair products that were good for the enviment!" (*Girl's Life*). On the other hand, their strategies for addressing environmental issues were frequently tied to their purchasing behaviors rather than conservation of resources. Another article in *Girl's Life* on eco-friendly fashion garnered over 50 comments in 8 hours, with most posts referring to the products as "cute" and thanking the magazine for posting the story.

This is not to suggest that consumption is a gendered strategy for addressing environmental issues. In fact, eco-friendly products are found at all ends of the spectrum from cars to washing machines to candy wrappers. Rather, the types of products the girls talked about buying in their pursuit of environmental responsibility—makeup, grooming products, clothing, etc.—tapped into the dubious relationship between gendered product consumption and empowerment (Budgeon, 1994). By buying these products girls are continuing to accept the link between feminist action and the purchase of beauty and fashion products. If "making a difference" or "taking action" on environmental issues is linked simply to the purchase of eco-friendly beauty and fashion items, then environmental activism is reduced to product consumption. Beyond offering only a mirage of empowerment, consumption contributes to environmental problems that exist.

Gender appeared to play a role in the way the girls talked about environmental issues and also the way they engaged with one another. Despite the fact that that some articles solicited strong feelings about environmental topics, global warming being the most common, the girls still engaged in a friendly, non-aggressive manner. This is likely linked to the gender-typical role of female as nurturer rather than competitor. In response to an article about global warming, one comment argued against the existence of global warming. This started a long string of responses about why the girls believed global warming is a reality. However, the interactions were typically polite with girls prefacing their comments with "No offense or anything . . ." or "Gosh you're all gonna hate me. ha ha . . ." or "alright, so i understand every-ones point of view in this, and to me, everyone has a correct view of this, yeah, per-haps . . ." Prior research has suggested that in group interactions females are less likely to express an opinion, than are males, and they are more likely to behave in prosocial ways (Wood & Karten, 1986; Carli, 1989). It appears that the readers of these magazines are posting qualified opinions in an attempt to avoid the percep-tion of antisocial or aggressive behaviors.

"me and my friends" working together

For the readers, environmental action was often situated in relationships—relation-ships with parents, friends, schoolmates, and other peers. The girls wrote about the environmental activities of their families, and concerns that they had with family members' environmental behaviors. One girl wrote, "I'm a vegetarian, and me and my mom are both eco-freaks, so we buy mostly organic food at my house. i like it. It tastes better, its better for the environment, and better for me" (*CosmoGIRL!*). They wrote about trying to change family members' behaviors "ok i am big on the recycling paper and cans but my dad just won't start i do save paper and take it to my moms to recycle but how can i get my dad to go greener as well? ne advice?" (*CosmoGIRL!*). One girl planned to use the information she learned in the article to argue for a change she wanted to make in her family.

> HHAHAHAHAHAHAH! i now have a very good argument against my parents getting a fake tree next year. We have cut down a real tree every year of my life, but my parents don't want one anymore. now i can tell them that getting a real tree from a tree farm saves the envi-ronment because they can be turned into "mulch." If my dad wants to go green with LED lights why not the 'whole 9 yards'? YES! (*Girl's Life*)

Friends also played an important role in environmental behaviors. A number of girls wrote about starting clubs with their friends or purchasing green product for their friends.

> OMG that is so cool!!! i'm totally buying a shirt for my friend for her b-day. it will be a cute surprise, because all my friends and me are doing projects on global warming right now at school, and we want to start an earth saver club! :) (*CosmoGIRL!*)

The decision to make a change was sometimes understood in the context of a friend group, "its really cool that a popular mag has decided to make a different to our world…it really influence me and my friends to help make a difference and put an end to climate change" (*Girlfriend*). Time and again, the issue of working in the context of social groups emerged. The girls also talked about schools changing policies or behaviors to be more environmentally friendly, and one mentioned her scout group working on an environmental project.

For these young girls it appears that environmental behaviors can be individual (purchasing clothes or beauty products) or in the context of family and peer groups. Environmental behaviors, however, can also be understood as a community effort, and this emerged in other comments made by the girls. An article on tips for going green solicited a number of responses from girls complaining about how their communities are not doing enough, and lamenting the fact that they have not been able to make an impact on the community. As one girl wrote, "ive been trying to get the message out but its hard because i live in a weathy town and no one seems to care" (*CosmoGIRL!*). Another girl echoed her sentiment:

> i come from a wealthy town also and nobody really cares about saving the earth. Our school hardly even recycles. i was staying late one day and the janitor took both the trash and the recycle bin and threw them in the waste. i was shocked.

I want to "make this world a better place!"

The most encouraging comments from the girls are the ones about what they are currently doing, and what they hope others will do also. These young girls felt passionately about environmental issues and were empowered to make changes in their lives. One girl wrote, "I am so concerned about the enviroment I became a vegetarian" (*Girlfriend*). Another wrote about taking action in the face of apathy among peers:

> i am a green person all ready, n me and my friend made a 'save enviroment' club at my school…some people jointed…but most didn't care…but now i will send that list to everyone. N see wht happens next (*Girlfriend*)

They demonstrated an enthusiasm for addressing environmental issues by offering common environmental practices.

> i'm the sort of person who turns of lights and turns off electricity. .i think we all need to turn off electricity we're not using and turn off dripping taps, have shorter showers and so much more. We need to take action! (*Girlfriend*)

A few girls talked about taking action in a new media environment as a way to demonstrate their commitment to environmental issues. Writing about a website sponsored by Greenpeace, one girl said, "i am so focused on saving the whales, a while ago i googled save the whales and i found that [virtual origami] and i made a whale and I called it chester" (*Dolly*).

The interest in environmental activism seemed to spread from girl to girl. When one wrote, "i put up the official posters for world environment day in my school and it was a great success" (*Girlfriend*) the next post said "i'll put up an official poster." Girls seemed to be inspired by the content of the articles and by each others' posts.

However, the examples of the girls taking action and recommending action were limited in their scope. While they understood environmental issues and the need for behavior at a personal, social, and community level, their recommended behaviors were almost always personal. Besides purchasing eco-friendly products they most commonly recommended behaviors were taking shorter showers, recycling, unplugging appliances (cellphone charger and computers), turning off lights, and using refillable water bottles. In order for young girls to be empowered to move beyond a simplistic understanding of their role in environmental issues, they need to move beyond offering simplistic solutions. With few exceptions, the discussion around environmental issues focuses around their own behaviors, how they can change personal grooming habits or eating habits to "make a difference." But, a full understanding of environmental issues requires a higher level of understanding.

A few posts offered hope that a more sophisticated understanding of environmental issues may emerge among readers. Posts on an article about supporting an environmental cause through purchasing flip-flops made the following statements:

> its great ppl are using even flip flops to stop global warming, but we need CHANGES. Cars and construction are the main effects of global warming, but ppl are too addicted to those to start using a healthier alternative transportation source. People are changing the goods that are EASIER for US to get used to, like sandals for instance. We are overlooking the harder habits to change, like cars. PPL need to stop with the luxuries that are easy for them and harmful to our planet. (*Seventeen*)

> Wow, here is a novel idea, rather than buying these flip-flops, which you probably don't need and which likely contributed to environmental degredation during their manufacturing, why don't you simply donate the money you would have spent directly to efforts to stop global warming (*Seventeen*)

CONCLUSION

This study found that online magazine article comments are a place where young girls talk about environmental issues and strategies for addressing these issues. The goals of this study were to explore how teen girls engage with online magazine content about environmental issues, how gender and identity play a role in girls' understanding of environmental issues, and what strategies girls use to address environmental issues.

The frequency of comments on environmental articles in this study varied with article types. The trends in commenting suggested that articles that spotlight green products or that offer simple to-dos (i.e., "10 Steps to Green Living" *CosmoGIRL!*) receive more comments than do issue feature or event articles, as evidenced by Table 12.3. But, a closer reading of the comments revealed that the content of those comments differed. In fact, comments on issue feature tended to include a healthy debate about weighty issues, such as recycling or global warming. By contrast, responses to product and how-to articles reflected the readers' appreciation for the products or suggestions with very little depth of content and little interaction among readers. Although issues articles received fewer comments, the nature of the comments suggested that when magazines cover environmental issues in a thorough manner, teen readers are motivated to formulate their opinions and express them. Rather than being passive consumers of information, they become active contributors to a dialogue about environmental issues. Unfortunately, this happened infrequently in the magazines examined in this study.

Gender and identity played a key role in teen girls' discussions of environmental issues as well. A number of the girls linked their environmental consciousness to their identities, calling themselves "green." Green identities among girls appeared to be linked to religion but not necessarily to gender; however, strategies for addressing environmental issues did appear to be to some degree gendered. Often girls are socialized to believe that their power resides in their beauty and their purchasing power, and this emerged in their discussions of environmental issues as well. Readers seemed to prefer articles that recommended consuming eco-friendly gendered products (including beauty products and fashion products) as a way of addressing environmental issues. Rather than challenging the dominant culture of consumption as an environmental solution, responses to these articles supported it.

Although consumption was the predominant strategy offered by the articles in this study, the teens often suggested other environmental behaviors including recycling, changing eating habits (becoming a vegetarian) or drinking habits (avoiding bottled water), and reducing electricity use. These suggestions rarely emerged in response to articles on consumption, but did appear on issues articles, event articles, and non-consumption-focused how-to articles. The teens also saw solutions for environmental issues residing in relationships on a number of levels—personal, social/peer, family, and community. The readers appeared to feel empowered to take personal actions, such as turning off electricity and recycling, and some wrote about environmental behaviors in the context of family and peer groups. What was lacking in their comments was an understanding of and engagement in behaviors on the societal and global levels. These include getting involved in public sphere behaviors such as joining civic groups that address environmental issues, participating in campaigns to raise awareness of issues and solutions to issues, or volunteering for an environmental organization. Teen girls with a nuanced understanding of environmental issues and the need for their participation in environmental solutions will be more likely to participate in these higher levels of activism. Media play a role in this.

While the link between bold activist action, like that taken by Wyness, and the content of online versions of teen girl magazines may not be a direct one, media that educate girls about the need for environmental activism will contribute to their empowerment. For magazines to cultivate teen girl readers that believe they can address environmental issues in a meaningful way, content will need to shift from consumption-frame to activist-frame.

NOTES

1. The population of online teen girl magazines was compiled from multiple lists found through Internet searches. Searches for terms "teen girls magazines," "teen magazines," "girls magazines," and "youth magazines" produced a list of 15 magazines. The website of each magazine was reviewed to see if it was currently active, and if it contained content specifically for teen girls. In the end, 12 magazines were reviewed for content in this study. The full list can be found in Table 12.1.

2. Only magazine with print issues were considered in the study, not online zines, for two reasons. First, the chapter examines how placing magazine content online and creating a forum in which teens can respond to it allows them to interact with content and with each other. It also opens a window on how teens perceive the content of the magazine articles, providing insight into how article topic can influence perception. Second, likely the type of content found in zines would vary from that found in online versions of print magazines, introducing another variable into the study. A cursory review of the online magazine gURL.com found few traditional articles on environmental issues with posted comments and many more forums on environmental topics that were not associated with traditional articles. For the sake of consistency, only online versions of print magazines were reviewed.

3. The analysis did not include forums, chat rooms, and other online venues for discussion on the website. Only comments to articles were examined. This allowed the author to draw a relationship between the content of the articles and the subsequent comments.

4. Following is a brief description of the six magazines whose articles and comments are discussed in this chapter. *CosmoGIRL!*, based in the U.S., is a teen girl magazine with a focus on beauty, fashion, and celebrity. The print version of *CosmoGIRL!* was discontinued in December 2008. *Dolly* is an Australian-based teen girl magazine whose print version is distributed monthly. Like the other magazines, it claims to cover beauty, fashion, and celebrity news. Also published in Australia *GirlFriend* magazine tends to reflect a more progressive perspective on girlhood, with articles on lifestyle portraying more than beauty and fashion. *Girl's Life* which serves teen and tween girl in the U.S., focuses on girls' achievements and encourages a balanced perspective on

girlhood. *Seventeen* magazine which targets older teens is also published in the U.S. The focus of the magazine is primarily fashion, beauty and health. The print version of *ElleGirl* magazine, based in the U.S., was discontinued in 2006, but the online version has continued. The focus of the magazine is fashion and beauty for older teens.

5. This subhead and the four that follow it are direct quotes from posts analyzed in this study. The quotes are left intact to reflect the voice of the posters.

REFERENCES

Arcury, T. A., Scollay, S. J., & Johnson, T. P. (1987). Sex differences in environmental concern and knowledge: The case of acid rain. *Sex Roles, 16*(9/10) 463–472.

Ballentine, L. W., & Ogle, J. P. (2005). The making and unmaking of body problems in *Seventeen* magazine, 1992–2003. *Family and Consumer Sciences Research Journal, 33*(4), 281–307.

Bayerl, K. (2000). Mags, zines, and gURLs: The exploding world of girls' publications. *Women's Studies Quarterly, 28*(3/4), 287–292.

Botta, R. A. (2003). For your health? The relationship between magazine reading and adolescents' body image and eating disturbances1. *Sex Roles, 48*(9/10), 389–400.

Brown, L. M., & Gilligan, C. (1992). *Meeting at the crossroads*. New York: Ballantine Books.

Budgeon, S. (1994). Fashion magazine advertising: Construction of femininity in the "postfeminist" era. In L. Manca & A. Manca (Eds.), *Gender and utopia in advertising* (pp. 62–70). Lisle, IL: Procopian Press.

Budgeon, S. & Currie, D. H. (1995). From feminism to post modernism: Women's liberation in fashion magazines. *Women's Studies International Forum, 19*(2), 173–186.

Carli, C. (1989). Gender Differences in Interaction Style and Influence. *Journal of Personality and Social Psychology, 56*(4), 565–576.

Clark, L., & Tiggemann, M. (2006). Appearance culture in nine- to 12-year-old girls: Media and peer influences on body sissatisfaction. *Social Development, 15*(4), 628–643.

Currie, D. (1999). *Girl talk: Adolescent magazines and their readers*. Toronto: University of Toronto Press.

de Vreese, C. H. (2007). Digital Renaissance: Young Consumer and Citizen? *The ANNALS of the American Academy of Political and Social Science, 611*(1), 207–216.

Dryzek, J. S. (2005). *The politics of the earth: Environmental discourses* (2nd ed.). Oxford: Oxford University Press.

Eagles, P. F. J., & Demare, R. (1999). Factors influencing children's environmental attitudes. *Journal of Environmental Education, (30)*: 33–37.

Fry, K., & Lousley, C. (2001). Girls just want to have fun with politics: out of the contradictions of popular culture, eco-grrrls are rising to redefine feminism, environmentalism and political action. *Alternatives Journal, 27*(2), 24–29.

Guzzetti, B. J., & Gamboa, M. (2004). Zines for social justice: Adolescent girls writing on their own. *Reading Research Quarterly, 39*(4), 408–436.

Kelly, D. M. (2006). Frame work: Helping youth counter their misrepresentations in media. *Canadian Journal of Education, 29*(1), 27–49.

Kelly, D. M., Pomerantz, S., & Currie, D. H. (2006). "No boundaries"? Girls' interactive, online learning about femininities. *Youth and Society, 38*(1), 3–28.

Hess-Bibber, S. (1996). *Am I thin enough yet?* New York: Oxford University Press.

Hunter, L. M., Hatch, A., & Johnson, A. (2004). Cross-national gender variation in environmental behaviors. *Social Science Quarterly, 85*(3), 677–694.

Labre, M. P., & Walsh-Childers, K. (2003). Friendly advice? Beauty messages in Web sites of teen magazines. *Mass Communication & Society, 6*(4), 379–396.

Lee, K. (2008). Making environmental communications meaningful to female adolescents. *Science Communication, 30*(2): 147–176.

Lenhart, A., Hitlin, P., & Madden, M. (2005). Teens and technology. Pew Internet and American Life Project. Retrieved July 28, 2009, from http://www.pewinternet.org/Reports/2005/Teens-and-Technology.aspx

Lenhart, A., Madden, M., Smith, A., & Macgill, A. (2007). Teens and social media. Pew Internet and American Life Project. Retrieved July 28, 2009, from http://www.pewinternet.org/Reports/2007/Teens-and-Social-Media.aspx

Lyons, E., & Breakwell, G. M. (1994). Factors predicting environmental concern and indifference in 13–16-year-olds. *Environment and Behavior, 26*(2) 223–238.

McRobbie, A. (1991). *Feminism and youth culture: From* Jackie *to* Just Seventeen. Boston: Unwin Hyman.

McRobbie, A. (2008). Young women and consumer culture: An intervention. *Cultural Studies, 22*(5): 531–550.

Pattee, A. S. (2004). Mass market mortification: The developmental appropriateness of teen magazines and the embarrassing story of standard. *The Library Quarterly, 74*(1), 1–20.

Potts, D.L. (2001). Channeling girl power: Positive female media images in "The Powerpuff Girls." *Studies in Media & Information Literacy Education, 1(*4), 1–9.

Sarkio, H. K. (2003). Teenage girls in the virtual world: Cyborgs or gendered beings? Unpublished doctoral dissertation, University of Minnesota.

Schahn, J., & Holzer, E. (1990). Studies of individual environmental concern: The role of knowledge, gender, and background variables. *Environment and Behavior, 22*(6) 767–786.

Steiner, L. (1995). Would the real women's magazine please stand up…for women. In C. Lont (Ed.), *Women and media* (pp. 99–108). Belmont, CA: Wadsworth.

Wood, W., & Karten, S. J. (1986). Sex differences in interaction style as a product of perceived sex differences in competence. *Journal of Personality and Social Psychology, 50*(2), 341–347.

Zobl, E. (2004). Persephone is pissed! Grrrl zine reading, making, and distributing across the globe. *Hecate,* 30(2), 156–175.

CHAPTER THIRTEEN

"Community, Content, and Commerce"

Alloy.com and the Commodification of Tween/Teen Girl Communities

SHARON R. MAZZARELLA & ALLISON ATKINS

INTRODUCTION

According to a March 2005 issue of the youth marketing industry newsletter, *Youth Markets ALERT*, "the time and loyalty kids and teens devote to online communities and blogs are forces that most marketers would love to tap into" ("Marketers Working," 2005, p. 1). Indeed, the article cites January 2005 ComScore Media Metrix data on the "most-visited Web sites among kids age 13–17," which show the site Alloy.com (Alloy) ranked seventh with 585,000 unique visitors during that time ("Marketers Working," 2005). Today, that number is almost double at 902,000 monthly uniques, 65% of whom are girls between the ages of 12–17 (Alloy Media & Marketing, 2010b). Interestingly, the *Youth Markets ALERT* article classified Alloy as an "online community." Reporting on the same ComScore Media Metrix study in the next issue of the newsletter, *Youth Markets ALERT* included a table showing Alloy ranked as the number one "most-visited *retail* Web site among teens age 13–17" during that time period ("Teens Go Online," 2005, emphasis ours). Is Alloy.com an online community or is it a retail site? This is one of the questions we take up in this chapter.

Background

Begun in 1996 as a "'media platform to reach hard-to-reach young consumers,'" Alloy, according to its co-founder, Matt Diamond, attempted "'not just to sell products but to be a brand that could reach [teens] and be a conduit for corporate America'" (Schnuer, 2004, p. S16). A subsidiary of Alloy Media & Marketing (AM+M[1]), Alloy is targeted to girls aged 12–24 with an average user age of 15.3 years. According to the AM+M site, Alloy is:

> The leading online destination providing teen girls with vibrant community, content and commerce. Alloy.com combines interactive applications, user generated content, the hottest apparel and accessories, with the web's most exciting promotions for a robust advertising environment. (Alloy Media & Marketing, 2010b)

In their analysis of online teen girl magazines, Labre and Walsh-Childers (2003, p. 382) assert that girls are the "hot new market" for fashion creators and advertisers. With young girls having greater purchasing power than before (Martens, Southerton, & Scott, 2004) and the growth of technologically innovative advertising tools, the Internet has become a popular vehicle for reaching this population, in particular through its celebration of a particular brand of normative, commodity femininity (Labre & Walsh-Childers, 2003), something AM+M realized early on.

While Alloy ostensibly serves as an online catalog for girls seeking access to the latest fashions, it has become an interactive, magazine-like virtual community for tween/teen girls, offering them content in such categories as *Entertainment*, *Style*, *Guys*, and *Astro* (Astrology). The Web site Mindgum.com ("Click Cliques," n.d.) argues that Alloy and other such sites are popular with tween and teen girls because "they combine aspects of a magazine (articles, reviews, horoscopes) with shopping, while at the same time creating a virtual community where kids can communicate with their peers." In fact, Alloy is what Alissa Quart (2003, p. 5) identifies as a classic "magalog"—combining elements of both magazines and catalogs in order to reach young consumers. Moreover, it is a magalog that is the centerpiece of AM+M's overall integrated and synergistic strategy for reaching the youth market.

Alloy Media + Marketing

A subsidiary of Alloy, Inc., AM+M describes itself to potential investors as:

> a widely recognized pioneer in nontraditional marketing. Working with AM+M, marketers reach consumers through a host of programs incorporating Alloy's diverse array of media and marketing assets and expertise in direct mail, college and high school media, interactive, dis-

play media, college guides, promotional and social network marketing. (Alloy Media & Marketing, 2010c)

The corporate structure of AM+M includes multiple subdivisions, two of which are directly relevant to our discussion of Alloy. The first is Alloy Media which includes Alloy.com and which "connects companies to their target audience through innovative, nontraditional media and marketing properties" such as Web sites. The second is Alloy Entertainment which is described as "an ideation leader in the youth market producing books, television and film" (Alloy Media & Marketing, 2010g). The latter is behind the highly successful book and movie *Sisterhood of the Traveling Pants* (the movie version of which was advertised heavily on the Alloy Web site) as well as the *Sweet Valley High, Gossip Girl,* and *Vampire Diaries* book series[2] among other successful TV and book projects. During the time of this project, the *Gossip Girl* television program, airing on the CW network, was being heavily advertised on Alloy. AM+M also owns the AMP advertising agency—an agency specializing in helping clients reach young consumers.

Luring potential investors and clients with its claims of a "database of 20+ million names" available for direct marketing (Alloy Media and Marketing, 2007b), AM+M has amassed a vast network of youth-oriented online outlets including channelone.com, candystand.com, and gurl.com among many others. According to their Web site, "Alloy reaches the highest concentration of teens, tweens, and young adults through our network of targeted sites to offer our clients innovative and integrated ad solutions reaching this audience in meaningful ways" (Alloy Media & Marketing, 2010a). Many of these sites have been acquired within the past 5–7 years purposely to strengthen and diversify AM+M's reach into the youth market and its ability to cross promote its products. For example, AM+M acquired Delia's (a then-competing tween/teen girl clothing catalog) in 2003 "thus boosting Alloy's database by 40% to 27 million young names" (Briggs, 2005); and the high school social networking site Sconex in March 2006, which gave AM+M access to Sconex's 500,000-plus registered users (Wasserman, 2006). In addition, in December 2007, AM+M created TEEN.com, an online advertising network offering advertisers the opportunity to target their products/services to "the highest concentration of teens online in a narrowly targeted and highly scalable way" (Alloy Media & Marketing, 2007a, p. 1). The network provides such companies as Verizon Wireless, Proctor & Gamble, and the CW Network both "display and integrated advertising" opportunities (Alloy Media & Marketing, 2007a, p. 1). Interestingly, an AM+M press release specifies that AM+M will handle the process of "ad unit placement across its partner properties" (Alloy Media & Marketing, 2007a, p. 2). By January 2009, AM+M was boasting their "'TEEN.com Network' [was] Now the #1 Online Community For Teens According to comScore" (Alloy Media & Marketing, 2009a).

LITERATURE REVIEW

The Youth Market

According to AM+M's September 2007 *Investor Presentation* (Alloy Media & Marketing, 2007b) the youth market is expected to grow "exponentially" over the next 5 years and marketers will need to continue their move toward "nontraditional advertising" in order to reach this market. *Tweens* (young people aged 8–14) in particular, according to AM+M, spend $51 billion of their own money each year and influence an additional $170 billion spent *on* them each year (Alloy Media & Marketing, 2010f). Similarly, AM+M labels *teens*, a third of whom carry a credit card, "a force in consumer spending, part of a highly influential $175B consumer market" (Alloy Media & Marketing, 2010e). AM+M considers itself to be a pioneer in marketing to this generation of youth. According to the *Boston Globe*, "this total pursuit of teens and tweens was largely an Alloy innovation" (Mehegan, 2006b, n.p.).

Corporations like AM+M have learned that one way to reach the tween/teen market today is to create virtual spaces for them. In a day and age when actual physical spaces for youth (e.g., parks, activity halls, and so on) have disappeared, the virtual spaces of online marketers have become welcoming places for the young as they combine entertainment, advice, friendship, community, and shopping (Cook & Kaiser, 2004; Labre & Walsh-Childers, 2003; Martens et al., 2004; Russell & Tyler, 2002, 2005). When it comes to sites targeted to girls, it is clear they promote products by celebrating a female identity grounded in normative or idealized femininity. Moreover, much of what they sell are products promising to facilitate the transition from girlhood to womanhood, products that often result in prematurely sexualizing girls. All the while, these companies position themselves as friends or big sisters who understand what tween/teen girls are going through, and who simultaneously provide a social space/community for girls.

Constructing the Teen and Tween Girl Consumer

While Alloy identifies its target audience as females aged 12–24 and lists Alloy in its "teen," rather than its "tween" online sites, it is clear from its content and clothing that they are also targeting the tween girl. Moreover, as evidenced by the previously-mentioned AM+M statistic that 65% of users are aged 12–17, tween girls are also visiting the site (Alloy Media & Marketing, 2010b). Despite the fact that the word tween is used routinely by academics, marketers, pundits, parents, the media—almost everyone but young people themselves—it is imperative to understand the marketing origins and connotations of the term. Generally considered to be either a hybrid of teen and between or a contraction of between (although no apostrophe is used) (Lamb & Brown, 2006), there is no disputing that the word was coined in the 1980s by marketers to refer to children (defined primarily as girls) between the ages of 8–14.[3] In fact, our search of the LexisNexis database found that the term first appeared in U.S. newspapers in 1989, and "by 1998, the Tween concept was well entrenched in market circles" (Cook & Kaiser, 2004, p. 218). In their informational and advice book for parents, Lamb and Brown remind us of the corporate origins of the term tween when they assert that: "As a psychological category tween falls short; as a marketing strategy it is brilliant" (2006, p. 5).

Many scholars argue that corporations targeting tween girl consumers take advantage of the fact that tweendom is "an aspirational social identity," in that young people in this age group seek to move "up the age prestige ladder"—a form of "anticipatory enculturation" (Cook & Kaiser, 2004, p. 206). At the same time, "teens now aspire to dress as if they were women in their twenties" (Quart, 2003, p. 16). As such, marketers focus on girls' coming of age, something that is sold to girls as empowering (Cook & Kaiser, 2004; Russell & Tyler, 2002). According to Cook and Kaiser (2004, p. 223), the tween girl category seems "to encode anticipatory status and identities to be acted out in the present all the while preparing the ground for entry into a particular articulation of heterosexual female culture."

Stocked with what can best be described as transitional products (Cook & Kaiser, 2004; Martens et al., 2004; Russell & Tyler, 2005), tween girl marketers target the confused "betwixt and be tween" (Cook & Kaiser, 2004, p. 203) girl child. The anxieties that are the hallmark of the pubertal and pre-pubertal years are relieved through the acquisition of aspirational products—makeup, jewelry, halter tops, and so on. In fact, part and parcel of the construction of the tween/teen girl identity is this concept of "normative femininity"—a narrow, culturally prescribed vision of what the ideal woman/girl should be like. Two primary components of normative femininity are physical attractiveness (in a conventional, socially defined way) and a focus on relationships (Wood, 2007), notably heterosexual relationships. Moreover, one way to achieve the former, and at least the appearance of the latter, is with clothing, accessories, and makeup—"the commodities needed to perform normative femininity" (Hains, 2007, p. 199). In fact, as Russell and Tyler (2005) remind us, to be a young girl means "to be a child, to be a consumer, and to be feminine" (p. 227). While tween and teen girls as ideal consuming subjects are targeted via a wide range of media outlets, it is the Internet that is the most intriguing as it has rapidly become a space in which girls engage in identity play and exploration (Mazzarella, 2005).

The Internet as a Space for Girls

In 2001, the Center for Media Education declared teenagers to be "the *defining users* of [the] digital media culture" who are "as comfortable growing up with digital media as their parents' generation was with the telephone and TV" (Montgomery, 2001, p. 1). That study reported that almost three quarters of young people aged 12–17 were online. Even more recent statistics by the Pew Internet and American Life Project found that while Americans of all ages are online, over 90% of teens aged 12–17 are, compared with just over three-quarters of adults in their 40s and nearly three-quarters of adults in their 50s (Jones & Fox, 2009).

Contrary to public perceptions, it is not only boys of this generation who are wired. An August 2000 study reported that girls between the ages of twelve to seventeen were then considered to be the fastest growing group of Internet users (Rickert & Sacharow, 2000). While the press has been quick to frame the Internet as a dangerous place for girls (Edwards, 2005) or report that girls are not as Internet-savvy as boys, the gender gap, indeed, appears to be lessening. Early research evidenced significant gender differences in how boys and girls used the Internet (Lenhart, Rainie, & Lewis, 2001; Tufte, 2003), with girls more likely to use the Internet for social communication such as e-mail and instant messaging and boys more for playing/downloading games and downloading music (Lenhart et al., 2001). Indeed, Tufte, likened this gender difference to the "best friend culture" (2003, p. 72) in which girls tend to engage. More recent scholarship, however, has shown that, "over time, adolescent boys' and girls' online activities have become more similar than different" (Gross, 2004, p. 646), notably boys' increased tendency to use the Internet for social communication.

Indeed, tweens and teens of both genders often expand their social networks through the Internet (Alloy Media & Marketing, 2006). Internet usage allows the young to communicate with one another, seek information confidentially, and express their thoughts and ideas (Mazzarella, 2005). A 2006 study of tweens and teens aged 8–18 conducted by AM+M and Harris Interactive reveals the role online social networking sites play in allowing youth "to practice social behaviors, to try out different personas in their exploration for identity" and in nurturing friendships (Alloy Media & Marketing, 2006, n.p.). According to AM+M executive, Samantha Skey, the new friendship circles afforded by online technology in general and social networking sites in particular "extends to brands endeavoring to reach this influential audience as advertisers look to use the power of youth connectivity—and the evolving definition of 'friend'—to enable online propagation of their messages'" (Alloy Media & Marketing, 2006).

Given what we know about the strategies employed by AM+M as well as how marketers in general have constructed the tween/teen girl consumer, this study proposes the following research questions:

RQ1:   How does AM+M's flagship online property, Alloy.com, construct an
           idealized version of the tween/teen girl?
RQ2:   Is Alloy.com an online community or a retail site?
RQ2a: Does Alloy.com function synergistically as an outlet to promote
           other AM+M properties?

METHODS

In order to address these research questions, the second author monitored Alloy.com
during the week of October 16–22, 2007. Specifically, she analyzed one each of the
main sections—Entertainment, Style, Guys, Life, Astro (Astrology), Quizzes, and
Boards—one day of the week. Each section was examined for topics covered; presence of advertising (banner ads and links to other corporate sites); links between
"editorial" content and products advertised; role of celebrities; messages about dat-
ing/romance; messages about body/appearance; the ways in which the site works to
create a community; and evidence of how Alloy constructs a tween/teen girl identity. During the initial week of data collection, the second author kept notes on all
of the above-mentioned topics using an open-ended, qualitative coding sheet. The
notes were then passed along to the first author who, during January 2008, revisited the site's archives to verify the second author's findings, adding more specific
examples and quotations to the notes. Although this second phase was conducted
three months later, almost everything on the site is archived, and the first author
was able to view the exact content that was available during the initial October 2007
phase. The two authors then met to discuss and compare their findings and arrive
at a consensus regarding interpretations of how Alloy.com constructs the ideal
tween/teen girl—how it constructs the ideal "Alloyer."

CONSTRUCTING AN IDEALIZED VERSION OF THE
TWEEN/TEEN GIRL

"Hey all new Alloyers," exclaims a user on one of the popular message boards welcoming girls who have recently become posters and have, thereby, entered into a
community of mostly tween/teen girls known to each other as "Alloyers." But what
does it mean to be an Alloyer? If we were to deconstruct the prototypical Alloyer
(i.e., the way Alloy.com constructs an idealized version of the tween/teen girl), we
would describe her as (1) trendy, stylish, and normatively feminine (traits to be
achieved by being a consumer), (2) pop culture savvy, and (3) boy-crazy.[4]

Being Trendy and Stylish: Alloy and Commodity Femininity

In the way that fashion and style allow girls to experiment with identities and to fit in with particular social groups (Martens et al., 2004), the "Style" section of Alloy deluges the user with messages about the importance of style through its numerous subsections. If she is careful, the Alloyer can, in these various subsections, learn about the current popular looks ("Get This Look") by following the latest trends ("Trendspotter," "Fashion Seen," "Style Features," "Style Slides") without violating any fashion dictates ("Oh No She Didn't!"), and then be praised for a job well done ("Style Child"). Through its emphasis on style, Alloy seems to be functioning as the quintessential popular girl—being looked up to and dictating style trends while ridiculing and ostracizing those who do not measure up, for example, those identified as being in need of makeovers ("Oh No She Didn't!").

Like many youth-oriented marketers who promote the idea of commodity-based image transformations (Martens et al., 2004; Russell & Tyler, 2002, 2005), the "Oh No She Didn't!" subsection of "Style" identifies girls in need of fashion help. Fortunately, these girls can find and purchase a more acceptable and trendy image through Alloy's "Get This Look" section, but it is not just clothing that can transform the average Alloyer into a paragon of normative, idealized femininity. As is true of most fashion magazines targeted to women and girls, Alloy shows how physical imperfections can be cured through makeup, creams, and hair products. For example, at the time of our original wave of data collection, Alloy featured the "Clinique Boot Camp,"[5] in which the Clinique cosmetic company offered commodity solutions to users' beauty problems, even allowing users to e-mail Clinique directly for advice. The phrase "boot camp" implies not only a transformation, but also a process of whipping raw recruits into shape. Clinique presented itself as having the products and information necessary to transform a typical girl into the idealized, older, even sexualized normatively feminine woman so valued on Alloy in general and in the culture at large.

Similarly, the "Style" section identifies other favorite products and "how to" steps for applying makeup. For example, on October 17, 2007, actress Alexis Bledel (*Sisterhood of the Traveling Pants*) was featured. To get Alexis's look, users are told they need shiny hair and "smooch-worthy" lips. Specifically, girls who want to look like the popular actress need to purchase "Pantene Pro-V Ice Shine Conditioner" and "L'Oréal's Endless Lip Color." To make it even easier to fix dull hair and lackluster lips, a link for each product takes girls to an online drugstore, where they can buy the corrective products. Even the "Astro" (astrology) section offers beauty advice in its "Beauty Scopes," subsection by offering a beauty product-related horoscope. For example, the first author's Beauty Scope (Aquarius) for the week of October 18, 2007 read:

Things might be going your way, but don't get *too* comfortable! If a friend of yours is experiencing a streak of bad luck, listen and be sympathetic—don't preach and talk about how great *you're* doing. Instead, spread the love (and this cranberry lip gloss) and be thankful for what you've got!

The scope then identified her "Berry-licious Lip Gloss" as Lip Glaze (in Cranberry) by Stila and her "Perfect Lip gloss" as Smooch Me! Lip Lacquer (in Go Figure) by Pinkie Swear. Not surprisingly, clicking on the names of each product took her to the Sephora.com cosmetic store Web site where she could purchase her desired product.

If girls need beauty and fashion advice for everyday life, they are even more in need of it for special events. For example, on October 17, 2007, one of the "Style" headlines read "Homecoming Hair: Want Your Fave Celeb's 'do? Get expert style tips from the pros!" Similarly, a range of style and beauty quizzes found in the "Style" subsection of "Quizzes" deal with the concept of making oneself over. Quiz titles include, "What Winter Trend Should You Try?" "Is Your Style Red Carpet Ready?" "Do You Need a Makeover?" and "What's Your Hair Color Personality?"

Considering that the first author was not aware that her hair had a "personality," she decided to take that quiz that began with the introductory statement:

Do people ever tell you that you would make an *awesome* blonde or a brunette? Apparently something about your personality just screams a certain hair color. Not sure what it is? No worries! Take our all-new SuperQuiz to see what your hair color personality is! We'll take your answers, and come up with a hair color that's been custom made for you.

After taking a quiz consisting of questions ranging from her favorite musical performer to her after-school activities, from her thoughts about boys to her goals in life, the first author was labeled a "Natural Brunette" (which she is). The results went on to read:

Being a natural brunette, you exude sophistication and earthy vibes. You're intelligent and charming. While you might not go out of your way to get attention, you have a soft glow about you that makes you stand out. Introverted and occasionally shy, your biggest challenge is to let more peeps see your fun-loving side. Try dark blonde highlights for summer, and you'll get tons of compliments—and have tons of fun. But don't forget to pamper your hair, too. Keep your hair healthy and shiny with Sunsilk's Color Boost products.

For us, the key words here are the last four—words that are hyperlinked to the Sunsilk Web site announcing "We're here to help." This quiz appears to be an example of what AM+M refers to on its Web site as "editorial integration"—the opportunity for advertisers to integrate their messages directly into the "editorial" content of Alloy. In fact, in describing the editorial integration opportunities available on Alloy.com, AM+M includes custom quizzes (such as the above), sponsored polls, horoscope sponsorship or integration, and "feature articles or reviews with editorial call-outs" among several others (Alloy Media + Marketing, 2010d).

Another way in which Alloy promotes an idealized, normative femininity is by encouraging the acquisition of products, in particular products targeted to older girls and young women that can make teens and tweens feel older and more powerful (Cook & Kaiser, 2004; Russell & Tyler, 2002, 2005). In fact, the use of makeup by tween/teen girls is presented by Alloy as the norm. For example, the "Fashion Seen" section features young girls' pictures each Thursday. Other Alloyers can click on specific pictures and read a short biographical sketch about each pictured girl. The sketches typically include questions about their fashion style. Questions include "What's your fave beauty product?" "How much time do you spend on your make-up?" "What's the most you've ever spent on a product?" "What's your morning makeup routine like?" The most telling thing about this list of questions is the question that is *not* asked. One would assume the first question to precede this list would be the basic "Do you wear makeup?" By not asking this basic-level question, it is assumed that the typical Alloyer *does* wear makeup. So the reader who herself does not wear makeup is subtly sent a message that "all of the other girls your age are doing it." This assumption further perpetuates the message that girls need to adapt to the dictates of normative femininity as they become young women (Cook & Kaiser, 2004; Labre & Walsh-Childers, 2003; Russell & Tyler, 2002, 2005).

Being Pop Culture Savvy: Alloy and the Cult of Personality

In addition to being a consumer, being an Alloyer means being pop culture savvy. Given the importance of celebrities in youth culture (Duits & van Romondt Vis, 2007; McRobbie, 1991; Sweeney, 2008), not to mention the media's current obsession with "young Hollywood" (notably starlets and socialites such as Paris Hilton, Britney Spears, Lindsay Lohan, the cast of the *Gossip Girl* television program) (Sweeney, 2008), it is not surprising that a magalog like Alloy will devote a significant amount of space to young celebrities—both in terms of style and gossip. Echoing McRobbie's (1991) concept of girls' bedroom culture, Sweeney reminds us that visiting the typical adolescent girl's bedroom will, most likely, reveal a plethora of celebrity and pop culture images adorning the walls—a phenomenon she likens to "an expression of visual identity" and "the performance of the Teenage Feminine." Girls' walls, she asserts "provide a canvas on which to dialogue with popular culture" (Sweeney, 2008, p. 5). Alloy's abundant use of celebrities and pop culture references function, in a way, as a means to "dialogue" with tween/teen girls, and is in recognition of the importance these pop icons play in girls' lives. Moreover, the manner in which Alloy presents young celebrities is telling. Specifically, they present female celebrities as role models to be emulated and male celebrities as romantic idols to be "crushed on." We will discuss male celebrities more in the next section, but here we focus on female celebrities.

Alloy offers users a range of features on popular female celebrities including Britney Spears, Rihanna, and Carrie Underwood—young women more in the aspirational rather than actual age range of tween/teen girls—many of which highlight the need for girls to aspire to look like a celebrity. For example, in one section, following a picture and brief biographical update of an individual celebrity, girls are told how to "Get this look." It is not surprising that girls will relate to young female celebrities since celebrities, as Sweeney (2008, p. 5) reminds us, function as "powerful meta-cultural concepts which provide gateways to our fantasy versions of our selves." Based on their findings of a study of how of tween girls in Amsterdam "make meaning from celebrities," Duits and van Romondt Vis (2007, p. 18) assert that celebrities provide girls with

> a tool to express their identity. Through appropriating the celebrity to their own lives the girls actively construct their identities....It is not imitation, but rather legitimization of behaviour. Celebrities offer lifestyles the girls can aspire to or avoid, and which, at some points, provide them with possibilities for and empowerment in their own lives.

According to the Web site, Alloyers should not only emulate the appearance of celebrities, but they should also know everything about them—a message Alloy transmits in part through its "Daily Gossip" section. The use of the word "daily" is telling as it implies that girls should check back with the site each day or risk dropping out of the loop. In this way, the site becomes part of a girl's everyday routine. If quick tidbits of daily gossip are not enough, more can be found under "Gossip Roundup," "The 10," "Celeb Blogger," and "Star Slides," each of which provides a wealth of celebrity-related information.

The "Life" section of Alloy offers an interesting way to encourage links between real life and fiction in its "Life Slide: TV Advisers" section. Every few days a series of questions are asked such as "How should you handle peer pressure?" Users are then taken through a series of still images from particular television programs (for the above question it was *Gossip Girl*) along with a plot scenario that relates to the quandary posed by the question. Following the scenario, an Alloyer gives her own take on the scene and offers advice to other Alloyers. In this example, Alloy is not only drawing links between television and real life, but is also providing advertising for one of its own products, *Gossip Girl*, a blatant form of what McAllister calls "integrated plugola" (2007, p. 252) "where media content promotes subsidiary licenses of the same media owner."

Across multiple sections, Alloy celebrates what are primarily young, female, and "sexy" celebrities—what Sweeney refers to as "Lipstick Lolitas" (2008, p. 43). The

"Entertainment" section provides girls with all of the latest gossip on them; the "Style" section teaches girls how they can look like them; and the "Guys" section instructs girls on how to emulate their dating styles. For example, an archived piece from August 3, 2007 featured "Celeb Dating Do's and Don'ts." The female celebrities featured under this title included Lindsay Lohan, Jessica Simpson, Beyoncé, Heidi Montag, Paris Hilton, and Kirsten Dunst. Although slightly older than the typical 15.3-year-old Alloyer, their fan base consists largely of tween/teen girls aspiring to be like them. In this way, girls are presented with a celebration of older, sexualized, commodified role models.

Being Boy Crazy: Alloy and Enforced Heterosexuality

Being an Alloyer also means being boy crazy—an enforced heterosexuality characteristic of normative femininity. While marketers encourage girls to conform to normative femininity in order to receive attention from males (Labre & Walsh-Childers, 2003; Martens et al., 2004; Russell & Tyler, 2002, 2005), Alloy goes one step further by providing a "Guy Guide" through which girls can learn about how guys behave—a decoder ring or sorts promising to help girls understand guys. For example, the "Guy Guide" offers answers to such questions as "Why Doesn't He Call?" "Should You Make a Move?" and "Is He Ex-Obsessed?"

In addition, each week, the "Dude Decoder" asks a guy a question about which girls are concerned—or at least about which they are *told* they should be concerned. For example, questions include "How would you like for your crush to approach you?" or "What do girls do that boys like/dislike." Girls are encouraged to email their questions for guys to answer. In this way, the site is a safe way to learn about the inner workings of the male mind, but it also places extreme emphasis on the belief that girls need to look and act in a way that is acceptable/pleasing to boys. For example, on October 18, 2007, the subject under "Crush Alert" was "Cute Boys and What They Like in Girls." Not surprisingly, Alloy's emphasis on being appealing to guys is one way in which they are able to market clothes, as girls are told they need a look that makes them appealing to guys. Luckily for them, the same Web site that sends them this message also offers the products necessary to achieving this guy-desired look.

Once girls have succeeded in attracting the opposite sex, they can tell their stories on either "He Did What?!" or "PDA." For example, on "Guy Features" a segment titled "PDA" allows a girl to submit a picture of herself with her boyfriend along with answers to questions about their relationship. Given that a primary component of normative femininity is an emphasis on relationships, a big part of being a successful Alloyer is having a boyfriend and a relationship that is worthy of other

Alloyers' attention. By reading these features, girls can gain a deeper understanding of what guys expect from girls—or at least what AM+M wants girls to think guys expect from them. These articles function as self-help tomes, teaching girls how to look and act in a way that is attractive to boys.

Of course, just the presence of a pull-down menu about "Guys" evidences the enforced heterosexuality perpetuated by Alloy. Certainly, girls finding themselves attracted to other girls can focus on the celebrity section where pictures and stories about attractive, young, female starlets abound, but there is no *official* endorsement on the part of Alloy of anything other than a heterosexual identity. Alloy is not the place for queer girls to find like-minded peers. For that, they have to go elsewhere (Driver, 2007).

ALLOY.COM AS A MARKETING TOOL

Given its origins as a more traditional tween/teen girl clothing catalog, it is not surprising that its online version has a commercial imperative. But Alloy.com functions as more than a way to market clothing; rather, it also works to market other AM+M properties and partners to Alloyers, something that is accomplished in part through Alloy's focus on celebrities.

AM+M, Alloy.com, and Corporate Synergy

During the time of our study, one of the daily gossip items was about *Gossip Girl* star, Chace Crawford who, we were told "was spotted snuggling up with *American Idol's* Carrie Underwood this past weekend." During this same week, Chace was included in the "Guy Slides" section's feature on "TV Crush List." The first of several young males featured, users are told by the editors: "We're totally hooked on *Gossip Girl*. Can you blame us? Super hot Chace is one of the main characters, and we love his tousled hair and deep baby blues. Before *Gossip Girls* aired, Chace visited our office, and girls—he is even dreamier in person (we swear!)."

But it's not just AM+M-affiliated television programs that are marketed to girls through Alloy. The "Life" section features a subsection on "Books" which includes "Books We Love." During the week of our data collection, two of the books that were highlighted were products of AM+M, *Forever in Blue: The Fourth Summer of the Sisterhood* (a sequel to *Sisterhood of the Traveling Pants*) and *It Had to Be You: The Gossip Girl Prequel*. The section features each book's cover and a brief plot synopsis with a link to "get more information." Clicking on the link for *Forever in Blue: The Fourth Summer of the Sisterhood* takes the user to a Random House Web site called "Sisterhood Central" (2008), "your source for all things sisterhood." Similarly, clicking on the link to "get more information" for *It Had to Be You: The Gossip Girl Prequel*, takes the user to an Alloy Entertainment Web site called "Gossip Girl: The Official Book Site" (2008). In the case of the Gossip Girl book, girls can do more than "get more information." They can also "read the first chapter" and "buy the book" directly from the Alloy site, further evidence of Alloy's extensive use of "integrated plugola" (McAllister, 2007, p. 252) in advertising its own products.

Alloy.com and Cross-Promotion

In addition Alloy plays a role in a range of cross-promotional efforts of AM+M and other related companies. For example, each section/subsection of Alloy features banner ads for a range of products—some created by Alloy, most not. Some of the products featured in banner ads during the week of our study included: Pizza Hut, T-Mobile, Orbitz, Zwinky.com, LowerMyBills.com, *Nature of the Beast* (ABC Family movie), Advil, Verizon, and *Gossip Girl* (CW television series). Clearly, what began as a clothing catalog designed to sell Alloy clothing to tween and teen girls has morphed into a vehicle for delivering tween and teen girls to other marketers.

Perhaps the most blatant and interesting example is the cross-promotional deal set up between Verizon Wireless and the CW television program *Gossip Girl*, both of which are prominently advertised on Alloy.com and, as mentioned earlier, are listed as clients of AM+M's TEEN.com online advertising network. As already mentioned, *Gossip Girl* is a book series packaged by AM+M which has been spun off into the CW Network TV program. According to *Advertising Age* (Steinberg, 2007), Verizon Wireless beat out four other rival wireless providers to be the official phone of the program, meaning, among other things, that *Gossip Girl* characters can all be seen using Verizon Wireless phones. A visit to the program's Web site (Gossip Girl, 2008) reveals more banner ads for Verizon Wireless—specifically, an advertisement for Verizon's V CAST phones through which users can exclusively access of a range of Gossip Girl-related content including "juicy gossip" and "daily dish" about the program "right on your phone" "exclusively from Verizon Wireless." Clicking on the ad takes the user to a Verizon Web site (2008) providing teasers for a plethora of Gossip Girl-related content including videos, music, wallpaper, and more—all of which can only be accessed for real using a Verizon V CAST phone. Such synergistic cross-promotion related to youth-oriented media is not unique to AM+M. Disney pioneered it (Wasko, 2001), but it is the interactivity of new media (wireless phones and Web sites, for example) that makes it all seem so much brazen in this case.

Online Community or Retail Site?

While barraging users with a range of advertising messages, like many corporate Web sites for tweens/teens (Mazzarella, 2008), Alloy simultaneously provides spaces for girls to interact with each other and with the Alloy staff. In general, the Internet allows girls to expand their social groups to include girls from many different places and backgrounds (Mazzarella, 2005), but, in this case, their only commonality is Alloy. They become friends because they are Alloyers first. Just as the mall has become a place to shop and spend time with friends (Russell & Tyler, 2005), the Internet has become a place where girls can interact with one another and learn about fashion, pop culture, boys, and shopping. In terms of what is being offered to customers, Alloy is actually *more* of a social space than the mall in part because AM+M is actively *working* to construct Alloy as a social community. Yet, in many ways it is a *re*-active not an active community. For example, nearly every feature is followed by a "You Say" message board, where girls can react to the content by expressing their thoughts and ideas. Polls are also popular features that allow Alloyers to express opinions that are guaranteed to be heard by Alloy staffers—or more likely Alloy marketers, as such polls serve as just another way to gather consumer data from users who must register by providing personal information in order to participate on many of the more "social" activities on Alloy.

In fact, each section offers some means by which girls can react to (and interact with?) the content provided by Alloy. The "Entertainment" section features post-article boards on which girls can leave comments and even respond to other girls' comments. Under "Style," girls can give their opinions on trends by voting to "Trash It or Flash It." In the "Guys" section, girls can be featured with their boyfriends under a "PDA" slide to which other girls can respond. "Life" offers a "Sound Off" section where girls can express their opinions on highlighted topics such as "Should Middle Schools Distribute Birth Control?" The "Quizzes" section allows girls to take fun quizzes that relate to teen/tween lives and even share results with friends via Alloy. (By January 2008, Alloy was even encouraging girls to join their "new Quiz Community"—a feature in which girls could "create an Alloy profile," "upload pics," and "find friends & compare quiz results.")

But it is the message boards where Alloyers come together. Alloy's message boards are so popular that there are even boards on which only girls who have posted at least 100 times can participate. At the time of the initial phase of data collection, there were a total of 4,877 members on the boards, and consistent, frequent posting is encouraged. Alloy recognizes the top ten posters and, much in the same way the size of one's Facebook friends list is an index of popularity and a cause for boasting, the girls often discuss their own rank in the list of posters. Indeed, an

AM+M/Harris Interactive survey of 8–18-years-old found that, with the widening of social circles facilitated by the Internet, "the number of friends young people attract to their social network profiles is an indicator of their status among peers" (Alloy Media & Marketing, 2006). While these boards provide some opportunity for girls to constructively interact with other girls by asking for and providing advice from/to each other, in other ways, they function as part of the Alloy marketing machine. On one board, for example, Alloyers share their "Alloy dreams"—the real-life dreams they have allegedly had about Alloy.com.

While message boards are extremely popular with Alloyers, they are often yet another venue by which they are inundated with messages of both commodity and normative femininity. For example, on one message board providing a space for Alloyers to "talk" with Alloy's editors, one editor stated, "My favorite thing about the summer is all the cute clothes. It's way cuter than all the bulky winter stuff." Participating in the boards are ways in which editors behave as one of the Alloyers. They seem to be friends of tween/teen Alloyers, by answering questions, offering advice, and responding to questions quickly. However, their messages are often plugs for Alloy products. For instance, the editor mentioned above was encouraging girls to get excited about Alloy's cute summer clothes.

According to Mitchell and Reid-Walsh, such commercial Web sites for young people can

> encourage interaction, either by children playing with built-in components of the site, or interacting with other fans, or even corresponding with the site producers through email or online chat. In some sites there appear to be possibilities for creativity, resistance, and limited subversion. (2002, pp. 149–150).

The question for us becomes whether, within this hypercommercialized environment, Alloy provides spaces for girls to create, resist and subvert. We would say the key word from the Mitchell and Reid-Walsh quote is "limited."

CONCLUSION

With the rising popularity of the Internet and its documented importance to young people, marketers are increasingly turning to nontraditional media to reach the lucrative but difficult-to-reach youth demographic (Cook & Kaiser, 2004; Martens et al., 2004; Russell & Tyler, 2005). AM+M has made a business out of this practice. In the case of Alloy.com, they have created an online community to capitalize on girls' transition from childhood to adulthood and their need for transitional products (Cook & Kaiser, 2004; Martens et al., 2004; Russell & Tyler, 2005). Alloy and other such companies profit by creating communities in which they act as friends and older siblings to young people undergoing such life transitions (Mazzarella,

2008) in part by celebrating an image of normative femininity (Cook & Kaiser, 2004; Russell & Tyler, 2002, 2005).

Alloy.com is the quintessential example of a commercially created Internet community for girls. By encouraging girls to be trend- and beauty-conscious consumers, pop culture savvy, and boy crazy, Alloy is able to capture the attention of girls seeking information and community in addition to an online shopping catalog. The creation of the idealized female image has also created a community of Alloyers who find attention, friends, advice, and fashion on Alloy. In other words, the content of Alloy and the opportunities that girls have to express their thoughts and relate to one another have essentially created a *community of young consumers*.

The Web site Mindgum (n.d.) argues that "The success of such virtual communities speaks of a physical deprivation of such interaction among today's youth." Without actual physical spaces to call their own, the young are turning to the virtual spaces offered by the Internet. Many of the chapters in the original anthology *Girl Wide Web* (Mazzarella, 2005), as well as the other chapters in this book, look at the manner in which girls are turning to the Web as a "safe space" in particular in which to express/try on their identities as well as to create communities with other girls. This phenomenon has certainly not gone unnoticed by marketers desperate to find new ways to target their products to this highly desirable target demographic. There is an important difference, however, between girls *creating* their own spaces, such as the blogs, personal Web sites, and games discussed in the other chapters in this book, and corporations such as Alloy Marketing & Media *providing* such spaces in exchange for girls' exposure to consumer messages and rampant product placement. In answer to our research question of whether Alloy.com is an online community or a retail site, we assert it is a retail site masquerading as an online community. The next step, of course, is to study how girls themselves negotiate their experiences on Alloy.com

NOTES

1. We are using the exact acronym Alloy Media and Marketing uses to refer to itself, AM+M.
2. AM+M describes itself as the "largest packager of books for [the] teen market," publishing over "30 new books per year" (Alloy Media and Marketing, 2009). Recently, AM+M's book packaging strategies have come under increasing scrutiny and criticism both in terms of its extensive use of product placement and allegations of plagiarism (Mehegan, 2006a, 2006b).
3. Cook and Kaiser (2004) identify a 1987 *Marketing & Media Decisions* article by Hall as first introducing the term.
4. Interestingly, shortly after this project was completed, Alloy added a "community" feature to the Web site. Participating girls could create a profile and interact with other Alloyers including "Alloy," a virtual "friend," created by the company. We found it interesting that "Alloy" describes

herself as "boy-obsessed gossiping fashionista" (Alloy Profile, 2008)—the exact three character-istics we use to describe what the Web site would have one believe the typical Alloyer is.

5. The Clinique Boot Camp was no longer on the site during the second wave of data collection. An entry on one of the message boards in January 2008 indicated that it was only a short-term feature.

References

Alloy Media & Marketing (2006. October 31). Teens Set New Rules of Engagement in the Age of Social Media. [Press Release]. Retrieved January 30, 2010, from http://www.alloymarketing.com/investor_relations/news_releases/index.html

Alloy Media & Marketing (2007a, December 17). Alloy Media + Marketing Launches TEEN.com—Premier Youth Ad Network Reaching over 17 Million Users with Highest Concentration of Teens Available Online. [Press Release]. Retrieved January 30, 2010, from http://www.alloymarketing.com/investor_relations/news_releases/index.html

Alloy Media & Marketing (2007b). *Investor Presentation*. Retrieved October 22, 2007, from http://www.alloymarketing.com/investor_relations/presentations/index.html

Alloy Media & Marketing (2009a, January 15). Alloy Media + Marketing's "TEEN.com Network" Now the #1 Online Community For Teens According to comScore. [Press Release]. Retrieved January 30, 2010, from http://www.alloymarketing.com/investor_relations/news_releases/index.html

Alloy Media & Marketing (2009b). *Investor Presentation*. Retrieved January 30, 2010, from http://www.alloymarketing.com/investor_relations/presentations/index.html

Alloy Media & Marketing (2010a). *Alloy Digital Network*. Retrieved January 30, 2010, from http://network.teen.com/advertise/

Alloy Media & Marketing (2010b). *Alloy.com & Delia's.com*. Retrieved January 30, 2010, from http://www.alloymarketing.com/mediakit/network/index.html

Alloy Media & Marketing (2010c). *Corporate Profile*. Retrieved January 30, 2010, from http://www.alloymarketing.com/investor_relations/

Alloy Media & Marketing (2010d). *Specs: Alloy*. Retrieved January 30, 2010, from http://www.alloymarketing.com/mediakit/specs/specs_alloy.html

Alloy Media & Marketing (2010e). *The Youth Network: Teens*. Retrieved January 30, 2010, from http://www.alloymarketing.com/media/teens/index.html

Alloy Media & Marketing (2010f). *The Youth Network: Tweens*. Retrieved January 30, 2010, from http://www.alloymarketing.com/media/tweens/index.html

Alloy Media & Marketing (2010g). *What's Next*. Retrieved January 30, 2010, from http://alloymarketing.com/

Alloy Profile. (2008). Retrieved June 13, 2008, from http://www.alloy.com/profile/Alloy/

Briggs, J. A. (2005, April 11). Hey, kids, listen up. *Forbes*. Retrieved January 30, 2008, from http://www.forbes.com/forbes/2005/0411/120.html

"Click cliques; Teens online: Balancing community, content and commerce." (n.d.) *Mindgum*. Retrieved January 26, 2005, from http://www.mindgum.com/click.html

Cook, D. T., & Kaiser, S. B. (2004). Betwixt and be tween: Age ambiguity and the sexualization of the female consuming subject. *Journal of Consumer Culture, 4*, 203–226.

Driver, S. (2007). *Queer girls and popular culture: Reading, resisting, and creating media*. New York: Peter Lang.

Duits, L., & van Romondt Vis, P. (2007). Girls make sense: Girls, celebrities and identities. *Conference of the International Communication Association.*

Edwards, L. Y. (2005). Victims, villains, and vixens: Teen girls and Internet crime. In. S. R. Mazzarella (Ed.), *Girl wide web: Girls, the Internet, and the negotiation of identity* (pp. 13–30). New York: Peter Lang.

Gossip Girl. (2008). Retrieved January 23, 2008, from http://www.cwtv.com/shows/gossip-girl

Gossip Girl: The Official Book Site. (2008). Retrieved January 23, 2008, from http://www.gossipgirl.net/

Gross, E. F. (2004). "Adolescent Internet use: What we expect, what teens report." *Applied Developmental Psychology, 25*(6), 633–649.

Hains, R. C. (2007). Inventing the teenage girl: The construction of female identity in Nickelodeon's *My Life as a Teenage Robot. Popular Communication, 5*(3),191–213.

Jones, S., & Fox, S. (2009, January 28). *Generations Online in 2009.* Washington, DC: Pew Internet and American Life Project. Retrieved January 30, 2010, from http://www.pewinternet.org/Reports/2009/Generations-Online-in-2009.aspx?r=1

Labre, M. P., & Walsh-Childers, K. (2003). Friendly advice? Beauty messages in web sites of teen magazines. *Mass Communication & Society, 6*(4), 379–396.

Lamb, S., & Brown, L. M. (2006). *Packaging girlhood: Rescuing our daughters from marketers' schemes.* New York: St. Martin's Press.

Lenhart, A., Rainie, L., & Lewis, O. (2001). *Teenage life online: The rise of the instant-message generation and the Internet's impact on friendships and family relationships,* Washington DC: Pew Internet and American Life Project. Retrieved March 17, 2004, from http://www.pewinternet.org/

"Marketers working on tactics for reaching youth online via blogs and communities." (2005, March 15). *Youth Markets ALERT.* New York: EPM Communications.

Martens, L., Southerton, D., & Scott, S. (2004). Bringing children (and parents) into the sociology of consumption: Towards a theoretical and empirical agenda. *Journal of Consumer Culture, 4,* 155–182.

Mazzarella, S. R. (Ed.). (2005). *Girl wide web: Girls, the Internet, and the negotiation of identity.* New York: Peter Lang.

Mazzarella, S. R. (2008). Coming of age with Proctor & Gamble: Beinggirl.com and the commodification of puberty. *Girlhood Studies: An Interdisciplinary Journal, 1*(2), 29–50.

McAllister, M. P. (2007). "Girls with a passion for fashion": The Bratz brand as integrated spectacular consumption. *Journal of Children and Media, 1*(3), 244–258.

McRobbie, A. (1991). *Feminism and youth culture: From* Jackie *to* Just Seventeen. Boston: Unwin Hyman.

Mehegan, D. (2006a, April 29). Viswanathan book deal raises more questions. *Boston Globe.* Retrieved January 23, 2008, from http://www.boston.com/ae/books/articles/2006/04/29/viswanathan_book_deal_raises_more_questions/

Mehegan, D. (2006b, May 8). "Opal" aided by marketing firm that targets teens. *Boston Globe.* Retrieved January 23, 2008, from http://www.boston.com/ae/books/articles/2006/05/08/opal_aided_by_marketing_firm_that_targets_teens/

Mitchell, C., & Reid-Walsh, J. (2002). *Researching children's popular culture: The cultural spaces of childhood.* London: Routledge.

Montgomery, K. C. (2001). *Teensites.com: A Field Guide to the New Digital Landscape.* Washington, DC: Center for Media Education. Retrieved July 10, 2003, from http://www.cme.org/teenstudy/

Quart, A. (2003). *Branded: The buying and selling of teenagers.* Cambridge, MA: Perseus.

Rickert, A., & Sacharow, A. (2000). *It's a Woman's World Wide Web.* Media Matrix & Jupiter Communications. Retrieved July 7, 2003, from http://pj.dowling.home.att.net/4300/women.pdf

Russell, R., & Tyler, M. (2002). Thank heaven for little girls: Girl Heaven and the commercial context of feminine childhood. *Sociology, 36*(6), 619–637.

Russell, R., & Tyler, M. (2005). Branding and bricolage: Gender, consumption, and transition. *Childhood, 12,* 221–237.

Schnuer, J, (2004, November 11). Alloy. *Advertising Age,* p. S16.

Sisterhood Central. (2008). Retrieved January 23, 2008, from http://www.randomhouse.com/teens/sisterhoodcentral/home.html

Sweeney, K. (2008). *Maiden USA: Girl icons come of age.* New York: Peter Lang.

"Teens go online to connect." (2005, April 1). *Youth Markets ALERT,* New York: EPM Communications.

Tufte, B. (2003). Girls in the new media landscape. *Nordicom Review, 24*(1), 71–78.

Verizon Wireless. (2008). Retrieved January 23, 2008, from http://products.vzw.com/index.aspx?id=featured_shows&show=gossipgirl

Wasko, J. (2001). Manufacturing Disney: The manufacture of fantasy. Cambridge, UK: Polity Press.

Wasserman, T. (2006, March 29). Youth-targeted media company expands its teen reach. *Brandweek.* Retrieved January 27, 2008, from http://www.brandweek.com/bw/news/tech/article_display.jsp?vnu_content_id=1002273691

Wood, J. T. (2007). *Gendered lives: Gender, communication and culture* (7th ed.). Belmont, CA: Wadsworth.

Contributors

Allison Atkins (B.A., Clemson University) is a grant coordinator in the Office of Substance Abuse Prevention and Education at the University of South Carolina, where she is also obtaining her M.Ed. in Higher Education Administration. She completed her Clemson University undergraduate honors thesis on how the transnational corporation Proctor & Gamble homogenizes and commercializes female puberty across multiple countries in its many national "beinggirl" Web sites.

Michelle S. Bae (Ph.D., University of Illinois, Urbana-Champaign) is currently an assistant professor in the Art Education Department at Buffalo State College, SUNY. She has worked as an artist, a media educator, and a supervisor/curriculum developer for undergraduate student-teachers in digital media technology and visual culture. Her intellectual curiosity and interest has revolved around teenage girls' Web cultures and cultural productions, including image-making, video-making, and Web site development. Her ethnographic research reflects interdisciplinary approaches encompassing art and media education, communication, women's studies, and Asian American studies. She has presented papers at regional, national, and international conferences and conventions on such topics as children's art, youth culture and production, media criticism, visual culture and pedagogy, globalized media and multiculturalism, and cyber culture and identity, and a contemporary qualitative inquiry. She has published book chapters in the field of art education and women and gender studies.

Kristine Blair is Professor and Chair of the Department of English at Bowling Green State University, Ohio. Her publications have focused on gender and technology, electronic portfolios, and online teaching, and her most recent work includes the co-edited collection *Webbing Cyberfeminist Practice: Communities, Pedagogies, and Social Action* (Hampton Press, 2009).

Denise Sevick Bortree is an assistant professor at Penn State University. Her research interests include volunteerism, environmental communication, and online communication among adolescents.

Ivana Chalmers (Bachelor of Journalism, Rhodes University) works at Northwestern University in Doha, Qatar. Her previous research included the effectiveness of television as an educational tool. Prior to joining Northwestern University in Qatar, Chalmers was involved in fashion video production and editing for London Fashion Week. Her research interests include media influence on gender perception and the influence of technological advancement on interpersonal communication.

Naydene De Lange is an associate professor in the Faculty of Education of the University of KwaZulu-Natal where she teaches in the School of Educational Studies, and heads up a multi-study research niche area on rural education in the age of AIDS. She has written extensively around the use of participatory video and other visual methodologies to address HIV&AIDS and is the co-editor of the book *Putting People in the Picture: Visual Methodologies for Social Change*.

Jill Denner is the associate director of Research at Education, Training, Research Associates, a non-profit organization in California. She has a Ph.D. in Developmental Psychology, and has been developing and doing research on after-school programs for girls since 2001. Her recent research focuses on how computer game design can increase IT fluency and computational thinking in middle school, with a focus on girls and Latinas. Dr. Denner has published numerous journal articles, and co-edited two books: *"Beyond Barbie and Mortal Kombat: New Perspectives on Gender and Gaming,"* published by MIT Press in 2008, and *"Latina Girls: Voices of Adolescent Strength,"* published by NYU Press in 2006.

Erin Dietel-McLaughlin is a doctoral candidate in the Rhetoric and Writing Program at Bowling Green State University, Ohio. Her research interests focus on intersections of new media, democracy, and literacy, and her dissertation work examines the vernacular rhetorics of Web 2.0 spaces.

Meredith Graupner Hurley is a doctoral candidate in the Rhetoric and Writing Program at Bowling Green State University, Ohio. Her research has focused on computer-mediated communication, writing assessment, and her dissertation work examines the integration of technology throughout the graduate curriculum.

Rodda Leage (M.F.A., Saint Mary's College) is a lecturer in the Department of Communication Studies at Northwestern University in Evanston, Illinois. She has taught at their Qatar branch campus for 1 year. Her teaching and research interests range from issues of gender and popular culture to creative writing. She is interested in how technologies can be used as a source of empowerment within different cultures and communities.

Jacob Martinez (Masters in Instructional Science and Technology, California State University at Monterey Bay), has more than 6 years experience working with at-risk Latino youth in Santa Cruz County, including designing and implementing youth programs that focus on engaging youth with science and technology. He was the Project Coordinator for the Girl Game Company, an after school technology program for middle school Latina girls. Prior to working for ETR he was the Academic Coordinator for the Math, Engineering, Science Achievement (MESA) program at the University of California at Santa Cruz.

Sharon R. Mazzarella (Ph.D., University of Illinois) is Professor and Director of the School of Communication Studies at James Madison University. Her research interests are in girls' studies and the representational politics of mediated portrayals of youth. She is editor of *20 Questions about Youth and the Media* (2007, Peter Lang), *Girl Wide Web: Girls, the Internet, and the Negotiation of Identity* (2005, Peter Lang), and co-editor of *Growing Up Girls: Popular Culture and the Construction of Identity* (1999, Peter Lang).

Claudia Mitchell is a James McGill Professor in the Faculty of Education, McGill University, and an honorary professor in the Faculty of Education, University of KwaZulu-Natal. She is the co-author/co-editor of several books on girlhood, childhood culture, and media including: *Researching Children's Popular Culture* and *Seven Going on Seventeen: Tween Studies in the Culture of Girlhood*, *Girlhood: Redefining the Limits*, and a two-volume encyclopaedia, *Girl Culture* (2007). She is the co-editor of a new journal *Girlhood Studies: An Interdisciplinary Journal*.

John Pascarella (Ph.D., McGill University) is a high school English Language Arts teacher in New Jersey and last worked as a Course Lecturer in the Department of Integrated Studies in Education at McGill University while completing his doctoral studies. His thesis examines the uses of new media and critical theory in the preparation of pre-service teachers in Canada and South Africa.

Paola Prado (Ph.D., University of Miami) is Visiting Assistant Professor, Advertising and Public Relations, at the School of Journalism & Mass Communication at Florida International University. Her research focuses on the adoption of information and communication technologies for development and social change in Latin America and the U.S. Latino market. Dr. Prado is the co-creator of the "Comunicadores para el Desarrollo" journalism and multimedia workshop program, which trains community reporters in under-privileged rural areas in the Dominican Republic. A pioneer in online media, Dr. Prado directed content for the Latin American and U.S. Latino arm of RealNetworks and led U.S. operations for ElSitio.com. She began her professional career at the Reuters TV news agency, where she produced and licensed world coverage for television broadcast. Later, she went on to head affiliate relations for Spanish-language cable news network TeleNoticias and for the Weather Channel Latin America. Dr. Prado is fluent in English, French, Portuguese, and Spanish.

Narissra Maria Punyanunt-Carter (Ph.D., Kent State University) is an associate professor of Communication Studies at Texas Tech University in Lubbock, Texas. She teaches the basic interpersonal communication course. Her research areas include mass media effects, father-daughter communication, mentoring, adviser-advisee relationships, family studies, religious communication, humor, and interpersonal communication. She has published over 30 articles that have appeared in several peer-reviewed journals, such as *Communication Research Reports, Communication Quarterly, The Family Journal,* and *Journal of Intercultural Communication Research*. She has also published numerous instructional ancillaries and materials.

Jason M. Smith (B.A., Lubbock Christian University) is a graduate student at Texas Tech University. His focus is on communication in the media and symbolic interactionism, specifically the self and its influences.

Lillian Spina-Caza (M.S., Syracuse University) is a doctoral candidate and HASS Fellow at Rensselaer Polytechnic Institute in Troy, New York. Before returning to academia, she worked for more than a decade as a producer, director, and writer of educational film and video programs for young people. Her hands-on production experience informs her current research, which explores new approaches to empirically study children's imaginative, self-directed play in emergent digital environments.

Carla E. Stokes (Ph.D., University of Michigan) is a health educator, life coach for teen girls, and founder of Helping Our Teen Girls In Real Life Situations, Inc. (HOTGIRLS)®, an Atlanta-based 501(c)(3) nonprofit organization dedicated to improving the health and lives of young black women and girls. She came of age in the "golden era" of the hip hop generation and taught undergraduate courses on representations of women in hip hop culture and black women's health in the Department of Women's Studies at the University of Michigan. Her dissertation, "Representin' in Cyberspace: Sexuality, Hip Hop, and Self-Definition in Home Pages Constructed By Black Adolescent Girls in the HIV/AIDS Era" won honorable mention in the 2004 University of Michigan Distinguished Dissertation Awards competition and was published in *Culture, Health & Sexuality* and featured in the *New York Times*. She completed a post-doctoral research fellowship at the U.S. Centers for Disease Control and Prevention, Division of HIV/AIDS Prevention, and is currently writing a book and curriculum based on her research and work with girls. She can be reached at http://www.drcarla.com.

Jean Stuart teaches in the School of Language, Literacies and Media Education in the Faculty of Education of the University of KwaZulu-Natal, South Africa, where she is also the director of the Centre for Visual Methodologies for Social Change. She completed a doctoral study working with beginning teachers and visual methodologies to address HIV&AIDS, and is currently heading up a research study on youth as knowledge producers in the context of AIDS. She is he co-editor of the book *Putting People in the Picture: Visual Methodologies for Social Change*.

Jacqueline Ryan Vickery (M.A., University of Texas at Austin) is a doctoral student in the Department of Radio-Television-Film at the University of Texas at Austin. Her research interests include social and cultural aspects of new media, particularly with relation to childhood and youth. In addition to presenting at several national conferences she has been published in *Girlhood Studies*. She was Senior Co-Coordinating Editor for the online academic journal *FlowTV.org* from 2008–2010 as well as a senior coordinator for the 2008 Flow Conference. Additionally she is a facilitator for the Teen Reporter Intern Program at *Latinitas* magazine in Austin.

Jaime Warburton (M.F.A, Sarah Lawrence) is a poet and assistant professor of Writing at Ithaca College. Her teaching and research interests hinge on the intersections of gender and sexuality with popular culture and children's literature, themes she has also explored in her poetry. The 2006 Thomas Lux scholar, she co-directs the biannual WomenSpeak conference in Ithaca, NY, and has presented her work on fan fiction, gifted in girls in literature, and sci-fi robot couples around the country.

mediated youth

Sharon R. Mazzarella
General Editor

Grounded in cultural studies, books in this series will study the cultures, artifacts, and media of children, tweens, teens, and college-aged youth. Whether studying television, popular music, fashion, sports, toys, the Internet, self-publishing, leisure, clubs, school, cultures/activities, film, dance, language, tie-in merchandising, concerts, subcultures, or other forms of popular culture, books in this series go beyond the dominant paradigm of traditional scholarship on the effects of media/culture on youth. Instead, authors endeavor to understand the complex relationship between youth and popular culture. Relevant studies would include, but are not limited to studies of how youth negotiate their way through the maze of corporately-produced mass culture; how they themselves have become cultural producers; how youth create "safe spaces" for themselves within the broader culture; the political economy of youth culture industries; the representational politics inherent in mediated coverage and portrayals of youth; and so on. Books that provide a forum for the "voices" of the young are particularly encouraged. The source of such voices can range from in-depth interviews and other ethnographic studies to textual analyses of cultural artifacts created by youth.

For further information about the series and submitting manuscripts, please contact:

SHARON R. MAZZARELLA
Communication Studies Department
Clemson University
Clemson, SC 29634

To order other books in this series, please contact our Customer Service Department at:

(800) 770-LANG (within the U.S.)
(212) 647-7706 (outside the U.S.)
(212) 647-7707 FAX

Or browse online by series at WWW.PETERLANG.COM